From the best-selling Japanese edition of Captain Hara's book, Fred Saito of the Associated Press and Roger Pineau—assistant to Admiral Morison on the U.S. Navy's official history of World War II—have prepared a book of paramount interest to all who want to know the facts about the great naval battles of the Pacific War.

Errors in U.S. accounts of famous sea battles are set right by inside reports of high-level Japanese strategy meetings and Hara's eyewitness account of six years of war. At times sharply critical of famous Japanese admirals, Hara also gives credit to Japanese and "enemy" officers whose daring and seamanship were proved in the savage battles of the Pacific.

Illustrated with eight pages of photographs from official U.S. and Japanese Navy files, and filled with exact maps of naval actions, this is a book for the permanent shelf of works on sea warfare.

JAPANESE DESTROYER CAPTAIN

Pearl Harbor, Guadalcanal, Midway—
The Great Naval Battles
as Seen Through
Japanese Eyes

CAPTAIN TAMEICHI HARA
of the Imperial Japanese Navy

with Fred Saito and Roger Pineau

Naval Institute Press
Annapolis, Maryland

Naval Institute Press
291 Wood Road
Annapolis, MD 21402

Teikoku Kaigun No Saigo by Tameichi Hara
© 1967 by Tameichi Hara
All rights reserved.
First published in the Japanese language in 1967 by Kawade Shobo, Tokyo.
This English edition published by arrangement with Mikihito Hara in care of
Tuttle-Mori Agency, Inc., Tokyo.
English translation copyright © 1961 by Captain Tameichi Hara, Fred Saito,
and Roger Pineau.

First Naval Institute Press paperback edition published 2011.
ISBN: 978-1-59114-384-0

The Library of Congress has catalogued the hardcover edition as follows:

Hara, Tameichi, b. 1900.
  [Teikoku Kaigun no saigo. English]
  Japanese destroyer captain : Pearl Harbor, Guadalcanal, Midway — the great naval
battles as seen through Japanese eyes / Captain Tameichi Hara of the Imperial Japanese
Navy with Fred Saito and Roger Pineau.
      p. cm.
  Includes index.
  ISBN-13: 978-1-59114-354-3 (alk. paper)
  ISBN-10: 1-59114-354-3 (alk. paper)
    1. World War, 1939–1945—Naval operations, Japanese. 2. Hara, Tameichi, b. 1900.
3. Ship captains—Japan—Biography. 4. World War, 1939–1945—Personal narratives,
Japanese. I. Saito, Fred. II. Pineau, Roger, 1916– III. Title.
D777.H313 2007
940.54'5952092—dc22
[B]   2006030097

Printed in the United States of America.

19 18 17 16 15 14 13 12   9 8 7 6 5 4 3

CONTENTS

MAPS

FOREWORD

As Japan began to get back on its feet after World War II, the Japanese public came to consider that war with detachment, and growing numbers of persons began to demand that the story be straightened out. Several excellent books were written by my colleagues in response to the demand. Most of these books, by former Imperial Navy flyers, are properly reflective of the authors' aerial background.

I was urged by many friends to tell the story from the surface side. It has not been an easy job, for destroyer men are trained in fighting not writing. This book, indeed, could not have been produced but for the all-out co-operation of friends too numerous for mention here. I can state, however, that all persons referred to by name in this book were either interviewed by me or voluntarily submitted their statements to me.

I am particularly grateful to my friend Ko Nagasawa who, as Commander in Chief of the new Japanese Navy, 1954–1958, not only gave me his own accounts willingly, but also instructed the Navy's Historical Section to co-operate with me. I am much indebted to all the naval historians who contributed so much to this work by allowing me to use the results of their research and study.

I trust this book will provide a comprehensive view of the Japanese side that will complement the many excellent American books which, in almost every case, are sadly lacking in accurate Japanese information. Accounts based solely on interrogations of Japanese survivors and veterans by the conquerors in the early days of the occupation were too often subjective.

In writing this book my greatest effort was to render as objective an account as possible. To do so, I had to be ruthlessly critical not only of myself, but also of friends who had helped me devotedly. It is a human trait, and the failing of every military officer, to try to cover up his friends' mistakes, if not his own. It has involved real pain, indeed, for me to avoid that failing.

My critical and straightforward account may hurt the feelings of many colleagues and possibly of those who fought against me. I hope, however, that all such readers will take a broad view and try to understand that it has been my desire to offend no one personally.

After surviving the sinking of my destroyer off Okinawa in April 1945, I was assigned to the Kawatana Torpedo Boat school near Sasebo and Nagasaki. My new command was to provide training for guerrilla warfare tactics in anticipation of American landings in our homeland.

Emperor Hirohito's surrender order of August 15, 1945 reached me at Kawatana while I was engaged in training young men to assume disguises as women or priests in order to fight enemy invasion troops. I surrendered the Kawatana base to a United States Navy detail headed by Captain Francis D. McCorkle on September 23, 1945.

The American captain astonished me by behaving more like a friend than a conqueror. He asked my permission to have as a souvenir a speedometer from one of the Shinyo Suicide Torpedo Boats then moored at Kawatana. I was delighted to oblige.

Since the end of the war, I have been working at a salt transport company. My two daughters were happily married in 1957, one to a merchant ship officer, the other to an office worker. My son Mikito is in senior high school. My wife, Chizu, is healthy and happy.

Tokyo, February 25, 1958
Tameichi Hara

PROLOGUE

1

Japan's Imperial Navy had an over-all wartime inventory of 25 aircraft carriers, 12 battleships, 18 heavy cruisers, 26 light cruisers, 175 destroyers and 95 submarines.

But it was the destroyer flotillas, totaling never more than 130 at any one time, which shouldered the heaviest burden of the war. They were the work horses of the Imperial Navy.

These destroyers were assigned not merely as fighting ships, but also as escorts to transports, and even *as* transports for many months of the war—particularly from early 1943 to mid-1944 when most of the larger Japanese warships were being "conserved" at a safe distance from the battle zones.

Japanese destroyers took part in scores of intense sea battles and scored many brilliant victories in the early days. These victories demonstrated the superiority of Japan's destroyer seamanship over that of the Allies.

Starting in mid-1943, however, Japanese destroyers had to work month after month without proper maintenance or upkeep, and without adequate rest or replenishment for their crews, until they lost supremacy over their Allied counterparts. That was largely owing to the amazing Allied development of scientific equipment and also to the growing superiority of Allied aircraft.

Nevertheless, Japanese destroyers fought gallantly and valiantly until the end of the war. I think their records deserve a full presentation for posterity. Although destroyer actions do not compare in scale to the larger and more famed battles like those at Coral Sea, Midway, the Marianas, or Leyte Gulf, which were largely fought by airplanes and capital warships, the efforts and achievements of destroyers in the lesser battles—which tend to be gradually forgotten—are worthy of being recorded in detail.

Japanese aircraft carriers played the lead role at Pearl Harbor—which was after all a one-sided action—as well as in three subsequent large operations that ended in complete defeat for the Japanese at Midway, the Marianas, and Leyte Gulf.

Japanese battleships treasured by the high command and "conserved" at every cost, fared even worse. *Musashi*, 72,400 tons, which consumed fuel at the rate of 30 large destroyers, took part in only one action in the war. It was sunk in Leyte Gulf before there was even a chance to level its nine 18-inch guns at any worthy targets.

Yamato, her sister ship, participated in only two battles. At Leyte, it broke off before the cornered American light carriers. Five months later, it sortied for Okinawa on a suicide mission and was sunk in the East China Sea more than 300 miles short of its goal.

But Japan's little destroyers worked throughout the war escorting much larger ships, sinking enemy ships and submarines, and transporting troops and supplies.

My happiest duty in the Imperial Navy was in destroyers, and that is where I spent most of the war. During the war my Navy friends called me the "Miracle Captain" and my destroyer *Shigure* was nicknamed "Indestructible." I don't think such compliments were really deserved. The officers who died in the 129 Japanese destroyers lost during the war covered a range of ability just as in any other navy, and many of them were better than me. The fact that I survived was entirely a matter of luck.

Among the survivors are others who were as capable, and more so. Thus far they have all been silent about their war records, perhaps in accord with the ancient Oriental saying: "Defeated men should not talk about their battles."

I have decided to challenge this precept, not for myself, but to give proper credit to the destroyers and the men who sailed them. That the war was lost does not detract from their credit and achievement. If this writing seems to be too much about myself, the reader is reminded that I am merely trying to present a typical Japanese destroyer man, with his typical merits and faults—nothing more.

This book cannot give a full history of every Japanese destroyer. Particularly inadequate is my account of destroyer *Yukikaze*, which survived eight major operations and battles until the last day of the war, and, in my opinion, deserves an entire book to itself. But the man for that job is her 1941–44 skipper, Captain Ryokichi Kanma, who, I hope, will eventually write his own account in full detail.

2

On April 7, 1945 Japanese light cruiser *Yahagi* endured a 90-minute aerial attack by American Avengers and Hellcats in which she absorbed six torpedoes, twelve direct hits by 250-pound bombs, and numerous smaller bomb hits. This punishment proved to be too much for even that gallant warship.

She had sortied from the Inland Sea early that morning with eight destroyers and the giant battleship *Yamato*. Their goal was Okinawa where they were to make a suicide attack against the American invasion forces. Clearly a suicide attack, because the Japanese warships were provided with enough fuel to reach Okinawa—not enough to return.

Now, less than 100 miles from Japan, the fury of an enemy attack had struck the *Yamato* task force, and light cruiser *Yahagi* was sinking.

As her skipper, I was standing on *Yahagi*'s bridge as the waves lapped closer. Near me on the bridge stood Rear Admiral Keizo Komura, commander of the escort force. All around us were signs of the havoc worked by the enemy attack. Bodies and debris were everywhere in *Yahagi,* hardly anything remained intact after the withering air attacks. The ship was listing 30 degrees to port and sinking fast. Admiral Komura was uninjured and, though blood streamed down my left arm, I was unaware of having been hit.

In a last look around, I saw that battleship *Yamato*, some 6,000 yards ahead, was still fighting. Two of our eight destroyers were already sunk. Three others were burning, dead in the water, and sinking. The other three were zigzagging desperately.

"Let's go," said Komura. I nodded. We took off our shoes and jumped into the water. The next moment the ship went down, dragging us down toward the bottom of the East China Sea. The gigantic whirlpool of the sinking ship caught us like a mighty fist, and I writhed and struggled in vain. I ran out of breath and gulped sea water. All around me was inky darkness. Was I dying? Not yet. I kept struggling. I would never know how many minutes passed, but it was a long time to me. Suddenly the clutch of the immense fist seemed to loosen. In the darkness a faint suggestion of light above me showed that I was going up. A stream of foam came from my nose as again I gulped in water. I kicked and struggled as the black darkness gave way to blue sky and daylight.

With startling, unbelievable suddenness I was back on the surface. Dazed, unthinking, and barely able to keep afloat, I was heartened to see that *Yamato* was still fighting. Scores of American planes swarmed gnatlike over and around her, launching their deadly missiles, but the giant ship still fought on. This encouraging sight helped to rouse me from my stupor. But the sight was short-lived.

At 1420 a frightening pillar of fire and white smoke came belching from the battleship, hiding everything. The smoke towered 20,000 feet into the sky.

While I watched the smoke gradually lifted, revealing nothing. The great battleship *Yamato*, pride of the Imperial Navy, had vanished into the sea. The Imperial Navy was finished.

I shuddered. Hot tears gushed from my eyes and streamed down my checks. I clung morosely to a piece of floating debris.

I was finished. Since the beginning of the Pacific War I had gone out on more than 100 sorties; and while countless friends and comrades fell, I always came back victorious. Now I tasted miserable defeat for the first time in my career.

Suddenly many things from the past flooded to mind as I knew there was no chance for my survival.

I recalled the heated discussion of the day before when three admirals and ten ship captains contemplated the orders for what was to be the last sortie of the Japanese Navy. Not one of us had seen any hope of success. *Yamato* with my cruiser *Yahagi* and eight destroyers had to sail for Okinawa with fuel enough for only a one-way trip. We were to reach Okinawa and, as warships on a suicide mission, there expend all our ammunition against the American fleet. We were blasted into the sea less than halfway to the target.

I saw vividly my family at home. Suddenly, their faces blurred as rain began to fall. I wept, mumbling aloud, "Farewell, Chizu. You have been a good wife, and a good mother to our children. Farewell, daughters Yoko and Keiko, and son Mikito! After your father's death and the defeat of your fatherland, you will face untold miseries. Ah, forgive your father! Try to remember me as a man who fought and did his best."

Then I heard a voice singing. I was not alone! I looked around to find that there were scores of other sailors in the water. Gradually they all joined the chorus, despite training instructions not to exhaust themselves thus. In this grim setting I listened to the haunting strains of the ancient *Song of the Warrior:*

If I go away to sea,
I shall return a corpse awash;
If duty calls me to the mountain,
A verdant sward will be my pall;
Thus for the sake of the Emperor
I will not die peacefully at home.

My weeping stopped and I closed my eyes to see again my childhood, school days, our cadet training cruise, the glorious battles in the Java Sea, the Solomons. . . .

part one

BORN A SAMURAI

1

I was born October 16, 1900, in a suburb of Takamatsu City on the northern coast of Shikoku Island facing the scenic Inland Sea.

My family was poor. I was the last of five children. My parents had to work their small plot from dawn to dusk. Like most of the farms in Japan, which is one of the most densely populated countries in the world, ours was less than one acre. It did not produce enough to support our family, so my father labored at night in a home workshop making crude farm tools for sale.

Most of my recollections of my parents are of their days and nights of toil; they had little or no time to play with us children. From early childhood my two brothers and two sisters had to help in supporting the family.

My grandfather, Moichiro Hara, was nearly 70 when I was born. He nursed me and played with me. He had been a real samurai in his youth, and he exerted a great influence on me.

Until 1871 the people of Japan were divided into four estates or classes. In that year all the feudal fords relinquished their titles and estates to the Emperor.

Before that time the ruling class was the samurai. As a member of that class, my family had served the lord of Takamatsu for centuries. The samurai's duty in time of peace was to administer local affairs and to keep constantly in training for a military emergency. In return, the samurai's livelihood was insured by his lord. So the samurai lived proud and aloof from the mundane routines and considerations of the merchant, artisan, and peasant classes.

With his status and privileges gone, a samurai found it hard to adapt himself to a new mode of life. Most samurai ended up as failures working at trades for which they were untrained. My grandfather was no exception. It was all he could do to cling to the small farm granted him on separation from the feudal clan. It is curious how closely my own life was to follow the course of my doting grandfather's.

The Imperial Navy was disbanded after Japan's surrender in World War II, and I, a naval captain, was without a job. The Allied occupation denied pensions to all former military officers and barred them from holding public office. Thus for several postwar years my family eked out a living only by selling personal belongings and doing manual labor. Despite this, I have never regretted my choice of a naval career. I am grateful for the many lessons my grandfather taught. Those lessons helped me to win battles and enabled me to survive defeat in that great war. The toll of my crews throughout the war was lower than that of any other Imperial Navy captain with equivalent combat experience.

My grandfather was wonderfully good to me. Because my mother was so busy, he tended and cared for me throughout my infancy. As I began to walk, it was he who took me along to nearby shrines. He would watch me, play with me, and buy candies for me.

As I began to talk, he told me endless samurai stories. My mother told me later of grandfather's hope that I would restore glory to the family, for he thought I was the brightest child of the five.

I can close my eyes now and see the white-haired old man sitting erect in the samurai manner morning and evening before the family altar. The altar contained the tablets of his ancestors, as well as that of his own lord, Yori-chika Matsudaira of Takamatsu. This daily routine of worship and reciting Analects of Confucius was never varied or disturbed until he became seriously ill.

As he lay on his deathbed surrounded by the family, he called my name and asked that I come close. As I was just six, my parents brought me to his side and put my hands in one of his. The other hand clutched his treasured samurai sword, which he finally placed in my tiny hands. He coughed and struggled to say, "Tamei, this is yours. Now listen carefully to your grandpa's last words."

All of us were silent as the dying old man went on falteringly.

"Tameichi Hara! You are the son of samurai and you will remember that. 'A samurai lives in such a way that he is always prepared to die.' Don't misinterpret that teaching. Never seek an easy death, for that would be against the true spirit of Bushido.

"I have told you many times about fine samurai who suffered great hardships to achieve their missions. Try to do likewise. Always be on guard, and redouble your efforts to better yourself."

Though I was too young to understand all he said, the dying man's expression of great affection for me was clear and unforgettable.

The following year I enrolled in grammar school. Throughout its six years of courses, I stayed at the head of the class and graduated as the first honor pupil of my family.

We were still poor. My brothers, ten years and eight years older than me, were already working. Neither they nor my two sisters went beyond grammar school. Seeing my fine school record, the brothers persuaded Father to send me to middle school, saying, "We'll help with his expenses." So it happened that I was able to continue my education. I will always be grateful to my family for making this possible.

I passed the middle school entrance examination and was one of five applicants fortunate enough to be chosen for admission. The school was one of the best in Japan, open only to carefully selected children. In five years there, I could not achieve top honors, but I finished about tenth in the class of 150 boys.

As that schooling drew to an end, I had to think about a career. Naturally I aspired to higher education. But college or university required expenditures that were prohibitive for my family. The only advanced education available to me was in government-financed institutions. This meant either a normal school and study for a teaching career, or a military school. I was of samurai blood. My choice was the military. I had not forgotten my grandfather's last words.

2

Upon graduation from the Takamatsu Middle School in March 1918 I applied for the Military Academy in Tokyo and also for the Naval Academy at Eta Jima near Hiroshima. I applied for both because my chances were small of winning either. My preference was the Navy but, failing that, the Army would have been acceptable because I could not afford to wait another year for the next examinations.

My grandfather had been a cavalryman. Why did the Navy have so much attraction for me? Perhaps my spirit was simply responding to the tradition of my ancestral region. Takamatsu and its environs have a special naval significance, for it was here that the Japanese Navy had its beginning.

The Inland Sea is to Japan what the Aegean was to ancient Greece. Early Japanese life revolved and developed around the Inland Sea with its thousands of picturesque islets, just as the Greek culture began on the shores of the Aegean.

The first major naval battle in Japanese history was fought off Takamatsu in February, 1185. The following month a naval force was collected at Takamatsu and it formed the nucleus of a winning fleet at Dan-no-ura in the greatest Inland Sea battle ever recorded in Japanese history.

In the 13th century when Kublai Khan's mammoth Mongolian fleet with 200,000 men attempted the invasion of Japan from northern Kyushu, the Takamatsu contingent again played a vital role in destroying the enemy at Japan's shore. Michiari Kono, a famed admiral from near Takamatsu, is noted in history books as the man who climbed victoriously on board the Mongolian flagship in the crucial battle of 1281. The entire Mongolian armada was demolished at Hakata Bay. Thereafter many Japanese fleets streamed out from the Inland Sea in "retaliation sorties" against the Chinese mainland.

These medieval Japanese fleets functioned somewhat in the manner of modern commandos. Unlike the Mongolian armada, they did not carry large numbers of land troops, for they did not aim at permanent occupation of mainland China. Crack Japanese sailors would land on the continent, chew up the immediately opposing Chinese troops, and return with loot. Chinese history shows that these Japanese commando raiders attacked the China coast until well into the 17th century and contributed to the toppling of many a dynasty, including that of the famous and powerful Ming.

My desire for a navy career was no doubt inspired by the naval heritage of my native province.

The Naval Academy at Eta Jima was one of the most highly competitive educational institutions in Japan. Enthusiastic youngsters who failed the first examination would wait a full year, or even two, for another chance. But my family situation would not allow a year of idleness, so I also applied for the Military Academy.

Entrance examinations for the Academies were given in principal cities throughout the country. In April, the month after my graduation from Takamatsu Middle School, I went to nearby Marugame for the Army examination. It did not seem too difficult and I felt sure that I had qualified.

The next month I traveled to Honshu—my first waterborne journey—to take the Navy examination at Hiroshima. Takamatsu Middle School had sponsored class excursions to Honshu, but I had never joined because of lack of funds.

It was quite exciting for an 18-year-old country boy to make this trip for the first time, and all alone. Hiroshima was already the largest city in Western Honshu. Its busy, thriving streets bewildered me.

I registered in a modest-looking hotel, located in a back alley, away from the busy thoroughfares. This was my first such experience and, as it turned out, my choice of lodging was not wise. In Japanese hotels a guest's meals are served in his room by a maidservant. Mine was in her early twenties, pretty, and friendly. So friendly, indeed, that she made me very nervous.

"Would you like to have liquor, sir?"

"No, miss, I'm not of age to drink and, besides, I am taking the entrance exams for Eta Jima tomorrow."

"Oooh," she squealed, "so you are going into the Navy. How nice! You will be a terrific officer. Will you come back to this hotel in uniform after you are in school? I'd like to see you again."

This conversation made me uneasy. In my typical Japanese upbringing I had never before talked with young women, except my sisters. It upset me to have this girl keep asking me questions. I barely managed a few curt words of reply each time, and I heaved a deep sigh of relief when she left. I opened a few books I had carried along. I was anxious to study and prepare for the Eta Jima examinations. I pored over textbooks for several hours but simply could not concentrate. A guest in the next room seemed to be having a drinking bout with his maid. Between drinks they sang. This was awful. I realized ruefully that I had picked the wrong hotel.

I gave up around midnight and asked at the front desk to have my bedding prepared. In a Japanese hotel room there is no bed. When a guest wants to retire, servants spread futon (bedding) on the matted floor.

That aggressively friendly maid reappeared and prepared my bed. But instead of leaving she insisted on helping me change, and fold and arrange my clothes. I was plainly embarrassed.

"Young gentleman," she said mockingly, "you look strained. You need a massage. If you aren't trim and fit tomorrow, you may flunk."

She ignored my stammered protest and started to massage my back. I gave in.

"My name is Noriko and I am from neighboring Yamaguchi province," she went on. "I have been working as a hotel maid for nearly three years. Sometimes the job is difficult because not every guest is a gentleman like you."

I was silent and, although the massage was relaxing, her words made me more strained than before.

"I have no more duties tonight," she whispered. "You may keep me."

Her voice was low, but it struck me like thunder, and I trembled. "What do you mean?" I croaked.

"Oh, come, young man, don't play the fool. A handsome boy like you must have known dozens of girls. You better have a good time tonight so you can face the examinations tomorrow with real composure."

"Oh, please leave me," I begged. "I have never had any girl. I have never spoken to any girl but my sisters in my life. Tomorrow's examinations are very, very important to me."

"You seem to think I'm a bitch," she said in a tone of hurt and anger. "I offered to stay with you simply because I fell in love with you at first sight. Also I know you'll be denied girls for the four years you're at Eta Jima. I am not a bitch. I will not charge you for my companionship. Listen! All is quiet next door. They are in bed."

That was too much for me. I earnestly begged her to leave. Finally she stalked out of the room, giving me a last look of utter scorn.

This awkward incident so disturbed me that I could not sleep. I took the exams next day, but suffered badly from lack of sleep. I did not feel confident about any part of the examinations. I returned to Takamatsu, disappointed and dispirited.

About ten days later I received notice that I had passed the military examination and should report to Tokyo in August. I had about given up the idea of a navy career and was fairly resigned to being in the Army, when a telegram announced that the Navy had also accepted me. I shouted, "Banzai!" and leaped with joy.

3

Eta Jima, Japan's Annapolis, was a shrine and a subject of dreams to millions of youngsters in prewar Japan. Every year hundreds of young aspirants, each with fine scholastic records and recommendations, would compete for the few public or unsponsored openings for admission. One would expect such a selective system to produce brilliant naval officers. But many graduates of this exclusive school were far from brilliant, and some failed completely to live up to the nation's expectations. What I say about Eta Jima and its system is not intended as an indictment; I wish only to present the facts and let the reader judge them.

I was enrolled on August 26, 1918. On that day I put on the snow-white uniform with seven shiny brass buttons and became a real samurai. With the uniform I wore the short, ornamental dagger, just as my grandfather had worn it in his youth.

Eta Jima is a small island facing the spacious harbor of the naval port of Kure, near Hiroshima, in the Inland Sea. Our course of studies at the Academy lasted four years. Except for summer vacations and a few short days of home leave, we lived on this island in complete isolation from the outer world.

Three days after my enrollment, as I was about to enter my dormitory, a third-year man shouted harshly at me, "Halt!" When I did, he hurried over and demanded angrily, "Why did you fail to salute me?"

I did not know what to answer, as I had not even seen him until after his command.

"Attention!" he roared. "Stand with your feet apart and be prepared. I'm going to knock out some of your laxity."

He hit me in the face with his fist a dozen times. If I had been standing at attention, his first blow would have knocked me to the ground. This treatment came as a great shock to me. I trudged into my billet bruised and bleeding.

The next day at breakfast a senior discovered that my uniform was improperly buttoned, and I received another dozen blows on my swollen face. My second assailant was stronger than the first. My left ear kept ringing all the rest of the day.

When a plebe was singled out for discipline, all other students in his platoon were lined up and given one blow. All plebes were subjected to this unique system of discipline, from which there was no respite. Each Sunday the 180 freshmen were assembled on the parade ground and made to stand at attention for four or five hours under the broiling sun. Instructors and their upper classmen "assistants" kept watching and ordering us. The hours of this Sunday lesson were punctuated by almost continuous fist beatings.

After a few months of such treatment the newcomers became sheeplike in their obedience. Every man's face bore evidence of the brutality we endured. My ear trouble became chronic, and I suffer from it to this day.

For some of the boys the rigors of this discipline did not seem to be too much of a shock. They had perhaps grown up in a similar environment. In some Japanese homes a stern father chastised his children liberally. In many provincial schools the boys were treated tyrannically by their teachers.

For me it was different. I was the proud son of a samurai family. No member of my family had ever tried to hit me. In my schooling harsh methods of discipline were never employed.

Perhaps I was spoiled to some extent. Perhaps I was not ready for a military career. At any rate, the Eta Jima discipline outraged and embittered me. Even today I remember those early days in the Academy with a bad taste in my mouth.

Certain of my seniors were sadistic brutes. They took singular delight in terrorizing freshmen. To this day I feel a revulsion at seeing these men, even though we have since shared the labors and miseries of war, and the same luck in surviving it.

We were roused by bugles each day at 0530, and we studied and drilled until lights out at 2100, without a moment of relaxation. The harsh Sunday routine continued for six months. Freshmen were then given their first day off and life became a little more bearable. All regular beatings ended with our plebe year.

On days off, no students were allowed to leave the immediate vicinity of the town. Sunday routine was to climb hills, hike around the island, or sprawl in the club.

One of my most outstanding classmates was Ko Nagasawa. He came from northern Japan, was a most personable character, and did not seem to mind the Spartan discipline of the Academy. He often amazed me with his wise-cracks after savage discipline by instructors or elder students.

He and I stood near the top of our plebe class of 180 men. He served well in command and staff duties during the Pacific War, joined the new Japanese navy in 1954, and became its top admiral in 1956. In the Eta Jima days he was liked and respected by all his classmates but no one foresaw such a future for him.

I know that many of my comrades look back on their Academy days with sweet nostalgia. But, because of the physical punishment alone, I do not share their feelings.

Letters from home often bore disconcerting news. They were another cause for my unhappiness at the Academy. First came the sad news that my elder sister, Uta, had died of tuberculosis. Because she left two small children, my other sister, Kiyo, was persuaded to marry Uta's widower. Kiyo wrote me of her reluctance and then of her eventual resignation. That situation disturbed me greatly, for I was very fond of Kiyo.

A year later Kiyo deserted her husband and stepchildren and returned home. In those days such an act was a total violation of behavior for a Japanese woman. But I could not blame her. I knew that she must have had good reason.

Such developments coupled with the Spartan campus life served to keep me in a state of almost constant distress and depression for the first three years. There was a new commandant for the Academy during my last year. This was Vice Admiral Kantaro Suzuki, the first truly great man in my life.

Admiral Suzuki was in command for just two days when he summoned a faculty meeting. In a burst of anger he sternly forbade all physical discipline. "This school is supposed to produce fine officers, not cattle," he stormed.

Suzuki thereupon instituted a series of sweeping reforms in the entire Academy system. He sought to encourage the students' interest and thus their desire to learn, and he was unalterably opposed to all forms of brutality.

It was my feeling that Admiral Suzuki should have come much earlier. Unfortunately for the school, Suzuki did not stay long. He was too big a man for Eta Jima, or even the Imperial Navy. He was retired comparatively early to become chamberlain to the Emperor. In 1945 he became premier and steered the nation in its surrender to the Allies. After him a procession of mediocre admirals commanded Eta Jima, and Suzuki's reforms were gradually forgotten.

On July 16, 1921, I graduated fortieth out of 150 students. My parents were happy and proud when they learned it. I knew, however, that I could have done better.

4

The year of my enrollment at Eta Jima marked the end of World War I. Japan took part in that war on the side of the Allies. The nation sustained no war damage, and Japanese businessmen made enormous wealth during the war.

With the armistice came world peace and a tremendous depression in Japan. Even at Eta Jima, secluded though it was from the outside world, the economic depression was much in evidence and reflected by the general atmosphere.

Within the year of my graduation the five great naval powers—Great Britain, the United States, Japan, France and Italy—concluded a disarmament agreement, setting a maximum tonnage for their naval ships.

The 150 cadets of my class were assigned to cruisers *Izumo* and *Yagumo*. I was in the latter. These 6,000-ton warships had been Japan's main strength in the Sino-Japanese War of 1894–5. Any 25-year-old ship is difficult to operate. A warship of that age is more a liability than an asset.

We youngsters, however, were so happy that we could hardly restrain ourselves from shouting with joy. We knew we would soon be leaving on a world cruise. Nothing could dampen our buoyant feelings. The ships were decrepit and awful to look at. But none of us cared.

For a month the two cruisers drilled in coastal waters around Yokosuka. Our individual chores and assignments were sheer drudgery. Many of us began to look back on Eta Jima days as if they had been kindergarten time.

There is an old saying in the Imperial Navy: "Navy castes are made up of officers, NCOs, cattle (meaning enlisted men), and lastly, cadets." In other words, it was generally accepted that the life of Eta Jima graduates in their initial shipboard assignment was more miserable than that of any recruit.

Japanese warships were never built with any idea of comfort for their occupants. They had no regular sleeping quarters for enlisted men or cadets. At night we spread hammocks in any available space to sleep. Meals consisted of rice and barley with some canned fish or meat.

The life of enlisted recruits was miserable. But they each had one specific job to learn, and could concentrate on that. A cadet, however, had to learn every shipboard duty—from boilerman to sextant operation—in the fine manner worthy of Imperial Naval officers. We had no time to call our own.

After a seemingly endless month of arduous training, the two superannuated ships left Yokosuka for the United States on the first leg of the world tour. Many Japanese youngsters were attracted to a naval career largely because of this chance to see the world.

As the cruise ships weighed anchor there was much joy and hilarity among the cadets. We thought our ordeals were over. How wrong we were. We had failed to reckon with the merciless waves of the Pacific Ocean. Every one of us fell helplessly ill two days after we left Yokosuka. Even I, a rugged healthy young man, retched in agony throughout the first leg of the voyage.

When we arrived at Honolulu a fortnight later, the young cadets staggered weakly down the ramps. I felt like kissing the ground to thank God for the end of that murderous ordeal at sea. My school nickname, "Dolphin," seemed singularly inappropriate on this occasion, and this sorry fish lost 30 pounds in the two-week ordeal. So did many others.

Vice Admiral Hanroku Saito, who commanded the training cruise, decided to spend a week in Hawaii. This decision was partly in response to the enthusiastic welcome and hospitality of the Japanese population of the islands, but more largely to enable us cadets to recuperate.

Our next port was San Diego, whence we cruised south, passed through the Panama Canal, and arrived at New York on October 29, 1921, more than two months after we had left Yokosuka. The five-power disarmament conference was then going on in Washington. It is possible that the arrival of our ancient, outmoded ships at that particular time may have been a calculated move.

Japan in those days was taking great pains to conceal its true strength. The battleships *Nagato* and *Mutsu*, completed in 1920 and 1921, were supposed to be conventional 32,600- tonners, with eight 16-inch guns, capable of only 23 knots. The truth was that these 35,000-ton warships with a maximum speed of nearly 27 knots were definitely superior to the U.S.S. *Maryland*.

Japan was also not bragging about the completion in 1921 of the world's first aircraft carrier, the 9,494-ton *Hosho*. Nor was the world told about the 1,345-ton *Shimakaze*, the new wonder destroyer. She was armed to the teeth with four 4.6-inch guns and six torpedo tubes, and could speed at 40 knots. Meanwhile two floating junk piles, clumsily manned by cadets, crawled unpretentiously around the American coast.

The people of New York City were most hospitable to us when we visited there. On a sight-seeing tour, for example, four of us walked into Wanamaker's Department Store, and a pleasant gentleman, who may have been the manager, took us to pose for a picture with him. I regret that I have forgotten his name.

Of the four boys in the picture, only the one on the left end, later Captain Matao Machida, and I have survived. Machida became a technical officer and specialized in the development of optical weapons. Living in Tokyo, he is an executive of the Canon Camera Company, producer of fine miniature cameras and lenses.

From New York we steamed across the Atlantic. By that time we had our sea legs and, too, that crossing was far more peaceful than the Pacific. We visited England and France before sailing through the Mediterranean Sea and the Indian Ocean toward home. We returned to Japan on March 9, 1922, after an absence of almost seven months.

By that time the outcome of the Washington Conference was announced. The results were most unsatisfactory to the Imperial Navy, and many high-ranking officers requested retirement as a consequence.

The disarmament agreement concluded at Washington in 1921 permitted Japan to maintain only 315,000 tons of battleships, as against 525,000 tons each for Britain and the United States, and 175,000 tons each for France and Italy. Aircraft carrier strength was limited to 81,000 tons for Japan, 135,000 tons each for Britain and the United States, and 60,000 tons each for France and Italy. As regards cruisers and other warships, the agreement set a ceiling on individual ship size of 10,000 tons but put no maximum on numerical count.

The agreement brought tears to the eyes of many Japanese naval officers. Battleship *Tosa*, 39,900 tons, launched in 1921, had to be sunk, and her sister ship, the *Kaga*, was converted to a carrier. Cruiser-battleships *Akagi* and *Amagi*, both 34,364 tons, were also ordered converted to carriers. *Akagi* was eventually converted, but *Amagi*, while in process, was demolished by the great earthquake of 1923. The high command was also obliged to destroy the design blueprints of four 47,500-ton battleships. These drawings had just been completed in 1921 after great effort by many technicians over a period of many months.

Naval opinion in Japan regarded the Washington Conference as a case of pure power politics which resulted in a terrible defeat for Japan. Many people were reminded of the enactment of the anti-Japanese immigration law in California in 1913, which caused the abrogation of the Anglo-Japanese alliance after World War I. Also brought to mind was the American boycott of the League of Nations after it had been formed under American guidance.

It was in this mental climate that Japan first came to consider the United States as a "potential enemy." Young officers, and cadets like myself, had no experience by which to measure this consideration, but that was the theory which our superior officers drummed into us daily.

My class of cadets all received commissions as ensigns shortly after our return from the world cruise. Five of us were assigned to duty in cruiser *Kasuga*. In our new role we at once had many things to be concerned about, but the "potential enemy" was not one of them.

The new assignment was not too inspiring for me. It brought to mind the Japanese adage, "It takes at least ten years to make a qualified seaman." *Kasuga* was not as aged as *Izumo* or *Yagumo*, but she had seen service in the Russo-Japanese War of 1904–5. I reminded myself, "You're still a trainee. Don't covet such a modern dreadnought as *Nagato*. Be patient! It's only six years since you enrolled at Eta Jima."

I reported on board *Kasuga* in May 1922. When the ship weighed anchor our destination was Russia. At first the assignment appeared to be a continuation of the world tour. *Kasuga*, however, was not on a mere training cruise. Its mission was to protect the Japanese residents of Siberia, then in the throes of a postwar revolution. Hundreds of Japanese had been massacred by Russian rebels at Nikolaievsk in 1920. Two years later Siberia was still in turmoil.

The experience for me was much as it had been on board *Yagumo* in that we did not fire a single shot. Since the destruction of her fleet by Japan in 1904–5, Russia had no warships to oppose us.

Kayuga's cruise in northern waters was my first shipboard experience in dense fog. In June we landed at Vladivostok, the famed Siberian port whose many sloping hills are reminiscent of Nagasaki. The misery of the defeated Russian people torn by civil war was shocking. What I saw in Vladivostok was in striking contrast to what I had seen in New York and the other thriving port cities of victorious countries. It occurred to me then that a nation must never lose a war. It was beyond any possible dream that Japan would suffer a fate such as that of Czarist Russia, let alone that it would come to pass within a mere 23 years.

After Vladivostok we visited Odomari, the southernmost port of Sakhalin, which had been ceded to Japan by Russia after the war of 1904–5. One could not then have dreamed that the sleepy, primitive port of Odomari would be wrested back by the Russians in 1945 and turned into the major naval base that Korsakov is today.

The Imperial Navy high command disdained the use of modern, fast ships for the unopposed operations in Siberia. But officers of keen diplomatic ability were chosen to lead the operation, because Japan was not then at war with Russia, and the operation involved many ticklish problems.

Kasuga's skipper, Captain Mitsumasa Yonai, was the second great man I served under. Like Admiral Suzuki, who had carried out sweeping reforms as commandant at Eta Jima, he had my highest respect and admiration. But these two men were strikingly different. Admiral Suzuki was a sharp, strong and outspoken character, Captain Yonai was taciturn. Still in his early forties, he was a strikingly handsome and dignified man. During the six months I served in *Kasuga*, I never saw him scold an officer. Yet the morale of his crew was extremely high. Every member knew he was with one of the greatest leaders the Imperial Navy ever produced.

Captain Yonai and Admiral Suzuki shared only one characteristic: they would not tolerate brutal methods of discipline. Yonai's own exemplary conduct was so stimulating that no stringent discipline was necessary in his command.

We junior officers were at first startled to find our commanding officer joining us during off-duty hours. He would nod at each of us in turn to grapple with him. After our recent arduous training at Eta Jima, we were pretty good at judo, and knew it, so our approach was timorous at first. Yet we soon learned that none of us could throw him to the mat. I tangled with him on occasion, and although he never took the offensive, he would stand like a rock and defeat the most fierce and aggressive assaults. Invariably his much younger opponents would come away from such encounters groggy, if not in a state of complete collapse.

It was during this tour of duty that I attended my first banquet. It was held ashore in a restaurant when our ship anchored and the local mayor or naval commandant was host. Pretty geisha girls in fancy kimonos served at the banquet. They played music, performed dances, poured *sake* (rice wine) for hosts and guests and kept the party alive by conversing in a refined and skillful manner. These pretty girls were a dazzling sight to me.

In a Japanese party there is an interesting practice called *kampai*, or "dry cup." In approaching a friend, one fills a cup with *sake* and invites him to drink. The friend drinks the cup dry, rinses it in fresh water, refills it with *sake*, and returns the cup to the well-wisher. The friend's only excuse for not drinking the offered cup is that he believes himself to be drunk.

I saw every one of 40 or 50 guests and hosts reaching and going through the *kampai* routine with Captain Yonai, one after another, and he would never decline. When most of the other guests were helpless, if not sprawling on the floor, Yonai sat straight as a stoic samurai although he had obliged all well-wishers and had drunk almost as much *sake* as all the other guests combined. His capacity in all things—like his judo ability—was unfathomable.

I learned that Yonai had been a naval attaché at the Japanese Embassy in Moscow before his assignment to *Kasuga* and he had trained well in vodka drinking bouts with the Russians. Yonai was also fluent in the Russian language.

At the end of such a party, I looked with awe at Captain Yonai sitting like a steel rod, while the others tumbled in disorder. The geisha girls would usually gather around him, doing their utmost to attract and please the handsome, dignified captain, but he was never known to "linger" with any of them.

It was a misfortune for Japan that Yonai had so comparatively few tours of shipboard duty. The Imperial Navy generally assigned its brilliant officers to headquarters duty ashore, and so the outstanding men were usually sadly lacking in shipboard experience.

Admiral Suzuki had been retired before the outbreak of the Pacific War. He had no voice in shaping naval tactics, strategy or policy. Yonai was opposed to the war, but his "defensive" approach was unsuccessful in dealing with the jingoistic Army officers who far outnumbered men of his caliber, and he was not successful in getting consideration for his views.

The episode is now famous in Japan of how Admiral Isoroku Yamamoto, Commander in Chief of the Combined Fleet in 1941, offered to relinquish his post to Yonai so that he could personally command the Pearl Harbor attack force. Unfortunately Yonai declined, but I believe he could have done every bit as well if not better than Yamamoto in that crucial post.

My tour in *Kasuga* ended on March 30, 1923, after I had requested assignment to specialist school. I had come to the realization that much more study was essential if I wished to be an officer like Yonai. From April to December, I received concentrated instruction in torpedoes and gunnery at Yokosuka.

While I was at Yokosuka Japan experienced her worst earthquake of modern times. It struck on September 1, 1923, in the vicinity of Tokyo and Yokohama, and damage to both cities was multiplied by ensuing fires. The damage was almost as heavy as they received from American bombings in World War II. Martial law was established in the area for a month, and I was put on emergency duty to help enforce it.

One of my outstanding impressions from that catastrophe was the prompt American help extended to these two stricken cities of Japan. United States warships raced to Tokyo Bay with relief supplies. That manifestation of unrestrained American good will was shattering to the indoctrination I had been getting against the "potential enemy."

As the year and my schooling were closing, there were decisions to be made about the direction of my career. The careers of officers in the Japanese Navy during the 1920s followed certain definite patterns. Headquarters officers were men with the best Academy and specialist school records; they received further education at Staff College. Yonai and Yamamoto belonged to this group. Battleship and cruiser officers had the second best records in Academy and specialist schools, but were usually without Staff College education. Officers with third best records in the schools were assigned to destroyers. Submarine officers, fourth rank at the Academy, received postgraduate study at submarine schools. Aviation officers, ranking fifth at the Academy, volunteered for study at aviation school. Last came the auxiliary-ship officers, who received no specialist schooling after Eta Jima.

It now seems absurd that aviation was drawing only fifth-rate naval officers in those days. The next 15 years saw marked changes in this situation, when flying came to attract the top men in each class. But that situation serves to explain why Japan failed to adjust from battleship to aircraft carrier dominance, even after air power proved itself as the decisive factor in the Pacific War. The officers who had the controlling voice in the high command thought only about battleships. Officers who were experts in air power did not have enough voice to make themselves heard.

Japan's top aviation officer of the war, Vice Admiral Takijiro Onishi, for instance, flunked the entrance examinations to the Staff College. So did I, and thus a career in destroyers was indicated. But it must be noted that brilliant students do not necessarily make good fighters.

My record at Yokosuka was not good, a matter for which I had no one but myself to blame. Out of complacence, after the long regimen of Eta Jima and subsequent training duties, I had taken to drink. Perhaps it was in childish emulation of Admiral Yonai, but I drank very heavily and often reported to class with a hangover. That was certainly bad.

Upon graduation from the school, I was assigned to sea again. I groaned at learning that my ship was *Hatsuyuki*, an obsolete third-rate destroyer. She was a 20-year-old ship of only 381 tons. By modern definition she was more of a destroyer escort, or even a sub-chaser, than a destroyer. But she could still run at 29 knots, compared to *Kasuga*'s maximum of 18 knots. It was the fastest ship I had ever been in. The speed fascinated me. Otherwise the new assignment was little more than a continuation of the training voyage. *Hatsuyuki* was based at Port Arthur, the southernmost naval port of Manchuria, to protect Japanese nationals living in Manchuria and North China. For a year we cruised around Kwantung Peninsula, dropping anchor from time to time at Yingko or Tientsin.

But shipboard life had greatly changed for me. An ensign, and one of the ship's few bridge officers, commanded about 60 crewmen. Life in such a ship is not always easy. Meals were never good. At sea, the crew completely gave up the luxury of a bath. We lacked water even to wash our faces, so no one bothered about shaving. In rough or stormy seas the ship was most uncomfortable, and we had to hold fast to supports for long hours at a time. The crew, however, was like one big family. Every man was well acquainted with every other. Harsh discipline was never necessary. I began to feel at home and enjoy my duties. I was satisfied with my decision for a destroyer career.

In December 1924, 1 was promoted to lieutenant junior grade and transferred to *Sanae*, a destroyer of about 1,000 tons. This was not much different from my assignment in the *Hatsuyuki*. In *Sanae* we cruised around Manchuria and North China for a year.

In December 1925, came the long-coveted duty when I was designated chief navigator of *Amatsukaze*, a first-line destroyer of 1,300 tons. Here was my first real fighting ship in the seven years since my enrollment in Eta Jima. It was thrilling to run the 37.5-knot ship. I was no longer a fledgling trainee but a real navy officer. It was a realization of great glory, wonder, and achievement.

Years later I would find out how wrong I was.

5

Names of Japanese ships must sound strange to foreign readers. Many Westerners during the Pacific War called a Japanese ship "Maru." It must be noted, however, that warships or other government ships do not have names ending with *Maru*. *Maru* has always been and still is used only for merchant ships or fishing boats.

Maru literally means circle, round or chubby. In medieval Japan, *Maru* was frequently used for childhood names of boys. For example, in his childhood Hideyoshi Toyotomi, the famed warlord of the 16th century, often considered Japan's Napoleon, was called Hiyoshi Maru, which may be translated literally as "chubby (or lucky) sunny boy"; and as a youth Yoshitsune Minamoto, the great 12th century general, was called Ushiwaka Maru, meaning "healthy and strong as a calf."

The Japanese people, by way of personification, came to add *Maru* to ship names. In the last 100 years *Maru* has been dropped from the names of all government ships. Japanese warships, like those of other nations, are classified so that all ships of a given type have names of the same category. Hence anyone familiar with the system can tell at once from its name whether a ship is a battleship, cruiser, destroyer, and so on.

Japanese battleships were always named after ancient provinces or mountains. Famed *Yamato* was christened for the province of Japan's most ancient capital city, Nara, in Central Honshu. This word was also used in ancient times to mean the whole country of Japan. This may explain the close attachment felt by the Imperial Navy for the greatest battleship ever built. Her sister ship, *Musashi*, was named after the province immediately north of Tokyo. Exceptions to this practice are *Haruna* and her sisters—*Kirishima*, *Kongo*, *Hiei*. Originally classed as battle cruisers, and named for mountains, they retained those names even after they were reclassified as battleships in 1930.

Heavy cruisers were traditionally named after mountains, and light cruisers were given the names of rivers. Carriers usually bore poetic names having to do with flight. *Hosho*, the world's first keel-up carrier, built in 1921, means "Soaring Phoenix." *Hiryu* and *Soryzi*, of the Pearl Harbor attack, may be translated "Flying Dragon" and "Blue Dragon," respectively. *Kaga* and *Akagi*, which perished along with the two Dragons at Midway in June 1942, are exceptional names for carriers because *Kaga* is a province and *Akagi* a mountain. The explanation is that these ships were converted from a battleship and a cruiser.

Submarines and sub-chasers had only numbers. Large submarines had the letter "I" for a prefix, while, the numbers of smaller ones were prefixed by "RO." The numbers of sub-chasers were prefixed by the letters "SC."

First-class destroyers were given meteorological names such as *Hatsuyuki* (First Snow), *Fubuki* (Blizzard), *Shimakaze* (Island Wind), *Amatsukaze*

(Heavenly Wind), *Akitsuki* (Autumn Moon), *Fuyutsuki* (Winter Moon), or *Yugumo* (Evening Cloud). Second-class destroyers were named for trees, flowers, or fruit such as *Sanae* (Rice Seedling), *Sakura* (Cherry) or *Kaba* (Birch).

When a Japanese warship was scrapped, a new one often inherited the old name, but without any signifying numeral like "II." Thus I served in two different ships named *Amatsukaze*.

My first assignment in *Amatsukaze* allowed me to be in the homeland on active duty for the first time. The destroyer was based at Kure, which is within a stone's throw of Eta Jima. After living at sea for many months, shore life was quite strange. Whenever I walked in the busy streets of Kure, sailors snapped to attention and saluted me smartly. On board ship or at naval stations it was perfectly ordinary and expected, but somehow it gave me a queer sensation to be in military uniform among the civilian populace.

For seven years I had lived in austerity, under harsh discipline and constant training, with hardly any chance for pleasure and relaxation. Now twenty-six years old, I was chief navigator of a modern destroyer. My monthly pay of 75 yen (then equivalent to $37.50) was quite a sum in those days. Here, I suddenly realized, was my first chance to enjoy a youthful fling.

One Friday night two other lieutenants and I decided to have our own private party in a Kure restaurant. We called for three geishas, at one yen per hour each. They sang and danced for us, kept our cups filled with *sake*, and maintained clever conversation which livened the party and made the time pass quickly.

The party broke up in time for our return to the ship by the 2300 deadline. As we departed one of the girls whispered to me, "Lieutenant, do come back alone tomorrow night and ask for me again. My name is Utamaru. Please remember me." This petite geisha was the youngest and prettiest of the three. I looked into her tender eyes and nodded.

The following night I returned alone to the restaurant and booked her. She sang prettily and danced gracefully, but her greatest charm for me was her lack of sophistication. She was eighteen and had been in the profession for a year.

"I was your age eight years ago," I said, "when I enrolled at Eta Jima. You know Eta Jima?"

"Yes, sir, I know it well, for I am from nearby Nomi Jima."

She had a lovely smile. I felt instinctively that her feeling for me was something more than merely professional.

Again, suddenly, I recalled being her age and my flustering experience at the hotel in Hiroshima on the eve of my entrance examinations for Eta Jima. That hotel maid had been too overwhelming for any 18-year-old boy.

Now the situation was reversed. I emptied many cups of *sake* and got tipsy, but I no longer cared. I had a 24-hour pass, and she lingered that night with me.

The status of a geisha is generally not well understood by foreigners. She is not a prostitute. Her job is to brighten a party and make it gay. If she lingers with a patron she does so of her own free will. It is not a routine of her occupation. My restaurant bill, including her fees, came to about 10 yen. Two days later, I was back again. I had fallen seriously in love with the girl and knew it. Within two weeks I had spent a whole month's salary.

She realized what was happening and worriedly confronted me, "You must not ruin yourself. Why don't you rent a modest room where I can visit you, so that you won't be squeezed of money."

I took her advice the following month when my destroyer returned to Kure from its routine cruise. After renting a room I went to the old restaurant, booked her again, and told her of my "shore base." I was truly skeptical about the possibility of her coming to my room. Utamaru, as was customary, had received from her employer a substantial cash advance at the start of her career. Her widowed father, an impoverished farmer with five other children, received that money. Her earnings, from which the advance was repaid, were divided with her employer. A geisha had to buy new, expensive kimonos every season and there was seldom enough income to repay her debt and have anything left to save.

To my surprise and delight, Utamaru appeared the following evening at my room. It was sheer joy to be alone with her. Everything else seemed unimportant. Indeed, I was even unaware of how great a sacrifice it was for her to come to my place. I thought she was merely forfeiting an evening's earnings and I gave her five yen in a spirit of some generosity. The fact was that her employer demanded extra money if she went to a non-restaurant place, where the customer was then supposed to pay double the usual charge of one yen per hour. Unwilling to tell me of this situation, she paid the difference out of her own pocket. And while her debt snowballed she continued to keep our rendezvous.

Ignorant of her desperate circumstances, I was having troubles of my own. Every month my salary was spent to the last penny. But I was young and in love, and youth seeks only the joys of life, taking them for granted. The cares must seek out youth. It was five months before they caught up with me.

I was just going ashore early one evening in October 1926, when an orderly brought word that the captain wanted to see me. I found him in his quarters, alone, pacing back and forth. His dour look made a chill run down my spine.

"Lieutenant Hara? Be seated. I have something personal to discuss with you."

His tone was strangely detached, and he was restraining himself with effort. I wondered what he wanted to discuss.

"You have been in service long enough to know that, in destroyers, unlike bigger ships, we live like a family. As your commander, I ought to know your personal problems and be your consultant."

"Yes, captain, you are right, sir."

"Well . . . uh, I don't wish to meddle in your private life. You are young, single, and entitled to enjoy your youth. But don't you feel you are overdoing it?"

"Sir?"

"I mean your girl friend. I don't blame you for occasionally entertaining a geisha. Yes, occasionally, but you must be going broke living with this girl. That is a bit too much, son. How old are you now?"

"I shall be 26 on the sixteenth of this month, sir."

"Why don't you marry and settle down? You are fully eligible. Your record has been very good. There are thousands of respectable families who would be delighted to have you as a son-in-law."

"Well, captain. It does not seem to me that a junior officer's life is too adaptable to marriage. I simply have not thought of getting married."

"Hmmmm . . . and so you live with a geisha?"

"I guess you are right, sir."

"You stupid idiot! I had never figured you for such a moron. The Imperial Navy cannot tolerate an officer's living with a geisha. Are you mad? Are you out of your mind?"

"Forgive me, sir, but I do not feel that Utamaru is a woman of ill repute. If my living with her is objectionable, I'll apply for permission to marry her."

"The Navy will never approve it! Don't you realize you will ruin your career? I have had a letter of complaint from her employer. Do you realize that your girl has run two thousand yen in debt because of you? Your conduct is most unbecoming an officer. Change your way or you are finished as a naval officer. I am disgusted talking to you. Get out!"

I got out quickly. Depressed and miserable, I trudged back and groped for a solution to my problem. There did not seem to be any. In desperation I finally decided to ask my brothers for help and advice. That night I wrote to both of them: Shigeru, an employee of the South Manchurian Railways, and Sakutaro, who worked in Kobe at a salt transportation company.

They replied promptly with bristling letters that showed them to be as outraged as my squadron commander. But, good brothers that they are, each enclosed a few hundred yen, saying it was all they could raise to help liquidate my shameful life. Yet both admonished that they would disown me unless I gave up my "immoral life" once and for all.

The most difficult part of the whole ordeal was my last meeting with Utamara. She was perfectly calm, however, and said quietly at the end. "I have never even dreamed of becoming the bride of an officer like you. I have behaved according to my own desires, and I am solely responsible for the debt I have chosen to incur. The few months shared with you have been the happiest time of my life.

"Do not worry about my future. I have recently heard from my aunt in the United States. She is married to a successful Japanese emigrant and has suggested that I come to America. I am planning to accept her invitation.

"You must marry into a good family and become a great naval officer. Concentrate on your studies and forget about me."

Utamaru was a fine woman. Her real name was Harako Takai. I have never heard of her since, but I hope that she is living happily in America.

6

On December 1, 1926, 1 was promoted to lieutenant senior grade and was enrolled again in the In-service School at Yokosuka. For a year I studied in the advanced course of the Destroyer Department. This course was open to officers recommended by squadron commanders as potential future skippers.

I was in the mood for a change of scenery and atmosphere, and Yokosuka is some 300 air miles east of Kure. There I was able to fling off the torpor which followed the catastrophic end of my romance. I pursued new studies which filled my time too full for personal sorrow. I was also preoccupied with the growing tension in China.

The Chinese mainland in those days was contested by two major warlords—Chiang Kai-shek in the south and Chang Tso-lin in the north. Chiang's force gained the upper hand early in 1927, and had occupied Nanking by March 24. There Chiang's forces made a major mistake. It is a historical fact, although now eclipsed by the later and more publicized Japanese acts, that Chiang's troops sacked Nanking, broke into consulates and molested Japanese, British, American, and French nationals.

Three British and American warships bombarded Nanking. The Japanese navy landed a token force in Nanking to protect Japanese residents. As a result, Chiang apologized to these nations and broke away from the Communists.

In May, 1927 Japan landed its army troops on the Shantung Peninsula in North China in an attempt to prevent further incidents. This act, however, served only to fan anti-Japanese sentiment in China.

To present-day readers, such landing actions may seem awkward. In fact, however, China was a country torn by civil war, with two governments and without unified sovereignty. Japan's right of garrison had been acknowledged since the end of the Russo-Japanese war in 1905. Still the Japanese action irritated the Chinese, and both governments encouraged anti-Japanese demonstrations.

In the summer of 1927, the second disarmament conference was held at Geneva. Japan adamantly demanded that the limitation of its naval ships be boosted from the previous 60 per cent of either Britain or the United States to 70 per cent. The two leading naval powers would not yield. The conference broke down. The five powers had to compromise on the agreement of 1921.

These world developments provided a strong impetus for me to get to work and study hard. By the time of my new assignment, destroyers and cruisers were assuming more importance than they ever had in World War I.

Upon graduation from the command school, I was reassigned to shipboard duty—this time as chief torpedo officer in destroyer *Susuki* (Pampas Grass). This assignment extended over a period of two years, longer than any of my previous tours of active duty. The ship cruised in China waters, mostly between North China and Formosa, occasionally dropping anchor at Tsingtao, the key port of Shantung Peninsula, then the crucial tinderbox of China.

Our squadron was at Keelung, Formosa on April 1, 1928, when we heard that Chiang Kai-shek had started a long northward drive toward Shantung. This news sent our squadron racing to Tsingtao. There the situation appeared calm, so we returned to the Pescadores on April 15.

The infamous Tsinan Incident occurred only two weeks later. The northern troops, demoralized at their imminent defeat, started looting in Tsinan, capital of Shantung. The Chiang force captured Tsinan on May 1, but went on to sack the city, as they had done in Nanking two years earlier. Fourteen Japanese residents were killed, more than 20 others were missing and all of the 114 Japanese houses were looted and completely demolished.

The Japanese Army rushed troops from Manchuria and Korea to the scene and restored order. This "big stick" policy, however, resulted only in embittering the Chinese. And this incident sowed the seed for the large-scale Japanese invasion which occurred later.

In late 1928, I was at Kobe and met my brother Sakutaro, who urged me to get married. I laughed and said, "Knowing of my bad background, do you think I am really eligible?"

Sakutaro, who has always been a good brother to me, replied seriously, "Let me find some good candidates for you." I told him to go ahead, but I did not think he'd have any luck.

About a month later, I received a letter from my brother enclosing a young lady's photograph and a few brief remarks in which he recommended her highly as a likely bride for me.

Miss Chizu Asayama, 22, was the adopted daughter of Japan's biggest leather goods manufacturer. The letter said that her foster-mother preferred a navy officer as the girl's husband because she wanted to live with her, and a seaman is away from home much of the time.

The photo convinced me that she was an exceedingly beautiful woman. She was a graduate of Tokyo's highly reputed Ochanomizu Girls' Higher School. A daughter of a wealthy family, my brother wrote, her trousseau would contain all necessary apparel and her dowry included five good-sized houses to be rented in Kamakura, a high-class resort town near Yokosuka.

The whole thing sounded unreal to me. Why would such a girl pick a man with my background? She could easily have chosen an honor graduate, assured of becoming an admiral. Her family would certainly hire a private investigator to check on my background. I suspected that she might also have an undesirable background relating to men.

I showed the letter to my devoted orderly and asked his opinion. The NCO solemnly replied, "Lieutenant, my brother is a regular police detective. If you wish, sir, I'll have him investigate her background."

I agreed and a month later his brother supplied me with a full report which said that Miss Asayama was unimpeachable.

I first met her early in March, 1929 for about an hour. Relatives of both sides were present at this important meeting. On the following day I notified her family of my acceptance and she reciprocated. This was done in the traditional manner of marriage arrangements in Japan. Westerners may consider it strange to make such an important decision after just one meeting. Actually marriages arranged in this fashion in Japan have proved more successful than many marriages based solely on romance.

The meeting was arranged only after full screening had satisfied both sides that the other was acceptable. After such a meeting a proposition is seldom declined unless a serious defect is discovered.

The wedding ceremony was held at a Shinto shrine in Tokyo on May 25, 1929, while my destroyer stopped over at Yokosuka. I was granted two days off for the occasion. Immediately after the ceremony we took a one-day honeymoon trip to Atami hot springs, some 50 miles southwest of Tokyo. On the following day I returned to Yokosuka alone. My new wife left the train at Oiso, another resort town midway between Atami and Yokosuka, where her family lived. For some time thereafter, I lived a strange married life, meeting my wife only once in every few months.

Six months later I was transferred to *Akikaze* (Autumn Wind), a 1,500-ton destroyer. This new assignment, as the destroyer's chief torpedo officer, lasted for a full year.

In April 1930, Japan, Great Britain and the United States reached another disarmament agreement in London which established ceilings for auxiliary warships. The 1921 ceilings on capital ships were maintained. This result set Japanese naval officers in a frenzy. They were infuriated at the result which put Japanese naval strength in heavy cruisers, light cruisers, and destroyers at 62, 70, and 70 per cent of the United States. And submarine strength was established at parity by the agreement.

It is difficult today to explain why these results were so unsatisfactory to the Japanese Navy. Japan had insisted on at least 70 per cent of America's strength in heavy cruisers. And parity in submarines was disappointing because Japan then had 77,900 tons compared with America's 52,700 tons.

All these arguments later proved silly when American industrial capacity produced naval ships in volume which overwhelmed Japan in the Pacific War. But in 1930, Japanese naval officers argued vehemently about the limitation. They insisted that Japan had been forced to swallow American terms at London. They came then to consider the United States not merely a potential enemy, but a probable enemy. All maneuvers from then on were carried out on the theory that the "hypothetical enemy" was the United States.

On November 8, 1930, my wife was delivered of our first child. We named her Yoko. Four weeks later I was assigned as chief torpedo officer to the destroyer *Fubuki* (Blizzard). During my one-year tour of duty on board this ship, I developed a friendship with another of the unforgettable people in my life. He was our squadron commander, Captain Chuichi Nagumo.

Nagumo was an instructor when I attended the Yokosuka school. He had then just returned from a year of study in the United States. He was one of the most brilliant destroyer experts in the Imperial Navy. It was certainly enlightening to live with him for a year. Nagumo encouraged me to study hard by loaning me various books he had obtained in the United States. Nagumo liked me and insisted that I should enroll in the Staff College.

In those days I never imagined that this officer, later vice admiral, would one day command great Japanese task forces in attacks on Pearl Harbor and Midway. Following the Midway debacle Nagumo was subjected to all kinds of criticism. In my memory, however, he remains a brilliant and aggressive naval officer, and a most kindhearted man.

7

Despite Captain Nagumo's daily interest and encouragement, I failed to pass the Staff College entrance examinations. Instead, in September 1932 I was appointed an instructor. This may sound puzzling, but such a development was not unusual in the Imperial Navy. My choice of this program meant that I was giving up the chance of a career as a headquarters staff officer to become a specialist.

In the three years following my marriage I had been tackling a private project. I did not discuss its details with anyone, knowing too well the audacity and the possible impact of my studies. I knew, too, that the reaction of my colleagues would be to scoff if they learned of my intentions.

Captain Nagumo had encouraged me in preparation for the Staff College. I read every book he recommended as well as his own dissertations on American mobilization potential, made during his studies in the United States. But I simply could not concentrate. I knew the importance of my private project, and it kept me from applying myself to other studies. Even with Captain Nagumo's support I flunked the Staff College examinations.

My project was completed in mid-1932. It had involved thousands of complicated calculations. In short, I had proved mathematically the faults of Japanese torpedo doctrine and established a new manual. The published results created a sensation in the Imperial Navy.

It is very hard to establish new doctrine in a military organization. Most career officers trained in an old theory are conservative-minded and react unfavorably to anything new. I was exceptionally fortunate. There was practically no objection to my new theory, and the Imperial Navy torpedo manual was in fact scrapped and replaced with a manual based on the results of my work. Thus it was that I came to be assigned to teach my theory at the Staff College.

I still take more pride in my achievement of correcting Japanese torpedo doctrine than in any other activity of my naval career, including my accomplishments in World War II. It is not easy to explain my theory in detail without using many calculations involving algebra, geometry, trigonometry, and calculus. Simply told, however, it evolved in this way.

After graduating from the Yokosuka Specialist School in 1923, I was generally assigned to destroyer duty, and usually as torpedo officer. I studied and trained religiously on the subject of torpedo firing. For almost three years the torpedo manual was my bible. Every week our squadron would go out on torpedo-firing maneuvers. The torpedoes were fired without warheads, as an economy measure, but were set to run just below the target to simulate a direct hit. After three years of intense training and practice, my score was such that I began to have doubts about my marksmanship. I seldom scored any direct hits.

My early reaction at the failures was to berate myself and work harder to improve. I trained frantically until I could tell at a glance through binoculars the distance and speed of the targets. After checking my judgment with instrumental measurement and finding that I was accurate, and still not scoring hits in practice, I began to be suspicious of the Navy's torpedo doctrine.

A destroyer's punch is packed in its torpedoes. A destroyer, usually about 300 feet in length, knifes through the waves at 30 knots or more, closes on its enemy ship, opens fire with all guns, and finishes off the opponent with torpedoes. A Japanese destroyer carried only 16 torpedoes. From two sets of four torpedo tubes fore and aft, eight "fish" could be released at two-second intervals. Once the first set of eight was released, it usually took about 10 minutes to reload the tubes. Therefore a torpedo officer's assignment was very important. A destroyer's small guns are no match for the tremendous fire-power of a battleship. If the first spread of eight torpedoes fails to strike home, the odds are completely against the smaller ship. It would be sunk easily during the ten minutes needed to reload the tubes. And that was how umpires of our war maneuvers ruled.

My destroyer was, thus "sunk" many times while I could only stand on the bridge, watch my "fish" miss the target, and grit my teeth. When I observed that other destroyer torpedo scores were as poor as mine, I gradually came to the conclusion that direct hits were little more than pure chance. I began to doubt the basic formula.

The accepted doctrine was to cover a total spread of 20 degrees in firing the eight torpedoes. After careful analysis of all the many factors concerned, I concluded that the 20-degree spread resulted in hits only if my destroyer, describing a hyperbolic curve at 30 knots, released its torpedoes at the peak of the hyperbola, at a target 2,000 meters distant, starting to draw away on an evasive curving course at 20 knots. Over a period of many weeks of maneuvers I discovered that the opposing squadron was apt to start its evasive turning before my ship was ready to release torpedoes. Also I discovered the necessity of considering every element of computation anew, including the 2-second interval between each of the eight torpedoes.

This research was eye-opening for me. As my studies progressed, I applied each new step of my theory in our practice maneuvers, and my marksmanship improved steadily. By the time I was serving under Captain Nagumo, I had achieved a reputation as the highest scoring torpedo officer in the entire navy. That was probably one reason why Nagumo was so interested in me, and why my theory was so readily accepted by the Navy in 1932.

My manual revolutionized the Imperial Navy's torpedo doctrine. Within a year of its promulgation there was an improvement in torpedo marksmanship throughout the Navy.

A very important technical development for Japanese torpedo tactics came in 1933 when Rear Admiral Kaneji Kishimoto and Captain Toshihide Asakama of the Kure Torpedo Institute developed a torpedo propelled by oxygen, instead of compressed air. This oxygen-fueled torpedo, a top secret of the Imperial Navy, was superior to the torpedoes of every other nation.

	Speed (knots)	Range (meters)	Explosive charge (kilograms)
Japan (61 centimeters)	49	22,000	500
	36	40,000	500
U.S.A. (53 centimeters)	48	4,000	300
	32	8,000	300
Britain (53 centimeters)	46	3,000	320
	30	10,000	320

The Japanese torpedo, in addition to being much faster and longer ranging than the best American or British torpedoes, had another great advantage. Ordinary torpedoes, driven by compressed air, leave a long, white, telltale track which is easily detected and evaded by a fast ship. But an oxygen-fueled torpedo runs without leaving a trace on the surface.*

The introduction of my new torpedo manual and the invention of the oxygen-torpedo were a great boost for the morale of Japanese destroyer men. Ship design was being improved steadily at the same time, until destroyers were fast becoming the darlings of the fleet. Destroyer officers were no longer concerned about Japan's numerical disadvantage dictated by the last disarmament agreement. They realized the great supremacy of the Japanese destroyer fleet, which they figured would play a major role in any war to come.

They failed to reckon with the miraculous development of electronic weapons by the United States and the overwhelming superiority of American air strength. These were the most decisive factors in determining the outcome of World War II.

This is not to say that there was complacency in our efforts. Our training was more strenuous than ever in promoting familiarity with the new mighty torpedoes. Standard daily orders were to close within 500 meters of the target before releasing these long-range torpedoes. Every officer was told to recover the torpedo even though in practice they were fired without warheads.

---

*Japan's oxygen-fueled torpedo remained a well-guarded secret. Not until after the war did the U.S. Navy learn its full characteristics.

We did obey this second order, because a single torpedo then cost 5,000 yen ($2,500). Moreover, we knew we must not take any chance that this torpedo might fall into alien hands and its secret be discovered. Sometimes an entire fleet would comb a wide area of the ocean for many hours to recover one errant torpedo. On stormy days we even cancelled maneuvers for fear that a torpedo might be lost.

The orders for closing to 500 meters were not, however, taken seriously. I never heard of anyone doing it in maneuvers, although later I sank three American destroyers by this method. The enemy's course during battle is too unpredictable. In order to torpedo his ship, the attacking destroyer must approach the course of his target, close quickly, fire, and then break off in a curve. A high-speed destroyer cannot slow down quickly to avoid a collision—and mid-ocean collisions are usually fatal. Also, to close with an enemy within 500 meters means braving dangerous gunfire.

In maneuvers we usually fired torpedoes at a range of about 2,000 meters. In actual warfare, the average distance was probably 4,000 to 5,000 meters—a distance which still outranged American torpedoes. In all fairness, however, I must cite the bravery of American destroyers. In my experience they always tried to close to within effective range of their torpedoes.

I was promoted to lieutenant commander on November 15, 1933. By this time I was the father of two daughters. It was twelve years since my graduation from the Naval Academy, and I felt like a full-fledged navy officer at last. It was elating to realize that, thanks to my work on torpedo doctrine, I was one of the youngest commanders in the Imperial Navy and was even ahead of my classmates who had been admitted to the Staff College.

8

For Japan the period from 1931 through 1937 was marked by a series of internal and external troubles which are now far more interesting to contemplate than they were to endure. These troubles were to culminate in the Pacific War. I cannot properly evaluate these fateful steps toward war because I lived through this period involved in my own studies and shipboard assignments. But a listing of the major events of those years may serve to indicate the path Japan was striding, headlong to war.

On September 18, 1931, the Japanese Army clashed with Chang Hsueh-liang's troops near Mukden, Manchuria. The fire of war quickly spread to the whole of Manchuria, where Japan destroyed the opposing Chinese troops and promptly established the puppet empire of Manchukuo.

On May 15, 1932, a dozen young army and navy officers stormed his office and assassinated conservative Prime Minister Tsuyoshi Inukai.

In March, 1933, Japan withdrew from the League of Nations after that world body had accused Japan of aggression in Manchuria.

In December, 1934, Japan notified the United States and Britain that she was scrapping the naval disarmament agreement.

In August, 1935, Lieutenant Colonel Saburo Aizawa, a fanatic extreme rightist, walked into the office of Lieutenant General Tetsuzan Nagata, Military Affairs Bureau Chief in the War Office, and slew him with his sword.

On February 26, 1936, hotheaded officers of the First Division attempted a *coup d'état*. Divided into small groups, they stormed the homes of senior statesmen, and assassinated four of them. This was the most grievous of Japan's internal incidents, but it fell short of the planned nationwide rebellion.

As a lieutenant commander, I was given command of a destroyer for the first time on November 1, 1934. I served as Judge in a Navy court martial in 1934 and again in 1935, thereby acquiring some knowledge of law, so the 1936 coup came as a horrible shock to me. My destroyer, *Nagatsuki* (Long Moon), attached to the Combined Fleet, was then operating around Southern Kyushu. Emperor Hirohito ordered the Fleet to rush to Tokyo Bay. His Majesty was incensed at the attempted coup and sternly ordered the army and navy to crush it. Fortunately the rebels surrendered before we had to fire on them. But I was dismayed at the gravity of the situation. I could no longer remain aloof, absorbed in my studies.

The so-called China Incident started on the 7th of July, 1937, at the Marco Polo bridge near Peiping. The army tried to keep the trouble contained in the vicinity of Peiping. But steadily growing anti-Japanese sentiment in China touched off incidents at several other places.

On the 23rd of August, that same year, I received my baptism of fire in a most unanticipated fashion. In that month, hordes of Chiang Kai-shek's army started an offensive in Shanghai against the Japanese residents, who were defended by about a division of Japanese marines (actually navy personnel trained for land operations). The marine division fought gallantly against heavy odds. For a time, however, it appeared that the Japanese were doomed, and the army commandeered a squadron of four destroyers to rush reinforcements from Nagoya to Shanghai.

One of the destroyers in the command was a new ship. *Amagiri* (Sky Mist) was of the very latest design. Although I was generally conceded to be the navy's top torpedo expert, my assignment to this ship had been a great and pleasant surprise.

Amagiri, a 2,370-ton destroyer, picked up some 300 army troops, armed to the teeth. They were packed like sardines into every available space in the ship. The four-ship squadron eased stealthily out of the big commercial port of Nagoya at midnight and made the 1,000-mile voyage to Shanghai in two days at the economical speed of 20 knots.

We sneaked into Shanghai harbor under cover of darkness, and I brought my ship quietly alongside a railroad pier at Woosung. The soldiers jumped quietly but quickly from the deck to the pier. Without warning, we were raked by bursts of machine-gun fire from the top floors of a darkened building some 50 yards away. *Amagiri's* six 127-mm. guns promptly replied with ferocious salvos at the unseen enemy. Sweat streamed down my forehead as I issued orders from the bridge.

It was fortunate that the enemy—apparently guerrillas or partisans—did not aim well. None of my men were hit, nor were any of the army troops. After a few salvos from our guns, the ominous building was silenced. I saw our soldiers dashing in with light machine guns, rushing into action, and ordered: "Pull away from the pier!"

We failed to achieve a "surprise," but the landing was still effective. Our ships were followed by others carrying Nagoya's third division. Two additional army divisions reached Shanghai from Kyushu. These efforts reversed the tide of battle and the Chinese offensive petered out. The Japanese drove all Chinese forces from Shanghai.

If the Japanese forces had stopped there, subsequent disaster might have been prevented. But the high command lost its head, kept pushing to the west, and in December, 1937 the Army occupied Nanking. The wishful thinking of army officers proved wrong when Chiang Kai-shek did not surrender upon the loss of his capital. He merely retreated to Hankow, then to Chungking, and kept resisting for eight more years.

While the army was pushing to Nanking, my squadron was employed to blockade the mainland coast. This assignment was quite dull, since our warships cruised completely unchallenged in Chinese seas. Once a week or so, we would halt a leisurely junk and inspect its cargo. If we found it to be carrying contraband, a few shells from the destroyer would sink the junk after its crew had been removed. As I say, the job was none too stimulating.

In November I took *Amagiri* back to Japan and the following month I was assigned to command of *Yamagumo*, another brand-new destroyer. After shakedown, I returned to China waters and the blockade assignment. While the war continued relentlessly on the mainland, I made my monotonous daily cruises, glumly watching the world situation. That was all I could do.

The Munich conference was held in September, 1938. In Europe Adolf Hitler's power was rising.

I was promoted to commander in November, but my monotonous China assignment continued until the end of March, 1939. For the next few months my outfit was ordered to our naval base at Chinhae, South Korea, mainly for training.

World War II at last exploded in Europe on September 3, 1939. Two months later, I was assigned to one of my rare tours of shore duty. I reported to the Naval Station at Maizuru where my duties were to train merchant skippers in combat movements. This was obviously in preparation for any "emergency" that might arise. This did not mean that the Imperial Navy had already made preparations for attacking Pearl Harbor. The merchant ship training was purely routine in view of the full-scale war developing in Europe.

Three cabinets fell during 1939 indicative of the political crises then boiling in Japan. A cabinet was formed in January, 1940 by my old esteemed superior, Admiral Mitsumasa Yonai. Admiral Yonai knew Japan would be engulfed in total war once she joined an alliance with the two Axis powers. He made Herculean efforts to resist a Tripartite Pact.

Army hotheads believed the Axis was winning the war and would soon end it, dividing all the spoils between Germany and Italy. When they found out they could not persuade Yonai to join the Axis, they simply decided to scuttle his cabinet, and the War Minister quit. Under the old Japanese constitution a war minister had to be an Army man, and when General Shunroku Hata resigned in mid-1940, no other general would accept an offer from Yonai. Thus his cabinet fell on July 21.

I did not realize the significance of that event at the time, but today it is clear that his resignation lifted the last roadblock in the way of war in the Pacific. By coincidence, Franklin D. Roosevelt was re-elected that year for his third term as the president of the United States. Soon America and other Allied powers began putting pressures on Japan. Such pressures had no effect but to antagonize the Japanese Army leaders who were actually running the nation since the fall of the Yonai Cabinet.

The next cabinet, under Prince Fumimaro Konoye, concluded the Tripartite Pact with Germany and Italy in September, 1940. Konoye struggled for a year against the jingoistic Army and the Allied economic pressures. Konoye's efforts were not rewarded, and he resigned in October, 1941.

part two

PEARL HARBOR TO GUADALCANAL

1

The ninth of October, 1941, is an unforgettable day for me. On that day there were some 200 warships of the Combined Fleet assembled in Hiroshima Bay. It was most unusual for the entire Combined Fleet to gather thus in one place.

I was skipper of the 2,500-ton destroyer *Amatsukaze* (Heavenly Wind), one of four similar ships which had just been added to the Second Fleet's Destroyer Squadron 2. These four brand-new ships were designated Destroyer Division 16.

This was a beautiful autumn day. The anchored warships lay motionless on the surface of the bay. Its mirror-like water reflected the blue mountains of the distant horizon. Countless sea gulls skimmed to and fro between the ships. All else was still and peaceful.

A signal hoisted from flagship *Nagato* at 0900 attracted the attention of all lookouts. The flags read: "All ships W.Y.Z." This was an unusual code signal meaning: "All commanding officers will report to the flagship." It started a flurry of activity in every ship. A few minutes later, my motor launch was carrying me toward *Nagato*. Her spacious stern deck was quickly filling with hundreds of officers, young and old, by the time I arrived.

Among those present I quickly spotted my immediate superiors, Rear Admiral Raizo Tanaka, Destroyer Squadron 2 commander, and Vice Admiral Nobutake Kondo, 2nd Fleet Commander. Everyone appeared grave and serious. The atmosphere was oppressive despite the crisp autumn weather. Three bells sounded in *Nagato*, signaling 0930, and all crew members disappeared, leaving on deck only ship captains of lieutenant commander rank and above. The unusual precautions served to increase the tenseness.

Commander Hajime Yamaguchi, one of the Combined Fleet adjutants, shouted from near the podium:

"Gentlemen, attention please! The Commander in Chief will be here in a moment."

We all stood at rigid and silent attention as Admiral Isoroku Yamamoto appeared on deck. His steps were clearly audible in the hushed silence as he strode to the podium. Admiral Yamamoto returned our salute, and began to speak:

"It is an exceeding pleasure for me to see you all on this occasion. Our Combined Fleet has completed preparations for war. We will continue our training on that basis.

"The current situation suggests Japan may be forced to take up arms against America, Britain, Australia, and the Netherlands rather than succumb to strangulation through their blockade.

"We are undoubtedly in the most serious crisis of our history. Once the nation decides on war against the Allies, it is the duty of Combined Fleet to defend our nation and defeat the enemy. I believe this task is possible, but only if every one of you exerts his utmost effort. I expect each of you to do his duty along with me, so that we can fulfill our destiny in case of an emergency."

Yamamoto's brief words were delivered in a low voice, yet they struck like a thunderbolt. Every officer was stunned. I felt frozen in my place.

Admiral Yamamoto clamped his jaws as he stopped talking and looked around as if trying to look into the eyes of each individual. He looked more glum than stern as he walked slowly away from the podium.

Vice Admiral Matome Ugaki, Yamamoto's chief of staff, spoke next, giving an analysis of the situation. He told the shocking results of the Allied embargo. Japan was running short of such critical supplies as petroleum, iron ore, rubber, zinc, tin, nickel, and bauxite. He explained the high command's conclusion that Japan would reach a point of collapse within a year or two if the present situation continued. He said that the high command had finally adopted a strike-back strategy against the Allied stranglehold.

"It may be that this meeting of all Combined Fleet officers. . . ." and at this point Ugaki faltered. "This may be the last meeting of its kind. We may not be able to see each other again in this fashion.

"From now on we are going to undertake the most rigid kind of training. Let me wish for your health. Also let me caution you: no matter how strenuous the training is, you must always see to it that your men have proper rest and sleep. We must see to it that no man falls from overwork. Each of us must be fit . . . always, even if we are preparing for certain death."

At the end of Ugaki's long briefing there was a hushed silence. Commander Yamaguchi announced that the meeting was over, and Admiral Yamamoto departed with his staff officers. The others began filing out.

I remained stunned, with Yamamoto's and Ugaki's words still ringing in my ears. As a mere commander it would be some time before my boat would come alongside to take me back to *Amatsukaze*. Suddenly I shook off my stupor and headed toward the midship hatch. I was determined to talk with Ugaki alone.

Our paths had crossed before so Ugaki was no stranger to me. Twice in the past I had been assigned as an umpire during Combined Fleet maneuvers. On one of these occasions Ugaki had been chief of the umpire panel and I had then had opportunity to have long discussions with him.

As I reached the hatch, a senior admiral emerged and I saluted hastily. It was my good friend Vice Admiral Chuichi Nagumo, then commander of the First Air Fleet. He returned the salute, and smiled as he spoke my name and we exchanged greetings. As he shuffled away, his broad shoulders drooped forward; it occurred to me that his wry smile was little more than a frown. I was startled to see Nagumo in such a mood. Nagamo had always seemed to me a robust and hearty man, who would usually rush up to an old friend, pat his shoulder and shout excited greetings.

The aggressive admiral's queer mood disturbed me as I clambered down the narrow ladder and reached the cabin of Admiral Ugaki.

I knocked at the door, and entered upon his booming bid to do so. Ugaki was seated at his desk. He was not in a buoyant mood.

"Sir, may I talk with you for a few minutes?" I ventured.

"Certainly, Hara," he answered. "Be seated."

I hesitated, and there was a clumsy silence before my voice came again. "Admiral Ugaki, my behavior may impress you as an extreme impertinence, but I am doing this entirely on my own discretion, and hope that you will understand. I hope you will not consider me a man who challenges, or flinches at, drastic orders. . . ."

"I know you well, Hara. Don't be shy. Go ahead and say what you wish to say. Have you come to discuss the wisdom of opening a naval war against the Allies?"

"That's right, sir. I am just a destroyer specialist with a narrow, limited perspective, and certainly am not qualified to criticize a formula worked out by top brains of the high command. Excuse my outspokenness, Admiral Ugaki, but I am skeptical of this whole strategy. Could we avoid total war by by-passing, say, the Philippines? If it is resources that force us to offensive action, could we not strike at just the Dutch East Indies for the time being?"

Ugaki forced a smile, much like Nagumo's. He cleared his throat and said: "I'll tell you, Hara. Your opinion was shared by a number of high-ranking officers, but it was ruled out. The decision has already been made. One thing I must emphasize. We have made the decision, and are prepared for the worst. As you know, Admiral Kichisaburo Nomura, our ambassador in Washington, is now engaged in last-ditch negotiations for a compromise. Career diplomat Saburo Kurusu will soon join him as a special envoy and the two will redouble their efforts. We are not seeking war. But if we are given no other choice, we'll have to strike hard and fast. That was the theory finally adopted by the high command."

I groaned silently, realizing that it was of no use to discuss the matter any longer. I asked to be excused and Ugaki said, 'Take care of yourself. You are the best destroyer officer in the navy. We shall depend on you. See you again, Hara."

That meeting, however, turned out to be the last for Ugaki and me. He survived when two twin-engined (Betty) bombers carrying Yamamoto and his staff were attacked in April, 1943 by a score of P-38 fighters. The attack occurred near Bougainville, in the Solomons. Both bombers were shot down and Yamamoto was killed. But Ugaki lived until the last day of hostilities when he headed for Okinawa in a suicide bomber on the final Kamikaze attack of the Pacific war.

To this day, I do not know if Ugaki himself was among those who had opposed the Pearl Harbor attack formula. I have always felt, however, that both he and Nagumo were opposed. Yamamoto was adamant in his insistence on that formula, yet even he was quoted as saying, "The Imperial Navy can fight strongly for only two years." Yamamoto was also said to have wished that Japanese statesmen could work out an honorable peace before a catastrophe occurred.

I walked back to the deck, still stunned. The younger officers were still gathered around in small groups. I heard one swashbuckling lieutenant commander say, "We destroyer men must forestall and beat the outnumbering enemy. The whole war will probably hinge on our fighting."

I nodded and thought to myself, "Perhaps he is right." I returned to my small cabin in *Amatsukaze* and took Sun Tzu from the bookshelf. This ancient Chinese classic on strategy and philosophy has been the bible of warriors for some 2,500 years.

The immortal classic opens with this statement: "The art of war is of vital importance to the state. It is a matter of life and death, a road either to safety or ruin. Hence it is a subject of inquiry which can on no account be neglected."

The third chapter concludes: "In waging war, to conserve one's own nation intact is more important than defeating another nation. To conserve one's own division is more important than to vanquish an enemy division. A commander who fights 100 times and wins 100 times is not the very best commander. A truly great commander wins over an enemy without fighting.

"If you know the enemy and know yourself, you need not fear the result of a hundred battles. If you know yourself, but not the enemy, for every victory gained you will also suffer a defeat. If you know neither the enemy nor yourself, you will succumb in every battle."

This advice, sound as it is, failed to provide any solace. I decided that the book was too philosophical and tossed it aside. Its words of wisdom were probably appropriate for a monarch or a commander in chief, but not for a low-level officer like me. My glumness continued.

While I had been following current events quite closely, I failed to consider that the military leaders could have already decided on war. The historic conference on board *Nagato* coincided with the resignation of Prince Konoye and his cabinet. His successor was General Hideki Tojo. Belatedly I realized that this change of regime at such a critical time raised an ominous shadow.

For several days I kept groping for a means of preparing myself for total war. After Sun Tzu I read various Imperial Navy manuals, none of which offered any solution. "Do I know the enemy's strength and my own strength?" I asked myself.

I was called the best destroyer officer. In maneuvers I was always victorious, finishing off the "enemy" with accurate torpedo hits. Often I would make my "kills" by releasing only half of a regular eight-"fish" salvo. This was an indication of my strength; what was the enemy strength?

I had only a vague idea. If the ratio of the London disarmament conference still prevailed—which was highly doubtful, since Japan had scrapped the treaty in 1934—the United States and Britain had a combined strength of 10 as against Japan's 3 to 3.5. This would mean I must sink at least four enemy ships and keep my own destroyer intact in the war. If every commanding officer in the Imperial Navy succeeded in so doing, we might break even. That was highly improbable. As Admiral Nagumo had told me many times, the tremendous industrial potential of the United States was another formidable unknown factor unfavorable to Japan. It is no wonder that all these thoughts left me gloomy and pessimistic.

More days of strenuous effort finally made me realize that I was, after all, a fighting man, not a high-ranking commanding officer. I concluded that my job was to be prepared to fight and, keeping my ship and men intact, sink any opposing ships. I could not allow myself to dwell on the overall problems of war, but must fight to the best of my ability in my limited role.

It is strange that in 1941 I should finally find answers to my problems in a book written 300 years earlier, *Go Rin Sho* (*The Five Wheels*), by Musashi Miyamoto. It enabled me to achieve the composure I had long groped for. These are the memoirs of a fabulous swordsman who survived 66 duels and later became one of Japan's greatest artists and philosophers.

Compared with Sun Tzu, Miyamoto's memoir is quite obscure. A literal translation of his prose would make little impression on Western readers. Miyamoto was born in 1584 and lived in an age of chaos. As a youth he was a genius with the sword. To attain sword fame in those days it was necessary to challenge other swordsmen of reputation, and it was no mere sport. Just as boxers in Western countries formerly fought without rules, Japanese swordsmen in those days often dueled to the death. Their swords were made either of hard wood or razor-sharp steel. When used by an expert, a wooden practice sword could easily maim or kill an opponent, so there was little difference between the two weapons.

Miyamoto's 66 consecutive wins—a wonder in any time—are considered and analyzed by the battler himself in this book. Throughout his account of these battles runs the consistent theme, "Not to adhere to any set formula or principle, but to adapt to each situation." This theory is extremely difficult to put into practice, particularly in struggles where a split-second mistake can mean death.

Upon reading this I was positive that here was the solution I had been seeking. By adapting to each situation I might help to overcome the overwhelming strength of the Allies. I am now convinced that it was because I put this belief into practice that I was able to make a good record in the Pacific war, and to survive.

2

"Operation Phase One" was ordered on November 7, 1941.

The Combined Fleet quickly but unobtrusively broke up and scattered. My destroyer, with its three sister ships of Destroyer Division 16, quietly slipped into the nearby naval port of Kure. I was unaware that major components of the First and Second Fleet went north to a rendezvous at Hitokappu Wan (Tankan Bay) in the Kuriles to become a part of the greatest Japanese task force ever assembled.

Our ships were put through a careful check-up in Kure. Nonessential items were unloaded. Sick crew members were ordered ashore, and they were quickly replaced. Only the commanding officers knew what the operation could possibly develop into. Crewmen were told merely that we were going to the South Pacific on a training cruise.

The high command was taking no chances. All leaves and furloughs were canceled. My last leave had been in September. I had taken a night express train from Kure for the 16-hour ride to my home in Kamakura, a resort town near Yokosuka. But the tiring ride was fully rewarded by the joyous reception I received. My two daughters, who leaped and danced in greeting my return, were joined by my son, Mikito, aged two, who was just beginning to talk. I was able to stay at home only one full day. The children grieved at my leaving, and I shared their feeling. I hugged each of them, saying, "Your daddy will be back soon." The recollection made me want to see them again before the "operation," which might deny my ever returning home.

"Operation Phase Two" was ordered on the 21st of November, 1941.

On the following day, Vice Admiral Chuichi Nagumo's task force was completely assembled in the fog-shrouded bay of Etorofu Island, in the

Kuriles. On November 23, eight destroyers of Destroyer Divisions 16 and 24 slipped quietly out of the Kure harbor and moved toward Terashima Strait, a familiar training area in northern Kyushu. For four consecutive days, we fused and prepared all shells and torpedoes in our ships. Doctors were kept busy administering various shots to the crews.

Our two-division squadron moved out of the Strait and headed for the Pacific Ocean at 1800 on November 26. At the same time Nagumo's task force sortied from Tankan Bay headed for Hawaii. Our immediate destination was Palau, in Japan's mandated South Sea islands. All commanding officers were notified to form a small task force at Palau for attacks on Mindanao Island in the Philippines, simultaneous with the attack on Pearl Harbor.

On the 2,000-mile cruise from Terashima, our radio transmitters were sealed, as were those of the Nagumo task force. But radiomen were working around the clock on their receivers. As our ships departed from homeland waters, there was a radio message: "Press reports U.S. Secretary of State Cordell Hull on 26 November handed Japanese Ambassadors Kichisaburo Nomura and Saburo Kurusu a note, apparently outlining final U.S. stand on negotiations."

As we were passing Formosa on November 28, we picked up a message from the local headquarters: "Two submarines of undetermined nationality, but presumably United States, observed moving northward in waters east of Formosa."

"Operation Phase Two" authorized commanding officers to take "hostile actions only in absolute necessity." I clenched my fists and spoke on the intercom to my sonar officer: "Alert, alert. Possibly hostile submarines reported operating nearby."

A professionally cool reply came through, "Roger, Roger. All sonar gear functioning properly. Will let you know if anything is picked up."

On December 1, our radio picked up this message: "British naval force of five warships, including battleship *Prince of Wales*, is now speeding to the Far East."

All the tense atmosphere ended when the green Palau island emerged on the horizon. We entered its port at 1300 the same day. The climate had changed from winter to summer in five days. Green coconut trees on the beach were soothing and restful. But my relaxation was short-lived. The atmosphere in Palau harbor was tense. There were scores of vessels at anchor, including many transports. Soldiers were going through drills, climbing up and down rope ladders on their ships. War appeared close at hand.

As I stood on the bridge, my first inclination was to set rigid watches. After a while, however, I decided that was pointless and ordered the ship's store opened for the crew. Everyone was also directed to take a bath—the first since we had left Kure a week before. At the first chance I took a dozen of my ship's officers to make a study of the harbor topography. Actually I planned this little excursion as a chance for my boys to relax. We toured the harbor leisurely by boat and had a chance to take it easy for a full day and night.

In the evening of the following day, December 2, we received a historic radio message from Combined Fleet Headquarters:

"Niitaka Yama Nobore 1208."

Literally translated, it meant, "Climb Mt. Niitaka (the highest mountain in Formosa) 1208." I gulped at reading this message, and felt its significance even before opening the sealed secret cipher book. The words meant: "Start war against the Allies 8 December."

Shortly afterward all his ship captains were gathered around Rear Admiral Raizo Tanaka for instructions on the Davao attack. In his short briefing Tanaka repeatedly cautioned: "Remember that negotiations are still being carried on in Washington. We must be prepared at any moment to receive a message calling off the whole operation, if negotiations turn out to be successful. Then we do only one thing: turn around and return to Japan."

I spoke up. "Here at Palau we are only 500 miles east of Davao, a key American naval base in the Philippines, and 700 miles southwest of another important American naval base at Guam. With so many of our warships assembled here, there must be a number of American submarines keeping watch against us. What should we do in case we contact unfriendly submarines from now on?"

Tanaka replied: "We shall have to sink them, even though Phase Two authorized us to take hostile acts only out of absolute necessity."

With that the meeting broke up, and each commanding officer returned to his ship, affecting an air of composure. Actually it was not difficult to maintain a poker face under the circumstances. I was still skeptical of the wisdom of fighting the Allies, and everything about the plan seemed unreal. I felt, or perhaps wishfully thought, that the "operation" would be called off at the last moment. An inner voice repeated the words of Sun Tzu, "A truly great commander wins without fighting." I had no inkling that the Imperial high command had concluded on December 1 that the Hull note was an ultimatum demanding Japanese capitulation without fighting, and had decided to go to war against the United States and its Allies.

For three days, December 3–5, we conducted rigid around-the-clock maneuvers within the harbor. In a final examination of shipboard conditions all nonessential items were removed.

On December 6, at 0130, our six destroyers and one cruiser steamed out of the spacious harbor at Palau. Our mission was to clear the waters of hostile submarines, paving the way for the carrier and two heavy cruisers to sail to Mindanao. Many transport's standing by in the atoll harbor were scheduled for other parts of the Philippines and also the Dutch East Indies.

We steered out of the narrow cut in the western part of the atoll and immediately combed the waters with sonar gear. There was nothing untoward until around 1600 hours the first day out when the sonar officer reported an alert:

"What appears to be a submarine, bearing 60 degrees to starboard, distant 2,500 meters."

I turned the ship in the indicated direction and barked orders, "Prepare to release depth charges!" Simultaneously the ship sounded a long whistle. Signal flags ABX ("We are attacking with depth charges") were hoisted to let my companion ships know of our action.

The sonar officer spoke again. "Ten degrees to starboard, 2,000 meters. Sound indicates submarine certain."

I adjusted *Amatsukaze*'s heading accordingly and proceeded at 12 knots. Looking around I saw that my men were ready for action at the depth charge launchers, awaiting my next order. The sonar officer continued to report angles and distances, as we closed on the target. I was tense with the excitement of a hunter approaching his quarry, but calm with thoughts of myriad details that had to be considered. As we came within striking distance I realized it was now or never and almost shouted, "Boost speed to 21 knots." Depth charges must be dropped only after a destroyer has boosted its speed, otherwise it will be damaged by its own weapons. But at the last instant I made my decision and swallowed the words. Instead I shouted, "Depth charge action canceled! Depth charge action canceled!"

It was one of the most important decisions I made during the war. My act on that day may be hard to understand for Western readers who may feel that I disobeyed orders in not carrying out the attack.

My decision was based on the following reasoning. The zero hour was set for December 8, two days hence. It was not warranted to attack a submarine on the high seas before it showed any hostility to us. At the first word of the sonar detection of the submarine, I became involved in a mental struggle. My concern for peace was great. My first thought was whether my present action might wreck the chance for peace. In addition to that lofty consideration, I was also concerned with the tactical situation at the moment. A successful depth-charge attack is not easy, particularly when the opponent is expecting it. If the target should escape, the outcome would be quite disagreeable. The submarine would radio its headquarters and every United States warship would be alerted for the next encounter. When one wavers like that in making a decision, I knew from maneuvers and practice experience, it is doubly hard to score a hit. So I called off the attack.

Rear Admiral Raizo Tanaka was watching me from his cruiser *Jintsu*, 5,950 tons. He has never questioned me about my queer behavior of that day. Perhaps he understood and shared my feelings.

After giving up the chase of the submarine, I turned around and joined the other ships. Presently we were joined by the carrier *Ryujo*, with two heavy cruisers and two destroyers out of Palau. The 12-ship task force assembled in a ring formation, boosted speed to 18 knots, headed straight to the west. We were soon out on the wide ocean, out of sight of all land, and even of other ships. From time to time a school of dolphins would catch the eye, but aside from them there was only sea and sky.

At the first opportunity I ordered my crew to assemble on deck and apprised them of our destination and mission. Their calm reaction at hearing this news was a surprise to me. Evidently they had already sensed the momentous nature of our orders from the extraordinary training and caution that had preceded our sortie.

The officers and men returned to their posts. I sat on the bridge and pored over charts of Davao and its environs. The ship was quiet, the ocean calm. Darkness came and all was peaceful. Our ring formation steamed on observing full blackout precautions.

"Captain Hara, a radio message."

I turned toward the courier. Seaman Second Class Takeo Murata had been on board only a month, having come as one of several replacements. The 17-year-old sailor saluted me and stood at attention.

I said, "Thanks, Murata," and unfolded the paper he handed me. I felt excitement at the thought that this might be an order countermanding the war operations. It was only an intelligence report.

"One *Bristol*-class sea-plane tender and one destroyer anchored in Davao harbor at 1800 hours 6 December."

I sighed and resumed the still watch on the dark ocean.

"Commander Hara, a radio message." Murata was at my side again, sweat dripping from his youthful face. He must have run from the radio room. Good boy! Suddenly I felt sorry for this lad who was sharing the destiny of war with full-grown men.

The new message read: "No enemy ship in sight at Legaspi at 1900 hours, 6 December."

The next messages received were two press reports. "Ambassadors Nomura and Kurusu have resumed talks with Secretary of State Hull and President Roosevelt regarding the latest American proposal . . ." and "Foreign Office spokesman said today that passenger ship *Tatsuta Maru*, which left Yokohama last week for Los Angeles, was instructed to visit Mexico. It is now scheduled to arrive Los Angeles 14 December, depart on the 16th, and arrive at Manzanillo on the 19th. . . . "

These items certainly implied nothing of a war move. Who could have discerned in these messages that *Tatsuta Maru* would be ordered to turn around for Japan 30 hours later?

The following day, December 7, passed in similar vein. The tense but monotonous voyage was punctuated for me only by the arrival of routine messages like those of the preceding night. Our second night on the ocean, my watch showed midnight, and the deadline had arrived with no order countermanding the operation. We were still many miles from the attack launching point—50 miles east of Cape San Augustin and 100 miles east of Davao.

Suddenly I felt the strain of two days and nights on the bridge and dozed off in my chair, leaving Lieutenant (j.g.) Toshio Koyama, my young but capable chief navigator, in command. Cool drops awakened me when our formation stabbed into a blinding rain squall on the dark ocean. It was 0330 of D-day, December 8, 1941. How stupid to be napping on such an important day! I cursed myself and phoned the radio room for any new messages. There were none. The squall had passed, but I could not shake off my drowsiness. It was awkward and irritating to be so drowsy that I could not concentrate on the war that was about to break.

At daybreak (0500) 20 light bombers and fighters were launched from carrier *Ryujo*, then 50 miles east of San Augustin and 100 miles from Davao. The sight of these planes had a rousing and inspiring effect on me. While I still lacked any feeling of enthusiasm for the imminent war, I now stood on the bridge of *Amatsukaze* as a professional, grimly determined to carry out orders.

With the departure of *Ryujo*'s planes, destroyers *Hayashio*, *Natsushio*, *Kuroshio*, and *Oyashio* broke from our ring formation and dashed forward in column formation at 30 knots for a coordinated attack on American forces in Davao Bay. The other eight ships fell into line formation, 1,500 meters between each ship, and steamed alternately east and west in this unusual formation, awaiting the return of *Ryujo*'s planes.

Ryujo was the only aircraft carrier used in the Philippine operation. It had originally been planned to use her, together with two converted carriers, in the attack on Luzon. But their plane-carrying capacity was so limited that it was decided to strike at Luzon with land-based planes from Formosa and use the carriers elsewhere. *Ryujo* thus moved to Palau and the two slower carriers were sent back to Japan in a last-minute change of schedule.

The sun shone intermittently, through occasional breaks in the clouds. There was practically no breeze, and we sweated out four and a half hours on the ocean in our monotonous back-and-forth, marking-time movement. Nineteen of the planes returned to *Ryujo* at 0930. The 20th, a bomber, had to be ditched because of engine trouble. We learned later that the crew was rescued by destroyer *Kuroshio*.

The task-force attack on Davao was a complete flop. Our planes and destroyers hit an empty bag. The two American warships reported there had vanished before our arrival. There was no air or ground opposition to our forces. Our planes strafed and set on fire only two American seaplanes which appeared to have been abandoned in the bay. The planes circled over Davao more than two hours. Not a single plane arose from the Davao airfield, or from any other base. It was a most peculiar operation.

The attitude of American military forces in Davao that day still remains a mystery. Whatever their judgment, they must have notified their headquarters of our onslaught. Yet Manila headquarters sat idle and kept all planes parked on Clark Field when our Formosa-based planes attacked some four hours after we had withdrawn from the Davao area.*

Meanwhile cruiser *Jintsu*, with destroyers *Hatsukaze* and my *Amatsukaze*, broke away from the task force formation and headed toward the mouth of Davao Bay to join the four destroyers returning from their fruitless sortie. The rendezvous was completed at 1400. I was astounded by the endless volume of radio reports of our brilliant exploits at Pearl Harbor and Clark Field. None of it seemed entirely real.

I was brought to sudden reality, however, by the appearance of a B-24 bomber. It flew at about 30,000 feet and seemed to have spotted our ships. Admiral Tanaka decided to make a feint, before rejoining *Ryujo*, to prevent discovery of our carrier by the American bomber. We made a 180-degree turn and cruised at 18 knots for one hour, then turned 90 degrees and ran at 21 knots, before switching 60 degrees again to rejoin *Ryujo*.

The B-24 kept rambling overhead without trying to attack, and finally gave up shadowing our ships before we turned toward our original position. This bomber was another mystery to us. Where it came from and what it was supposed to be doing has never been figured out.

By the time we got back to the point 50 miles east of San Augustin, new orders came for me and the skipper of destroyer *Hatsukaze*. Accordingly we

---

* The mystery of U.S. Air Force unpreparedness at Clark Field is still unresolved. As Louis Morton wrote in *The Fall of the Philippines,* "All forces in the Philippines had knowledge of the attack on Pearl Harbor hours before the first Japanese bombers appeared over Luzon. A dawn raid at Davao had given notice that the Japanese had no intention of bypassing the archipelago. The early morning bombings on Luzon gave even more pointed warning that an attack against the major airbase in the Islands could be expected. Colonel Campbell testifies that Clark Field had received word of the approaching Japanese aircraft before the attack. Colonel Eubank states that no such warning was ever received. Other officers speak of the breakdown of communications at this critical juncture. There is no way of resolving this conflicting testimony. . . . General Arnold, eight years after the event, wrote that he was never able 'to get the real story of what happened in the Philippines.'" About the results of the attack, there is perfect agreement. Of the modern combat bombers, 18 of the original 35 B-17's were destroyed. Fifty-three P-40's, three P-35's and about 30 miscellaneous observation planes and smaller bombers were also lost. "Thus after one day of war," Morton writes, "with its strength cut in half, the Far East Air Force had been eliminated as an effective fighting force." Japanese losses: 7 fighter planes.

raced toward Legaspi to join the cruisers *Myoko* and *Nachi* which had gone ahead. The carrier and two escorting destroyers had already left for Palau. Admiral Tanaka's flagship *Jintsu* and the four other destroyers followed.

I stayed for a week in Legaspi waters, on patrol against American submarines and surface ships carrying possible reinforcements. None appeared, so the duty was boring. But we all knew the importance of safeguarding this rear area in support of the main Japanese landing operation in Luzon.

The only excitement I had during the assignment was the 24 hours starting at 1710 on December 9, when my radioman monitored a message from submarine I-65 reporting the discovery of two British warships which were racing toward the Japanese landing convoy in Malaya. Thereafter the radio brought a steady stream of reports about the Japanese attack against the British battleship *Prince of Wales* and cruiser *Repulse*. Sweat streamed down my face as I read message after message about this action some 1,000 miles away.

My immediate feeling about this distant action was complex. It was a mixture of awe and admiration of the British Navy for its quick deployment. Also I was suddenly full of enthusiasm for battle and a desire to engage the enemy. But these thoughts of participating in the current battle were purely wishful because I had my own assignment where I was.

When the first reports came in concerning action against the British ships, I was greatly concerned. There were only two Japanese cruiser-battleships in Malayan waters at the time. They were *Haruna* and *Kirishima*, both 27,500 tons. Built in 1912 and 1913, they were the oldest warships in service in the Imperial Navy. I did not think they would be any match for Britain's "unsinkable" *Prince of Wales* and the combat-seasoned *Repulse*.

The flood of early messages from the vicinity of Malaya was bewildering and disturbing. Rear Admiral Shintaro Hashimoto (Commander Destroyer Squadron 3) reported that it would be difficult for his ships to make early contact with the British force. Submarine I-65 reported at 0430 on the 10th that it had lost sight of the British force because of rain squalls. Then radio signals began to jam each other and no intelligible broadcasts came through to us.

It was curious that not a single American warship would come out to fight us in the Philippines. But the British navy was now driving us panicky all over the area. Atmospherics suddenly cleared at 1400, and we picked up this message: "No aerial escorts observed above the British force." Many more messages started coming in rapid succession:

"22nd Air Squadron bombs enemy battleship at 1420."

"Enemy battleship torpedoed at 1430."

"Aerial torpedo hit direct on enemy cruiser 1440. It now lists heavily to port."

"One of five enemy destroyers set afire."

"One enemy battleship exploded and is sinking at 1450."

Now I was bewildered. Unbelievable things were happening. Japanese airplanes alone had sunk the *Prince of Wales* and *Repulse*!

The Japanese attack on Pearl Harbor never really impressed me as a measure of air strength because the enemy was taken unaware. As a destroyer specialist, my perspective was undoubtedly narrow. But the victory against the British in Malaya really shocked me. I had never considered airplanes to be so powerful.

My obstinacy was such that, even after the spectacular Malayan battle, I could not change my perspective. My confidence had been shaken, but I still believed that, since planes were hampered by weather, surface ships must still play a vital role, especially in all-weather battles. Thus, while I was forced to the realization that planes were certain to play an ever-increasing part in warfare, I clung stubbornly to the importance of my own field of interest and endeavor—destroyers.

It may well be that this very stubbornness, by maintaining my confidence in destroyers, increased my skill and enabled me to score the successes I did in the Pacific War and still survive so many savage battles.

I considered at length the British loss of that battleship and cruiser to aerial attack. But I could not possibly envisage that three years and four months later Japan would be suffering a parallel loss, and that I would be in command of the Japanese cruiser.

3

On December 15 the high command, satisfied with the smooth progress of landing operations at Luzon, no longer deemed it necessary to patrol Legaspi waters, and ordered our ships back to Palau. An American counteroffensive in the Philippines was written off at that time. While refueling at Palau further orders arrived for us to escort landing vessels to Davao.

At 0700 on December 17, a convoy of 12 transports laden with an Army regiment steamed out of Palau in three echelons. Seven destroyers and two small patrol vessels served as escort. The operation was commanded by Admiral Tanaka in cruiser *Jintsu*.

Forty-five minutes after leaving Palau, I was standing on the bridge of *Amatsukaze* when my sonarman reported a submarine just 2,000 meters distant, bearing 80 degrees to starboard. This was almost an exact repetition of what had happened on "X-Day." This time there was no hesitation. We closed to 1,000 meters, boosted speed to 21 knots, threw overboard six depth charges, then, turning 230 degrees, we dropped another six. The charges were set to explode at 30 meters. We observed no indication on the surface of the effectiveness of our efforts. I resumed the escort position at the right wing in front of the second echelon of four transports, and the convoy zig-zagged on at 10 knots.

At 1300 the same day, destroyer *Kuroshio* on the port wing of the first echelon reported, "Enemy submarine spotted. In co-operation with a friendly antisub patrol plane, we attacked it with depth charges. A large quantity of heavy oil floated on the surface. We consider the submarine sunk."

This message was dismal news for us in *Amatsukaze*. I silently showed it to my officers. They groaned in disappointment.

On December 20 before daybreak, the convoy entered the quiet of Davao Bay without challenge from a single plane or ship. A landing operation was not new to me. My experience at Shanghai five years earlier had initiated me in enemy gunfire. Our orders at Davao were to hold fire unless challenged. We wanted to occupy the place intact, with a minimum of destruction. Two echelons had already landed successfully farther down the bay.

The escort ships moved slowly into the port, which appeared quiet and peaceful. A platoon of my men shoved off from *Amatsukaze* in a small motor-boat with the assignment of disarming and capturing small vessels at anchor in the port. Within minutes, some 200 troops suddenly emerged on the pier and opened fire on my men in the motorboat. A lookout shouted: "Gunfire on boat; some of our men appear to be hit!"

I shouted orders, "Port guns open fire." This was indeed a repetition of the Shanghai landing. A clumsy repetition for which I cursed myself.

Our six 120-mm. guns rotated and fired. None of the shells hit the enemy, some 2,000 meters away, but they scattered and fled. Second and third salvos followed. The pier was promptly emptied of troops.

"Cease fire," I ordered. But the fourth salvo was already on its way. One of the six shells hit a small oil tank some 50 meters from the pier, and it burst into flames.

The developments in this operation were far from my expectations. I had repeated a series of clumsy mistakes. I was no longer a swell-headed destroyer expert, but a humbled, penitent man, who was also disgusted with himself. The motorboat, meanwhile, returned with one dead. The following day I officiated at the funeral of Petty Officer 2/c Tsuneo Horie, the first of my men to fall in the war. The oil tank burned on for three days and nights.

For a week after the landing, we were kept busy rescuing Japanese residents of the area. Since Davao had the largest Japanese colony in the Philippines, it was too bad that this operation was so many days delayed. Fortunately, only a few had been killed by retreating enemy troops, and we freed from prison camps the Japanese who had been hurriedly rounded up at the start of the war.

It was not long before word came of casualties inflicted on other Japanese destroyers. Ships which took part in the Wake Island operation evidently fared worse than we did at Davao. On December 11 destroyer *Kisaragi* was sunk by U.S. Marine planes based at Wake. *Hayate*, a teammate of *Kisaragi*, was sunk the same day at Wake by marine shore batteries. How could they have been so clumsy?

But others were still more clumsy, I learned. Destroyer *Shinonome* hit a mine and sank at Miri, Borneo. Highly classified reports said it was not determined whether the mine was Dutch or Japanese.

I was infuriated to learn that destroyer *Sagiri* was torpedoed and sunk by a submarine, also off Borneo, on December 24. A cat eaten by a mouse! How could a destroyer be so stupid! It was ascertained later that the successful submarine was the Dutch *K-16*.

Destroyer *Kuroshio* of my own division, flushed with the achievement of sinking an enemy submarine, also managed to lose face. It was caught napping December 23, apparently in the belief that there were no enemy planes around, when suddenly one emerged from out of the sun. This B-17, a Flying Fortress, came in at low level to drop its bombs, one of which hit the ship and seriously wounded four sailors.

These stories were never made public. They were buried deep beneath the spectacular Japanese exploits which were given wide publicity. When I learned of the losses I could not help feeling worried. As has been said, war is a series of mistakes. But Japan could not afford mistakes. My mounting anger at such losses was changing me from the irresolute, wavering skipper of a month before to a new man, fierce and determined.

Frustrations continued along with our successes in the early days of the war, and on January 4, 1942, another occurred which was maddening to me. On that day 14 major warships, comprising almost the entire Japanese surface force of the area, lay moored in the small harbor of Malalag on the western coast of Davao Bay. The harbor mouth is quite narrow, and the commanding admiral of the fleet had ordered it closed with an antisubmarine net.

I was eating lunch when the lookouts shouted, "Air raid!" We looked up and saw nine land-based 4-engine bombers at 30,000 feet. We knew these were enemy B-17s, Flying Fortresses, because Japan's only 4-engine bombers at that time were Kawanishi flying boats ("Emily").

Mess gear flew in every direction as officers and men scrambled to get to battle stations and into action. But what could we do? With the mouth of the small harbor closed, we were helpless. We could do nothing. Our guns would not reach the planes' altitude, and not a single Japanese fighter plane was airborne.

I could only cross my fingers as the bombs came curving down. Fortunately the American bombers, apparently new arrivals at Java, did not carry heavy bomb loads, and their aim was not good. One 250-pound bomb did score a direct hit on the No. 2 turret of cruiser *Myoko* in the center of the harbor. More than 20 were killed and 40 others wounded. Splinters of that bomb reached seaplane tender *Chitose*, moored 500 meters away, and damaged five planes on her deck. Not one Japanese plane was able to take off in time to pursue the raiders.

My *Amatsukaze* was so near the beach we could not move an inch to evade the bombs. Luck alone saved us. I had never felt so miserable as on that day when I watched the 12,374-ton *Myoko*, our teammate since X-Day, limping out of Davao Bay on its way back to Japan for repairs.

We could not afford this kind of stupidity.

4

In January, 1942, I took part in the invasion of the Netherlands East Indies, supporting the landing operations at Menado and Kendari. In both landings, there was little opposition from the local garrisons, but the poor quality of our air support was an ill-omen for the future. The Japanese Navy did not have enough planes to cover our landings, and the few planes we saw were manned by second-rate flyers. Without proper training, they reported "ghost" ships that did not exist, bombed whales that they mistook for submarines, and even shot down our own transport planes in the confusion of air battles.

My own experience in hunting submarines had been no more satisfying. On the night of January 31, while escorting transports to a landing at Bill Bay on Ambon Island, I caught a submarine on the surface with my searchlight. We failed to hit with three salvos, and it got away.

Regretfully I signaled our failure to the other ships, warning that the enemy had probably escaped unscathed and might come back. I sweated out the next two hours. The enemy sub might choose our slow troop-laden transports as easy targets. Our sonar watch was reinforced, but they picked up no further trace of the submarine. My uneasiness continued, however, until 0100 when our convoy reached the landing point.

The landing started at 0120 on February 1, with no pre-invasion bombardment from our warships. That was not in accordance with the original schedule. After my encounter with the sub, the enemy must have been fully alerted, and I was itching for a chance to bombard. I thought it meaningless to attempt an invasion against alerted enemy forces, with no pre-landing bombardment.

Nevertheless no bombardment orders came from the flagship. Admiral Tanaka explained to me after the war that he had omitted bombardment, figuring that the ground opposition, even though alerted, would be weak. An even more binding reason, Tanaka explained, was that he had orders to "conserve ammunition as much as practicable." That may sound ridiculous to Americans, but it was a grim reality to Japan. In the prosecution of that stupendous war we were constantly reminded of the need for "conserving." At the same time we were experiencing American "saturation bombings" and massive pre-landing bombardments that were incomprehensible to us.

Navy gunners were trained constantly to hit the target with opening salvos. Range-finding salvos, as used by Americans, were completely out of the question for us. That was an additional reason for my displeasure at the poor marksmanship of my gunners in shooting at the enemy submarine.

The landing troops, as I had anticipated, were stopped at the beach by enemy ground fire. Commander Konosuke Ieki, in charge of the invasion troops, signaled at 0200: "We are pinned down and the landing is thwarted." But he would not ask for support bombardment.

On the bridge of *Amatsukaze* I squirmed with vexation. The situation was disgusting in every respect. At 0320 the landing troops finally signaled that the beachhead was secured. But there was more trouble ahead. At 0500 they radioed: "Enemy fortress guns cover our flanks."

Word came at noon by radio that Commander Ieki had been killed in action. It was ridiculous. Why did he have to die like that? A preliminary bombardment and continued shipboard fire support would have spared his life and many others. Stupid, stupid!

That sad news was followed shortly by orders from Vice Admiral Raizo Tanaka: "All escort vessels close beach to pick up casualties." *Amatsukaze* loaded 30 dead and 90 wounded. Meanwhile the ground fighting was stalemated. We could not shoot now because of the confined ground situation.

Japanese float planes from tender *Chitose* finally appeared early the following day and attacked the enemy's fortified positions. Still there were no fighters or bombers from carriers *Hiryu* or *Soryu*. I simply could not understand why aerial co-operation was so inadequate.

The seaplanes, coming in six at a time, were manned by brilliant flyers. They attacked enemy gun positions with telling effect. At one time they tangled with five enemy bombers, apparently from the Dutch East Indies, and shot down two of them. No Japanese planes were lost.

The Dutch-Australian garrison surrendered in the first evening of the invasion, February 1, 1942. Two hundred garrison troops were taken prisoner. They told us that some 70 mines were laid at the main harbor on the southern side of Ambon Island. Our minesweepers spent a week on the hair-raising job of sweeping the narrow harbor. Three of them were hit by mines and sank with their crews.

Two days after the surrender, a transport moored near the mouth of the mine-filled harbor signaled: "Ship under torpedo attack from seaward." And indeed it was. Fortunately none of the torpedoes found targets, but the alert sent me into action immediately. I figured that these torpedoes must have come from the very same submarine that had fooled me three days earlier. I was grimly determined to find and sink it.

For five hours sleek *Amatsukaze* chugged about at a snail-like 11 knots. Our insensitive sonar gear would not function effectively if the ship moved any faster. An aggressive submarine could make an easy mark of such a slow target, even though it was a destroyer armed with deadly antisubmarine weapons. I thought of destroyer *Sagiri* sunk by a submarine torpedo near Borneo in December.

When a destroyer is patrolling, concentrating on spotting an enemy, it is fully on guard. If any sub was attracted by *Amatsukaze*, snailing at this tempting speed, I felt ready for it. But we picked up no trace of the submarine. As the slow hours stretched into five, the situation developed into a war of nerves.

At 2134 a sonarman shouted exultantly. "Submarine! distant 2,400 meters, bearing 10 degrees to port."

I ordered: "Everybody to combat station! Prepare depth charges. Eight charges. Set for depth of 50 meters!"

The sonar officer chanted in a calm professional voice: "Sub at 1,800 meters, 40 degrees to port.

"The sub now at 1,300 meters, 50 degrees to the left. It seems to be swerving to the left."

Amatsukaze's course was adjusted to the new bearings. At 2153 the sonar officer shrieked in dismay, "Lost track of sub!"

Strangely calm at this news, I immediately judged that the sub had slipped into a blind angle. It and *Amatsukaze* must be cruising on an identical course. Japanese sonar in those early days operated on the principle of sending out sound waves and calculating an object's distance by checking the rebounding waves. These devices were not sensitive enough to pick up a sub's engine noises directly.

My head was filled with calculations of bearings, angles, and distance. The answer came almost reflexively: "The sub is 180 degrees, or dead ahead, moving at 9 knots, now 1,000 meters away, at a depth of about 30 meters." I ordered speed boosted to 21 knots, and looked at the second hand of my watch. I rapidly diagramed the two ships' navigation curves. At 2158 we released eight depth charges when I believed the enemy sub was directly below.

I put *Amatsukaze* about and turned back, poised for another series of a depth-charge attack. The surface of the sea gave off a strong odor of Diesel oil in the dark night. We could see nothing. The smell of oil grew stronger. We were well aware of skunk tactics used by submarines under attack. By releasing oil while submerged they try to induce pursuers to believe they have been sunk. We searched the site diligently for two hours, but picked up no trace of our quarry.

I wrote the sub off as sunk, but there was no exultation in me. Four days passed and there were no other reports of the sub. It was obvious that I had scored a "kill." I realized grimly that there is little real cause for elation in warfare. I learned a great deal from the Ambon operation.

On the 9th of February, I returned to Davao, in escort of the transport *Kirishima Maru*, and carrying some of the wounded and dead who had fallen at Ambon. The voyage was uneventful.

Peace and quiet was restored completely in Davao. Hostilities in the Philippines were now limited to Bataan Peninsula and Corregidor Island. Other scenes of war had moved far to the south. Davao had not seen an enemy plane in more than a month.

Huge bundles of letters from home awaited us. There were also many packages and "comfort kits" sent by relatives and other friendly civilians in the homeland.

On arriving at Davao I enjoyed a long, leisurely bath, for the first time in 20 days. When a Japanese destroyer was on combat assignment, even its skipper willingly skipped the luxury of a bath. I relaxed in my small cabin, after ordering my crew to bathe and take it easy. The ship's store was ordered opened. It carried liquors, candy and toilet goods. Men were allowed to buy and drink liquor on board with the sanction of their skipper.

Small as my cabin was, it was still the best quarters in the narrow ship. The six-by-nine-foot space was filled with a bed, toilet equipment, a small round table, a wardrobe, and a sofa and stool. On the table was a photograph of my family.

Murata, a young sailor, delivered my mail, which included packages and letters.

"Did you receive your mail, Murata?"

"Yes, sir, I did."

He beamed, saluted and turned around.

I opened a letter from my wife dated January 4. She reported that the three children and herself were well and happy. A postscript, however, reported disturbing news. "The day before yesterday, I took the children to Tokyo for a visit with relatives. Our maid was away, and when I returned to Kamakura the door lock was broken and all our valuables were gone."

That was distressing. My wife was from a good family and was totally unused to this kind of thing. In my anxiety about this I downed several cups of sake (rice wine).

There was a package from my eldest brother, who lived in Osaka. It contained a waist band with 1,000 stitches, handmade with crimson thread, a traditional Japanese charm against enemy bullets. My brother's wife wrote that she had stood at a downtown street corner to solicit 999 other women to contribute a stitch each to it. Gratefully I put it about my waist although I held no belief in the superstition.

A letter from my brother contained further distressing news. His eldest son, Shigeyoshi Hashimoto, 25, a machine-gun officer in the 4th Army Division, had died in December of tuberculosis. This nephew had been my favorite. I closed my eyes and mumbled a prayer for him. Feeling depressed, I stopped opening the mail, had a few more drinks, and walked out onto the bridge. It was a lovely day. The harbor looked beautiful under the bright tropical sun. The duty officer sat gazing wistfully at the shore as I approached.

He stood up and saluted. "Announce that I am authorizing shore leave tomorrow for all hands. They will be organized into three groups and each will have three hours of liberty."

The lieutenant's eyes lit up with excitement and he immediately started to spread the good word. Not one man in my crew of 300 had been ashore during the past 50 days, so the announcement was received with great joy.

I returned to the cabin and opened another letter. It was from Kure but the sender's name on the back of the envelope was unknown to me. The letter read: "I am Hinagiku, one of the geisha girls, who served in the party before your departure to the war." I groaned. I, the father of three children, certainly had not anticipated a love letter from a geisha girl. The letter was filled with prosaic good wishes which ended on a decidedly sour note. "The landlady of the restaurant has reminded me that you forgot to settle the account before your sudden departure. We should be happy if you will pay the attached bill at your convenience."

This certainly put me to shame. I was disgusted to realize that at my age I could be so shiftless. I had a sudden desire to get drunk, and downed another bottle of sake.

The last package was from Hiroshima and I knew by the childish handwriting of its sender that it was a "comfort kit." Japanese school children made these little gift packages on their own and sent them with a note to some unknown serviceman at the front. My package yielded a set of picture postcards showing the famed Hiroshima landscape, a sketch by the sender, a bunch of envelopes, and a letter pad. An accompanying note read: "I am a nine-year-old school girl in Hiroshima. All of us school children here are studying hard. We sincerely pray you will fight hard for the sake of our nation."

This was the only really heartening letter of the day. I stopped drinking, and began writing replies, first to the unknown Hiroshima girl: "My dear Young Lady, Thank you very much for your very kind comfort kit. I am the commanding officer of a destroyer. I am grateful and happy to receive your sincere good wishes. . . ."

The following day I went ashore with the first of my crew headed for their 3-hour liberty. It was good to see that the streets of Davao had not been damaged. They were crowded with crews from other warships anchored in the harbor. Housewives of Japanese residents in the city had set up refreshment stands with signs reading, "Please help yourself to coffee and tea. Served free by your fellow countrymen."

Filipinos were also walking the streets peacefully. The girls with their elaborate hairdos and bright ribbons and the men with brilliantly pomaded hair presented a gay picture. It was surprising for me to note, however, that most of them were barefoot. In Japan no one walks barefoot on a city street; anyone who can afford it owns a pair of shoes, those who cannot, wear wooden clogs. I was intrigued by the native scene.

Theaters were showing the latest American movies to packed audiences. On side streets I noticed a number of houses marked: "Japanese military recreation center." Many sailors and soldiers were queuing up in front of them. These were brothels whose Japanese, Korean and Okinawan occupants followed wherever the Japanese military moved.

I noted a sudden uneasiness among the men, obviously because of my presence. I said to my lieutenant, "Let's part here. I must go to headquarters. I'll meet you at noon. Caution your chiefs to count noses at the pier."

"Aye, aye, sir," grinned the lieutenant.

As we parted the men shouted gaily, "Bravo! Long live our skipper!"

5

On February 27–28, 1942, I took part in the Battle of Java Sea. That action is worthy of note as one of the few major sea battles of World War II in which no planes were involved except for reconnaissance. Accordingly, it deserves a full description and analysis.

There have been many books by both Allied and Japanese authors which purport to tell the story of this action. Most of the Allied books were written too soon after the war. The authors' feelings seem still to have been running too high to permit objectivity and historical detachment. Nor do the Japanese books thus far impress me as being either objective or accurate. Part of this shortcoming is attributable to a lack of source documents, to be sure, but defeated and dispirited commanders are really not capable of giving objective accounts of their battles.

Most of the commanding officers of the Allied ships in this battle were killed during the action. Therefore it is not possible to reconstruct all the details of the Allied side.

Rear Admiral Takeo Takagi, the top Japanese commander in the battle, was killed at Saipan in 1944. He was survived by his chief of staff, Captain Ko Nagasawa, now a top-ranking admiral of the new Japanese Navy, and Nagasawa's assistant, Lieutenant Commander Kotaro Ishikawa, who was Takagi's Intelligence Officer. Before writing this chapter I had long discussions with each of them as well as other surviving officers involved in the battle.

The Allied fleet made first contact with the Japanese convoy off Surabaya and reached out in an effort to destroy it. At the outset the Allied column of 3 heavy cruisers, 2 light cruisers, and 11 destroyers managed to box the 41 slow transports of the convoy as well as its escort of 10 destroyers and 2 light cruisers. The transports were loaded with a division of army troops. There were also 2 Japanese heavy cruisers assigned to this operation but they lagged some 150 miles behind the convoy.

With all their initial advantage of position and numerical superiority, the Allies failed to sink a single Japanese vessel in this encounter. Though the many errors committed by both sides seemed to offset each other, the really decisive factor, in my opinion, was morale.

It is interesting to compare this battle with what took place at Leyte Gulf in October, 1944. There the Japanese fleet, led by Vice Admiral Takeo Kurita, played an almost identical role to that of Dutch Rear Admiral K. W. F. M. Doorman's forces in the Java Sea battle.

At Leyte Gulf Kurita cornered four of the enemy's light carriers, slow and vulnerable, and could have dealt them a shattering blow. But he turned around at the critical moment and gave up a brilliant chance. That was exactly what the Allied fleet did in the Java Sea.

Kurita went to Leyte with grim determination, but with full realization that he had no chance of winning against the overwhelming forces of the enemy. It is important to note that psychological background before criticizing his seemingly foolish reversal.

In February, 1942, a sense of hopelessness reigned among Allied officers at Surabaya. They saw little or no chance of survival. The Allied fleet of 15 fighting ships was licking its wounds. All these ships knew that they were likely to face a real showdown within a week.

Allied commanders recalled the Pearl Harbor attack and the sinking of *Prince of Wales* and *Repulse* two months earlier. They had almost refused to accept the news at first, and there was still disbelief in their minds. But facts piled on facts. Singapore had just fallen. Complete occupation of the Philippines appeared imminent. The Japanese were surging to the south, reducing one outpost after another.

The Imperial Navy's mighty task force, commanded by Vice Admiral Chuichi Nagumo, was known to be moving in the waters of the South Pacific. It appeared to enemy eyes as a mammoth super-armada. They simply had no way of knowing just how huge it was, or how many carriers Japan had. This confusion sprang in part from the fact that the enemy could not tell whether attacking Japanese planes came from carriers or land bases.

The massive air raids on the Philippines, carried out a few hours after Pearl Harbor, were believed to have come from Japanese carriers. Actually the planes came from Formosa. A series of bomber attacks over Java were also carried out by land-based Japanese planes from Jolo, Balikpapan and Kendari. To Allied officers at Stirabaya, these planes appeared to have come from Japanese carriers in the Java Sea.

On February 1, a small American task force attacked the Marshall Islands. Nagumo's task force promptly rushed out from Truk on a 1,500-mile sortie to the Marshalls. Allies at Surabaya, hearing of this movement, thought it was now safe to go out and attack the Japanese. Their four cruisers and seven destroyers steamed to Balikpapan, hoping to repeat the achievements of Commander Paul Talbot.

The Japanese were not napping this time. Sixty Japanese bombers and fighters which had come from Formosa to Kendari, swooped down on February 4 and damaged the Allied fleet. These ships limped back to Surabaya, stunned by what they believed to have been carrier-borne Japanese planes. The whole affair was a nightmare to them.

On the 19th another event—impossible in the eyes of the Surabaya headquarters—occurred right over their heads. Allied intelligence reports said the Nagamo Task Force had turned before reaching the Marshalls and was

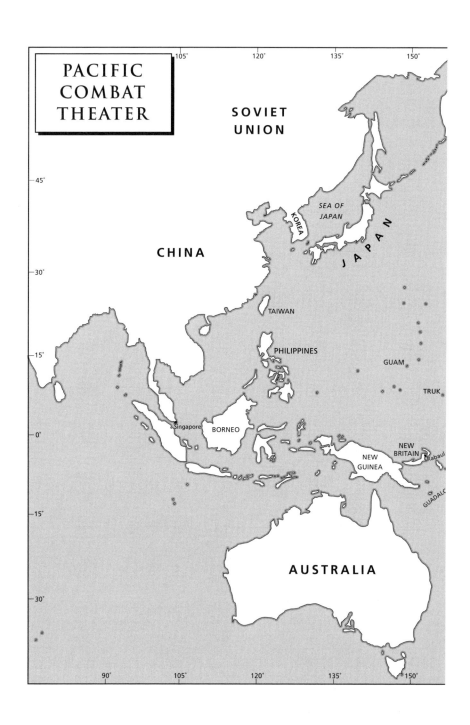

PACIFIC
COMBAT
THEATER

SOVIET
UNION

45°

CHINA

30°

KOREA

SEA OF
JAPAN

JAPAN

TAIWAN

15°

PHILIPPINES

GUAM

TRUK

0°

Singapore

BORNEO

NEW
BRITAIN

Rabaul

NEW
GUINEA

GUADALC

15°

AUSTRALIA

30°

105°   120°   135°   150°

90°   105°   120°   135°   150°

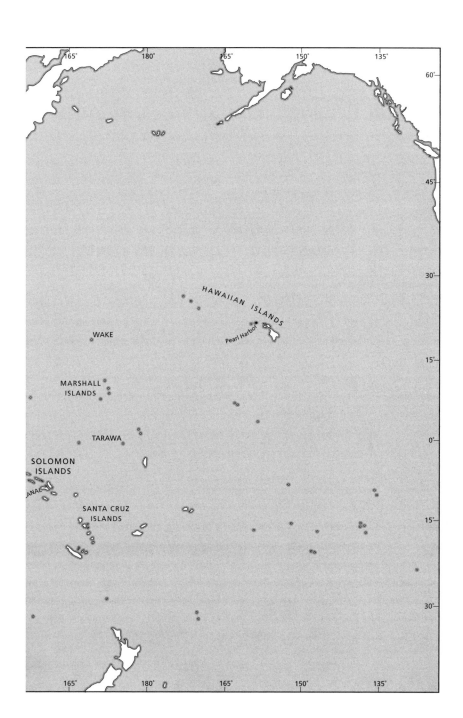

165°   180°   165°   150°   135°

60°

45°

30°

HAWAIIAN ISLANDS

WAKE   Pearl Harbor

15°

MARSHALL
ISLANDS

TARAWA   0°

SOLOMON
ISLANDS

ANAL   15°

SANTA CRUZ
ISLANDS

30°

165°   180° 0° 165°   150°   135°

headed toward Australia. Early that morning Nagumo hurled 188 bombers and fighters in a devastating raid on Port Darwin.

About noon the same day, 23 Zero fighters swarmed over Surabaya and shot down 40 Allied fighters, mostly P-36s, in a brief air melee. Even if the intelligence man at Balikpapan had reported accurately that these Japanese navy fighters had flown 450 miles from Formosan bases, the Allied officers would probably not have believed it. They were all convinced that the Zeros were from carriers.

Later that same day, a group of Japanese bombers from Kendari struck a secret enemy airfield at Djombang, near Surabaya, and destroyed P-40s, Buffaloes, and British Hurricanes based there. Japanese combat planes were fast gaining respect in the eyes of the enemy. It was no chance thing that Britain's proudest battleship had fallen victim to their attack. The same fate could meet any of the remaining ships at Surabaya.

Against this background the commanding officers at Surabaya on February 20 mulled over the latest reports that two massive Japanese convoys were heading toward Java. One convoy of 41 transports with some 20 escorting warships left Jolo for Surabaya on February 19. The other, with 56 transports and 15 escorts, had left Camranh Bay, Indochina, two days earlier heading for Western Java.

The high command at Surabaya must have been in agony. If the Allied fleet went out to tackle one of the Japanese convoys it might win a battle. But it would not then have a chance of defeating the second convoy. The most difficult factor for the enemy, however, must have been the unpredictability of Nagumo's mighty task force. It might turn up at any moment to swing its sledgehammer blows at the Allied fleet, now devoid of air cover. Meanwhile, Japanese planes were able to come and go at will.

At the Japanese high command, Admiral Isoroku Yamamoto, commander in chief of the Imperial Combined Fleet, had met with his staff officers on February 17 aboard battleship *Nagato*, moored at Hashirajima near Kure in Central Japan. He had already ordered Nagumo to turn around and hit Port Darwin without pursuing the small American task force. "We must secure oil and other resources of the Dutch East Indies. That is of higher priority than pursuing any small American force."

Yamamoto doubtless had in mind the outline of his forthcoming Midway Operation. When his staff had studied all intelligence data and reported to him, Yamamoto concluded that the Allied surface fleet in Surabaya was "no potential threat" to Japanese actions. And he ordered the two convoys, each carrying an Army division, to weigh anchor. "The landing operation does not require the support of a major task force," Yamamoto ruled. So Nagumo pushed 220 miles north of Port Darwin on February 19.

On February 20 Yamamoto held another staff meeting. It was decided that the Allied fleet was "completely demoralized" and "no longer in shape to attempt any major action." Yamamoto canceled his earlier plan of using land-based planes as air cover for the Japanese convoys. Nagumo was ordered to the Indian Ocean "to sink Allied warships expected to be fleeing from Surabaya."

This audacity resulted in jeopardizing the operation of at least the convoy which I escorted. The 41 transports were in two columns, 600 meters between ships, and two thousand meters between columns. They zigzagged sluggishly at 10 knots. The formation was spearheaded by four minesweepers on a line of bearing with 3,000-meter intervals, followed at 3,000 meters by three destroyers, similarly spread. Then came cruiser *Naka*, the flagship, flanked by two small patrol ships. One destroyer to port and one to starboard guarded the middle section of the long transport columns.

Another escort group, consisting of Destroyer Division 2 which included my *Amatsukaze* and three other destroyers, led by Rear Admiral Raizo Tanaka's flagship *Jintsu*, was in position farther out on the port side. This group had taken part briefly in the Timor Island landing operation after Ambon and we had joined the convoy at Macassar on February 25. Two heavy cruisers, *Nachi* and *Haguro*, followed haughtily behind the convoy at a distance of some 200 miles.

The 20-mile-long convoy was quite a spectacle. An obvious laxity prevailed in the transports with their ill-trained crews. Many transports emitted huge clouds of black smoke from their funnels. Many used their radios in violation of "no-transmission" orders, or failed to observe blackout rules at night.

Enemy submarines could have had a field day against such easy targets. Most disturbing, however, was the dreadfully slow pace of the trailing heavy cruisers—the only ships of the force which packed a real punch, in case the enemy fleet chose to attack us.

The weather was beautiful; sparkling sun by day, and bright moonlight silvered the sea every night. Even at night, trained eyes could span the length of the entire force. Five Allied submarines had been observed by our reconnaissance planes, but none menaced our ships. To this day, I do not understand why enemy submarines failed to come out.

On the morning of the 26th, the sea south of Borneo was calm. I awakened from a brief nap and pored over the latest information. Our reconnaissance planes and intelligence agents reported a formidable mine field all along the Surabaya coast, adding to the hazard of many sunken ships. The reports also said, 'The Allies are still flying bombers, including some B-17s recently arrived from Africa, and fighters at Malang and other small strips."

The situation certainly did not warrant all our optimism. At 0800 a PBY Catalina float plane suddenly slipped out of the clouds to the southeast and headed toward my ship.

"Enemy plane dead ahead! Open fire!" I yelled.

An antiaircraft machine gun fired one burst as the PBY dropped a bomb— a bit too early—which raised a large water pillar about 500 meters ahead. The plane swerved, gained speed and disappeared into the overcast. The whole action was so brief that we didn't even have time to get excited.

This was most unusual. The more I thought about this awkward attack the more puzzled I was. If the plane was on reconnaissance—as it must have been—it was foolish to have made its presence so obvious. It was still more ridiculous for the plane to drop just one bomb at a destroyer. A transport would have been a much more profitable target. In a way it was good to know that the enemy was aware of our operation.

A lookout called attention to a big white ship to port heading in our direction. Using large binoculars I saw what appeared to be a hospital ship of about 4,000 tons. Its presence in this area was the second puzzle of the day.

We hoisted flags ordering it to stand by for inspection, and sped toward the ship. Through binoculars I watched a small elderly man, apparently the ship's skipper, on deck hastily putting on a uniform. His hands were shaking and he appeared very nervous. As we closed I read the name *Optennote*, and our Ship Register confirmed that it was a Dutch hospital ship.

Lieutenant Goro Iwabuchi and six armed petty officers rowed over in a boat and boarded the ship. An hour later they returned to report some 15 doctors and nurses on board, in addition to the crew. I asked for instructions and Admiral Tanaka replied, "Even a hospital ship is objectionable in this area. Take it to the rear to anchor among our supply ships."

I spent all morning chaperoning the hospital ship. After handing it over to the care of the Supply Squadron Commander, I rushed back at 26 knots and rejoined the escort at 1415. A few fighter planes from Balikpapan flew cover over the convoy. They came after the PBY had attacked us, and stayed overhead until about 1900. By that time a cool breeze had sprung up. I lit a cigarette and asked the navigator the time of sunset. Lieutenant (j.g.) Toshio Koyama answered that the sun would set at 1948.

My smoke was interrupted by the staccato sound of anti-aircraft guns. Seeing that cruiser *Jintsu* was firing, I ordered, "Battle Stations! Air Attack!" Looking up I saw two B-17 bombers coming out of the cloud deck some 4,000 meters high, and yelled, "Open fire!"

The 12.7-centimeter guns swung up to 75 degrees, but still could not bring the planes into range. The smaller guns were completely ineffective, but they fired as if their noise might scare the bombers. The B-17s, apparently from Java, dropped six 500-lb. bombs. Four of them fell about 1,500 meters to starboard of *Amatsukaze*. Two hit the water some 500 meters on destroyer *Hatsukaze*'s port hand. Poor marksmanship!

The bombers attacked our fighting ships, instead of troop-laden transports, that meant that the enemy wanted to knock out our fighting ships, so his fleet could tackle the whole convoy. This was alarming, and I felt braced for the challenge.

The morning hours of the following day, February 27, were uneventful. Our crew continued with routine training. Then at 1150, just when everyone was ready for lunch, four big bombs exploded without warning. Huge columns of water rose about 200 meters ahead of destroyer *Yukikaze*, cruising 3,000 meters to the right of my ship.

The preceding day we had seen the bombers before they attacked. Today we were caught unawares, and belatedly I again discovered two B-17s flying just below the 4,000-meter cloud cover. The Flying Fortresses had certainly achieved surprise. It was only inept bombing that spoiled their chance.

Their aiming again at the highly maneuverable warships puzzled me. Why didn't they hit at the sluggish transports? One hit by a 500-lb. bomb could easily have sunk a transport and disrupted the whole Japanese schedule. Today, years after the battle, I still believe that was a big mistake.

Japan also made a serious error in launching this operation without sufficient air cover for the surface forces. But that mistake was offset by the ineffective and unwise tactics of the Allied planes.

Ten minutes after the B-17 encounter, the convoy altered course 90 degrees for Surabaya. Until then we had been heading westward—in a feint movement. We were already 60 miles north of Surabaya. Soon afterward a Japanese scout plane from Balikpapan flashed a report: "Five enemy cruisers and six destroyers, 63 miles 310 degrees from Surabaya at 1200 hours. This force is heading on an 80-degree course at 12 knots."

Nachi, 12,374 tons, one of the two heavy cruisers following us far to the rear, immediately catapulted its scout plane to maintain contact with the enemy fleet. The fleet was surprisingly near and apparently headed toward us. Was it coming to fight us? We waited uneasily for further scout plane reports.

Two long hours passed. At 1405 the *Nachi* plane radioed that the enemy force of 5 cruisers and 10 destroyers was continuing on the same course. With two of our cruisers 150 miles to the rear, the enemy fleet was definitely more powerful than our escort. Admiral Takagi ordered the transports to turn northward.

I no longer felt the tropical heat. Cold sweat ran down my back. We had blundered into a trap. If the enemy picked up speed immediately, he could easily tear our convoy to shreds and sink the transports like clay pigeons. I shuddered at the prospect. The two forces drew steadily closer, and I wondered why the enemy fleet still cruised at a mere 12 knots. At 1510 *Nachi*'s scout plane radioed an amazing message: "The enemy fleet has turned around and is headed toward Surabaya."

Admiral Takagi, on *Nachi*'s bridge, laughed. "The enemy ships were merely staying clear of our air raids on Surabaya. The enemy is in no shape to fight us. We will stick to our original plans and schedule. The force will turn and head south again."

At 1630 there was another surprise message from the *Nachi* scout plane. "The enemy fleet has turned around again. The double column formation is now shifting to single column. The enemy is gaining speed and is headed on a course of 20 degrees." Ten minutes later, another message came: "The enemy speed is 22 knots. It is heading directly for our convoy."

There was no longer any doubt about the enemy's intention. I checked the chart and found that the distance to the enemy fleet was 60 miles. If both sides ran at 20 knots, we would meet within an hour and a half.

Takagi, suddenly glum and angry, ordered the transports to turn around once again. He also ordered the cruisers to catapult their observation planes, and the escort ships to line up into fighting formation. Cruisers *Nachi* and *Haguro* belatedly began to pick up speed.

My flotilla quickly formed in a column—cruiser *Jintsu* followed by the four destroyers. The transports turned around and fanned out. Their movement was painfully slow. They were mostly requisitioned merchant ships and their crews were untrained. It was distressing to watch their disarray.

Many were baffled at the repeatedly changing orders and they were unable to respond quickly.

Most irritating of all was the slow arrival of *Nachi* and *Haguro*. They were so many miles to the rear. Each of these two heavy cruisers packed a punch equal to that of ten destroyers. Without them I did not see how we could fight the powerful enemy fleet. If the enemy increased speed to 30 knots they might arrive at any moment. If that happened, what could we do?

At 1700 the chaos subsided as the transports resumed an orderly formation escorted by patrol ships and minesweepers. Behind our flotilla, four other destroyers formed up. The other flotilla, consisting of cruiser *Naka* and seven destroyers, brought up the rear. The Japanese warships now sped at 24 knots, ready to fight. I scanned the horizon as we cruised around the 2-mile-long column, but found no trace of our two heavy cruisers. I mumbled profanely in my vexation.

"Enemy ship!" shouted Warrant Officer Shigeru Iwata, who, gifted with amazing eyesight, was the chief spotter on the bridge. I looked where he was pointing. I saw several masts to the south. They soon became visible to everyone on board. From pictures I had studied, the masts were clearly recognizable as belonging to the Dutch cruiser *De Ruyter*. "*De Ruyter* is distant 28,000 meters (about 20 miles)," Iwata chanted. "It is closing rapidly."

I turned around. *Nachi* and *Haguro* were still not in sight. There was, in fact, nothing to be seen but the many Japanese transports, sluggishly fanning out behind us. I shouted, "Gunners and torpedomen, get ready. Our target is the lead cruiser in the enemy column!"

All noises in my ship were suddenly hushed. We were heading for our first major sea battle! The silence was broken by Iwata's voice, "Commander, look! *Nachi* and *Haguro* there!" I looked around and saw the long-awaited cruisers on the eastern horizon. They were far away, but could make it. Good! I nodded. The time was 1730.

The enemy ships suddenly altered course to the west and began running almost parallel to us. This was another puzzling development. The enemy must have seen our column formation. Why did he refuse to go straight ahead? By staying on his original course, the enemy could have chosen broadside targets while keeping himself only thinly exposed to Japanese gunfire.

That enemy movement again enabled us to gain time. Admiral Takagi leaped with joy when he saw the enemy, still 36,000 meters distant, swerving to the parallel course. "Now I can catch up with our fleet," he yelled. At

1746 Takagi's battle orders were issued: "Deploy in three columns and head on course 170 degrees (south)."

One minute later cruiser *Naka* opened fire at the enemy 22,000 meters away—too far for its 14-centimeter guns. Realizing the mix-up, Takagi hurriedly changed his orders: "Keep course parallel to the enemy." Cruiser *Jintsu* and her four destroyers swung out and moved some 10,000 meters along the western course of the force. *Jintsu* fired its six 14-centimeter guns at *De Ruyter*, 18,000 meters away. The shells were wasted. The four destroyers watched glumly. At that distance, their 12.7-centimeter guns were also useless. *Nachi* and *Haguro* started shooting their 20-centimeter guns from a distance of 25,000 meters. Their shells were equally ineffective.

The Allied fleet swerved again—gradually to the southwest—increasing the distance from our ships. The enemy guns were now blazing, but the distance was also too great for them. All their shells were wasted. At 1805 Rear Admiral Shoji Nishimura, commanding Destroyer Squadron 4, apparently lost patience with the ineffective gun duel over a widening distance.

Nishimura's cruiser *Naka* and his seven destroyers released 43 torpedoes at the enemy, then estimated to be more than 15,000 meters distant. The oxygen torpedoes, pride of the Imperial Navy, could run 40,000 meters at a speed of 36 knots. But released at such a distance even they could not be expected to hit moving targets—except by sheer chance. Of these torpedoes a dozen or so blew up after running a few thousand meters. There is no explanation of why they exploded. It may have been a mechanical failure, or perhaps some of them collided and their explosions induced the others to explode. The other torpedoes went on, but hit nothing. They, too, were wasted. Allied officers must have been astounded at the range and spread of these torpedoes. It must have been quite nerve-wracking.

After the torpedo attack, the Allied fleet turned sharply to the south. At 1827 eight Allied planes appeared. They flew on some 20 miles ahead of us and headed for our transports.

About a dozen Zero fighters, which had been called in from Balikpapan at the time our escort ships had deserted the convoy, gleefully pounced on the enemy bombers. All of the enemy planes were shot down before they released any bombs at the Japanese transports. This attempted enemy air attack was yet another puzzling development of the day.*

---

* The hapless attackers were light bombers of the Netherlands Air Force.

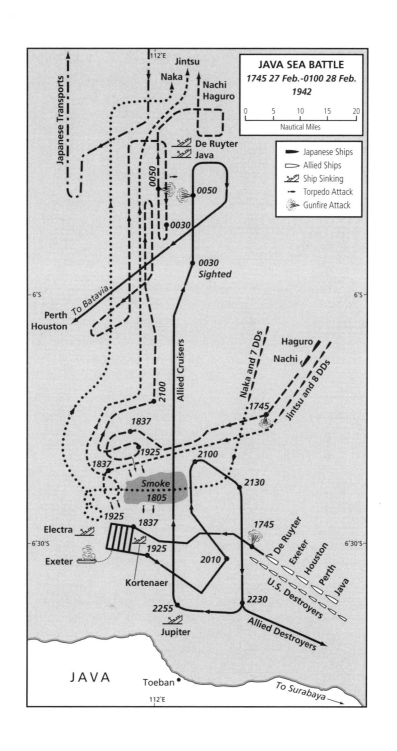

JAVA SEA BATTLE
1745 27 Feb.-0100 28 Feb.
1942

0   5   10   15   20
Nautical Miles

Japanese Ships
Allied Ships
Ship Sinking
Torpedo Attack
Gunfire Attack

Japanese Transports

112°E

Jintsu
Naka
Nachi
Haguro

De Ruyter
Java

0050

0050

0030

0030
Sighted

To Batavia

6°S   6°S

Perth
Houston

2100

Allied Cruisers

Naka and 7 DDs

Haguro
Nachi

1745

Jintsu and 8 DDs

1837

1925

2100

Smoke
1805

2130

1837

1925

1837

1745

De Ruyter
Exeter
Houston
Perth
Java

6°30'S   6°30'S

Electra

Exeter

1925

Kortenaer

2010

U.S. Destroyers

2255

2230

Jupiter

Allied Destroyers

JAVA

Toeban

112°E

To Surabaya

It was cloudy with a lowering sun piercing the clouds from time to time. But dusk was fast approaching, and sunset would be at 1950. By 1833 Admiral Takagi determined that we were merely wasting ammunition and the possibility was growing that the enemy might flee under the dark of night if we continued the battle in that fashion. He ordered all ships "to close and charge the enemy."

The enemy fleet had again turned to starboard and was now heading due west. The Japanese ships also turned to the west, with guns blazing. Four minutes later, British cruiser *Exeter* was afire, causing sudden confusion in the enemy formation. The enemy ships promptly emitted thick smoke screens. (It was later learned that a 20-centimeter shell, from *Nachi* or *Haguro*, had hit *Exeter*'s powder magazine.) *Exeter*, in second position in the Allied column, lost speed rapidly. In slowing she swung to the left out of column, and barely avoided collision with following American cruiser *Houston*.

An amazing development followed when *Houston* also swerved to the left, and all the following ships did the same. Flagship *De Ruyter* alone continued straight ahead, and it was a few minutes before she discovered that the rest of the column had turned off. In turning around to rejoin them at full speed, she almost collided with a destroyer.

This sudden chaos in the Allied formation enabled us to close, and eight Japanese destroyers, including mine, went dashing in at 30 knots. The Allied fleet reformed, leaving the limping *Exeter* behind, and the guns of every ship were leveled directly at us. At 7,000 meters from the enemy fleet, destroyer *Tokitsukaze*, a little ahead of *Amatsukaze*, took a shell hit. *Amatsukaze* was enveloped by thick white smoke bursting from *Tokitsukaze* which blinded us. Shells rained all around, raising water pillars on every side, but still none reached my ship. I gritted my teeth and made a dogged dash as the enemy shells came closer and closer. I had to continue if I was to release my torpedoes effectively.

The enemy was heading northwest, directly toward us, in his first aggressive operation of the day. Six thousand meters to the enemy now. Sweat streamed down my face as I grasped the bridge railing. Not yet. Wait. We must close to at least 5,000 meters. Enemy shells were falling close, and could hit my ship at any moment.

At 1927 Rear Admiral Raizo Tanaka ordered his cruiser to release eight torpedoes. When *Jintsu*'s fish swished out of their tubes, I could hardly restrain an order for gunfire. A near miss dashed water on my face. My knees shook and my arms trembled at the time. I grow quite uncomfortable when I think of it even now. I was not worried about being a coward, but was concerned that my cool judgment might vanish, being under the fire of enemy ships for the first time.

I saw 16 more torpedoes spring into the water from *Yukikaze* and *Tokitsukaze*. At this I gave in and yelled: "Fire torpedoes!" Four other destroyers followed *Amatsukaze*'s lead. I calculated the chances of a hit. Very slim at 6,000 meters. Perhaps less than five per cent—3 hits out of the 72—I figured. How wrong this proved to be!

The enemy fleet made a rapid turn to the west, and I saw that at least half of our torpedoes would pass beyond the enemy bows. The rest of the "fish" reached the area of the targets but all seemed to have missed, when suddenly there was a tremendous flash. Dutch destroyer *Kortenaer* was hit and sank instantly. One hit out of 64 shots! What poor aiming and how excellent were the enemy's evasion tactics!

Rear Admiral Shoji Nishimura's cruiser *Naka* and his seven destroyers arrived presently and also released 64 torpedoes. The enemy again swung 90 degrees, this time to the north, in an unorthodox, fantastic movement, and all 64 of these torpedoes were wasted. The enemy then took two more 90-degree turns and the whole column turned around in a thick smoke screen. Such tactics were not to be found in the Imperial Navy manual. I just stood and gaped.

An enemy shell hit destroyer *Asagumo*, killing five and wounding 19, disabling its engine for a time.

After the torpedo release our Second Squadron and *Naka*'s Fourth Squadron drew their courses in looping curves and turned in a complex movement. The distance to the enemy fleet was steadily expanding. Our chances appeared to be lost. However, Allied behavior on this night was really inscrutable. After having made a 360-degree turn, the enemy had apparently turned heel and run under the thick smoke screens. But the Allied fleet then made two more rapid 90-degree turns and headed back straight to the north. The enemy intention remains a mystery. Perhaps they still wanted to make a drive against the Japanese convoy.

Japanese cruisers *Nachi* and *Haguro*, trailing far behind the two destroyer squadrons, saw the enemy and turned around. At about 2000 hours they released 16 torpedoes at a range of 16,000 meters. The distance was too great. The Allied fleet again made a 360-degree turn, and all these torpedoes were also wasted. The enemy fleet sped at full steam southward toward Surabaya.

The Japanese cruisers would not chase. The staff officers uneasily watched a series of about 12 explosions to the south. They had no idea what the explosions were and suspected that enemy submarines were attacking the Japanese destroyers. It was later ascertained that these explosions were simply their own torpedoes, which had traveled 40,000 meters to the south, hitting the shore. In the gathering darkness we could also see the Surabaya lighthouse, just 20 miles away.

At 2030 hours Takagi ordered all ships to break off pursuit and gather near the transports. The battle was indeed a series of blunders made by each side. Almost every man in Tanaka's Destroyer Squadron 2 was disgruntled at the order to break off action. Our ships had not expended as much ammunition as the others, and I also felt that we had forfeited a chance of giving hot pursuit and finishing off the enemy.

When Takagi saw that all the destroyers were turning to the north, he ordered *Nachi* and *Haguro* to halt and pick up the five scout planes catapulted from these cruisers earlier. Takagi almost paid with his life as a result of this decision. Only a serious blunder by the enemy saved him. It was technically difficult to pick up the planes ditching near the vessels. Later in the war many Japanese warships simply gave up their planes once they were catapulted. At that time, however, while Japan was winning, commanders were eager to recover catapulted planes. So Takagi was quite right in his decision to recover his flyers. He was entirely wrong, however, in thinking that the Allied fleet had fled to Surabaya.

At 2050 *Nachi* was trying to pick up the last of the five planes, when a lookout called: "Battleship Division 3 has arrived!" Commander Ishikawa looked through his binoculars. "Hmmmm, three-masted ships," he mumbled. "Yes, they look like *Haruna* and *Kirishima*."

"How did they get here? They were in the Indian Ocean just two days ago . . . ," the information officer remarked incredulously on the bridge of *Nachi*.

Thirty seconds later, Ishikawa screamed in rage: "Damn! Those are enemy ships, and four of them are heading toward us. They are only 12,000 meters away."

There was furor and commotion everywhere in the ship. The two cruisers were stopped dead. How could ships fight when they were dead in the water? And the crews were not at battle stations. A dozen flares were fired by the oncoming enemy. Admiral Takagi bit his lip so hard that he drew blood. He was in agony.

"Hurry up the plane recovery," he ordered. "All men to battle stations!" Spines tingled. One minute. Two minutes. Three minutes.

"The plane is caught!" yelled the winchman.

Takagi roared. "Engine, full astern!"

Nachi's engines shuddered to life. The ship slowly began to move backward, a plane dangling at its side by the winch cable. The enemy cruisers opened fire and near misses began dropping all around. Takagi ordered smoke as *Nachi* and *Haguro* got up to 18 knots, the minimum fighting speed. Both ships turned and opened fire but, knowing they were outnumbered, did not use searchlights. The ensuing gun duel, conducted at a distance of 12,000 meters, merely wasted ammunition on both sides. After ten minutes, *Nachi* and *Haguro* lost sight of the opposing ships, and the crisis was over.

But a new anxiety arose. Takagi said, "The enemy may be headed for our transports." The two cruisers went to 30 knots in frantic search for the enemy ships which 20 minutes earlier had given them such a scare. Takagi ordered cruiser *Jintsu*, some 5,000 meters away, to catapult its remaining plane and scout for the enemy. Admiral Tanaka responded quickly.

At 2145 the *Jintsu* plane radioed: "An enemy force of four cruisers and six destroyers is heading south." This news relieved the harried officers in *Nachi* and *Haguro*.

Evidently our two cruisers had encountered the enemy as he was making the last 90-degree turn of a 180-degree movement. The Allies had not expected to meet the Japanese in that fashion, and had pursued their planned course to the south. They thereby lost an excellent chance to maul our forces. Had they rushed in for a showdown, they could at least have crippled *Nachi* and *Haguro* and might have then massacred the unguarded transports.

The enemy naval force had taken a beating. Burning *Exeter* headed for Surabaya. Three destroyers were sunk. Six other destroyers, badly damaged, had also cleared the area. The remaining Allied ships regrouped close to the Java coast. There were four cruisers—*De Ruyter*, *Houston*, *Perth* and *Java*—and two destroyers which assembled in a series of their familiar turns.

They valiantly decided to head north in another attempt to challenge the Japanese. Unfortunately, they had already missed their best chance. The force made one 90-degree turn, then another. British destroyer *Jupiter* hit an

Allied mine and sank instantly. The five other ships did not retreat. They made one more turn, of 45 degrees, to head straight north, illumined from time to time by flares dropped from the *Jintsu* plane.

The moon was bright, but frequent rain squalls reduced visibility. The Allies headed for their final bid, driving through the darkness which was punctuated by Japanese flares.

Japanese warships were also being reformed and readied for a night action. Only a few had been hit; none sunk. All were in fighting shape, eager for a scrap. Heavy cruisers *Nachi* and *Haguro* kept watch to the north in accordance with steady reports from the *Jintsu* scout plane. At thirty-three minutes past midnight on February 28 there was a flurry on the bridge of *Nachi* as it appeared that the enemy was heading doggedly to the north.

Nachi and *Haguro* immediately swung northward, to parallel the Allied column, and slowed down to achieve a good attack angle. Economy of fuel and ammunition was a matter of great concern to the Japanese ships, so their gunfire was only intermittent. No hits were scored on the enemy ships. Some Allied accounts published after the war say the Allied fleet at the time knew nothing about the approaching Japanese ships. *Nachi*, however, reports that there was return fire but that it was ineffective.

At 0053 *Nachi* released eight torpedoes and *Haguro* four at targets bearing 60 degrees to starboard. The enemy ships were 10,000 meters distant. Encountering a brief rain squall, the Japanese officers crossed their fingers and hoped. At 0106 the dark night was suddenly lit by a tremendous fire pillar to the southeast. A torpedo had hit cruiser *Java* amidship. Four minutes later there was another explosion in the Allied column, and *De Ruyter* burst into flames to burn like a match box. Sailors on the decks of *Nachi* and *Haguro* shouted "Banzai!" They leaped and danced and slapped each other on the back with joy.

Admiral Takagi spoke coolly. "Let's finish off the remaining ships." *Nachi* and *Haguro* rushed northeast at full speed through little rain squalls. Failing to locate any other ships, they swung near the two burning ships. "Don't waste ammunition on them," Takagi said. "They are done for." The search was called off at 0300.

The last puzzle of the day was the movement of the American cruiser *Houston* and Australian cruiser *Perth*. And Takagi's fruitless search to the north was probably the last Japanese mistake of the battle. The other two Allied ships had turned around as soon as *Java* and *De Ruyter* burst into flames. They moved southwest, following the coast—a curious finale to their defiant northward sortie.

Nine minutes past midnight on March 1, destroyer *Fubuki* spotted two unidentified ships. They were located some 10,000 meters east of Babi Island, near Banten Bay, roughly 500 nautical miles from the scene of the Java Sea battle. Commander Yasuo Yamashita, *Fubuki*'s skipper, had no idea what these ships were. *Fubuki* swung around and followed some 8,000 meters behind the two mysterious ships. The ships were *Houston* and *Perth*, and the mystery is how they ever made the 24-hour voyage without being observed during the day by Japanese scout planes.

After the long hours of fighting in the running battle of the Java Sea, these ships were low in ammunition. They had made a 500-mile voyage at some 20 knots and were also running low on fuel. They were in no shape to strike back at a vastly superior Japanese force. The two ships, headed for fuel and ammunition supplies, must have been astounded to sight a 56-ship Japanese convoy in Banten Bay, ready for landing. They bravely started to shell these transports at 37 minutes past midnight.

Japanese destroyer *Harukaze* dashed forward to lay smoke screens. Destroyer *Fubuki* fired 9 torpedoes. Rear Admiral Akisaburo Hara's 12 escorting warships scrambled in confusion and chaos. *Fubuki* had notified them of "two mysterious ships entering the bay," but they were still not fully prepared for a battle. There were just too many opposing the two Allied ships. Some of the skippers told me later they were busy the whole time evading friendly shells and torpedoes.

Within an hour, however, both Allied ships were sunk. Three Japanese transports were badly damaged, and one—the troop command ship—was sunk. General Hitoshi Imamura, the top Army commander, was thrown into the sea and had to swim to shore. Japanese casualties were extremely light.

An investigation committee studied this confused battle but produced no solution as to how the Japanese transports were sunk. There were opinions that the transports had been hit by *Fubuki*'s torpedoes, which were fired from a distance of 7,000 meters. But other Japanese ships had released at longer ranges.

While all the transports completed their landing successfully near Surabaya, cruisers *Nachi* and *Haguro* were busy. They contacted another group of three remaining enemy ships about noon the same day near Bawean Island to the north. The two Japanese ships, reinforced by cruisers *Ashigara* and *Myoko*, sank the limping British cruiser *Exeter* at 1330. British destroyer *Encounter* was sunk ten minutes later, and U.S. destroyer *Pope* was finished off at 1530.

Only four American destroyers managed to flee from Bali Strait to the south. Four others were sunk by Japanese planes from the Nagumo Task Force. Not a single transport or warship was lost in the convoy headed by Takagi. He achieved his purpose with complete success, and the battle ended in a lopsided Japanese victory.

Nevertheless, Takagi was furiously attacked for "his series of blunders." He was particularly criticized for having opened fire at a range of 28,000 meters, and wasting ammunition. When the battle ended, *Nachi*, for instance, had only seven shells left for each of its ten 20-centimeter guns. Tanaka's *Jintsu* had practically no fuel and was almost adrift. Gunnery officers scorned Takagi, saying: "He's a submariner, and doesn't know how to use guns."

Takagi and his aide, Nagasawa, offered no excuses. Takagi was soon transferred to command of a submarine fleet. Nagasawa returned to Tokyo and was assigned to the personnel bureau.

This action taught many lessons. After my ship's first encounter and release of torpedoes, we remained outside the main scene of battle. But I observed much of the action and saw the fire pillars of *Java* and *De Ruyter* from a distance. This one battle meant more to me than all the hundreds of practice maneuvers in which I had participated.

6

Rear Admiral Raizo Tanaka ordered my destroyer to Bandjermasin for refueling in the afternoon of February 28, when he had determined that the waters near Surabaya were clear of all hostile surface ships. I was to escort the Dutch hospital ship we had halted before the battle opened, taking it to the nearest Japanese base in Borneo.

"Be sure to take on a maximum load of fuel on your way back," Tanaka cautioned, "because our other ships will have to refuel from you." Our flotilla had joined the operation from Timor and was badly short of fuel.

My ship *Amatsukaze* barely had fuel to reach Bandjermasin at the economical speed of 18 knots. Tanaka was properly doubtful that any of the other ships could have made it.

Passing Bawean Island, we sighted men in the water. Coming closer we found that there were some hundred Caucasians, apparently from Allied ships sunk in the midnight encounter. Hands raised in appeal for help, they cried, "Water! Water!"

The sight was pitiable. I had no personal hatred for the drowning enemy. But what could I do? My small ship could take 40 or 50 of them, at most. How could I discriminate and pick only half of these survivors? Moreover, my fuel supply was rapidly dwindling. If I should halt the ship—braving the chance of attack from possible enemy submarines—it was doubtful if we could make port.

I wavered, but could come to only one conclusion. I had to close my eyes to the miserable men floating in the water. I ordered a message sent to Admiral Tanaka: "More than 100 enemy survivors adrift 60 miles, 270 degrees from Bawean Island. Urge rescue effort."

The navigator took the ship cautiously past the drifting men. One of my lieutenants, who spoke good English, ran to the rail and shouted: "Hang on! Hang on! A rescue ship will come soon."

We made Bandjermasin with the Dutch hospital ship. After refueling and taking on board all possible oil, we headed back to Surabaya on March 1. Passing Bawean, I looked around but saw none of the Allied survivors. We had had no word of any rescue operation in these waters since the previous day, and I felt very depressed.

I reviewed the awkward battle of the Java Sea. It seemed strange to me that no enemy submarines had joined in the action. Perhaps the engagement was so brief that the submarines had no time to arrive on the scene. It was also puzzling that we had not seen more enemy destroyers. I was startled from these musings by the sight of a great rising of foam and water on our port hand, which had the appearance of a submerging submarine. I called to the sonarmen for a target report. The sonar officer replied: "Sir, our acoustic sonar can't receive effectively while we are steaming like this at 20 knots."

I looked back at the queer foam, already far behind, but kept my ship on course. I debated turning back until it was too late to do so. Why couldn't I act promptly and decisively? I cursed my indecision and the possibly lost opportunity.

Warrant Officer Iwata stepped forward, stood miserably at attention, and said, "Commander, it was my fault, sir. I should have spotted the sub before it submerged. Please blame me." Iwata was an expert lookout. His eyes were unbelievably keen. Where other spotters might observe the tiny image of a surfacing submarine at 10,000 meters, Iwata could spot them at distances up to 20,000 meters. But Iwata and the rest of us had been caught off guard.

We rejoined the Tanaka Flotilla soon afterward, and fueled cruiser *Jintsu* and the three destroyers which were almost bone dry. By 2030 on March 1 the fueling was completed. *Jintsu* and the four destroyers then formed up, 2,500 meters between each ship, in a hunt for enemy submarines. It. was a cloudy night with limited visibility, but the sea was calm, and we hoped to discover surfaced targets. Staring, straining, my crewmen clung to their posts, still bitter and angry from our midday failure.

A sub hunt by our ships, having no radar, was a game calling for great patience. Detection depended on the eyes of the spotters and our none-too-effective sonar equipment. Our five ships zigzagged at 18 knots for six hours but made no sightings. The patience of the crew was wearing thin and the spotters were exhausted.

In the early morning of March 2, lookout Migita shouted: "A black object, 40 degrees to port. It appears to be a submarine!" Every man on the bridge came suddenly alert. I raised my binoculars but could discern nothing in the darkness. Migita said abjectly, "It now looks like floating debris." This brought a general sigh of disappointment. Through binoculars I could see what looked like a broken native boat. With this letdown, fatigue returned, and for the next hour we had to fight against drowsiness.

At 0340 starboard lookout Bunichi Ikeda cried out, "An unidentified object, bearing 30 degrees . . . it may be a submarine." All eyes strained in that direction. Something was there. Then Ikeda shouted again: "Positive submarine."

Keen-eyed Iwata, the forward lookout, dejected at being scooped, turned and said, "Definitely a submarine . . . damn!"

I walked to the tripod on which Ikeda's big 20-centimeter binoculars were mounted, to get a close look. It was unmistakably a submarine, apparently in trouble, some 6,000 meters away. I shouted orders. "Make No. 2 Battle Speed (26 knots). Right, 50 degrees. Everybody to battle stations. Gunners ready for action. Ready searchlights! Ready depth charges."

The crew, freed from the wearying search game, responded gleefully to the orders. The deck, long still and quiet, was now a beehive of activity. The ship quickly picked up speed. An orderly ran from astern with the message that destroyer *Hatsukaze* was following us. "All right, tell the signalman to light up the blue tail lamp (showing 26-knot speed)," I replied. "*Hatsukaze* may want to co-operate."

Iwata shouted: "Surfacing submarine now distant 3,500 meters."

Lieutenant Akino hollered from his fire-control post, "Commander, guns ready to open fire, sir."

"We'll fire when target is at 2,500 meters, 60 degrees to starboard." The enemy submarine appeared to be adrift. Our six 12.7-cm. guns and the 90-cm. searchlight were rotated to the 60-degree angle. "Akino, observe strict blackout in turrets," I shouted.

We raced headlong for the target. At 2,700 meters, *Amatsukaze* came around to port, bringing all guns to bear directly on the submarine. "Shine searchlight! Open fire!" I yelled.

The submarine showed up clearly and the first salvo followed. I saw seven crewmen running around helplessly on the deck. A moment later, two yellow explosions burst among them, followed five seconds later by the second salvo! One of these six shells hit the target. Then the third salvo, and again one direct hit. The submarine blazed fiercely.

Hatsukaze's first salvo was over. The second salvo barely missed, and there was no third salvo. The submarine sank so fast that it had disappeared among the waves before we arrived at the spot.* We dropped six depth charges to cinch the job. We cut down our speed to 12 knots and combed the area together with *Hatsukaze*. Our sonars did not pick up any targets, but the area smelled strongly of heavy oil. We abandoned the search at 0359 and left the scene.

Two hours later we returned to the same area, because I wanted *Amatsukaze's* crew to view the heavy oil on the surface. Only a few officers on the bridge and the gun crew had seen the burning sub. I decided it was important to show everyone the fruit of their great strain and efforts. Oil was still rising at the place where the sub had sunk. It stretched out for miles on the surface of the sea and the scene made a great impression on my crew.

My elation over our first definite "kill" was diminished by the fact that our victim had already been in trouble when we attacked. It was too much like cold-blooded murder to sink a ship that could offer no resistance.

---

*This was submarine *Perch* (SS-176), but she was not finished off by this attack. She was attempting to mend earlier-inflicted damage when these two Japanese destroyers attacked. Submerging to evade Hara's attack and effect repairs, *Perch* surfaced early in the morning of March 3, and was finally scuttled by her crew when attacked by two other Japanese destroyers.

We continued our hunt the following night though the weather was quite bad, with intermittent driving rain. The big binoculars were almost useless because rain drenched their lenses. Visibility was not more than a few thousand meters.

Around 2030 I saw a dim, flickering, yellowish light several thousand meters away on *Amatsukaze*'s starboard bow. It blinked once and swiftly disappeared, like the flick of a lighted match. I pulled out my pocket binoculars and gazed in the same direction. Yes, someone was on deck smoking a cigarette. I estimated the distance as 4,000 meters almost due north and forward of *Amatsukaze*'s course.

The destroyer quickly picked up speed and dashed forward through the dark with all hands ready at battle stations. The target was made out to be a surfaced submarine. It was moving to the east at fairly good speed. We boosted speed to 26 knots and swung left to bring *Amatsukaze* on a parallel heading with the sub at a distance of 2,300 meters. Our searchlight showed the target to be a medium-sized submarine.

The first salvo roared. All the shells were over. The next moment, I saw two sinister lines of foam running a few feet ahead of our bows. "Torpedoes!" someone shouted, and a chill went down my spine. My dread was forgotten a few seconds later when two shells of our second salvo landed on the target. *Amatsukaze* was up to 30 knots, and the enemy torpedoes had missed us.

There was a third salvo, which scored one more hit, as fire broke out on the conning tower of the submarine. The flaming ship vanished quietly into the waves.

We swung rapidly to port and dashed to the submersion scene. Six depth charges were dropped. The sea billowed and boiled in the dark, and all was still but for the rain. There was no question about the fate of this enemy.

We cleared out at 2345 after combing the area for possible sonar contacts. There were no signs that the sub was alive.

Weather cleared the following day, and we returned to the scene of the night's action, 39 miles, bearing 245 degrees from Bawean Island. This spot, too, was marked by a long path of heavy oil. It rose to the surface like smoke belching from an undersea volcano. The crew was again called out to see the results of their teamwork. They were not as exhilarated as on the previous evening, but they looked contented and satisfied. While the crew was thus assembled on deck, I took the opportunity to speak to them: "You have seen the good results of our combined efforts. I am thoroughly satisfied with your fine job. We have been through much together in the months since this war started, without losing a single soul. Let us hope our good fortune may continue. You have done a fine job, but more will be expected of you from now on.

"Look at the stream of oil! That oil comes from an enemy submarine that has been turned into a huge casket for its crew of more than 100 men. They died because of the unpardonable stupidity of one man who smoked on the surfaced deck. I saw the match he lit and that gave us the initiative.

"Enemy seamanship was good. Their torpedo marksmanship was terrific. Despite all our advantage, *Amatsukaze* survived only by a very close shave. But for one stupid, careless man breaking blackout by smoking, this destroyer might well have been sunk and all 250 of us killed. This is war. I trust that each of you has learned a lesson from this.

"As you may know, I have been an inveterate smoker for 20 years. But last night when we sank this sub, I stopped smoking. I mention this—not to urge such stoicism on you, but to let you remind me of my pledge whenever I am tempted to do it again. As your skipper, I am responsible for your lives and thus I cannot afford smoking any longer.

"Now let us offer a humble prayer for our victims. Though enemy, they died for their nation and thus are deserving of our prayers."

After the brief prayer, I called up Ikeda, who had spotted the submarine adrift on March 2 and rewarded him with a bonus of ten yen (roughly $4) from my pocket, a package of towel, soap and cigarettes, and a certificate noting that he had earned 10 priority shore leaves. The meeting ended with an ovation for Ikeda. A number of his colleagues thronged about him with congratulations.

On March 6, *Amatsukaze* and *Hatsukaze* returned to Bandjermasin for fuel, ammunition and supplies. While there I visited the Dutch hospital ship, out of concern for the sailors we had seen adrift near Bawean Island a week earlier. It was a great relief to learn that most of them had been rescued and were in the hospital ship, which was filled with nearly 1,000 prisoners of war. Seeing the men cramped and huddled in the narrow spaces reminded me of my cadet days and the training cruise to America and Europe. Some of these prisoners could be men I had met. It was distressing to watch them and I made an earnest wish never to be captured.

The rest of March passed uneventfully. No enemy submarines were reported in the Dutch East Indies during the remainder of the month.

On the last day of March, *Amatsukaze* took part in the seizure of Christmas Island, some 200 miles south of Java. This isolated island was not only in a strategic position, but it contained very rich deposits of phosphorus ore. This operation was the easiest of any I had thus far taken part in or witnessed. There were preliminary bombings by a dozen bombers, and offshore bombardment by two cruisers and four destroyers. The British garrison surrendered at 0700, even before the landings had been completed. Some 100 British troops were taken prisoner. They were put to work loading our empty transports with phosphorus ore stacked high on the pier.

A sour note punctuated the second day of this simple operation. At 1805 on April 1, I saw in the water an eerie line of foam arrowing toward our flagship, cruiser *Naka*. This torpedo ran no more than 700 meters at an angle of 50 degrees from *Naka*'s starboard side. The cruiser swerved to starboard—but too late. The torpedo hit smack amidship and broke *Naka*'s foremast. The impact and explosion left a five-meter hole gaping in its hull. Miraculously, however, not a single crewman was killed.

Our four destroyers and two patrol ships ran wildly about, dropping many depth charges in an effort to get the attacking sub, but the enemy fled unscathed. I still marvel at the skill and daring of this submarine.* It had sneaked into the narrow area, braving four bristling destroyers, and fired its torpedo at extremely close range.

Although *Naka* had taken in 800 tons of water, her watertight compartments held and prevented her sinking. She limped back to Japan under escort of several destroyers. Back in the homeland it took weeks to effect her repairs. Such was the price of complacence. We all shared in this guilt, and I had learned another lesson.

---

* This attack was made by USS *Seawolf* (SS-197).

Picture taken at Sasebo in 1934, when the author was a lieutenant commander, with wife, Chizu, daughter Yoko (*left*), and daughter Keiko (*center*).

Destroyer *Amagiri*. In 1937 author Hara commanded this ship in carrying Army troops to Shanghai, where he had his baptism of fire on August 21.

Amatsukaze, launched in 1940, was the finest destroyer of her day. With 52,000 h.p. engines, she was capable of 35 knots and carried six 5-inch guns and eight torpedo tubes. Hara commanded *Amatsukaze* in the Philippines, the Java Sea battle, and the disastrous Midway operation. Off Guadalcanal, on November 12, 1942, *Amatsukaze* sank DD *Barton* and inflicted heavy damage on the cruisers *San Francisco* and *Juneau*.

Leading officers of the Imperial Navy's Second Destroyer Squadron in October 1941 shortly after the meeting at which Admiral Yamamoto revealed plans for the attack on Pearl Harbor. Shown here are Commander Hara (2nd row, 3rd from right) and squadron commander Rear Admiral Raizo Tanaka (front row, 4th from left), who sank one U.S. heavy cruiser and damaged three others in a brilliant action off Guadalcanal.

Vice Admiral Nobutake Kondo's fighting group rushing towards Guadalcanal November 14, 1942. Picture taken from aboard Kondo's flagship cruiser *Atago,* 12,986 tons. Cruiser-battleship *Kirishima,* 27,500 tons, in the center, followed by the cruiser *Takao,* 12,986 tons. (*Photo courtesy Mrs. Matsuji Ijuin*)

Lt. Jack Kennedy almost lost his life on the night of August 1, 1943, when one of Capt. Hara's destroyers cut his torpedo boat in half. Shown here is PT-109, the craft the president commanded. (*Official U.S. Navy photo*)

Rabaul was central supply base for Japanese forces in the Solomons and New Guinea. Famed "Tokyo Express" often sortied from Rabaul before U.S. air attacks made the port too dangerous. Here bombers score direct hit on Japanese corvette.

Destroyers *Shigure* and *Samidare* of the 27th Flotilla advancing along the eastern coast of Bougainville, October 7, 1943. A decrepit old ship, capable of only 30 knots, *Shigure* became under Hara's command the most famous destroyer in the Japanese Navy, completing numerous patrols and fighting three major battles without losing a man. (*Official Imperial Navy photo*)

Captain Hara's cruiser *Yahagi* sailed for Okinawa on August 6, 1945—the last sortie of the war. Without fuel for the return voyage, *Yahagi* was to sink as many U.S. ships as possible in a desperate attempt to save the home islands. Miraculously escaping near misses in this dive-bomber attack, *Yahagi* was finally sunk on the afternoon of August 7th, with a loss of 446 lives. Hara was one of the few survivors. (*Official U.S. Navy Photos*)

Battleship *Yamato,* 72,800-ton pride of the Imperial Navy, sailed from the Inland Sea on August 6, 1945, on a suicide mission to attack U.S. ships off Okinawa. The next day she was caught at sea by 386 carrier-based planes from Task Force 58 and severely pounded. Hara, whose *Yahagi* was sunk that same afternoon, saw the great battleship racked by a gigantic explosion. When the smoke cleared, *Yamato* was gone. (*Official U.S. Navy photos*)

part three

THE "TOKYO EXPRESS"

1

The Christmas Island venture marked an anticlimactic end to the first phase of Japanese operations in Southeast Asia. It was followed by a lull of more than a month in the Pacific.

On April 3, my ship bade farewell to the limping cruiser *Naka* near Surabaya and joined the fleet in the Java Sea. We arrived in Batavia the next day and left that afternoon for Macassar, where we had an easy five days, while engines and weapons were checked. I allowed my crew to go ashore in shifts. The city was buzzing with activity, peace was restored and business was normal. Stores were filled with goods of far greater variety than had been available in Japan six months before.

After the war many of my countrymen said that Japan should have concluded a peace in the spring of 1942, instead of waiting to swallow Allied peace terms after Japan had been bled white. But in the early months of 1942 there were no thoughts of suing for peace. Indeed, many politicians and military leaders firmly believed that the occupation of Southeast Asia was assured as permanent and that Japan, with the immense resources of this great region, would be invincible.

From Macassar we moved to Surabaya, and at last, on April 17, we were ordered to return to Japan. The men were jubilant. Drafted sailors dreamed of discharge and going home. They hoped for an end of war. Officers could hold no such rosy prospects, but they were as happy as the enlisted men at the chance of returning to Japan.

We left Surabaya to return to Macassar and the following day joined a group of destroyers escorting transports laden with ore, food and oil for Japan. The voyage was without event but pleasant. When we entered home waters and the islands of Japan loomed on the horizon, everyone jumped with joy. *Amatsukaze* and the other destroyers quietly entered our home port of Kure on the second day of May. The hundreds of tiny islands dotting the Inland Sea were a peaceful and welcome sight. Sea gulls swooped and cried, and small fishing boats tooted greetings to us.

Japan is so different from the tropics. The southern sea is indigo, radiant flowers glare in the broiling sun, and everything is garish. Back in Japan, all colors are sedate and soothing. We had missed the cherry blossoms of early April. But young leaves sprouting on the cherry trees were as much a treat to us as the blossoms.

The day after our arrival in Kure I ordered the ship's store to be opened. Duty orders were kept to a minimum so that everyone could take it easy. Lieutenant Goro Iwabuchi, my deputy, went ashore to arrange a ship's banquet. He booked a reservation at the Morisawa restaurant for a 240-man party, and reported, "The operator said he was not sure of providing food enough for us, because many other ships are holding similar parties in the city and buying up all available materials. But he has a good supply of liquor."

When the evening party was announced, *Amatsukaze* almost rocked with the joy of her crew. Lots were drawn to select the ten unlucky men who had to stay behind and guard the ship. The rest of us went ashore at about 1700. The bustling city of Kure was filled with sailors. Streets and sidewalks were jammed.

For our banquet, we brought enough canned food to supplement the restaurant's larder. There were only five geisha girls to serve our entire party. They were harried enough just trying to keep the more than 200 guests supplied with food and drink. To add to their chore these few girls had also to entertain us with singing and dancing. But free-flowing drinks soon saturated the guests and many enlisted men were soon volunteering to help the girls. My boys began to sing and dance.

In the course of the evening practically every one of my men came to offer me an individual toast. I responded to every well-wisher. I don't know how much *sake* I consumed in the process. Nothing but my rugged physique pulled me through the chain drinking that lasted until the banquet ended around midnight.

On the following day, three- to six-day leaves were authorized for all hands. The first third of the crew left for home that day, and I boarded a night train for my home. My heart brimmed with joy as the train reached Kamakura in the morning of May 4. It was a perfect day. Balmy sea breezes rustled the graceful pine trees covering this 800-year-old city.

My family was waiting to greet me on the station platform. Little Mikito, almost three, trotted with a hand in his mother's, shouting, "Daddy, Daddy!" I hugged him. He had grown so fast during my absence. Daughters Yoko, 12, and Keiko, 9, shouted, "Welcome home!" My wife, Chizu, smiled happily.

My home was only a 20-minute walk from the station, but I felt that this was a triumphant homecoming and hired a cab for the occasion. The children were wide-eyed, for they seldom rode in a taxi.

Back home we opened packages of presents I had brought from the south. The children shrieked with joy at sight of chocolates—a rare treat in those days. In the evening Mr. Tanzan Ishibashi, our good neighbor of many years, came to offer his congratulations. At his invitation, my family went to his home for dinner. Ishibashi was editor-publisher of the magazine *Toyo Keizai* (*Oriental Economist*). I knew him as a man of rare insight and wisdom, but never dreamed that he would one day be prime minister of Japan.

We enjoyed the dinner, and afterward I sat drinking *sake* with him. Being an economist, he was eager to hear of the situation in Southeast Asia. "Is our Navy powerful enough to control these vast areas and secure their rich resources for Japan's industrial workshops?" he asked.

With a man of his caliber there was no point in trying to hide the truth. "We have won a series of battles simply because the enemy outblundered us," I replied. "You know as well as I do of the immense productive capacity of the Allies. There is no room for optimism for Japan in this war." He was stunned by what I had to say. Censorship was so complete that he was unaware of many of the facts of this war.

In 1956, just before he became prime minister, my book of war experiences was published in Japan. Ishibashi wrote an introduction for the volume that made me blush. He wrote that our talk that evening in 1942 convinced him that I was more than an ordinary Navy officer.

The six-day leave passed quickly. Orders for my new assignment, calling for instant departure, might come at any time. Once orders were issued, there would be no time for an overnight trip to Kamakura. In order to be with my family as long as possible, I took them back with me to Kure on May 10. The children got a kick out of their first journey, especially when we registered in a hotel. When things were easy, we strolled in the streets or climbed the hills surrounding the city.

The officers' club delighted my family because it still served rich meals unavailable in town. My children talked about the club dinners for many years, particularly in the days of privation just after the Japanese surrender.

Jimmy Doolittle's surprise air raid on Japan in April was quickly forgotten. The B-25 bombers did very little damage. The Army announced that all of the attacking planes were shot down. Japan was so drunk with her own great victories and vast conquests that the Doolittle raid was no more than a fleabite.

Four days after my return to Kure, sweeping reassignments came for most of my crew. Practically all of my officers and half of the petty officers and men were transferred. Every day saw my experienced officers and men leaving for new ships, and new officers and recruits arriving to replace them. Such changes were going on throughout the Navy. I could not imagine what the high command was thinking. My trained crew was being broken up, and I resented it. Other skippers felt the same way. It would take at least two months to drill into shape this conglomeration of new men who had never worked together. And what would happen if we were called into action before they were ready?

When the Midway operation plan was revealed on May 20, I thought the high command must have lost its mind. This surprising news was whispered to me at the Kure Naval Station by Rear Admiral Raizo Tanaka. I gasped. "What? What does this mean, Admiral?" I stammered. "Are we going to conduct it with this crew?"

"Sshhhhh . . ." said Tanaka dispiritedly. "As a matter of fact I am not sure about it. I hope it's untrue."

Tanaka's flotilla of one cruiser and six destroyers sailed quietly from Kure on May 21. We went at 20 knots toward Saipan where "specific orders" awaited us. The day after leaving Kure, I heard angry shouts and the sound of someone being hit, and I went out on deck. There Lieutenant Kazue Shimizu, the new gunnery officer, was ranting at a sailor. As the hapless man stood there penitently, Shimizu hit him blow after blow with his fist. I was astonished.

"What's going on?" I demanded.

Shimizu turned toward me, his eyes still glowing with rage. "Commander, this man saw me but failed to salute," he spluttered. "I am disciplining him."

"Is that right?" I turned to the petty officer.

"That is correct, sir," he replied shamefully, his face flushed from the beating he had taken.

I was shocked to discover that the man was Ikeda, the expert spotter who had been cited for his discovery of an enemy submarine near Surabaya. I dismissed him with a strong warning, and asked Shimizu to come to my cabin. He looked bewildered, but followed me without saying a word. I closed the door of my cabin and offered Shimizu, standing at ramrod attention, a chair.

I was distressed at the scene but tried my best to restrain myself. "Shimizu, you may smoke if you wish. This is a man-to-man talk, not between a skipper and his gunnery officer. I don't want to criticize you or defend this sloppy man. But I must make it clear that I do not subscribe to maintenance of discipline by physical punishment. I don't know what your former skipper's policy was, but it is my belief that a destroyer crew must maintain perfect teamwork if they are to fight most efficiently. The 250 men of this ship must work as one man. They must be knit together in real harmony and friendship."

Shimizu saw what I was driving at. He looked down unhappily, but not without showing his disagreement.

"Maintenance of good teamwork and proper order is not easy. But I have done it without resorting to corporal punishment. It is hard, but worthwhile. If it is too hard for you, report to me for decision, the next time you are faced with a disciplinary situation."

Shimizu kept looking down in silence. I rang and asked my orderly to summon the three other department heads. All were new to my command. Lieutenant Shigeo Fujisawa, the chief engineer; Lieutenant (j.g.) Masatoshi Miyoshi, chief torpedo officer; and Lieutenant Kinjuro Matsumoto, chief navigator, quickly came to the cabin. They stood at attention, apparently alarmed at the sudden call. "I have just seen Shimizu strike a sailor," I said. "Since he did this in the open, I conclude that such things are taking place generally in this ship. I will not permit physical beatings of my crewmen. It must stop as of this moment. You have your orders."

The officers withdrew, and there was a bad taste in my mouth. I was helplessly angry. With my crewmen living under such conditions, how could I possibly build the kind of teamwork needed for the important operation which confronted us? I recalled my experiences at Eta Jima many years before, and still could not forgive the tyrants who had beaten me so freely. To beat men like cattle merely deprives them of the initiative so necessary in a destroyer which must be manned by a closely knit team. Only thus can a crew work with the split-second efficiency demanded in destroyer operations.

I decided to spend every spare moment in personal inspections of the ship. I heard angry voices, but saw no more physical discipline. Still I brooded about going into action with this unblooded crew.

The 1,400-mile voyage, however, was quiet, and we reached Saipan on the morning of May 25. Sixteen transports from Truk laden with 3,000 Army and 2,800 Navy troops had already arrived. Also in the harbor were more than a dozen sub-chasers, patrol ships, minesweepers and tankers.

At a tactical conference of skippers and commanders the following day, the Midway operation was officially announced. Documents containing details of the operation were handed to each officer. We thus received the orders assigning us to escort the Midway invasion forces.

The Midway Operation Plan went into effect on May 26, 1942. On the following day, the Nagumo Task Force sortied from the Inland Sea—destination Midway. The landing troops escorted by our destroyers left Saipan in the evening of May 28. Anticipating that enemy submarines were watching, we took a feint course to the west, then turned south from a spot directly west of Tinian. Simultaneous with our departure, Vice Admiral Takeo Kurita's squadron of three cruisers and two destroyers left Guam.

The mainstay of the Combined Fleet led by the new super-battleship *Yamato* departed the Inland Sea on the 29th. The previous day, when our convoy had departed from Saipan, was auspicious as the 37th anniversary of Japan's 1905 victory over the Russian Fleet at Tsushima Strait. A good omen, but instinctively I felt that something was wrong with this operation, and my heart was not buoyant.

The next six days passed monotonously. At about 0600 on June 3, one enemy float plane was spotted a few miles ahead. It went away after a short time, but there was no doubt that this plane had notified Midway of our approach. We were then 600 miles southwest of Midway.

In the late afternoon several large planes appeared from the south. Tanaka's flagship *Jintsu* opened fire and the enemy planes went away. They returned when the guns stopped, and *Jintsu* reopened its ineffective fire. The planes finally went away, but these actions were unnerving to us, as we were without air cover. The enemy planes came back at dusk and this time swooped head-on at us, so that they were identifiable as nine B-17 Flying Fortresses.

All destroyers opened fire, throwing the enemy's timing off. Bombs arcing down from the four-engined bombers fell 1,000 meters away. They turned around and went away, none hit by our shells. Later that night, four enemy planes sneaked in and launched torpedoes, one of which pierced the bow of oiler *Akebono Maru*, killing eleven men and injuring 13 others. Watertight compartments held and the tanker was able to keep pace with the slow transports.

We were well aware that we were advancing against a fully prepared enemy, but I was no longer ill at ease. The attempts thus far against our convoy had been furtive and feeble. The Nagumo Task Force could smash the enemy with its sledgehammer blows.

Dawn of June 5 brought murky weather with low, heavy clouds everywhere. There was practically no wind. As I stood on *Amatsukaze*'s bridge, my eyelids were heavy after a sleepless night. Breakfast was delivered while I brooded at the weather which would make it difficult to oppose planes that might suddenly emerge from the low clouds. I was alerted by a shout from the radio room voice tube.

"Commander, our main task force is sending out many urgent messages."

"All right, bring them to me promptly as each one comes in."

Within moments an orderly came running to the bridge and handed me a piece of paper. I scanned it, held my breath and froze. The message was from carrier *Kaga* and read: "We have been bombed and are afire."

Rapidly succeeding messages reported effective attacks delivered against carriers *Soryu* and *Akagi*, Admiral Nagumo's own flagship. Three carriers including the flagship set afire almost simultaneously! What was I reading? Was I dreaming? I shook my head. No, I was wide awake! I groaned and handed the messages to my officers. Lieutenant Shimizu's hands trembled as he read them, Lieutenant Matsumoto paled. Lieutenant Miyoshi was a study in incredulity.

I looked around. Our convoy zigzagged on its way. Other skippers and their officers must be reading the same shocking news. Staggering as these reports were, we had to continue as scheduled, having received no orders to the contrary.

The horrifying reports continued until there was no room for doubting their accuracy. The mighty Nagumo Task Force was being cut to ribbons. Still we received no change of orders. What was our high command doing? My grief over our carrier losses abruptly turned into black anger. Were we to fall into the trap as the main task force had done? Damn! Damn!

Operation Order No. 154 finally arrived at 0920 instructing our transports to turn "northwestward temporarily," and all the "fighting ships to attack the enemy north of Midway." The small escort vessels and 16 transports turned slowly from the formation and headed north. Our six destroyers and one cruiser boosted speed to 30 knots and raced toward Midway Island.

Even on this windless day, my speeding destroyer kicked up ocean waves sending showers of spray and foam to the bridge. But now I felt no exhilaration. At 1010 Operation Order No. 156 announced "postponement" of the Midway occupation plan and directed us to carry out offshore bombardment of Midway's ground installations.

We were still 300 miles from Midway, and ten hours seemed like a long time in approaching an alerted enemy target. We continued toward the goal without incident except for the continually depressing reports from the front. At 1430 on June 4, word came from *Hiryu*, the last of Nagumo's operational carriers, saying: "We have been bombed and set afire." And at 1615 Admiral Isoroka Yamamoto issued his third order of the day directing the remnants of Nagumo's force to engage the enemy in night battle. This order not only did not mention the loss of all Nagumo Force carriers, but it insisted that the enemy fleet had been "practically destroyed and is retiring eastward."

Even with my limited view of events in this battle, I did not understand how Yamamoto could have issued that order. It now appears that he was trying to prevent the morale of his forces from collapsing, but at the time I thought he must have taken leave of his senses.

At 2130 Nagamo radioed a report which ironically bared the falsehoods of the Yamamoto order. 'The enemy force of five carriers, six cruisers, and 15 destroyers moving westward. We are withdrawing northwestward escorting *Hiryu*." It took two hours for Yamamoto to issue his next order, still insisting on strikes at the enemy. This reached me as I watched a ship burning fiercely some 5,000 meters to the east. We checked its position on the chart and determined that this was *Akagi*. I recalled the sight of an enemy ship burning in the Java Sea. This time it was our flagship. What a difference! In the Java Sea battle the Allies outblundered the Japanese, but at Midway only the Japanese blundered.

Shortly before midnight we received orders announcing an end to the Midway Operation and instructing us to join with Yamamoto's main force.

2

The Midway Battle is termed the point at which the tide of the Pacific War turned in favor of the United States. Nagumo suffered a crushing defeat at Midway, to be sure, but that did not mean the entire collapse of the Navy. Yamamoto's Combined Fleet was intact, and Japan still had at least four carriers to match those of the U.S. Navy.

What really spelled the downfall of the Imperial Navy, in my estimation, was the series of strategic and tactical blunders by Yamamoto after Midway, the operations that started with the American landing at Guadalcanal in early August, 1942.

After the sour ending of the Midway Operation, Yamamoto took his Combined Fleet to Truk and then back to the homeland. When the Americans hit Guadalcanal, the mainstay of Yamamoto's Combined Fleet was anchored near Kure in the Inland Sea, 2,700 miles from the battle zone. Throughout the crucial operations around Guadalcanal, Yamamoto flung into the area one small fleet unit after another. His strategy seems ridiculous when judged by hindsight. How did it develop?

I rejoined the convoy of transports some 600 miles north of Midway on June 10, and helped to escort them to Truk, where we arrived on the 15th. Two days later, we all left for Japan. We arrived in Yokosuka June 21, and moved up to Kure three days later. All personnel were ordered not to talk about Midway. The real details of the battle were labeled "Top Secret" even to commanding officers. It seemed that the order called for absolute belief in the Imperial Headquarters communiqué, discounting Japanese losses, exaggerating American ones, and insisting that the battle had ended in a Japanese victory.

The Combined Fleet returned to the quiet of the Inland Sea, but not because it needed repairs. Serious wounds had been sustained by the Nagumo Task Force but other major units were practically undamaged. Yamamoto wanted to train his men after the sweeping reshuffle of a month earlier.

Yamamoto and the Navy High Command in Tokyo had not had the slightest suspicion that the Americans would launch a major offensive at Guadalcanal within two months after the Midway battle. They believed that it would be mid-1943 at the earliest before the Americans could mount an offensive.

From June 28 through August 5 I guarded merchant ships in the Tokyo Bay area. This easy assignment gave me a welcome opportunity to train my new crew.

There is no doubt that Yamamoto's withdrawal of the Combined Fleet to Japan waters at this time was a grave blunder. Most of the Combined Fleet should have been kept in Truk. Yet Yamamoto's strategy was not entirely without merit. Most of his 104 destroyers got respite and the training which was greatly needed. All these destroyers would soon be engaged in a series of intense, fierce battles lasting for more than two years. In these battles, destroyers assumed a leading role for the first time and probably for the last time in history.

Another great blunder was the piecemeal of commitment of destroyers in the Solomons, usually without help of planes or larger warships. Yet they fought gallantly against all odds. In addition to fighting, they also transported troops. The destroyers of the celebrated "Tokyo Express" were the real workhorses of the South Pacific.

Attrition was high. From the start of the U.S. Guadalcanal operation on August 7, 1942, to the Japanese "Dunkirk" from that island on February 7, 1943, 12 Japanese destroyers were sunk.

I took part in the continuing operations in Solomons waters from March through November 1943, in command of destroyer *Shigure*. Losses were higher than in the previous six months owing to the enemy's growing air supremacy and improved radar. My ship was the only one in the "Tokyo Express" to survive these battles without losing a man. Some 30 other Japanese destroyers were sunk in this period.

Japanese Navy people called *Shigure* (Autumn Rain) the "Ghost Destroyer" or the "Destroyer Indestructible," and I was nicknamed the "Miracle Captain." That was indeed the most glorious period of my career.

An old Chinese proverb says: "A lion uses all its might in attacking a rabbit." The American Navy acted exactly like this "lion" when it stormed Guadalcanal and Tulagi at daybreak on August 7, 1942. Ironically, the Japanese airfield at Guadalcanal had just been completed the previous day. Guadalcanal was occupied by 2,600 Japanese construction workers and defended by only 800 Navy troops equipped with a few artillery pieces and some machine guns. The Japanese air strength consisted of only nine float fighters and 12 unarmed flying boats.

The Americans annihilated the Japanese at Tulagi in two hours, and one battalion perished on Guadalcanal as quickly. At the time the Japanese "lion"—the Combined Fleet—was fast asleep 2,700 miles away in Japan's Inland Sea. But Yamamoto had a "watchdog" at Rabaul, 560 miles northeast of Guadalcanal, in Vice Admiral Gunichi Mikawa's 8th Fleet.

Mikawa's force, comprising five heavy cruisers, three light cruisers and one destroyer, steamed out of Rabaul at 1530 on August 7 and stormed the American invaders at midnight of the 8th. Mikawa's ships sank four American and Australian heavy cruisers, and damaged one cruiser and two destroyers in a 30-minute battle.* Mikawa's only loss was Cruiser *Kako*, sunk two days later by submarine *S-44* as his ships were nearing Kavieng, New Ireland. Mikawa achieved one of the most brilliant surface victories of the war. He erred, however, in failing to attack any of the supply-laden transports of Guadalcanal.

Mikawa has been sharply criticized for this blunder by both Americans and Japanese after the war. It is my belief, however, that Mikawa fulfilled his "watchdog" assignment. The real blame must rest with Admiral Isoroku Yamamoto who held his Combined Fleet in home waters.

When the American invasion was reported to Japan, the "lion" pricked its ears, but did not rise. Emperor Hirohito, vacationing at his summer villa in Nikko, upon hearing the news, said he would return to Tokyo immediately; but Admiral Osami Nagano, Chief of the Naval General Staff, went directly to Nikko for an audience.

"Your Majesty, it is nothing worthy of Your Majesty's attention," Nagano explained. He flashed an "intelligence" report from the Japanese Military Attaché in Moscow claiming that the enemy had only 2,000 troops at Guadalcanal, and that their plan was simply to destroy the airfields and withdraw from the islands. It is not known how this stupid intelligence report was obtained, but even more stupid were the high-ranking officers who must have ignored the many other intelligence reports. Finally on August 10, three days after the operation started, the 5,800 "Midway" troops standing by at Truk were ordered to Guadalcanal by Imperial General Headquarters.

The Yamamoto "lion" had closed its eyes again after hearing of Mikawa's "phenomenal win," and it slowly arose only after learning of the IGHQ order. The next day, August 11, Vice Admiral Nobutake Kondo's 2nd Fleet was detached from Combined Fleet for the 2,700-mile voyage to Guadalcanal. Vice Admiral Chuichi Nagumo stalled, saying that his new pilots were not

---

* Cruisers *Quincy, Vincennes, Astoria*, and HMAS *Canberra* were sunk; cruiser *Chicago* damaged. Destroyer *Jarvis* was damaged by air attack during the preceding day and was sunk by air attack the next day. Details in USNI *Proceedings* Feb. 1950, p. 119. "*Jarvis*: Destroyer That Vanished," by Cdr. J. C. Shaw.

yet ready; but, under prodding, he did have his ships ready to sortie with Yamamoto's Main Force on August 16. By that time American forces were firmly ashore on Guadalcanal.

Last-minute changes put my ship, *Amatsukaze*, under the command of my old friend Nagumo. *Amatsukaze* and 14 destroyers were assembled into Destroyer Squadron 10, around cruiser *Nagara*, Nagumo's flagship since the sinking of *Akagi* at Midway. The squadron was commanded by Rear Admiral Susumu Kimura, a destroyer expert.

We went south at an easy 18–20 knots. These destroyers were all capable of 33 knots, but high speed increased fuel consumption tremendously. Our schedule was to reach Truk around August 20, covering 2,000 miles in five days. Thence we would advance to Guadalcanal.

Halfway to Truk we learned of another Japanese blunder committed at Guadalcanal. On the night of August 18, six Japanese destroyers had landed 800 lightly equipped troops on the eastern coast of Guadalcanal. Apparently no one in the Japanese high command realized that the Americans had already poured some 20,000 well-equipped Marines into the island. The Japanese troops made a dogged advance through the jungle, only to be trapped two days later by the Americans in a mass slaughter. Fewer than 200 Japanese survived the onslaught and they fled in utter disorder.

The news shook Yamamoto. He immediately called off the scheduled stopover at Truk and ordered the fleet to rush directly to Guadalcanal. Belatedly Yamamoto had come to his senses. But the Army command clung to the myth that the invincible Japanese could shatter outnumbering enemy forces by their aggressive spirit. After the collapse of Colonel Kiyonao Ichiki's first regiment, the Army decided this time to throw in a brigade. This force, commanded by Major General Seiken Kawaguchi, was also defeated. But it was still a long time before the Army could decide to put a full division into the effort.

Yamamoto's complacency was completely shaken on August 20. That morning, a patrol plane searching about 500 miles west of Bougainville had sighted an enemy task force—at least one carrier, one cruiser and two destroyers—heading north at 14 knots.

Yamamoto had canceled the stop at Truk, but practically all ships were low on fuel. We had to refuel at sea from tankers before continuing our advance. Refueling at sea is always a hazardous and nerve-wracking operation, especially so in time of war. Both tanker and warship must slow to six knots, and several destroyers must patrol lest enemy subs or planes attack this tempting target. On this occasion our refueling took so long that it was 0400 on the 23rd before we arrived in position 400 miles north of Guadalcanal.

Two transports carrying another 1,500 troops under Colonel Ichiki, escorted by one cruiser and six destroyers of Destroyer Squadron 2, were 50 miles ahead of us. The plan was for half of Ichiki's vanguard troops to assault Guadalcanal followed by the other half after the first force had been landed. Additional support troops would be provided by the Kawaguchi Brigade whose convoy had left from Truk.

On the morning of August 23, Destroyer Squadron 2 reported that its ships had been spotted by enemy patrol planes, and Admiral Yamamoto was thus confronted with a problem. The most appropriate solution would have been to cancel the scheduled landing operations and engage in a decisive naval action. Yamamoto, however, ordered Destroyer Squadron 2 convoy with its Ichiki troops to reverse course "just for a day," and he gave no orders to the Kawaguchi convoy. He had decided to knock out the small American task force and then continue with the scheduled landing operation.

Some explanations are required here to explain Yamamoto's decision, bearing in mind that hindsight judgments can never appreciate the burdens of an on-the-spot decision. Since the China War it had been traditional for the Army to take the initiative and the Navy to follow suit. It was the Army's idea to land a battalion first, then the remainder of the regiment and then a brigade. To demand that the Army revamp this idea would have been to break with tradition.

If Yamamoto had known the strength of the enemy on Guadalcanal he would undoubtedly have taken the bold step and ignored the tradition. But somehow the facts of the situation failed to reach him. His prime concern was for the troops holding a beachhead on the east coast of Guadalcanal. Their annihilation seemed to be only a matter of time. Something had to be done to prevent the loss of this beachhead.

Yamamoto hastily formed a diversionary force of 10,150-ton *Ryujo*, the smallest Combined Fleet carrier, heavy cruiser *Tone*, and destroyers *Tokitsukaze* and *Amatsukaze*. This four-ship unit, led by Rear Admiral Chuichi Hara,* was to storm Guadalcanal and draw off the American task force reported heading toward Bougainville. The Nagumo Task Force with its nucleus of two

---

* No relation to Tameichi Hara, author of this book.

40,000-ton carriers was directed to turn northeastward and flank the enemy ships as they pursued Admiral Hara's decoy force.

We set off at 0200 on the 24th with 13,320-ton *Tone*—a weird-looking ship with all of its eight 6-inch main guns mounted on the bow deck—in the lead. *Ryujo* followed, flanked by *Amatsukaze* to starboard and our sister ship *Tokitsukaze* to port. We dashed toward Guadalcanal at 26 knots.

The assignment was not an easy one, but it was my first really important mission of the war. My muscles twitched with excitement as I stood on the bridge. Admiral Hara, in *Tone*, was one of the Navy's most brilliant leaders. I had known him since my Academy days when he had been an instructor, and I had full trust in him. Hara had led one carrier division of the Nagumo Task Force when it hit Pearl Harbor.

The big concern was *Ryujo*. Whenever I looked at this 10-year-old carrier I got uneasy. The best pilots were never assigned to older ships, and, after losing so many crack flyers at Midway, I was positive that *Ryujo*'s aviators were sadly inexperienced. I brooded over how this "decoy" would survive its first acid test in the war.

At 0713, as day dawned on the South Pacific Ocean, the first enemy contact was made with a Navy float plane. It followed us for many miles but finally turned away, evidently with enough information about our strength. I groaned. We went ahead according to schedule for four uneasy hours without sight of any more enemy planes. The sea was extremely calm. The sun shone intermittently through thick clouds. The weather, favorable for attacking aircraft, recalled memories of Midway. What a bad day, I thought.

At 1100 we were 200 miles north of Guadalcanal. Six bombers and 15 fighters zoomed up from *Ryujo* and headed for the island exactly on schedule. When *Ryujo* turned westward toward its rendezvous with these planes, my ship swung to port, keeping 2,000 meters from the carrier. I knew that the 21 planes sent off were not the ship's full complement, and wondered why *Ryujo* did not fly its nine remaining fighters as air cover. Looking at the cloud banks I speculated on how enemy planes might spill out of them at any moment to deal a fatal blow at the vulnerable carrier, just as at Midway. Gradually I became more and more irritated.

Another hour passed, and still no more fighters from *Ryujo*. I simply could not understand it, and mumbled angrily to myself. At 1230 the tube from the radio room brought an excited voice: "Commander, a message from a *Ryujo* plane says that the Guadalcanal bombing was successful."* I sighed in relief, but wondered just how effective only six bombers could be. I started to eat lunch which had been brought to me on the bridge.

I had just finished eating when I heard one of the lookouts call: "A plane, looks like the enemy, coming from 30 degrees to port." Through binoculars I saw an enemy plane rambling leisurely in the distance, slipping in and out of the clouds.

Signal flags went up, ship whistles blew, and guns were raised for antiaircraft firing. As the plane approached, another emerged from the clouds. They appeared to be B-17 Flying Fortresses, like our old friends at Davao. I turned toward *Ryujo* and stared openmouthed. All was so quiet and serene on board the carrier that I thought the skipper must be asleep.

To alert *Ryujo*, I told my gunners to open fire, although the enemy bombers were still out of range. *Tone* and *Tokitsukaze* immediately followed suit. At last two fighters zoomed up from *Ryujo*. The enemy planes turned tail, their reconnaissance completed. Our fighters climbed rapidly, but when they reached the enemy altitude, the B-17s had vanished into the clouds. The fighters came back and circled slowly over their carrier.

My patience ended, I was worried and furious. *Ryujo* would be helpless against enemy planes which might appear in strength at any moment. I jotted a note and called my signal officer. "Send this message to *Ryujo* by semaphore at once!"

A signalman ran up and briskly waved his flags: "From Commander Tameichi Hara, *Amatsukaze* C. O., to Commander Hisakichi Kishi, *Ryujo* Exec.: Fully realizing my impertinence, am forced to advise you my impression. Your flight operations are far short of expectations. What is the matter?"

The message was probably rude and certainly audacious. I don't know of any other Japanese naval officer who sent such a message during an operation. I addressed the message to Kishi because we had been classmates at Eta Jima. He was not responsible for flight operations, but my intention was to awaken the skipper and flight officer who were responsible.

Wondering what Kishi's reaction would be, I stared at the carrier and saw an answering signal: "From Kishi to Commander Hara: Deeply appreciate your admonition. We shall do better and count on your co-operation." *Ryujo*'s

---

* The airfield suffered only minor damage.

action response was prompt. Seven more fighters quickly appeared on deck. Their propellers went into action almost instantly, but they were too late, for at that moment my lookouts shouted: "Many enemy planes approaching."

It was about 1400 and *Ryujo* was turning into the wind to launch aircraft when scores of American dive-bombers attacked. I watched *Ryujo* anxiously. Other Japanese carriers could clear their decks of readied fighters in a matter of a few minutes. But not *Ryujo*.

I had many other things to do. My ship was moving out to a 5,000-meter distance from *Ryujo*, just as were *Tone* and *Tokitsukaze*, to fight the oncoming enemy planes. *Ryujo* radioed the 21 planes which had struck Guadalcanal, ordering them to go to Buka, midway between Rabaul and Guadalcanal, instead of returning to the carrier. Why didn't it call back some of these 15 fighters for interception?

I had no more time to speculate. The enemy SBD Dauntless bombers and Grumman fighters were pouncing on the sluggish carrier.* At least two dozen American bombers spilled their deadly charges around *Ryujo*, and fighters swooped low over the ship, machine-gunning everything in sight. *Ryujo*'s 12 antiaircraft guns fired sporadically without downing any of the attackers.

Two or three enemy bombs hit the ship near the stern, piercing the flight deck. Scarlet flames shot up from the holes. Ominous explosions followed in rapid order. Several more bombs made direct hits. Water pillars surrounded the carrier, and it was engulfed in thick, black smoke. This was no deliberate smoke screen. Her fuel tanks had been hit and set afire. Was she sinking? Had she sunk?

The enemy planes now turned from the carrier and headed against the other three of us. All guns opened fire as the planes swooped on us. My ship was making 33 knots and zigzagging frantically. Tremendous bow waves kicked up by the speeding destroyer drenched me on the bridge.

Amatsukaze weathered the 30-minute attack. Some of the bombers had saved their "eggs" for us. None hit my ship, but there were several near misses.

I breathed deeply as the enemy planes pulled away. Now I turned my eyes in the direction of *Ryujo*. The black smoke was beginning to dissipate, and the carrier emerged. Through binoculars I could see that *Ryujo*, in her death throes, had stopped all forward motion and was sinking! A heavy starboard list exposed her red belly. Waves washed her flight deck. It was a

---

* The attacking planes came from U.S. carrier *Saratoga*.

pathetic sight. *Ryujo*, no longer resembling a ship, was a huge stove, full of holes which belched eerie red flames.

Flagship *Tone* signaled: "Destroyers, stand by *Ryujo* for rescue operation!"

My ship immediately dashed toward the sinking carrier, but we were delayed when three planes appeared suddenly out of the clouds, causing general alarm. As they neared they were identified as returning Zero fighters. They circled slowly over their sinking home, as if bidding it farewell. One of them came down slowly near my ship, trying to ditch. *Amatsukaze* obligingly slowed down. The other two planes ditched alongside *Takitsukaze*. The three pilots were quickly rescued, but nothing could be done to save their planes.

Precious time was lost in this rescue work. It seemed to me *Ryujo* would sink at any moment. But the burning carrier, despite its many gaping holes, miraculously stayed afloat. Even the eerie flames spurting from the hull subsided—possibly because of the thousands of tons of sea water flowing into her.

Our hopes rose as *Amatsukaze* rushed to *Ryujo*'s side. I recalled miraculous cases of effective damage control which enabled badly crippled ships to limp back for repairs. Our approach to *Ryujo*, however, was again suspended, this time by two B-17s which emerged from the clouds. The two destroyers and *Tone* had to resume speed for a zigzag run. All guns opened fire at the two bombers, which fortunately made only a halfhearted attack. Or perhaps they were simply too inexperienced to aim properly at fast-moving targets on the ocean. All their bombs were wasted.

Dusk was approaching as the bombers departed and we resumed rescue operations. Thank God! *Ryujo* was still afloat, but without power. Maybe we could tow her to Truk for repair. My wishful optimism was shattered as we drew near. The fire had gutted everything. All weapons and facilities were destroyed. Bodies were scattered everywhere. The ship was listing some 40 degrees, and sinking visibly.

Presently a man started waving signal flags, which read: "We are abandoning ship. Come alongside to rescue crew." We quickly moved in along *Ryujo*'s submerging starboard deck. If the carrier sank—as it could at any moment—*Amatsukaze* might be carried down with it. It was clearly no time for hesitation, and I decided to take a chance.

The ocean, which had appeared calm, was actually rolling in long waves, causing the carrier's listing superstructure to pitch and brush frighteningly against the bridge of my little destroyer. Cold sweat ran down my back. Scores of strong seamen armed with long poles ran to the port side of my ship and held us off *Ryujo*. As long planks were set to link my ship with *Ryujo*, the wounded were helped and followed by the able-bodied who filed across to our ship, the officers carrying classified documents. The transfer was made very efficiently. More than 300 survivors boarded *Amatsukaze*.

Ryujo's list suddenly increased steeply. It was sinking now. "Evacuation finished?" I shouted. An officer at the end of the plank nodded and answered, "Yes, sir! Please cast off. It's getting dangerous!"

Amatsukaze's powerful turbines roared into action instantly. The destroyer responded quickly and moved desperately away. We had gone scarcely 500 meters when *Ryujo* disappeared among the waves. The tremendous whirlpool caused by its sinking made *Amatsukaze* bob like a cork. It was a close shave indeed! I was still breathing hard when a low voice behind me said, "Commander Hara, I . . . I do not know how to thank you. . . . "

I turned around and saw Captain Tadao Kato, of *Ryujo*, the last man in the evacuation line. This was the man I had cursed so many times only a few hours ago. Kato, haggard and pathetic, bowed to me and croaked, "Please accept my humble thanks on behalf of my men."

Suddenly I felt sorry for this general line officer, not a specialist, and my anger switched abruptly to Admiral Yamamoto who had chosen such a man for a "decoy" mission. "You need not thank me, Captain Kato," I replied curtly. "You look ill. Are you hurt?"

"No, Hara; not a bit. But . . . so many of my men were lost, and the ship!" Hands to face, he sobbed, no longer able to control himself. I feared he might collapse and called, "Orderly, quick, take Captain Kato to my cabin."

"Oh, no, Hara!" Kato protested. "Let me stay with my men, any place that won't bother your operation."

I let him do as he pleased, since every inch of my ship was jammed with the rescued crew of *Ryujo*. I pitied the old captain as he trudged toward the ladder. "Captain Kato," I called, "just a moment. May I ask if my good friend Kishi, your Exec, is safe?"

Kato turned back speechless, his haggard face wrinkled with the pain of sorrow. I understood and nodded. Kato lowered his head and went below.

I was stunned. My friend Kishi was dead. Kishi had a brilliant record as an aviation specialist. Had he been given a free hand by this line skipper from the beginning, things might have turned out better. I shook my head. There was still important work to be done. Mourning had to wait until duties were completed.

My ship joined *Tokitsukaze* and flagship *Tone*, and I was elated to find them unscathed like mine. They were still busy picking up some *Ryujo* crewmen who had jumped overboard. Meanwhile 14 *Ryujo* planes returned from the strike on Guadalcanal and circled overhead. Seven, including the only radio-equipped one of the flight, were lost. The remainder, accordingly, did not know they had been ordered to land at Buka. They had to ditch and our three ships picked up the crews, but all the planes sank.

The sun was setting as *Tone*, *Tokitsukaze* and *Amatsukaze* started eastward under orders from Nagumo to join his main task force. This day of the Battle of the Eastern Solomons—August 24, 1942—had been a long one for me, and it was not yet over. After cruising some 50 miles toward our scheduled rendezvous, we observed a group of Japanese warships moving slowly to the south with their searchlights blazing. They were searching for pilots who had been forced to ditch.

The night was black as pitch, the bombs and guns had been silent for hours, and I was beginning to feel the accumulated fatigue of a day-long battle following a sleepless night when these ships were sighted. I was thinking it would be good now to have a short nap when my signal officer reported that flagship *Shokaku* was blinking a signal to *Amatsukaze*:

"Admiral Nagumo directs Commander Hara to rescue two *Zuikaku* pilots adrift. Proceed at once to position KI N 21."

I replied immediately: "From Commander to Admiral Nagumo. *Amatsukaze* will proceed at once to KI N 21 and rescue *Zuikaku*'s pilots."

Turning to the charts I checked the indicated grid position and whistled. KI N 21 was 98 miles almost due south of our present position; and it was within 60 miles of the enemy task force position as reported at the time of *Ryujo*'s sinking. But orders were orders and this was no time for hesitation. My drowsiness vanished and I summoned my staff for consultation.

We could not afford to be off course by the slightest bit in this mission. I had no idea how the position of the pilots had been determined, but knew that our slim chance of rescuing them would be greatly reduced if there was any error in navigation.

Admiral Nagumo had been so good to me that, knowing he had chosen me especially for this mission, I was determined to live up to his expectations. We were approaching what might well be the jaws of the lion, but my men were willing and eager and I was with them.

Four hours of running at 24 knots put us in the approximate area. I slowed *Amatsukaze* to six knots. With no stars visible a sextant was of no use, so we had to rely on dead reckoning. When Ensign Hideo Shoji reported that we were in the designated grid position I called all spare crewmen to stand lookout, announcing that whoever discovered the first clue leading to rescue of *Zuikaku*'s pilots would be rewarded. The men ran enthusiastically to positions of vantage around the ship.

Since there were Japanese pilots down in this vicinity, I had to assume that enemy pilots might also have ditched here and that they were also being looked for. Accordingly, I could not allow the use of searchlights which might draw attention to our position. Our destroyer, snailing along at six knots, was as vulnerable to submarine attack as an old transport.

After half an hour of fruitless searching I became concerned about our fuel supply. In addition to all the other factors that had to be considered, *Amatsukaze* had used much fuel in its decoy mission with *Ryujo*, and we still needed enough to reach Rabaul, 500 miles away. With this in mind, I ordered small running lights placed on the sideboards. Within minutes a sailor in the bow sang out, "Floating object to starboard. Looks like a bottle."

I leaned from the bridge railing, saw the pop bottle reflecting the green running light, and shouted, "Good, they must be nearby." Cheered by this turn I ordered a weak signal light from the bridge to blink the name of the pilots' ship: "*Zuikaku! Zuikaku!*"

Another half hour passed and hope was waning when out of the darkness I saw a flick of a light off the port bow. It flickered again—some thousand meters distant—and went out, but this time I was sure. Turning in that direction, a boat was lowered from *Amatsukaze* when we had approached to within 100 meters and saw two men clinging to a raft. Ensign Hideo Shoji commanded the rescue boat. A blue-shaded light was used to assist the operation and Shoji paused halfway to the raft to report back that the men looked like Americans.

I grabbed binoculars for a close scrutiny. In the blue light they did look like Americans, but I ordered, "Rescue the men, whoever they are."

My knees were shaking. If these men were Americans it meant that our search must continue. But I was resolved to carry out my mission if it meant searching until dawn. As our boat reached the raft a flashlight blinked that these were the Japanese we sought, and I breathed a sigh of great relief.

With the men safely on board we headed north at 24 knots, and I relaxed in a chair for the first time in many hours. Our rescue mission of the day was a complete success.

Our decoy mission, on the other hand, had met a dismal end; and yet it had not been a failure. The sacrifice of *Ryujo* had deflected the enemy from the main Japanese force and permitted Admiral Nagumo to concentrate his full air strength against *Enterprise*. Still, the sinking of *Ryujo* as against the damaging of *Enterprise* was no advantage for Japan, since the latter carrier survived and was restored to service within two months.

Furthermore, the U.S. Navy bombed the Ichiki convoy and damaged cruiser *Jintsu*, the escort flagship. Six destroyers of the squadron closed Guadalcanal and bombarded it furiously during the night, but B-17s hit back the following morning and raked the ships for several hours. The convoy escaped to Bougainville, but not before destroyer *Mutsuki* had been sunk and transport *Kinryu Maru* sunk. Learning of the stiff opposition to be expected, the Kawaguchi convoy turned around and went back to Truk.

Thus the whole of this second encounter in the Solomons ended in a Japanese defeat—tactically and strategically. And Yamamoto's decision was proved wrong.

Two days after the operation I heard an Imperial Headquarters communiqué claiming that in the battle of August 23–25, heavy damage had been inflicted on a large American carrier, medium damage to a medium American carrier and a *Pennsylvania*-class battleship. The communiqué admitted to the loss of only one Japanese destroyer sunk, and heavy damage to a small carrier.

An American announcement said *Saratoga*'s planes had bombed a Japanese carrier and damaged a cruiser and a destroyer. It admitted considerable damage to *Enterprise*, but went on to say that the *Saratoga* and Marine planes had also scored hits on a battleship and two cruisers.

Ryujo had sunk before my very eyes, but none of the other three ships in our decoy force were even hit. American pilots apparently mistook transport *Kinryu Maru* for a battleship and destroyer *Mutsuki* for a cruiser.

From that day on, I distrusted all war communiqués, Japanese or enemy.*

When *Amatsukaze* rejoined the Nagumo Task Force around noon on August 25, I found new and pleasant orders waiting for me in the form of a message from carrier *Shokaku*:

---

* Actual losses for the Japanese were: carrier *Ryujo* plus 21 planes downed over Guadalcanal. For the U.S.: escort carrier *Enterprise* plus 17 planes destroyed in air combat.

"Admiral Nagumo congratulates Commander Hara for his fine, impressive job, and directs him to proceed immediately to Truk and land the rescued persons."

Amatsukaze again broke away from the Task Force and steamed alone to Truk. We reached the calm of that atoll the following day.

3

The great Han Dynasty of China was founded by General Liu Pang in 202 B.C. after he had emerged victorious from a series of many battles in a great civil war. One day, after gaining the throne, Generalissimo Liu was chatting with his chief of staff, General Han Tsin:

Liu: "How do you rate me as a general?"

Han: "I think Your Majesty can command, at most, an army of a few divisions."

Liu: "And what is your own ability?"

Han: "The more armies of as many possible divisions I command the better I work."

Liu: "How does it happen that I am an emperor while you remain a general?"

Han: "You are a born leader of leaders."

Liu was one of the greatest emperors and Han one of the greatest generals in history. Few admirals have enjoyed such high reputation as did Admiral Isoroku Yamamoto in World War II. He had great ability, but I feel that his reputation as a naval leader was greater than he deserved. I do not mean to compare Yamamoto categorically with Liu, but in respect of their actual abilities, they are comparable.

Despite Japan's miserable defeat in the Pacific War, the nation is still inclined to regard Yamamoto as a hero. Postwar writings have criticized other military and naval leaders, but not Yamamoto. If my remarks on Yamamoto seem severe it is not that I have any personal feelings against him; this is just the first writing by a Japanese military man to be at all critical of him.

To me Admiral Yamamoto was a born leader of leaders and for that he deserved the almost religious respect accorded him. But he was not qualified to command a million tons of ships and their crews. It was tragic that he was chosen to head the Combined Fleet.

Many of my colleagues believe that Yamamoto would have been an ideal Navy Minister, and there was a movement under way among certain Naval officers to have him named to this post. Their idea was that Admiral Mitsumasa Yonai should command the Combined Fleet. That move collapsed when Yonai, who strongly opposed war, refused, saying, "I am not a fighting admiral, and would only make things worse with the Army. Furthermore, if such a stiff-necked man as Yamamoto becomes Navy Minister he will surely be assassinated by Army hotheads."

The real trouble was the Army. When the war began the cabinet was headed by General Hideki Tojo. Admiral Shigetaro Shimada, the Navy Minister, was known to be a Tojo stooge. The Navy chief of staff, Admiral Osami Nagano, was not strong enough to oppose Army plans. In criticizing Yamamoto, his actions and inaction, consideration must be given to all these factors which served to hamstring him.

Throughout his career Yamamoto was known to be a superb gambler. He was skilled in all games of chance, especially poker. His decision to attack Pearl Harbor was a gamble which paid tremendous odds. It is strange, therefore, that Yamamoto never again played his cards for all they were worth, as a gambler should. The lessons of the Coral Sea battle were not applied to Midway, where Yamamoto split his forces—to his detriment—between his prime objective and the Aleutians. Yamamoto was undoubtedly preoccupied with preserving his forces.

My survivor-laden *Amatsukaze* entered the quiet of Truk harbor on the 25th of August, 1942. I fully expected to be ordered back to action as soon as our passengers went ashore. None of us in *Amatsukaze* imagined that we would stay more than a month at this haven during such a critical period of the war. At Truk I learned details of the Coral Sea battle of May 7–8, which had taken place while I was vacationing at home, and subsequent actions.

Japan's plans for an amphibious invasion of Port Moresby, a key Allied base on the southern coast of New Guinea, were thwarted as a result of this battle. Light carrier *Shoho* was sunk, and fleet carriers *Shokaku* and *Zuikaku* were so damaged that they could not take part in the Midway battle one month later. Against these losses the Imperial Navy claimed a victory in having sunk three enemy carriers. The enemy's actual losses in this battle were carrier *Lexington*, oiler *Neosho*, and destroyer *Sims* sunk; and carrier *Yorktown* damaged.

There was no doubt that Japan suffered a stunning setback, despite the official claim of victory.

One month later Japan was crushingly defeated at Midway where she lost carriers *Kaga, Akagi, Hiryu,* and *Soryu,* and heavy cruiser *Mikuma.* The U.S. Navy had carrier *Yorktown* repaired in time for Midway—to Japanese bewilderment—and she was lost in this battle, along with destroyer *Hammann.*

In July, the Japanese High Command committed another blunder in landing an Army division at Buna, on the east coast of Papua. The troops were to cross the Owen Stanley Mountains and attack Port Moresby. The entire division perished, more from natural causes—impossible terrain of jungle and mountains—than from enemy attack.

It is significant that the Allies started their Guadalcanal invasion on August 7, just as Japanese forces were committed and bogging down in Papua. Yamamoto blundered in his evaluation of the Papua and Guadalcanal operations. Just as at Midway he had divided his forces in making a simultaneous attack on the insignificant Aleutians, so with Guadalcanal he was forced to divide his efforts between that island and the Papuan Peninsula. The piecemeal Japanese offensives were ineffective, and the consequent division of forces and effort was disastrous.

On the night of August 24, while *Amatsukaze* was rescuing the two fliers, seven destroyers were storming Guadalcanal with little or no result. On the next two days our planes attacked the island without significant effect while the mainstay of his Combined Fleet maneuvered aimlessly around the Solomons. Yamamoto's irresolution was becoming apparent.

Four days later, the Ichiki Convoy tried again for Guadalcanal. Escorting Destroyer Division 20 took the brunt of Allied air attacks in which *Asagiri* was sunk and the other three destroyers—*Shirakumo, Yugiri, Amagiri*—were damaged. Yamamoto belatedly sent 30 fighters and three bombers from carriers *Shokaku* and *Zuikaku* to assist, but they arrived after the convoy had been forced to turn back to the Shortlands. Meanwhile, on a forlorn corner of Guadalcanal, the decimated vanguard unit of the Ichiki Regiment cried for reinforcement. At the Shortlands the troops were again loaded into six destroyers next day, the 29th, and this time the 1,000 soldiers were successfully landed after dark at Taivu Point on the north central shore of Guadalcanal.

Additional reinforcement by Major General Seiken Kawaguchi's brigade, originally intended for Papua, was on the way from Truk. They arrived at Bougainville in late August, and the first battalion was carried to Guadalcanal in three destroyers on the 30th. Eight destroyers brought in a 1,200-man contingent on the 31st. A third group was carried south by four destroyers on September 1, but they were turned back by stiff air opposition. The next day 20 Japanese fighter planes and 18 bombers pounded Guadalcanal, and the landing of the Kawaguchi Brigade was completed by a dozen destroyers on September 4th and 7th.

During all these reinforcement operations, *Amatsukaze* was stuck frustratingly at Truk. I knew how to use destroyers in putting troops ashore. I also knew that soldiers landed from destroyers could carry only light arms. I brooded over the fact that our lightly equipped troops, in whatever numbers, were no match for the heavily armed Americans on Guadalcanal.

Truk was quiet after the Kawaguchi convoy sailed. The calm of the harbor waters and the peace of the atoll were soothing to *Amatsukaze*'s weary crew. My men were happy, and took full advantage of our respite.

The atoll abounded with fish of many varieties and every motorboat brought fresh fish back to the ship. This meant a great treat for men who had been living on tasteless canned food, and we all enjoyed our fill of *sashimi*, the thin strips of raw fish which are such a delicacy.

One day I heard loud voices near my cabin, and went out to investigate. On the foredeck a cluster of men were gathered around a crude cage which held a falcon. The bird had been caught the day before when it perched on our mast. Moving closer I saw that a rat had been put in the cage. The falcon sat on its perch indifferently, eyes closed, while the rat scurried frantically about. The men watched in hushed silence as the bird blinked and suddenly darted at the rat, piercing out one of its eyes. Loud cheers. The bird whirred once around the cage and then deftly pierced the other eye. It was an impressive display of marksmanship and skill. With the rat blinded, the bird perched aloof again and showed no further interest. The men roared an ovation.

I returned to my cabin in no mood to enjoy such a performance. To me the bird seemed too much like a skillful attack plane, and the rat a destroyer.

The mainstay of the Combined Fleet ended ten days of fruitless roaming and entered Truk on September 5. The spacious harbor shrank considerably when filled with these 50-odd vessels headed by the 69,100-ton battleship *Yamato*.

For three days the skippers and commanders of the many fleet units met in the various flagships for detailed tactical conferences. The last meeting was held aboard *Yamato* with Admiral Yamamoto presiding. The preliminary discussions had dealt only with trivial matters. No one dreamed of contesting the basic operation formula already set. Criticism of basic concepts in the Imperial Navy would have impugned the top level admirals, and brought instant dismissal of the critic.

Thus all the preliminaries had been unproductive. Yamamoto was his taciturn self at the final conference. He cautioned against underestimating American fighting strength, and the session ended with the issuance of two simple instructions:

1. Keep the location and movements of our carriers unknown to the enemy.
2. Make initial air assaults against the enemy as strong as possible.

I returned to my ship with empty heart, feeling that the conferences had achieved nothing. Lieutenant Shimizu met me unhappily at the ramp. "What's the matter with you?" I asked.

"We failed to catch a single fish today. This super fleet of ours has exterminated every fish in the atoll in just three days."

On September 9, the Combined Fleet steamed out of Truk Atoll with *Amatsukaze* back in its original position as part of the Nagumo Task Force. Our plan was for an all-out assault on Guadalcanal on September 12 in concert with an offensive by Kawaguchi's ground forces. Instead, however, we spent the night of the 12th awaiting word that the Guadalcanal airfields were in Japanese hands. We continued impatiently to wait all through the next day. Late that night Naval Air Headquarters at Rabaul radioed, "According to our reconnaissance, the enemy airfields at Guadalcanal seem to be held by our forces."

Early next morning several scout planes from our force returned with full reports which completely refuted the Rabaul information. The long-awaited message from Kawaguchi reached us on the 15th saying his troops had met stiff enemy opposition, sustained heavy losses, and were forced to abandon the airfields. We stamped our feet in bitter anger.

In the afternoon of the same day, our patrol planes and submarines reported a large enemy task force of carriers and battleships 260 miles southeast of Guadalcanal. Lieutenant Commander Takaichi Kinashi, skipper of submarine I-19, in the first joyful message of that gloomy week, reported that he had torpedoed and sunk U.S. carrier *Wasp*.*

Our task force was ready and anxious to meet the enemy, but, after roaming idly for a week, our fuel ran low. We spent three days in fueling our ships some 200 miles north of Guadalcanal. Thus our best chances for engaging the enemy at this time were lost.

Meanwhile Admiral Yamamoto finally decided that at least a full division of troops was needed to reinforce Guadalcanal. So, having wasted tremendous quantities of fuel without accomplishing a thing, the Combined Fleet turned back to Truk.

At the same time Yamamoto ordered Rear Admiral Kakuji Kakuta, then training three new carriers, in home waters, to bring his ships to Truk as soon as possible. Yamamoto had decided to delay any further operation until after the arrival of Kakuta's Second Air Fleet, and Kakuta did not get to Truk until October 9. Thus Japan lost two months of precious time following the enemy landing on Guadalcanal before the Imperial Navy was ready for a full-scale counteroffensive.

4

Sun-tze, the military sage of ancient China, wrote in the eleventh chapter of his immortal Analects:

> The skillful tactician may be likened to the *shuai-jan*. Now the *shuai-jan*
> is a snake that is found in the Chang Mountains. Strike its head and you
> will be attacked by its tail; strike at its tail, and you will be attacked by
> its head; strike at its middle, and you will be attacked by its head and
> tail both.

In October 1942, Admiral Yamamoto's Combined Fleet was deployed for the first time in the manner of the *shuai-jan*. Its head was the Nagumo Task

---

* Hit by three torpedoes on September 15, *Wasp* was badly damaged, abandoned, and given the *coup de grace* by torpedoes from U.S. destroyer *Lansdowne* in position 12 25' S, 164 08' E.

Force, the body was Yamamoto's own battleship squadron, and the tail was the newly arrived ships under command of Admiral Kakuta.

Nagumo's teeth were 29,800-ton carriers *Zuikaku* and *Shokaku* which, fully armed and loaded, actually came to some 40,000 tons. Japan's foremost carriers, they boasted the best crews and pilots. They were supported by Kakuta's 27,500-ton converted carriers *Hiyo*, *Junyo* and 13,100-ton *Zuiho*. These were manned by newly trained crewmen and fliers, but their inexperience was offset by Kakuta's fierce aggressiveness. He was the youngest of Yamamoto's flag-rank subordinates, and a robust battler. He arrived at Truk vengeful at the loss of carrier *Ryujo*, which he had once commanded. It had been sunk in the Battle of the Eastern Solomons mainly because of boners by the high command of the Japanese Navy. He was still angry about the Midway debacle, too, where he had commanded the Second Carrier Striking Force which struck at the Aleutians. In that case the "tail" was extended too far to permit it to strike back when the "head" was attacked.

By October 1942, Imperial Headquarters at Tokyo had awakened to the grave situation and authorized Yamamoto to concentrate on Guadalcanal and "leave the Papuan operation as it stands." He was thus given a chance to be Sun-tze's "skillful tactician," but he was not given a free hand in carrying out his chance. The Army still held the initiative.

The Army brought its Second Division from Java to Rabaul and requested "a joint amphibious operation to Guadalcanal." The "amphibious operation" meant that the Army supplied troops and arms; it was up to the Navy to carry and support them. The Army had half of all Japan's combat planes, but it did not offer a single one to this operation. The Japanese concept of a "joint operation" was quite different from that of the United States.

When Guadalcanal landing operations were resumed, it was the famed "Tokyo Express" which carried the Second Division. These were ships of Rear Admiral Gunichi Mikawa's Eighth Fleet at Rabaul.

Rear Admiral Kakuji Kakuta's task force steamed out of Truk on October 10 to give air support to ground operations at the bitterly contested island.

My ship and one other destroyer had left Truk the previous day to hit Ndeni, one of the northern islands in the Santa Cruz group, which we suspected of harboring enemy flying boats. We arrived there only to find the island completely evacuated. We swung back north of the Solomons and on October 15 joined the Nagumo Task Force, which had left Truk on the 11th.

Mikawa's "Tokyo Express" landed the 10,600-man Second Army Division in eight trips between October 2 and 11 practically without loss. The operation was a complete success. The Allies apparently recognized the *shuaijan* deployment and took a cautious stand. The only clash was on the night of October 11 between Rear Admiral Aritomo Goto's Cruiser Division 6 and Rear Admiral Norman Scott's Task Force 64. The Japanese escort group was ambushed by TF 64 in the narrow waters between Savo and Guadalcanal Islands, in what has since become known as the Battle of Cape Esperance.

The American fleet of four cruisers and five destroyers had a numerical advantage over Japan's three cruisers and two destroyers. The furious fight ended with Japan losing cruisers *Furutaka* (sunk) and *Aoba* (damaged). TF 64 suffered the loss of destroyer *Duncan* (sunk), and destroyer *Farenholt* and cruisers *Salt Lake City* and *Boise* (damaged). This action was further costly to Japan in that Admiral Goto was killed. But the battle was valuable, too, as it cleared the American fleet from the area. Vice Admiral Takeo Kurita was thus able to bring battleships *Kongo* and *Haruna* close to the Guadalcanal coast on the night of October 13 for a point-blank bombardment of Henderson Field.

This was Yamamoto's first departure from his previous policy of "hoarding" the battleships. In all the earlier operations he had steadfastly refused to expose battleships at the fighting front. With air support available from a field just completed at the southern tip of Bougainville, Yamamoto gambled. The gamble paid off.

At 2300 on October 13, the two 27,500-ton warships closed to within one mile of the coast and slowed to a leisurely 18 knots. Their 16 big guns hurled 918 incendiary shells onto the airfield, which burned for a full 24 hours. Japanese troops on the island were thrilled and encouraged by this spectacle and urged the Navy to repeat the show. Yamamoto obliged and the next night Admiral Mikawa paralleled the coast in cruisers *Chokai* and *Kinugasa*, and sprayed the airfield with 752 shells.

But there were other chores for the Navy these days and nights and an important one was the delivery of heavy arms to equip the troops. While such undertakings were in progress the American task force worked its way back. The first effective American air attack hit on October 15, when six Japanese transports were sunk or put out of action. Another devastating attack came on the 17th. Early that morning two American destroyers carried out an audacious bombardment of supply dumps setting them afire. Seven American bombers returned that afternoon and finished the job.

The lack of motorized equipment for quickly moving landed cargo to places of safety thus cost the Japanese Army dearly. Brave men cried in anguish at the sight of these precious dumps in flames.

The American ships were spotted 110 miles south of Guadalcanal as they withdrew, but Kakuta's task force was 200 miles north of the island and so had no chance to engage them.

When Yamamoto reinforced the area, the enemy acted precisely in the spirit enunciated by Sun-tze in the seventh chapter of his Analects:

> When fighting a powerful force, one must hit when its morale ebbs. . . . A force's morale is keen when it sorties, gradually begins to flag, and ebbs as it is ready to return to camp. One should avoid a force while its morale is keen, and one should hit when its morale ebbs.

The two Japanese naval forces had been in the waters of the southern Solomons for more than a week without engaging any strong enemy force. Their initially high morale was waning.

Meanwhile, we were waiting impatiently for an all-out offensive on Guadalcanal promised by the land troops for October 20. The Army had at Guadalcanal its Second Division, from Sendai in northern Honshu. This outfit had occupied Nanking during the China War. Its ruthlessness had won it notoriety in the much-exaggerated "rape" of that city. The division had an easy time invading Java where it faced practically no opposition. But it failed completely to anticipate the rugged terrain and inclement weather of Guadalcanal. Now, with more than half of its newly landed equipment burned by the Americans, the Army troops were fighting a truly uphill battle.

Despite the urgency of the army's situation, the October 20 offensive was postponed repeatedly while the Navy stamped its feet in disgust. Ominously for Japan, Admiral Kakuta's flagship carrier *Hiyo* suddenly developed engine trouble on October 22. Frantic efforts by her engineers failed to correct the difficulty. Her engines, originally designed for a merchant ship, were not capable of the acceleration needed for a carrier. Kakuta transferred his flag to *Junyo* and ordered *Hiyo* back to Truk. It returned there at its best speed of six knots.

The stage was being set for an American onslaught against the Japanese Navy, as much as for land action on Guadalcanal. And now Kakuta's Task

Force had only one carrier. *Zuiho* had been transferred earlier to the Nagumo Task Force. The "Sun-tze snake was no longer lithe, and its tail had lost two thirds of its original stingers. Fresh, eager American naval forces were ready to strike.

5

In the late afternoon of October 24, Vice Admiral Chuichi Nagumo sat grimly in his cabin in carrier *Shokaku*. He had aged visibly since the Midway defeat. His hair was gray, his face sallow and deeply wrinkled. He stared at two pieces of paper. He had already read them dozens of times trying to puzzle out their meaning. One was a United Press story dated October 20 saying that the United States Navy was preparing for a major sea and air battle in the South Pacific. Nagumo asked himself what this meant. Was it a trap?

The other sheet of paper listed enemy ships spotted by Nagumo's scout planes since the arrival of his task force in the area:

Oct.	Carriers	Battleships	Cruisers	Destroyers	Others
12	0	0	1	1	2
13	2	3	5	6	0
15	0	0	2	2	2
16	1	3	8	15	0
21	0	2	3	2	0
23	0	2	1	2	0
24	0	5	3	19	0

"The enemy carriers have been missing for a week," Nagumo mumbled. "What does this mean?"

He stood up and slowly paced the room. The aging admiral stopped short, smiled, and thought of Sun-tze's advice that one should avoid engaging the enemy while his morale is keen, and one should strike when his morale ebbs. There was a knock at the door, and one of Nagumo's staff officers entered.

"Sir," Commander Toshitane Takada said as he saluted, "radiomen report they are suddenly getting great numbers of undecipherable messages, evidently from nearby enemy submarines and aircraft."

"Very well," Nagumo nodded. "Call chief of staff Kusaka quickly."

Rear Admiral Ryunosuke Kusaka, a heavy-set, energetic man, rushed into the room from the bridge a few moments later.

"How is the fuel supply of our ships?" Nagumo asked. "They are fueling from tankers, sir," Kusaka replied.

"Very well," Nagumo nodded. "Inform every skipper that a major action is imminent. Spread the formation as soon as the ships are fueled."

About the same time in carrier *Junyo*, Rear Admiral Kakuji Kakuta was listening to a radio broadcast from Hawaii. The commentator was predicting a major sea and air battle soon near the Solomons. Kakuta had been considering two sheets of paper identical to those of Nagumo's. Kakuta snorted and turned to his air officer, Lieutenant Commander Masatake Okumiya. "Well, what do you say, Masatake?"

This alert and intelligent little man, whose eyes sparkled from his impassive face—burned and scarred in an air crash several years earlier—cleared his throat and said quietly, "Sir, October 27 is America's Navy Day."

Kakuta, a burly battler, jumped to his feet and roared with laughter. "Very good, very good. Let's hustle and prepare a nice Navy Day gift for those cocky Yanks."

On board *Shokaku*, Nagumo still conferred with Kusaka. "What is our deployment now?" Nagumo asked.

"Battleships *Hiei* and *Kirishima*, cruiser *Chikuma* and seven destroyers of Rear Admiral Koki Abe are ahead of us, 60 to 80 miles to the south," Kusaka replied. "Rear Admiral Chuichi Hara's cruiser *Tone* and destroyer *Terutsuki* are 200 miles to the east. Rear Admiral Kakuta's force is 300 miles to the west."

"Any reports on enemy carriers?"

"No, sir."

The ensuing brief silence was broken by Nagumo who spoke hesitantly, meditatively, as if thinking aloud: "At Midway, the enemy struck us at a time of his choosing. Now, too, there is no doubt that the enemy pinpoints our position as if on a chessboard, but we are running blind. . . ."

Commander Takada, a staff officer, ventured to speak. "Excuse me, sir, may I suggest sending a message to *Yamato* (the Combined Fleet flagship, then at Truk) asking for instructions?"

Nagumo was silent. Kusaka closed his eyes for a few moments, then opened them and said, "All right, Takada, take this message: 'From Kusaka, First Air Fleet chief of staff, to Vice Admiral (Matome) Ugaki, Combined Fleet chief of staff: May I suggest halting our southward advance until we receive definite word that the Army has captured Guadalcanal airfields? There seems to be a possibility of our being trapped if we continue going like this.'"

Nagumo listened intently and nodded his concurrence. The message was sent and a grim silence descended on the cabin. Nagumo and his staff settled down to wait for an answer.

My destroyer *Amatsukaze* was cruising 2,000 meters to port of flagship *Shokaku*. We were part of the ring formation of one cruiser and nine destroyers which surrounded the flagship and carriers *Zuikaku* and *Zuiho* of Carrier Division 1. Nagumo and Kusaka had learned a bitter and costly lesson at Midway, and they were taking full precautions this time.

Shortly after midnight the long-awaited reply arrived from Truk. "From Ugaki to Kusaka: Your Striking Force will proceed quickly to the enemy direction. The operation orders stand, without change."

Kusaka bit his lip. Takada groaned. Nagumo snorted, then said calmly, "All right, start fueling the carriers."

The three carriers slowed down to take on oil in the dark of night. By daybreak of October 25 the painstaking process was almost completed when an orderly dashed into the admiral's cabin with a message. Nagumo was dozing. He awakened instantly and read the report from one of the patrol planes supposed to be circling above his carriers: "I have shot down an enemy plane, apparently a scout." Nagumo jumped to his feet.

"Cut refueling. Turn the carriers around and head due north!"

At 0530 the Nagumo and Kakuta forces retreated at 20 knots to the north northeast. As soon as Nagumo heard that the enemy scout plane had been shot down he ordered the drastic turn—something he failed to do at Midway—because he decided the enemy had obtained full information about the strength and composition of his force. The Americans failed to foresee this decision of Nagumo's, and a few hours later their planes searched vainly where his ships should have been.

Nagumo sent dozens of scout planes in all directions. But they sighted no enemy carriers. They did, however, see and report two Allied battleships, five cruisers and 12 destroyers. After running northward for 12 hours, Nagumo again directed fueling for all his ships, including the three carriers. At 1900 the two Japanese task forces reversed course and headed south at 20 knots.

It was a warm moonlit night. On weather decks, however, a breeze flapped flags and dried out sweaty clothes. Nagumo was again huddled with staff officers in the heavy atmosphere of his cabin. Everyone was glum. "We must presume that the enemy contact has failed," one said. "From the enemy radio activity, they may still be in contact with our vanguard units." Nagumo closed his eyes, as though in pain. Kusaka wiped sweat from his face. Commander Takada squirmed.

At 50 minutes past midnight, October 26, every alarm sounded on carrier *Shokaku*. "Air raid! Air raid!" Staff officers jumped. Takada dashed to the bridge in time to see four water plumes rising on the starboard side of carrier *Zuikaku*, some 5,000 meters astern of *Shokaku*. He held his breath until the water pillars subsided, and he saw that *Zuikaku* was still safe. The bombs had fallen at least 300 meters away from the carrier. Takada almost fell down the ladder racing to the admiral's cabin to report these events.

Nagumo and Kusaka were still in their chairs. When Takada reported what he had seen, the two admirals looked at each other and said exactly the same thing, "Let's turn around."

From the bridge of *Amatsukaze* I saw *Shokaku*'s signal light blink: "All ships turn 180 degrees to starboard!" and then the big black ship started its abrupt turn. A second blinker-light order followed shortly: "Speed of advance, 24 knots." And the third message came at 0130, as the turn was completed. "All ships of this force steady on course zero degrees."

The moon vanished into the clouds and an uneasy hour passed while we braced for an all-out attack by the enemy. Not a single enemy appeared. It was becoming evident that the plane which had hit—and so poorly—at *Zuikaku* had committed a grave blunder. It had sounded an alarm—a most vital alarm—to which the Japanese responded promptly, to the distinct disadvantage of the enemy.

Dawn of October 26 was to break at 0345 (Japan time; local or sun time in the Solomons was 0545). In the predawn darkness, red-shaded flashlights moved to and fro on *Shokaku*'s deck. It was plain that all hands were busy in the carrier.

At 0215 our radio picked up a report that the vanguard unit, then running far to our rear, had catapulted seven reconnaissance planes. Thirty minutes later, 13 scouts zoomed up from the decks of our carriers. Then the whole fleet turned about again and headed once more to the south.

By morning's light I saw *Shokaku* pilots near their planes, ready for battle at a moment's notice. Admiral Nagumo was clearly visible on the bridge, easily identified by his snow-white gloves.

About 0500 the radio-room voice tube suddenly came to life as Ensign Hideo Shoji shouted excitedly, "*Shokaku* scout plane reports a large enemy force at KHI7. Force consists of one *Saratoga*-class carrier and 15 other ships heading northwestward. 0450 hours." I was speechless at discovering that KH17 was 210 miles distant on bearing 125 degrees. We had figured that the enemy would be directly ahead of us, or even slightly to the right. Cold chills ran down my spine. My officers took a look at the chart and groaned.

Similar consternation was being felt on the bridge of every Japanese ship. Everyone suddenly realized how narrowly we had escaped an enemy trap. Had we maintained a southern advance without the two turnarounds and the northern run, the Americans could have struck at us from the rear and battered us into a disastrous defeat.

On *Shokaku*'s bridge, Admiral Nagumo grinned for the first time in many hours. He ordered an immediate air sortie, and planes began rolling down the deck. Everyone had learned at Midway that the slightest hesitation could cause a debacle. *Shokaku* and *Zuikaku* launched 40 bombers and 27 fighters within 15 minutes. Their speedy action was in marked contrast to the sluggish *Ryujo* operations I had witnessed two months earlier in this same area.

Two American scout planes cut through the overcast and suddenly swooped to spray a few bombs on carrier *Zuiho*. Their daring paid off. One bomb pierced the flight deck aft and exploded. The resulting fire was soon put under control, but the deck was ruined.

Zuiho's skipper signaled that she could launch planes, but could not receive any on her damaged deck. Nagumo reluctantly ordered *Zuiho* to withdraw after dispatching all her fighters.

Combustibles were removed from every ship's deck and all water pipes were opened. The enemy had located our forces and might appear in force any moment.

A second wave of Japanese attackers, including *Zuiho*'s 16 fighters, was launched by 0600. All carriers were now left without air cover. We had to strike the enemy first.

Meanwhile, in carrier *Junyo*, Admiral Kakuta angrily stamped his feet at learning that the enemy was 330 miles away. He ordered his ships to head southeast at full speed, and enthusiastic boilermen responded instantly. The bulky converted carrier reached her maximum speed of 26 knots in a record 10 minutes instead of the usual 20. *Junyo* sprang from the ring formation leaving behind her three escorting destroyers.

The destroyermen gaped at seeing the most sluggish carrier in service running away from them. It took the destroyers more than an hour to catch up with their darting flagship. The 330-mile distance to enemy targets was not prohibitively far. Kakuta could have had his planes return to the nearer *Shokaku* or *Zuikaku* instead of trying to range back to *Junyo*. But he wanted to close with the enemy so that he could juggle his few combat planes for as many attacks as possible.

The enemy's timing and movements were most adroit, but he failed to reckon that the smaller, more distant task force, with its lone carrier, would offer such a determined fight.

Starting at 0714 Kakuta sent out 29 planes in three attack waves to strike the enemy.

Breakfast that day was even more Spartan than usual. I was munching the emergency fare of biscuits and water when a scout bomber came in, wagging its wings for identification, to make a neat landing on *Shokaku*'s deck. Handling crews were at work on the plane as soon as it stopped, readying it for another sortie. The plane was quickly rolled to one side as six fighters sped down the deck to fly combat air patrol over our ships. An enemy onslaught was expected at any moment.

The first word from our own attack planes came at 0710 when they announced: "Enemy carrier sighted . . . all planes attacking." The 40 bombers and torpedo planes scored several direct hits and many near misses on carrier *Hornet* in a concentrated attack which lasted about 10 minutes in all.

My attention was diverted from this exciting news by the return of another bomber plane which tried to land on *Shokaku*'s deck. The plane was crippled and had to ditch near the carrier's stern. *Amatsukaze* raced to rescue the crew, stopped near the sinking plane, and lowered a rescue boat. While this operation was in progress, enemy planes were sighted. General alarm was sounded, and all hands went to battle stations. I glanced up and saw about a dozen dive-bombers approaching from out of a cloud bank at 2,000 meters. I continued our rescue operation, confident that the planes would choose carrier *Shokaku* for their target rather than my little destroyer.*

While *Amatsukaze*'s boat was returning with the two rescued fliers, all ships opened fire at the approaching enemy planes, and they were gleefully jumped by our six combat air patrol fighters. *Amatsukaze* joined the fray as quickly as possible. How different was Japanese response from what it had been two months earlier when carrier *Ryujo* had been under air attack!

---

* These planes were from *Hornet*: 15 Dauntless dive-bombers, and 6 Avengers.

Two enemy torpedo planes were hit by our fighters, blew up in smoke, and disappeared. One of our fighters rammed a third bomber, causing a terrible explosion which blotted out both planes in an instant. I saw two enemy bombers, apparently hit by gunfire, fall into the sea. Very strangely, I saw not a single American fighter. I wondered why these enemy attackers came without escort.

The number of enemy planes was decreasing. The skies were filled with white and yellow smoke from the barrage of our ships, antiaircraft fire. It appeared that we might pull through this raid unscathed. *Amatsukaze* was zigzagging at a steady 33 knots, but half of my attention was devoted to *Shokaku*, which needed all possible protection. I saw two enemy bombers pierce *Shokaku*'s gunfire and dive full toward the carrier from a height of about 700 meters. The planes arced up at the last moment and disappeared into the clouds. The next instant I saw two or three silver streaks, which appeared like thunderbolts, reaching toward the bulky carrier. Their impact raised flashes at the fore and amidship, near the bridge, of *Shokaku*. The whole deck bulged quietly and burst. Flames shot from the cleavages. I groaned as the flames rose and black and white smoke came belching out of the deck. The flagship was hit at last—and how vulnerable it was—by four bombs!

Shokaku turned, maintaining a speed of more than 30 knots. Apparently the engines were not damaged. The ship started to withdraw with two destroyers as escorts. Before leaving the area, Nagumo signaled instructions for me to escort *Zuikaku*, the only carrier of his force remaining in operation.*

I was still bewildered at *Shokaku*'s vulnerability. Why was it so weak, with all its crack flyers and efficient crew? *Ryujo*'s sinking was not too shocking, in view of its poor combat efficiency, but *Shokaku*'s defeat confounded me. No time, however, for such disturbing thoughts. There was work to be done. The enemy air raid was over. But more waves might be coming at any time to attack *Zuikaku*. Furthermore, *Zuikaku* had to retrieve the returning planes of all three carriers. It was obvious that some of these planes, particularly damaged ones, would have to ditch. *Amatsukaze* headed toward *Zuikaku* at full speed.

---

* Carrier *Junyo*, which also survived, was part of Kondo's Advance Force, and not under Nagumo's command.

An hour passed with no fresh assault by the enemy. We were grateful for a number of *Zuiho's* fighters which returned in small groups. Their pilots explained the mystery of the lack of fighter escorts for the bombers which attacked *Shokaku*. The first Japanese sortie of 40 bombers and 27 fighters had met the first air attack group of the enemy in mid air. Such a rare encounter was completely unforeseen by either side. Half of the Japanese fighters broke off to engage the enemy group. A furious free-for-all dogfight ensued high over the Pacific, midway between the opposing task forces.

All eight American fighters were shot down—but not in vain. They enabled the American bombers to carry out the attack which put *Shokaku* out of action. The Japanese attack group which went ahead with a reduced escort also had a difficult job hitting *Hornet*. Seven Japanese bombers were lost.

It appears that the group of 21 bombers and 8 fighters from *Hornet* hit our vanguard unit, while the smaller group of *Enterprise* planes hit *Shokaku*. Why this bigger force of *Hornet* planes chose the vanguard group of cruisers, instead of the two carriers at the core, still remains a mystery to me. The cruisers were then 120 miles ahead of us, having stretched out the original distance of 60 miles, as a result of Nagumo's turnarounds. The *Hornet* group must simply have failed to discover the core.

Only cruiser *Chikuma* in the van was damaged. Several bomb hits caused it to lose speed, and it was sent back to Truk with two destroyers in escort. American failure to follow through on their initial attacks left the initiative completely in Japanese hands. While *Hornet* was being abandoned, *Enterprise* was ruthlessly bombed by fresh groups of Japanese bombers. Kinkaid, seeing the operation fail, started to withdraw all his forces.

It took us too long, however, to realize that the enemy was being routed. With nightmarish memories of the Midway debacle still fresh, we could not imagine that the American and Japanese positions were now the reverse of what they had been at Midway.

After the brief but effective attack on *Shokaku*, live destroyers, including mine, surrounding *Zuikaku* had a field day rescuing ditched Japanese fliers. *Amatsukaze* rushed to pick up two bomber crewmen. The pilot was wounded in the left leg. He said, "Bullets hit my fuel tank. It was a miracle that the plane didn't explode."

Next, a torpedo-bomber touched on *Zuikaku's* deck but could not be stopped. The plane skidded wildly, turned over, and crashed into the ocean.

My ship raced toward the scene but plane and crew sank before we could reach them.

A fighter ditched alongside my ship. I ordered full speed reverse and halted in time to pick up the badly wounded flyer before the plane sank. While my crewmen applied first aid, the young pilot breathed his last, murmuring "Mother!" That day, *Amatsukaze* rescued 13 flyers from the sea. Three others died soon after being picked up.

The two remaining carriers worked furiously. *Junyo* joined *Zuikaku* in early forenoon and hurled a second attack wave of 15 planes at 1106. Five minutes later, *Zuikaku* flung 13 planes at the fleeing Americans. Kakuta's *Junyo* kept up its dogged advance and sent off a third group of attackers, made up of planes which had returned and refueled in the early afternoon.

But not every Japanese admiral was as aggressive as Kakuta. Vice Admiral Nobutake Kondo, deputy commander in chief of the Combined Fleet, led battleships *Kongo* and *Haruna*, escorted by about a dozen cruisers and destroyers. This unit, with its powerful bombardment punch, made only a halfhearted advance.

Also reluctant was Rear Admiral Koki Abe's vanguard unit of two battleships and five destroyers. His cruiser *Chikuma* with two destroyers had already left the battle zone. Exposed for the first time to a furious American air attack, Abe apparently was too cautious.

When orders came from Truk in the afternoon to "chase and mop up the fleeing enemy," it was too late. Kondo's fast ships dashed at 30 knots but could not shave the 300-mile distance to the fleeing enemy. Thus Kondo's blunder enabled the enemy to get away without additional loss or damage.

Destroyers *Makigumo* and *Akigumo* reached *Hornet* in the night. Two American ships near the helpless carrier turned and fled, and the Japanese destroyers finished off the burning hulk with four torpedoes.

Nagumo had returned to the area in destroyer *Arashi* early in the morning of October 27. The fires in *Shokaku* were brought under control shortly after noon. Nagumo transferred his flag from *Arashi* to *Zuikaku* and resumed command in that carrier. Many planes were sent out by *Zuikaku* and *Junyo*, but they were unable to find the enemy fleet anywhere within their 300-mile scouting radius. At 0630 on October 27 Nagumo called off the operation. All ships of his force gathered during the day, and turned triumphantly toward Truk.

The balance sheet of the Santa Cruz Battle follows:

United States	Japan
SUNK	
CV *Hornet*	
DAMAGED	DAMAGED
CV *Enterprise*	CV *Shokaku*
BB *South Dakota*	CVL *Zuiho*
CL *San Juan*	CA *Chikuma*
DD *Smith*	DD *Akizuki*
	Hoshizuki
74 planes lost	66 planes lost

Thus, numerically or tactically, it was a Japanese victory. The enemy had entered the fray with a tactical and psychological advantage, but complacence had cost them a high price. The enemy was able to strike at times and places of his own choosing. To his surprise, the head and tail of the Japanese opponent were versatile and flexible—contrary to Midway—and they struck back effectively with what force they had, in proper fashion as decreed by Sun-tze.

Despite Japan's numerical victory in this action, the strategic victory belonged to the enemy. As a result of this battle the Americans won valuable time which permitted them to strengthen forces and prepare for the next action. This was achieved at nominal cost because our center force, under Admiral Kondo, was lacking in spirit. If it had responded as it should have—and as did the head and tail—the destruction of the enemy forces could have been complete.

6

Jubilance over the Santa Cruz victory did not last long. Orders awaited Admiral Nagumo at Truk. On November 2, he was relieved from command of the Third Fleet, the official title of his task force, and transferred to the homeland as commandant of the Sasebo Naval Station.

On learning of this rotation, I went to see him, not knowing whether to offer congratulations or sympathy. Nagumo was a haggard old man. He seemed to have aged 20 years in the last six months. "Glad to see you, Hara," he beamed. "You have done a terrific job. I am proud of you."

I blushed and, after a clumsy silence, ventured: "You don't look good, Admiral Nagumo. Are you sick?"

"Oh, just a touch of flu," he replied casually. "Once back home I'll be in good shape, and return soon to join you in the fight."

"Yes, sir, Sasebo's climate will cure you, and you deserve a rest. You have been in combat continuously for a year. Compared with your duty, I've been on a pleasure cruise."

"Well, you'll have a tougher time from now on. All the carriers except *Junyo* are going home for repairs. And we have lost some of our best flyers. It will be some time before new flyers can be properly trained."

"I beg your pardon, sir. But are *Shokaku*, *Zuikaku*, *Zuiho* and *Hiyo* all going to be 2,500 miles away in home waters? Must we fight with only *Junyo*'s air support?"

"Yes, Hara. Damage to our ships was minor at Santa Cruz, but we lost a number of our best pilots and flight leaders. Just between us, Hara, this battle was a tactical win, but a shattering strategic loss for Japan. As you know, I made a special study of America's war potential during my stay in the States. Considering the great superiority of our enemy's industrial capacity, we must win every battle overwhelmingly. This last one, unfortunately, was not an overwhelming victory."

Nagumo was relieved by Vice Admiral Jisaburo Ozawa, a noted destroyer expert, whose ability as a task force commander was unknown. The news was received with mixed feelings. We knew that Nagumo was completely exhausted and not fit for combat duty. Everyone hoped that our new commander would "work a wonder" and lead us to great victories.

Next I visited Kakuta, who had been promoted, to congratulate him. The vice admiral was in high spirits, as usual, but he grew serious when we discussed the fact that his task force would be operating with the only Japanese carrier in the Southwest Pacific.

The atmosphere in Admiral Yamamoto's Combined Fleet headquarters was grim and tense when I paid my courtesy call. Since the 2nd Division had taken such a beating, the Army had decided to commit the 38th Division to Guadalcanal. The Army asked Yamamoto for his full support in providing transportation. He had no choice but to comply.

Yamamoto knew that all his units were particularly tired after the Santa Cruz battle. But he had to send them out again, and this time with insufficient air cover. Yamamoto rationalized that the enemy had suffered such losses at Santa Cruz that he must be equally exhausted. For a while in early November this rationale appeared to have substance when 20 Japanese destroyers succeeded in landing the entire 38th Division in runs made on the 2nd, 7th, 8th, and 10th without enemy obstruction. But the United States Navy, exactly as in the previous operation, was waiting only for correct timing. The Americans came back and clashed with the Japanese in a series of savage sea battles off Guadalcanal November 12–15.

I took part in the first of this series and found that Nagumo's prediction was right. It was much tougher than any previous battle of my experience. I torpedoed and sank cruiser *Juneau* and destroyer *Barton*, and damaged Rear Admiral Daniel T. Callaghan's flagship *San Francisco*. Two shells from American cruiser *Helena* mowed down 43 of my men while I stood uninjured in their midst. I was fortunate to survive the battle.

This was one of the most fantastic sea battles of modern history in that it was fought at almost point-blank range between 14 Japanese and 13 American warships. Japan lost one battleship and two destroyers. Of the American fleet only three destroyers and one badly battered cruiser survived. A number of the American commanding officers were killed. It was one of the worst United States defeats of the entire Pacific War. Yet Japan was not entirely happy with the results. In fact, the commanding Japanese officer was court-martialed and retired for his "disgraceful leadership."

The battle was extremely confused. True details, except for the final score, will probably never be known. I have sought to reconstruct the battle in as complete, objective, and unbiased a manner as possible. Rear Admiral Koki Abe, a destroyer specialist and a combat veteran, commanded the Japanese ships. He was known for his extreme caution, which his critics claim often amounted to timidity. In the Santa Cruz battle he had commanded the vanguard unit which withstood United States air attacks, but failed to give effective chase to the fleeing enemy forces at the end.

Admiral Abe was not enthusiastic when he received Yamamoto's orders to lead a 14-ship squadron in a shore bombardment with incendiary shells, as Kurita had done the previous month. Abe did not believe the Americans were so stupid that the very same formula of attack could succeed again against the jealously guarded island.

Abe's mood was bad—particularly after learning of the October 11 battle off Savo Island, in which his lifelong friend, Rear Admiral Aritomo Goto, was killed. Survivors told Abe that they had been caught off guard by the enemy's radar-equipped ships led by Rear Admiral Norman Scott. Abe also knew that Goto had died believing he was the victim of friendly gunfire. On the smashed bridge of cruiser *Furutaka*, he breathed his last murmuring "*Bakayaro! Bakayaro!*" ("Stupid bastard!") The dying admiral uttered this profanity at what he believed to be the Japanese responsible for his death—also, perhaps at himself.

It was an ignoble death scene for a commanding admiral, and Abe, unhappy to hear of it, was determined not to follow Goto's example. Abe rightly interpreted the unopposed landing of the 38th Division as a deceptive lull, like the one which preceded the Santa Cruz battle. He was prepared for the worst.

My *Amatsukaze* left Truk November 9 in a group of eight destroyers with light cruiser *Nagara*. These ships joined Abe's two battleships and three more destroyers near Shortland Island in the early morning of the 12th. At 0830 that day, some 300 miles north of our destination, we were sighted by a B-17. *Junyo* planes were sent up by Kakuta to repel it, and the enemy plane left without dropping any bombs. But there was no doubt that the American plane had learned all he needed to know about our movement. This early enemy contact increased Abe's natural cautiousness. Also, by this time he was reading reports about the enemy's successful reinforcement efforts of November 11 and 12.

At 1330 Abe called for a drastic change in formation. Our single column was ordered into a tight double-half-ring formation. Five destroyers spread out in an arc, 8,000 meters ahead of cruiser *Nagara*. Six other destroyers drew a half ring fanning out from *Nagara*, with 2,000 meters between each ship. Flagship *Hiei* and sister *Kirishima*, 27,500-ton battleships, followed in column behind *Nagara* with 2,000 meters between each of them.

This tight formation was completed by 1400, when we were within 200 miles of Guadalcanal. I thought the aim of this formation was to prevent surprise attack by submarines or aircraft during our approach to the target area. I never dreamed that Abe was so concerned over a surprise attack that he would stick to this complex setup throughout the operation.

While we proceeded south at 18 knots, *Hiei* catapulted a scout plane. An hour passed with no message from the plane. No enemy planes came, either. The weather suddenly turned bad. Thick clouds gathered rapidly, bringing a tropical rainstorm. It was a tremendous, driving downpour which covered everything in darkness. It became difficult to see the nearest vessel. Nerves tightened in *Amatsukaze* as we waited expectantly for orders to slow down and change to a less complex formation. No such orders came.

To Abe the storm was a blessing. He knew that, cloaked in such a rain squall, his squadron was safe from air, surface and submarine attack. At his staff officers' advice to slow down, he snorted, "We must maintain this speed to reach the target area in good time."

A rain squall on tropical seas is normally limited to a small area, and seldom lasts more than a few minutes. To our growing amazement this squall appeared to be endless. We continued to advance at 18 knots. Two hours passed without letup of the cascading rain. Sweat streamed down our faces and bodies, despite the torrent of rain which drenched us like rats.

In peacetime, a force commander would never take his ships through a blinding storm at such speed and in such a complex formation. Anything could happen. On that day, however, not a single hitch developed in the long, almost blind dash. This performance, which lasted more than seven hours, attests to the seamanship of Japanese destroyer crews. The same high proficiency kept us from shooting each other in the confused battle which ensued. American reports claimed that some of our ships fired on each other, but this is not true.

On *Hiei*'s bridge Abe was in a buoyant mood. To his drenched officers he said, "This blessed squall is moving at the same speed and on the same course as we are."

The first message came in from the scout plane: "More than a dozen enemy warships seen off Lunga." And Abe chortled, "If Heaven continues to side with us like this, we may not even have to do business with them."

The squadron pressed on. Hours passed, but the rain squall did not abate. If anything, it got stronger. In all the years of my career, I never experienced such a rain. It was completely enervating. My officers were bored and expressed their boredom. Ensign Shoji said: "Phew! This rain is killing me. I am fed up. Let us fight the Americans, not this rain."

We were nearing our goal at 2200, if all 14 of our ships had navigated accurately. On board *Hiei*, Abe pored over the charts. Being a destroyer expert, he knew the skill of each of his skippers, and he knew that Rear Admiral Susumu Kimura in *Nagara* was one of Japan's top navigators.

Abe had just received a message from the Army observation post on Guadalcanal, saying, "Weather now very bad here." The *Hiei* scout plane, unheard of since its Lunga report, had gone on to the airstrip on Bougainville, rather than attempt locating *Hiei* in the storm. Admiral Abe realized that an accurate bombardment was impossible in the storm, so he made his decision to get out of the southbound squall. Accordingly, *Hiei* radioed by ultrashort wave: "All ships stand by for a simultaneous 180-degree turn."

I responded immediately, "From *Amatsukaze* to *Hiei*, standing by for a simultaneous 180-degree turn." The "execute" signal usually follows such a message within 30 seconds. I peered anxiously at my watch. Timing is essential in such a maneuver if collisions are to be avoided. One minute passed. No orders. One minute and thirty seconds. Still silent. For God's sake, I thought, this can't be true. I hollered into the radio room tube, "No execute order yet?"

A nervous voice replied, "No, sir. Van destroyers *Yudachi* and *Harusame* have not yet acknowledged the stand-by orders."

Three minutes passed. The tube boomed again: "Commander, *Hiei* is talking to *Yudachi* and *Harusame* on medium-wave frequency."

"Oh, no," I cried. "Has *Hiei* lost its mind?" Medium-wave radio can easily be picked up by the enemy. Thus our advantage of the rain squall would be squandered by *Hiei*.

At 2200 the radioman shouted, "*Hiei* orders 180-degree turn for all ships."

"Righto," I yelled at the top of my voice. "Turn 180 degrees!" My destroyer turned cleanly. I looked around desperately, fearful that another ship would suddenly appear on a collision course. Nothing happened. The drastic course change in a complex formation had miraculously succeeded.

Hiei's next order was, "All ships slow to 12 knots." Abe would not take unnecessary chances. From his many years of experience, he knew the original formation must be considerably askew after seven hours of blind marching and the drastic 180-degree turn. He was right. The formation was certainly scattered. I found out later that, even before the *Hiei* order, the five destroyers arcing 8,000 meters ahead of *Nagara* had to turn around to keep from running aground on Guadalcanal. The van arc was thus broken into two and three destroyers, and, thus divided, the two groups drew increasingly apart. This factor had an important bearing on the battle as it developed.

The rain squall finally ended at 2240, more than 30 minutes after we began the backward run. Abe ordered another 180-degree turn, to take us back to the dangerous island. I was sure he would now form the force into a single column. Our complex formation was good for opposing attacks by small torpedo boats, but we would be stymied if an enemy stormed us in strength.

Abe, maintaining his cautious stand, steadfastly held to the formation. For the first time, I began to doubt his wisdom. In battle it is bad to doubt one's leader. But I thought it was meaningless to keep such a formation after exposing ourselves to the enemy by our use of medium-wave radio. The enemy was sure to locate us and to strike.

"Small island, 60 degrees to port," a look-out's shout ended my musing. Almost simultaneously another hollered, "High mountains dead ahead."

I turned to the left and saw the black, chunky form of Savo Island looming out of the darkness. Forward I saw the mountains of Guadalcanal barely visible against a dark background of clouds. Feeling that battle was imminent, I trembled in excitement and breathed deeply of the balmy night breeze. I shouted: "Prepare for gun and torpedo attack to starboard! Gun range, 3,000 meters. Torpedo firing angle, 15 degrees."

Silence prevailed in our ship as every man went to his battle station. In *Hiei*, Abe was studying various reports. Guadalcanal observers radioed that the rain had just cleared and that they could see no enemy ships off Lunga. Bougainville reported sending out float planes. Fifty minutes after the second turnaround the squadron was about 12 miles offshore. Abe was still undecided, and sighed wearily, "Tell *Hiei* and *Kirishima* to ready main batteries for Type-3 shelling." In the two ships, the huge, one-ton shells, each loaded with hundreds of incendiary bombs, were stacked up and ready around the turrets. The gunners were itching for fire orders.

At 2342 a message came in from *Yudachi*: "Enemy sighted."

"What is the range and bearing?" Abe roared. "And where is *Yudachi*?"

Abe had hardly finished his outburst when *Hiei*'s masthead lookout frantically shouted, "Four black objects ahead . . . look like warships. Five degrees to starboard. Eight thousand meters . . . unsure yet. Visibility bad."

Abe covered his face. "*Yudachi* was 10,000 meters ahead on our starboard bow. Ask him distance."

Commander Masakane Suzuki, Abe's chief of staff, shouted at the lookout, "Is eight thousand correct? Confirm."

"It may be nine thousand, sir."

Abe, visibly shaken, said in a faltering voice, "Tell *Hiei* and *Kirishima* gunners to replace all those incendiaries with armor piercing, and set turrets for firing forward." Abe staggered to his chair. He was in agony. Should he order the two battleships to turn around while they changed shells? He deliberated and finally decided not to, figuring that at such short range his battleships would be sitting ducks for the oncoming enemy. This indecision, it was later ruled, cost him his ship.

On the decks of the two battleships there was pandemonium. Almost every hand had left his battle station to help cart away the Type-3 shells. There was a stampede in the magazines, men pushing and kicking to reach the armor-piercing shells stored deep inside. At a range of 9,000 meters capital ships can fire with deadly accuracy. Just one shell landing on the deck of either of these battleships, stacked high with mountains of incendiary shells, could ignite it like a mammoth match box.

Hiei's signal officers screamed hysterically over the radio. Ultrashort wave, ordinary short wave and medium wave—all available frequencies were used to announce the presence of the enemy. Security precautions were thrown to the winds.

On *Amatsukaze's* bridge the notice came as no surprise. I watched uneasily, however, as *Hiei's* crewmen scurried like scared rats. My lookouts still could not see any enemy ships, and they squirmed. "No sweat, boys," I shouted. "We are well prepared to engage when the distance is down to 3,000 meters."

Mysteriously, for eight long minutes, no shells came from the enemy. Their combined speed of 40 knots meant that the two forces were closing at a rate of 1,200 meters per minute. And still no gunfire! What a contrast to the Java Sea Battle, when both sides started firing at a range of more than 25,000 meters. The pandemonium in *Hiei* and *Kirishima* was over. All incendiaries had been removed and the guns were ready to fire regular armor-piecing shells.

Why had the enemy allowed us to gain the precious eight minutes which saved us from catastrophe? Seeking an explanation, I have read American postwar accounts of the battle. The answer was complex and difficult to come by because most of the high-ranking officers in the American task force died in this action. All versions I read were based on fragmentary and often conflicting accounts by survivors. I learned, however, that the enemy's inability to open fire during the critical eight minutes was the result of an impossible deployment and confused command.

At 2341, when *Yudachi* reported her sighting, the enemy force was advancing in a single column headed directly against the core of the Japanese unit. From such a formation only the leading ship could fire. That accounts for the enemy gun inactivity at the outset, but it does not explain subsequent events. Why did they not swing sharply to the right to bring their turrets into firing position? Why did they not choose the other alternative of going close inshore to flank our ships to starboard? These questions still puzzle me.

There were other unusual things about this battle. One of these was the movement of our destroyer *Yudachi*. Her skipper, Commander Kiyoshi Kikkawa, was a close friend, and after the battle he explained this to me.

"My blunder was in being overcautious. I had been in the Bali sea battle the previous February. In that action my destroyer *Mitsushio* was flanked and badly damaged while I was directing our fire on a target in another direction. I never forgot that bitter lesson.

"On November 12 my *Yudachi* with *Harusame* was searching for the three other ships with which we had originally formed the vanguard arc. In our hunting we never guessed that the earlier mixup in the two 180-degree turns had brought the other three to the rear instead of the van.

"I was flabbergasted to see an enemy destroyer suddenly emerging from the darkness, and bearing down to strike us amidship. The nightmare of Bali flashed to my mind. Anyway, I was not ready to fire. We frantically turned away, radioing the discovery to *Hiei*, but we could not give positions because we did not know where we were relative to our own forces.

"We ran for a few minutes and I saw gunfire. I was covered with confusion and shame. I ordered *Yudachi* about to head back toward the American column. By that time every man in my ship was boiling mad—at our failure to hit the enemy.

"From then on, *Yudachi* fought valiantly until she sank. *Harusame*, however, went on to join *Nagara*. Apparently it lost track of us in the darkness. *Yudachi* was running on overboost at 35 knots."

Not only was the vanguard arc broken but also the inner ring. The seven hours of blind march and the two rapid 180-degree turns were too severe a test for any formation.

Hiei shone its searchlight at 2350 to find that *Nagara* was no longer 2,000 meters ahead, as it had been. The 36-knot cruiser had advanced some 5,000 meters ahead of its position and veered to port in front of destroyer *Yukikaze*, which was preceding my ship by 2,000 meters. When *Hiei*'s light spotted cruiser *Atlanta*, an estimated 5,000 meters away, the latter responded instantly with a full salvo of five-inch guns. Hastily aimed, all 12 shells fell some 2,000 meters short of *Hiei*.

Thirty seconds later, *Hiei*, swinging to port, opened with its eight 14-inch guns. A range of 5,000 meters is almost point-blank for guns of this size. Almost all the one-ton shells hit *Atlanta*. Rear Admiral Norman Scott and practically all other officers on the bridge were killed in an instant. Thus Abe's opening salvo avenged his friend Goto. It was one of the most accurate ship-to-ship bombardments of the entire Pacific War.

Hiei paid a high price for her use of the searchlight. Four American destroyers in front of *Atlanta* concentrated their fire on *Hiei* at distances ranging from a few hundred to 2,000 yards. Lead ship *Cushing* poured several main battery salvos and torrents of machine-gun fire onto *Hiei's* bridge. Badly aimed, however, these shells and tracers cascaded down around my *Amatsukaze*. The spectacle was so dazzling that for many moments I stood blinded on the bridge. Fortunately no hits were scored on my ship.

Cushing is reported to have released six torpedoes at *Hiei*. None hit. If they overran, none of my crewmen saw them. I am thus inclined to doubt the claim. *Cushing's* shells and tracers, however, kept crossing over *Hiei* and showering down around *Amatsukaze*, seeming to pin us down. Ahead to port was the black coastline of Florida Island, with its many reefs. I shouted, "Gain speed! Let's get the hell out of here to starboard!"

The ship responded quickly. It broke away from *Hiei* and, followed by destroyer *Yukikaze*, raced past to starboard of *Nagara*. I saw numerous American ships moving like wraiths in the darkness along the coast of Guadalcanal to the right. "Turn full right, flank speed!"

I decided to tackle the enemy ships and deal them a blow before they got in position to hit our confined formation. The next moment, the wraith-like images disappeared into the black coastline. Momentarily blinded by the shells and tracers, I blinked and stared frantically until tears came to my eyes. I gazed intently ahead. Three Japanese destroyers suddenly appeared from *Hiei's* right flank, preventing me from shooting at the enemy.

Despairing of offensive action at the moment, I looked at *Hiei*. Her rugged mast was in flames. American destroyer *Laffey* must have scored some hits. I cursed that misfortune and then noticed that the three friendly destroyers had started a swerve to port, obviously trying to cover *Hiei* from the rear. The three ships—*Akatsuki*, *Inazuma* and *Ikazuchi*—were newer ships and faster than mine. I planned to follow behind their column.

All of a sudden a couple of flares lit up ahead. Later I learned from Admiral Kimura that *Nagara* had fired them. Five or six enemy ships in a column emerged clearly. The nearest was 5,000 meters, 30 degrees on my starboard bow, approaching on a roughly parallel course. I gulped. My heart bubbled with excitement. This was the chance to prove my torpedo theory. Though adopted as doctrine by the Imperial Navy, it had remained unproved. This was my chance.

Lieutenant Masatoshi Miyoshi, my torpedo officer, yelled impatiently, "Commander, let's fire the fish!"

I answered, "Get ready, fishermen!" and barked instructions: "The target 30 degrees to starboard, is approaching. Adjusted firing angle, 15 degrees. Navigators, turn right, close in and follow a hyperbola."

The crew responded instantly. The distance closed steadily as the adversaries approached at a combined speed of 60 knots. Miyoshi glared at me eagerly, impatiently, but I ignored him. The enemy strangely failed to open fire. Even if they did, they could not catch me in the hyperbola run, though we were separated by only 3,000 meters. "Ready torpedoes, fire!" I yelled.

Eight big fish jumped in rapid succession and sped on their way. I watched prayerfully. It was 2354. Gusts of wind buffeted us on the bridge and we were showered by spray kicked up by the dashing ship. As we turned left again, slackening speed, another couple of flares filled the sky, limning a column of four enemy destroyers, a distance of only a few hundred yards between each. *Yudachi*, guns blazing, had cut in front of the American column, almost grazing the bows of *Aaron Ward*, which made a violent turn to avoid it.

The second ship, *Barton*, stopped short to avoid collision with *Aaron Ward*. At that moment, two minutes after the launching of my torpedoes, two pillars of fire shot high in the air from *Barton*. These fireworks subsided so quickly that I rubbed my eyes in disbelief. The ship, broken in two, sank instantly.

I heaved a deep sigh. It was a spectacular kill and there was a roaring ovation from my crew, but I didn't hear it. It was all too easy. My own feeling was one of satisfaction rather than exultation. It was the first real war-test of my theory, which was now a proved formula.

The flares burned down and out. In the renewed darkness, *Amatsukaze* looped out of her firing hyperbola, and headed back to the west, while I determined what to do. In the distance I could see *Hiei*, barely silhouetted by its own fires. We headed in her direction. A few minutes later we saw dim, intermittent flashes to port. The flashes outlined a sleek ship . . . with four masts! Definitely enemy, possibly a cruiser!

"Torpedoes, ready!" I ordered. "Target 70 degrees to port."

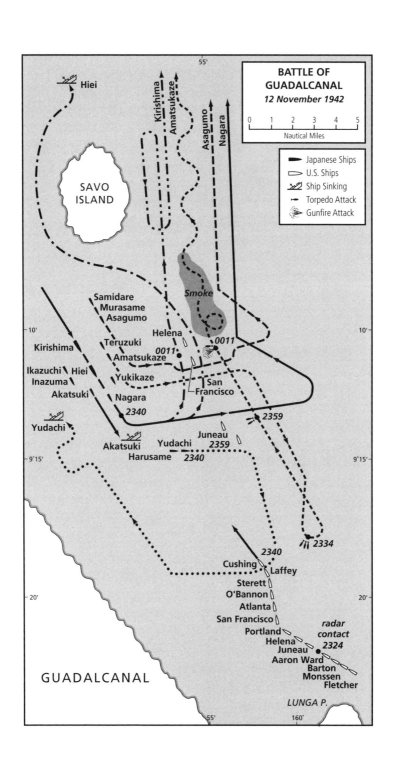

BATTLE OF
GUADALCANAL
12 November 1942

0   1   2   3   4   5
Nautical Miles

Japanese Ships
U.S. Ships
Ship Sinking
Torpedo Attack
Gunfire Attack

Hiei

SAVO
ISLAND

Kirishima
Amatsukaze
Asagumo
Nagara

Smoke

55'

Samidare
Murasame
Asagumo

Helena
0011

0011

Teruzuki
Amatsukaze

Kirishima

Yukikaze

San
Francisco

Ikazuchi Hiei
Inazuma
Akatsuki

Nagara
2340

2359

Yudachi

Akatsuki   Yudachi   Juneau
Harusame   2340   2359

Juneau
2359

2334

2340

Cushing   Laffey
Sterett
O'Bannon
Atlanta
San Francisco

Portland
Helena
Juneau
Aaron Ward
Barton
Monssen
Fletcher

*radar
contact*
2324

10'

9°15'

20'

10'

9°15'

20'

GUADALCANAL

LUNGA P.

55'   160'

"Torpedoes ready, sir," Lieutenant Miyoshi called back like a student answering his professor, with no trace of his earlier impatience.

"All right, hold it, hold it . . . hold it, the target is moving ahead. Easy, easy . . . easier target than the last. Miyoshi, use only four torpedoes this time, not eight . . . steady, steady . . . Fire!"

In hushed silence, the four deadly fish left at 2359. Three minutes and 40 seconds later, a large, reddish flame rose from our target. It was American cruiser *Juneau*, that had been exchanging gunfire with *Yudachi*. My crewmen roared with joy.

Lieutenant Shimizu, the gunnery officer, wanted to bombard the target and finish it off. I said, "No, Shimizu. Let's leave the spoil for our friend *Yudachi*. Don't be impatient. We'll have plenty of targets. Shelling at this stage would only expose our position to the enemy."

Amatsukaze went straight ahead. Meanwhile savage fights were going on in other places. Commander Hideo Sekino of *Hiei* later recounted to me how the flagship fought. Destroyer *Cushing*, after its attack on *Hiei*, was caught by fire from destroyer *Terutsuki*. The Japanese ship had advanced from its position on *Hiei*'s port quarter and, once *Cushing* fell under the scrutiny of Japanese searchlights, it was finished off by a point-blank salvo from *Terutsuki*.

The second American destroyer *Laffey* almost collided with *Hiei*. While skidding away from a close shave, *Laffey* let loose a torrent of machine-gun fire at *Hiei*'s mast, riddling the bridge. Captain Suzuki was killed instantly; others, including Admiral Abe, were wounded. *Hiei*'s big guns and *Terutsuki*'s torpedoes caught *Laffey* going away. The destroyer was hit mercilessly and sunk within a few minutes.

Destroyer *Sterrett*, next in line, fired torpedoes at *Hiei*. All missed. *O'Bannon*, following, shelled the battleship and scored many hits. *Hiei*'s internal communications went dead at this time, and the Japanese flagship started to withdraw from action.

This was just about midnight, and the fighting became terribly confused. A free-for-all followed. Destroyer *Akatsuki*, from her original position 2,000 meters to starboard of *Hiei*, had dashed forward and fired torpedoes which hit cruiser *Atlanta*.

Akatsuki thus became caught in fatal crossfire between *San Francisco* and an American destroyer, and was sunk with almost her entire crew. *San Francisco* was still battering *Akatsuki* when battleship *Kirishima* approached and finished off flagship *San Francisco* with deadly blows from its powerful

14-inch guns. *Kirishima* then left the area quickly in compliance with Abe's orders.

Commander Kikkawa, skipper of *Yudachi*, narrated the night's activities of his destroyer. "When we returned and crossed the American column I saw an enemy destroyer on the port beam coming directly at me. There was no time to aim torpedoes. While exchanging gunfire, I swung hard right to rattle the enemy's aim and timing.

"After running for a few minutes, I saw cruiser *Juneau* to starboard, on a parallel course. *Yudachi* fired eight torpedoes at her, but all missed. The cruiser answered with a powerful salvo, to which I could respond only with guns. That was bad. I felt I was pinned at last. A destroyer cannot outgun a cruiser. Then all of a sudden, a burst of flames rose from the cruiser. It stopped firing, spread smoke screens and quit the fight. It was your *Amatsukaze* that saved me."

When *Akatsuki* was sunk, the two Japanese destroyers next behind her vengefully attacked *San Francisco* and *Portland*. The latter responded with gunfire on *Inazuma* and *Ikazuchi*. At the same time unpredictable *Yudachi* was closing *Portland* on the port quarter. Kikkawa said, "I just repeated your tactics, Hara, and released eight torpedoes at the cruiser which was occupied with fighting in the other direction. The ship burst into flames when our torpedoes hit.

"Our jubilation was cut short when shells showered down on us. I was a victim of the same tactics we had just used and now we were being bashed by someone off our stern."

This must have been American destroyer *Aaron Ward*, which had been putting up a determined battle since *Yudachi* had crossed its path some 10 minutes earlier.

About that same time, my *Amatsukaze* was moving northwest toward the crippled flagship. The scene was strangely quiet. Dim, distant gunfire appeared like fireworks. It was impossible to tell who was fighting. I had decided to join *Hiei* which, with its deck fires, was the only ship that could be recognized. I asked if there were any important messages. A radioman replied, "No, sir, but we are not reading *Hiei*. Her communications must be out."

Glumly I looked at my watch. It was 13 minutes past midnight. A red flash far to the west proved to be another ship set afire. That was *Yudachi*. I screamed as a big ship suddenly appeared out of the darkness just in front of us. Lieutenant Kinjuro Matsumoto spun the helm frantically to the right.

There was nothing that the rest of us on the bridge could do but watch help-lessly as the ships drew swiftly closer. Just as a collision seemed inevitable, *Amatsukaze* responded to her rudder and we avoided a collision.

I wondered what ship it could be. We passed so close I could not see its whole shape. There was no apparent activity on board. It had no turrets, but it was not a merchant ship. It was familiar and yet I couldn't place it. This dis-turbed me as I knew every kind of ship and decided that this must be *Jingei!* She was a submarine tender, and had no turrets. But what was she doing here? The next moment I realized it could not be *Jingei*, and knew this must be an enemy ship. I jumped up and yelled, "Gunners! Torpedomen! Stand ready to port!"

Lieutenants Miyoshi and Shimizu shouted their readiness but, at the crucial moment, I wavered again. We must identify the ship for sure, and not fire at a friend under any circumstances. In desperation I ordered search-lights. Our target appeared unmistakably to be an enemy cruiser. I ordered Open Fire with everything we had.

Four torpedoes leaped out. They were the last of our full load of sixteen. All six of our 4-inch guns roared for the first time in this battle. Enthusiastic gun crews fired rapid salvos. Almost every shell hit the target in this point-blank bombardment. Explosions were so near that the blasts were shaking me. Fires shot up at scores of places. Yet the enemy seemed so taken by sur-prise that there was no counterattack.

Some 20 seconds after we opened the attack, four solid underwater sounds were detected. I held my breath, anticipating mighty explosions. Ten seconds passed, but there was no detonation. As the ship wobbled on, I realized my stupid mistake. Every Japanese torpedo had a safety device which prevented detonation under any circumstance within 500 meters of its launching, and our target was no more than 500 meters away. I cursed my stupidity. Through haste I had lost the chance to make a certain sinking.

One blunder usually follows another, and it did here. Wild with anger at myself, I forgot to order the searchlight to be turned off. Kikkawa had reminded me that a searchlight always attracts enemy eyes. And I had forgot-ten the lesson. The enemy ship swerved to the left, perhaps to avoid collision, but its movements were erratic.

Meanwhile my gun crews continued firing as though shell-drunk. Every shot was hitting home. The phantom ship wobbled on, spewing fire and smoke throughout its length. This was *San Francisco*, and our near-collision must have occurred just after Admiral Callaghan and his staff, as well as the cruiser's own staff, had been wiped out by other Japanese ships. The turrets, whose absence puzzled me, had been blown to bits by direct hits from *Kirishima*'s 14-inch guns.

All of a sudden shells were failing around my ship. I thought that the phantom ship had revived and was offering a last-ditch fight. Some shells hit *Amatsukaze*. "Gunners, don't budge an inch," I roared. "Finish it off." Evidently I was shell-drunk too. Our guns continued to pump shells into the enemy ship—my third blunder.

Actually there were no shells coming from the dying *San Francisco*. A shrieking voice came through the deafening roar of guns. Warrant Officer Shigeru Iwata was shouting at me from his observation post just above the bridge: "Commander, another cruiser is sniping at us from 70 degrees to port!"

My head snapped to that direction, and there was another enemy cruiser. I stood frozen from head to toe, but finally yelled, "Douse searchlight, stop shelling, spread smoke screen!" I had not finished the order when the third salvo from the new enemy, later identified as *Helena*, reached *Amatsukaze*. Two shells landed very near. I hunched my back and clung to the railing. The blast was so strong, it almost threw me off the bridge. The detonations were deafening. I got sluggishly to my feet, but my mind was a complete blank for several seconds. Next, I felt over my body, but found no wounds.

Looking around I saw with relief that all my nearby fellow officers were alive. What about others? I saw Iwata prostrate, hanging over the range-finding gear. "Iwata, Iwata," I cried. "What's the matter with you?" He did not move. Blood covered his head. A piece of shrapnel had pierced his skull, killing him instantly.

A shell had exploded at the fire director station immediately above Iwata's observation post. "Shimizu! Shimizu!" I called at his voice tube. "How are you?" No reply came through. "Radiomen! Report!" I shouted into another tube. This tube was also dead silent.

A second shell had pierced the deck slightly below the bridge and exploded in the radio room, killing everyone in it. The ship was still turning sharply to the right and was now starting into a loop. "Matsumoto, turn the helm!" I shouted.

"I did turn, sir, but there is no response!"

Flames rose from under the bridge, apparently from the radio room. More fires flared. *Helena* had really done a job on us. "Damn it! Let's return fire!"

A gunner struggled to the bridge, blood dripping from a shoulder wound. "Sir, the turrets won't move. The hydraulic system has failed."

An orderly came from the engine room, shouting, "The rudder mechanism no longer works, sir. The hydraulics have failed."

I talked to both men at once. "What happened to Shimizu? How's the engine? Any fuel fires?"

"Lieutenant Shimizu was blasted from the ship, sir, leaving behind only one of his legs."

"The engine works unimpaired, sir. The fuel has not caught fire."

"All right, you, Gunner, go get first aid. Matsumoto, go to the engine room and check. Send reports to me every three minutes."

The ship had come full circle on the ocean and was about to begin a second loop. *Helena*'s shells were still raining around, but very few were now hitting. Near-misses shook the ship violently. More fires were starting, but crewmen were active with water hoses. Our guns were still silent, and we had no torpedoes. If the enemy closed, we would be as defenseless as a bull in a slaughterhouse.

Amatsukaze's movements were getting more erratic and she started her second circle in dense smoke. The rain of shells diminished as the enemy ship at last began to move away. Good! He was not going to finish the job.

An orderly came with Matsumoto's message. "The hydraulic system is definitely out. We'll have to operate the rudder with manpower. Please confirm."

"All right, tell him to halt the ship for the shift to manpower operation right away."

Miyoshi winced and said, "Are we going to stop right here, sir? So near the enemy?"

"Certainly, before we encounter more enemy ships." One of the voice pipes squawked. It was Matsumoto reporting. "Commander, we have patched some of the damage."

"Good, Matsumoto. Stop the ship and shift the rudder for manpower operation."

As the ship slowly shuddered to a halt, the enemy shelling stopped completely. Apparently the enemy ship had turned around thinking that *Amatsukaze* was done for. Through the dense smoke I could no longer see the enemy ship. Actually *Helena* was having its own troubles, more serious than mine. As it had caught me unaware, so it was caught unaware by three freshly arrived Japanese destroyers. The trio—*Asagumo, Murasame* and *Samidare*—originally had been in the vanguard arc formation with *Yudachi* and *Haru-same*. Because of the drastic prebattle maneuvers, they had fallen to the rear just before the battle started. They finally came on the scene barely in time to catch *Helena*.

The enemy cruiser was battered helpless by three ships emerging from nowhere. Before it could determine who and where the new opponents were, *Helena* was defeated. *Murasame's* torpedoes delivered fatal blows but the cruiser miraculously drifted a few more hours before sinking.

Asagumo, Murasame's teammate, turned its guns toward another enemy ship approaching from the east. Destroyer *Monssen*, her identification lamps lit, approached naively in the belief that the three prowling ships were friendly. Her lamps were suicidal, just as my searchlight had been when it attracted *Helena*. Several rapid salvos disabled *Monssen*, and *Asagumo* finished her with torpedoes. *Monssen* had been followed closely by *Fletcher*, who, in no mood to challenge the Japanese trio, turned tail and cleared out.

Sterrett, one of the surviving enemy destroyers, claimed the sinking of a Japanese destroyer at this time and location with two torpedo hits. But there was no such Japanese destroyer. *Akatsuki* had sunk some time earlier, and *Yudachi* was still burning several miles to the west. It appears evident that *Sterrett* must have mistakenly sunk an American vessel. Her victim must have been one that was still barely adrift after absorbing a surfeit of Japanese torpedoes and shells.

Some American versions say that Japanese guns fired on Japanese ships near the end of this battle. After checking with all my friends who took part in the battle, and after examining damage to the surviving Japanese destroyers, I can definitely state that this contention is unfounded. On the other hand, many of my friends say that the American ships exchanged gunfire among themselves in this battle.

After *Amatsukaze's* helm and rudder were disengaged from the shattered hydraulic system, we resumed navigation. Luckily the engines were in good order, and we quickly picked up a 20-knot speed. It is always difficult to handle the rudder of a 2,500-ton ship manually, and *Amatsukaze* had been badly battered. Her gears were twisted and there were many gaping holes in the hull. The ship moved like a drunken man, skidding wildly from side to side. After a few painful minutes of watching this erratic movement I knew what had to be done, and spoke into the tube: "Matsumoto, I'll take over. This manpower operation requires experience. Your timing is off. From now on I'll give steering orders from up here and you pass them to your boys."

Ten husky men dripped sweat handling the rudder. It was a backbreaking task. But my chore wasn't easy. I had to keep shouting almost steadily. My voice croaked, and sweat streamed down my face. The veering movement continued, but the steering was less erratic.

At 0300 Miyoshi reported that all fires were under control. A few minutes later I saw *Hiei* to port. Her fires appeared to have subsided but the flagship was almost at a standstill. There were no Japanese ships around to offer help. I felt sorry for my friends in the doomed ship, but my ship was in no shape to help anyone. The most I could do was to keep her going in a northerly direction.

It was barely possible for us to negotiate the narrow waters of Indispensable Strait. Mustering all my strength and determination, I kept shouting directions into the voice tube, and we kept moving. At the first sign of daylight Ensign Shoji shouted, "Three enemy planes approach."

I ordered, "Miyoshi, take command of the guns. Do your best."

The torpedo officer darted from the bridge. An orderly reported shortly, "No guns rotate, and only No. 1 gun can be elevated skyward."

That lone gun fired rapidly as the planes came close. They overestimated our speed and released their bombs too early. The nearest one fell some 300 meters off our bows. After one pass the planes turned back toward Guadalcanal. More planes would probably follow, but brooding was of no use. We had work to do just keeping the ship moving forward, and we kept at it.

Our luck seemed about to run out when Shoji next reported, "Commander, a ship sighted 9,000 meters ahead, speeding straight for us! What should we do, sir?"

Instead of replying, I yelled into the pipe again: "Matsumoto, an undetermined ship is sighted ahead. Make your maximum speed. We can do nothing but ram if it is the enemy."

Shoji dashed out to prepare the crew for this drastic action. I glanced again at the ship. It was closing on us at a speed of well over 30 knots. After a tense minute I breathed a deep sigh of relief, and called my orderly to summon Shoji quickly. "It's a Japanese destroyer . . . yes, *Yukikaze*, unmistakably."

Shoji came back leaping and bouncing with joy and relief. From a distance of 3,000 meters a *Yukikaze* signalman started waving flags. They were distinct in the morning light: "Heartiest congratulations to *Amatsukaze*. We're heading to assist *Hiei*. Anything we can do for you?"

My signalman immediately relayed my answer, "Thanks for your greetings. Don't bother about us. Go ahead full speed. Enemy planes already spotted us, very probably *Hiei* too. Be prepared for air attack. Good luck!"

We passed *Yukikaze* on our port beam at a distance of 1,000 meters. Crews on deck exchanged greetings. Though they had traveled a long way together in the meantime, this was the first time the two ships had seen each other since early the previous day. *Yukikaze* had been stationed immediately ahead of *Amatsukaze* in Abe's complex formation. We had not been visible to each other for the many hours of our blind march. In the battle, *Yukikaze* and cruiser *Nagara* were among the first to withdraw from the area. *Yukikaze* had not received a single hit.

My warning to *Yukikaze* proved right. Scores of Marine bombers swarmed over *Hiei* and demolished her. Admiral Abe ordered *Hiei* scuttled before abandoning ship, as *Yukikaze* came alongside. It was this scuttling order which cost the jobs of Abe and Captain Masao Nishida, *Hiei*'s skipper, a few days later.

After passing *Yukikaze*, my ship slowed to its previous 20 knots. We were out of the hazardous strait and in a wide area. Our worries about shoals and reefs were over. But new worries cropped up. Daylight was unwelcome to a lone crippled ship, in an area infested by enemy submarines.

The sonar equipment in Japanese destroyers, as explained earlier, was not of a high standard. Even when in working order, it was useless when a ship was running at 20 knots or better. *Amatsukaze*'s sonar was completely dead at this time. "Matsumoto, you had better change your rudder detail every hour. We'll need real muscular strength to make any abrupt turns. Submarines may set on us at any moment."

Strangely enough, for the next 12 hours there were no attacks. Enemy submarines must have seen *Amatsukaze*. Perhaps there was no attack because they did not realize that the lone wolf was limping. *Amatsukaze* was running at a steady 20 knots. Its skidding to left and right must have seemed like an intentional zigzag pattern. Had they come close, they would have seen how beaten up and crippled we were.

About 1500 another Japanese destroyer loomed on the horizon. Knowing we had reached safety, I suddenly felt exhausted. Accurate navigation had brought us to a spot about 250 miles north of Guadalcanal, where Vice Admiral

Takeo Kurita's fleet was standing by to sortie that night. As we closed in, I found destroyer *Terutsuki*, another companion of the Abe fleet. My signalman sent a message inquiring as to the general situation.

A reply came quickly. "Welcome home, *Amatsukaze*. Our heartiest congratulations. You were reported lost hours ago. Few of us expected your return. Our fleet did well. Only *Hiei* and *Yudachi* were reported dead in the water. *Akatsuki* has not been heard from, and is considered lost. *Murasame* and *Ikazuchi* received shell hits, none vital. Again congratulations. You worked a wonder. We are proud of you."

As we approached *Terutsuki*, again most all of her crew moved to the railings and waved at us, calling, "Atta boy, *Amatsukaze*!" Several other ships repeated the same kind of welcome for us. But I felt no triumph at all. My heart was heavy with remorse at my blunders. *Amatsukaze* was already inside the formation of Kurita's ships, and was slowing down. His flagship, 27,500-ton battleship *Kongo*, emerged like a fortress. Her signalman was sending a flag message to us.

"From Admiral Kurita to Commander Hara: I salute your brave return and am pleased to inform you I have orders for you to go along in my sortie. I shall be proud to have you with us. Acknowledge."

I was astounded at this message, and replied promptly, "From Commander Hara to Admiral Kurita: Your compliments unwarranted. I return a cripple with loss of 43 crewmen including gunnery officer. We are in need of repair. We are on manual steering now."

A few minutes later *Kongo*'s message came: "Admiral Kurita orders you to return to Truk immediately. We repeat our respects to you all the same. *Bon voyage* and good luck! See you again!"

Kongo blurred through my tears as I read this warm message. I was choked up but managed to rasp into the voice tube, "Matsumoto, turn to starboard. We are going home."

"Yes, sir," Matsumoto replied. "Say, Commander, you sound tired. Why don't you rest? You have been shouting continuously for the past 15 hours. I have learned enough of the rhythm and timing from your rudder directions to handle it now."

"Thank you, Matsumoto, I guess you are right. You take over." I sat down for the first time in more than 24 hours. Minutes later I sprang from the chair. I had forgotten something. "Miyoshi! Shoji! We must conduct funeral services before dark."

Forty-three bodies—some mere token remains—were brought to the foredeck. Close friends of each of the deceased came forward, cleansed the bodies with hot fresh water and wrapped them in canvas. Precious distilled water was used freely for this ceremony. The wrapped and weighted bodies were dropped into the sea while buglers sounded a farewell and the crew saluted.

A sea burial is always sad. I had attended several such services, but never one so sad as this. When Miyoshi and Shoji consigned the first remains—a leg of Lieutenant Kazue Shimizu, the gunnery officer—to the sea, I wept. Shimizu, a headstrong man, had often argued with me, but he was a fine man and an excellent officer. If I had followed his recommendation and closed with *Juneau*, perhaps I would not have committed the blunders which cost his life.

Two petty officers stepped forward to take care of the body of Warrant Officer Iwata—the man who, by sighting *Helena*, had once saved the ship and crew. I walked down from the bridge. The crew stared. It was the first time I had left the bridge since the start of this operation. "Iwata was my friend. I will take care of his remains." The two men gaped when I doffed my uniform jacket and put it over Iwata. "Iwata, farewell," I murmured. "Rest in peace." Tears flooded my eyes as I stood at attention and saluted. Trudging back to the bridge, I saw many crewmen weeping like children, several wiping their eyes with their fists.

As I watched the setting of the big, fiery sun I pledged never to repeat my mistakes. It was completely dark by the time the funeral services ended. *Amatsukaze* circled the burial area once while the crew offered prayers in a final farewell to their 43 buddies, and then continued to the north.

Matsumoto, a young graduate of the merchant marine school, had learned the manual handling of the rudder very quickly. The ship advanced with a minimum of skidding, and 24 hours later, on November 14, *Amatsukaze* anchored in Truk's quiet atoll. At Truk I heard that Japanese submarine *I-26* had just torpedoed and sunk a crippled United States cruiser near Guadalcanal. It was years later, however, that I learned that this was cruiser *Juneau* which *Amatsukaze* had hit and disabled.

The battle ended unquestionably in a Japanese victory, but the win was purely tactical. Strategically the enemy had won because the Abe force failed to deliver a single incendiary shell to Guadalcanal airfields. Nine American warships were sunk, but not in vain. They contributed greatly to the American side in the bitter contest for this island.

Admiral Yamamoto at Truk was upset by the failure of Abe's mission. *Hiei* was the first Japanese battleship to be sunk in the war. Its scuttling infuriated Yamamoto, who had been quite lenient with earlier blunders committed by others of his men.

The high command in Tokyo was also stung. The anger of the top admirals did not abate when they heard of Vice Admiral Nobutake Kondo's failure, immediately following that of Abe. A panel of admirals was established to conduct a secret court of inquiry. Abe and Captain Nishida, *Hiei*'s skipper, were called to testify. They offered no defense of their actions or mistakes. The court's verdict was "retirement" for the two officers, almost the equivalent of the U.S. Navy's "dishonorable discharge." They were allowed pensions, but were barred from public office.

On the night of November 13, Rear Admiral Shoji Nishimura's squadron of three cruisers and four destroyers closed the coast of Guadalcanal and shelled the airfields. The shelling was so ineffective that Marine planes rose from these airfields next morning. They teamed with carrier *Enterprise* planes and swooped on a Japanese convoy of 11 transports, sinking or disabling seven of them. The planes also sank cruiser *Kinugasa* and heavily damaged three destroyers.

Admiral Kondo, deputy commander in chief of the Combined Fleet, was ordered to replace Kurita as leader of the next sortie on the night of November 14. Two 13,000-ton cruisers, *Atago* and *Takao*, under Kondo's direct command, were suddenly teamed with the original Abe fleet, less *Hiei* and three destroyers.

Admiral Yamamoto's choice of Kondo proved to be a disastrous mistake. It is still a mystery to me why Yamamoto thought so highly of Kondo, even after his halfhearted actions in two earlier important battles. Kondo's three battleships, small cruiser and nine destroyers encountered a clearly inferior American force of two battleships and four destroyers led by Rear Admiral Willis Augustus Lee. Despite his distinct numerical advantage, Kondo lost battleship *Kirishima* and a destroyer, while Lee lost only three destroyers.

Kondo's two fast cruisers were still intact. But Kondo ordered their withdrawal without even trying to give chase to the American ships. It was his third such halfhearted effort in four months.

Admiral Yamamoto, who was stern with Abe, was strangely lenient with Kondo. Many of Kondo's officers were ashamed of him and of themselves. They preferred not to talk about the battle. Kondo was the British-gentleman sort of man. He was amiable and affable to everyone and was known as a scholar. He was always good to me and I had great respect for him. But I must say that it was one of Yamamoto's greatest errors that he so greatly overvalued Kondo's fighting ability. Kondo might have been a great commandant of the Naval Academy, but he was a misfit as commander of a naval fighting unit.

7

At Truk *Amatsukaze* went alongside repair ship *Akashi*, whose chief engineer promptly came on board to inspect our damage. I acknowledged that our ship had been banged up a bit, but pointed out that she had made it back to port under her own steam, and concluded with my hope that *Amatsukaze* could be patched up without delay so that we might join the fleet again in a week or ten days.

The engineer smiled patiently and said, "Commander Hara, most skippers underestimate damage in their own ship, and, when engaged in battle, do things considered impossible in a normal voyage. Let's look around. I understand you fitted out this ship. Will you come along and explain her finer points?"

Amatsukaze was indeed my baby. As her fitting-out officer, I had been at her launching early in 1940 and had spent the next six months supervising her every need. She was the finest destroyer of her day, this 2,500-ton fighting ship, and I knew every inch of her.

The engineer and I spent a day going over her injuries. By the end of the tour my optimism had fallen flat on its face. In her hull we counted 32 holes larger than one meter in diameter. In addition there were five smaller holes which had been bored by dud shells. After 40 small shrapnel holes I stopped counting. That American cruiser had done a real job, which I had estimated as only three hits. The engineer was right. No longer a prize destroyer, *Amatsukaze* was but a floating wreck.

At the end of the tour we came to my cabin where I flopped into a chair, depressed and morose. The engineer said understandingly, "Let me congratulate you on magnificent seamanship in bringing your ship back at all, let alone in such good time. You have really worked a miracle, but it cannot be repeated."

I recognized the truth of his words, but was so dispirited that I had nothing to say. He continued, "As you must realize, we cannot concentrate all our efforts on your *Amatsukaze*. There are others that need repairs too. I estimate that it will take a month to patch up your ship enough to get back to Japan. There precision parts will be available and it should be possible to have *Amatsukaze* fully seaworthy in one month."

"But," I stammered, "there is evidence that the enemy can effect major repairs in much less than 60 days. Why can't we?"

I knew that the answer lay in the enemy's tremendous industrial capacity, so far superior to Japan's, and realized how embarrassing my question was. An awkward silence followed, until I spoke again, "Please do your best. I will stay with my ship. My men will cooperate with your repair crews in every possible way."

The engineer expressed his appreciation, saluted, and withdrew. I was left to brood, and again stroll the decks of my ship. Countless holes from machine-gun bullets made me feel that we were lucky not to have lost more than 43 lives.

Repairs were begun the following morning. For the next week I was busy showing off my "miracle" ship to visitors from battleship *Yamato* and other ships anchored in the harbor of Truk. Without exception they marveled that *Amatsukaze* had survived. Many visitors congratulated me but none asked my opinion of how to avoid such a fate in the future. I was more than ready with many recommendations, but no one asked.

It puzzled me that not one of the staff officers from Combined Fleet who visited my battle-scarred ship was interested enough to ask me for opinions or recommendations. When this lack of curiosity continued throughout the week I began to wonder about the ability of these men. It was disquieting to think that they, who were helping to form plans and strategy, were not interested in learning from recent battle experiences. Perhaps they were not as well qualified for their jobs as they should be. A most disturbing thought, indeed.

Two letters from Japan reached me at Truk. In a letter written on November 13, my wife told of conditions at home and concluded:

Little Mikito awakened suddenly last night and cried loud and long. I thought at first he was sick, but he finally explained that he had dreamed you were in danger. He said you looked pale and frightened. I wonder where you were last night and what you were doing. The newspapers tell of bitter battles in the south. I am worried about you.

Noting the date, I recalled the night of November 12–13 and its dangers. I must have looked pale when we were being battered by the enemy cruiser, because I certainly was frightened. How could my little son have seen it?

My mother, 82 years of age, had written the other letter. It concluded:

> I pray each morning and night at the family altar that our ancestors and the Merciful Buddha will protect you. Take care of yourself and come back alive.

My eyes filled with tears at reading this. My thoughts turned to the families of my dead crewmen, and I wept aloud. Letters of condolence must be written to those 43 families before I could reply to my wife and mother. The sun was setting when I finished this sad task eight hours later and walked out on deck.

A motorboat approached *Amatsukaze*. Another curious spectator, but the courtesies must be observed. I approached the ramp as the boat came alongside. The passenger shouted a cheery greeting as he came up and I recognized Commander Yasumi Toyama. He was chief of staff on Rear Admiral Razio Tanaka's Destroyer Squadron 2, based at Rabaul. I had previously belonged to this squadron, and we were old friends. He was in Truk for tactical conferences in Admiral Yamamoto's flagship *Yamato*.

"You look sick," he said. "What is the matter? Were you hurt in battle?"

"No, not a bit. I just feel let down. Anyone would after his ship had taken a beating like this."

"No, Hara, you should not feel bad. You did a terrific job. I had a good look at *Amatsukaze* from the motorboat. I knew you were the Navy's Number One torpedo officer, but never realized what a navigator you are. Any other skipper would have lost this ship."

"I can't agree, Toyama. We were just lucky that those countless enemy shells missed the engine and fuel tanks. Tell me, how is the squadron?"

"Ahhh," he groaned, "we are more a freighter convoy than a fighting squadron these days. The damn Yankees have dubbed us the 'Tokyo Express.' We transport cargo to that cursed island, and our orders are to flee rather than fight. What a stupid thing! It is doubtful whether we could fight anyway. Our decks are stacked so high with supplies for Guadalcanal that our ammunition supply must be cut in half. Our cargo is loaded in drums which are roped together. We approach near the island, throw them overboard and run away. The idea is that the strings of barrels will float until our troops on the island can tow them ashore. It is a strenuous and unsatisfying routine. But I want to hear about your battle and learn from your experience. Tell me all about it."

That was the first intelligent request I had heard in a week. I explained with enthusiasm and in detail our latest operation, noting our failings and the enemy's, and giving my fellow professional an over-all analysis. In conclusion I said, "Whatever our mission, we must always be ready for battle. I think it is wrong ever to consider fighting as merely secondary. Caution is necessary to be sure, but excessive caution is crippling. Please tell Admiral Tanaka not to repeat our mistakes."

He left the ship to catch a plane back to Rabaul. His quick visit to Truk and his remarks about the curious supply activities of Destroyer Squadron 2 indicated that the enemy undoubtedly had air supremacy at Guadalcanal. Japanese destroyers were even having trouble acting as fast freighters. Supplies of every kind were acutely lacking for Japanese troops on the island. Their daily distress calls emphasized shortages of food and medication.

Admiral Tanaka had been given responsibility for the stave-off-starvation missions Toyama had described. In these operations each destroyer would carry 100 or more drums of supplies in each nighttime delivery. Delivery consisted of jettisoning the strings of drums within 200 or 300 meters of the Guadalcanal coast. There Army troops were supposed to boat, swim, or wade out to retrieve the precious containers and haul them ashore, where they would be manipulated into the jungle and hidden from enemy air attack.

Tanaka's eight destroyers left Rabaul November 27 and headed southward to the Shortlands. The passage had to be made furtively. In the darkness of the 29th the squadron departed the Shortlands at 2245 for the final leg of the mission. Taking every possible advantage, the force feinted eastward toward Roncador Reef and Ramos Island. Then early in the morning of November 30, the eight destroyers, in single column, turned sharply south and headed straight for Guadalcanal.

An enemy patrol plane made contact with the squadron at 0800 and Admiral Tanaka realized that his secrecy of movement was broken. Soon afterward an observation post on Guadalcanal reported a dozen enemy destroyers off Lunga Point. Messages from other posts soon confirmed this movement of an enemy surface force around the island.

At 1500 Tanaka issued a directive to his squadron: "It is probable that we will encounter an enemy force tonight. Although our primary mission is to land supplies, everyone is to be ready for combat. If an engagement occurs, take the initiative and destroy the enemy."

The squadron reached the rendezvous point off Tassafaronga at 2100 and speed was slowed to 12 knots. A northeasterly breeze yielded a visibility of 9,000 meters. Tanaka's ships approached in single-column formation with *Takanami* as scout, 3,000 meters in the lead and slightly on the port bow of flagship *Naganami*. This was a flexible deployment for destroyers, and far more advantageous than the overcautious double-ring formation used by Admiral Abe on the night of November 12–13.

The American force which came to challenge Tanaka under Rear Admiral Carleton H. Wright repeated the formation used by Callaghan and Scott. They too were in single column, four destroyers in the van, five cruisers, then two rear destroyers, the whole led by destroyer *Fletcher* with its modern radar equipment. Two weeks earlier *Fletcher* had survived the Callaghan-Scott debacle from its position at the tail of the formation. When the action opened, the U.S. side had a distinct advantage of numbers.

Besides numerical inferiority, Tanaka was further handicapped in that the decks of his ships were stacked high with drums of supplies. Because of these cargoes the ammunition supply in each ship had to be reduced by one half. In addition to the reduction of shells for their guns, each of Tanaka's destroyers carried only eight torpedoes instead of their full quota of 16.

Admiral Wright's squadron had left Espiritu Santo early in the morning specifically to intercept Tanaka's destroyers which had been spotted by scout plane. At 2106 flagship *Minneapolis*'s radar first detected the Japanese force at 26,000 yards. Ten minutes later radar screens in *Fletcher* caught a target 7,000 yards on the port bow and the destroyer prepared to launch torpedoes. But five precious minutes were wasted before *Fletcher*, as well as destroyers *Perkins* and *Drayton*, were given permission to fire torpedoes. A total of 20 "fish" sped toward Japanese targets. None hit.

Meanwhile Admiral Tanaka was busy studying charts and the position of his ships. His cargo-dumping point was only 5,000 meters distant at 2115 when scout-ship *Takanami* reported. "Enemy ships bearing 100 degrees. Identified as three destroyers."

Takanami immediately launched eight torpedoes at these targets and opened fire with her guns. This was done on *Takanami*'s own initiative, without waiting for permission to open fire.

Until the five U.S. cruisers opened fire at this time, Tanaka had been unaware of their presence. Instantly Tanaka ordered. "Belay supply schedule! All ships, prepare to fight!"

One minute later, at 2122, Tanaka further ordered, "All ships, full battle speed!"

American gunners seemed to have aimed at only *Takanami*. She, at any rate, was the only Japanese ship hit. Many direct hits set her furiously afire, and she sank with all of her 211 crewmen.

With flaming *Takanami* as a shield, Tanaka made a daring 180-degree turn to bring his ships on a course parallel to the enemy column. He then speeded up to close with the enemy ships and *Naganami* swung to port after firing a spread of eight torpedoes at leading cruiser *Minneapolis*. The six other Japanese destroyers promptly followed *Naganami*'s example. These broadside launchings had far more precision than those of *Fletcher* and her companions who fired at targets approaching head-on. It was no wonder or surprise that the American torpedoes missed. They had been fired at an almost impossible angle, apparently without proper calculation of the many factors involved. The consequent poor marksmanship reflected a lack of training in torpedo technique.

Two of *Naganami*'s torpedoes, on the other hand, hit *Minneapolis*, shattering her bow, exploding a fireroom, and slowing the lead cruiser almost to a stop. *New Orleans*, next in line, narrowly avoided colliding with the flagship when a torpedo, apparently from *Makinami*, caught her port bow and exploded two forward magazines. The blast knocked off the cruiser's bow clear back to the No. 2 turret.

Cruiser *Pensacola*, next in line, also fared badly. While trying desperately to avoid a collision she took a torpedo hit which ignited fuel tanks, turning her into a floating torch. It was twelve hours before the flames were conquered and the crew knew that they could save her.

Light cruiser *Honolulu* followed *Pensacola* until that ship turned to port when the torpedoes began hitting. At that time *Honolulu* swerved to starboard to avert colliding and thus got out of the glare shed by her burning colleagues. She zigzagged away to the northwest and escaped being hit even by gunfire.

Northampton, the last cruiser of the enemy formation, could have seen little of the activity until she was upon her three flaming colleagues. She started to follow *Honolulu* but, seeing the Japanese ships dashing to the west, turned westward herself and opened fire with 8-inch guns. Hers was a hasty, blind shelling which scored no hits. But two Japanese torpedoes caught her port side, causing a monstrous explosion which swept her with flames and left *Northampton* to sink.

Tanaka's squadron swung northwest at full speed as soon as its torpedoes were launched, leaving behind a badly battered and confused enemy. *Honolulu*, the only undamaged cruiser of the American force, mistook rear-guard destroyers *Lamson* and *Lardner* for Japanese targets and blazed away at them until they turned and fled. The action had lasted about 15 minutes.

Flagship *Naganami* slowed down some 50 miles away from Guadalcanal and Admiral Tanaka took a count of his forces. Not one of his surviving seven destroyers had been hit by a single shell or torpedo, nor had they lost a man of their crews. It was a remarkable performance to have inflicted so much damage on the enemy at a cost of only one destroyer. But Admiral Tanaka was not jubilant. He grieved over the loss of *Takanami* and was glumly silent during the withdrawal while he considered returning to the battle zone to rescue survivors and re-engage the enemy.

A tally showed that four of his seven ships had spent all their torpedoes, one had fired only half of its supply, and the two others had fired none because of a bad angle during their firing ran. A total of 44 torpedoes had thus been expended. In light of this, Tanaka decided that his force was no longer in shape to engage the enemy. Accordingly, at 2330, he gave the order to return to Rabaul.

The high command took a dim view of this decision, even though Tanaka claimed to have sunk a battleship and two cruisers, and to have damaged four other cruisers. The facts were impressive enough, for Tanaka had sunk one and seriously damaged three heavy cruisers, at a cost of only one destroyer. But these statistics were not as persuasive with Tanaka's superiors as the fact that he had failed to unload the cargo so badly needed on Guadalcanal.

The Navy's displeasure with Tanaka was, reflected in his transfer to Singapore shortly after this battle, and then to Burma. These transfers, which took him away from the active fighting front, where his ability was so desperately needed, undoubtedly saved his life. Who knows what the Navy's shortsighted retributive policy may have cost in subsequent losses which Tanaka might have prevented?

Throughout the war, Tanaka never again held a responsible command afloat. Fifteen years after the Battle of Tassafaronga I visited him at his farm near Yamaguchi. In discussing the action he told me: "I have heard that U.S. naval experts praised my command in that action. I am not deserving of such honors. It was the superb proficiency and devotion of the men who served me that produced the tactical victory for us.

"In this I am not rejecting glory in order to escape criticism. I accept the principal criticism leveled by fellow officers. It was an error on my part not to deliver the supplies according to schedule. I should have returned to do so. The delivery mission was abandoned simply because we did not have accurate information about the strength of the enemy force. I believed that the enemy formation had four van destroyers and four more following the cruisers, as in the Callaghan-Scott formation of two weeks earlier. I saw no percentage in having our seven destroyers, low on ammunition and decks loaded with cargo drums, fight another running battle against eight U.S. destroyers. Had I but known that only one cruiser and four destroyers remained in fighting trim! . . ."

Tears came to his eyes when he spoke of destroyer *Takanami*. "We were able to defeat Admiral Wright's ships in this action only because of *Takanami*. She absorbed all the punishment of the enemy in the opening moments of battle, and she shielded the rest of us. Yet we left the scene without doing anything for her or her valiant crew."

However Admiral Tanaka may have felt about the Japanese effort at Tassafaronga, it is fair to consider what the U.S. Naval Historian, Rear Admiral Samuel Eliot Morison, had to say about this battle: "It is always some consolation to reflect that the enemy who defeats you is really good, and Rear Admiral Tanaka was better than that—he was superb. Without his trusted flagship *Jintsu*, his decks cluttered with supplies, he sank a heavy cruiser and put three others out of action for nearly a year, at the cost of one destroyer. In many actions of the war, mistakes on the American side were canceled by those of the enemy; but despite the brief confusion of his destroyers, Tanaka made no mistakes at Tassafaronga."

8

Before Admiral Tanaka's transfer to Singapore, there was time for him to lead several more transport missions to Guadalcanal. On December 3, he commanded a force of 4 cruisers and 11 destroyers which succeeded in delivering

1,500 drums of supplies to the shores of Guadalcanal. Tanaka was ready for a repetition of the Tassafaronga action, but the Americans apparently were not. Tanaka's phenomenal win had staggered the U.S. Navy.

There was no surface opposition, but some planes harassed the force and dropped a few bombs which slightly damaged one destroyer. It was a sour note in the operations that only 500 of the drums were picked up by the island forces.

Four nights later Tanaka was back again, this time with just 11 destroyers. Excessive repetition of a single formula in warfare is almost bound to fail, and this time planes from Henderson Field damaged two of his destroyers. On this night, too, Tanaka was confronted for the first time by a new kind of opponent—motor torpedo boats. Eight of these swift little PTs so harried his force that the reinforcement effort was called off and the destroyers returned to base.

Tanaka tried again on the night of December 11, using nine destroyers, and succeeded in dropping 1,200 drums of supplies. Air attacks on this convoy were ineffective, but the PTs struck again and hit flagship *Teruzuki* with two torpedoes which set her aflame. Her crew tried valiantly to save her but all efforts proved futile when the fires exploded her depth-charge stowage. Tanaka was injured when the torpedoes hit *Teruzuki*, but he transferred his flag and got home. In addition to the loss of his flagship, Tanaka was grieved by news that of the 1,200 drums transported and dropped on this run, only 220 reached Japanese hands.

Admiral Tanaka was hospitalized at Rabaul and there he dictated a memorandum to the high command recommending the withdrawal of forces from Guadalcanal. In reply he received orders assigning him to Singapore. This flat rejection of Tanaka's recommendation was unfortunate since it was becoming apparent that the island was no longer tenable. Submarines as well as destroyers were being used to bring in supplies, yet their combined best efforts brought only a trickle of what was needed to support the 20,000 troops.

Through these exciting days I remained at Truk. I felt sorry for Tanaka but could do nothing to help him. There was no new destroyer available for me so I could only watch as the skilled hands from repair ship *Akashi* worked over the scores of holes which cruiser *Helena*'s armor-piercing shells had put in my destroyer. *Amatsukaze* was patched enough that I was able to leave Truk on December 15 for the homeland where precision repairs could be made. The five-day voyage was uneventful. As we passed the island of Saipan

I saw a dozen Japanese planes and was curious about how they would react to our appearance. I was disappointed when not one of them even bothered to determine our identity. This nonchalance, if such it was, bespoke a laxity which was unwarranted and unforgivable while Japanese were being bled white in the Solomons.

I was almost able to forget the war, however, when we entered our home port of Kure. Sea gulls crisscrossed our bows in graceful greeting as we enjoyed the quiet of this peaceful and familiar harbor. It was so different from the savage waters of the Solomons; could it be that such contrasting places belonged to the same world?

When *Amatsukaze* was safely docked and arrangements were made for her thorough inspection and repair, I was able to take a week of home leave.

I arrived at my home in Kamakura on December 27. The week passed all too quickly, but it was a delight for me to be able to spend even that much time with my family. Kamakura is one of the most beautiful cities of Japan and I enjoyed revisiting its scenic places with my children, and hiking through the city and its surrounding hills. Pine trees hummed their eternal song to the balmy Pacific breezes. It was almost too good to be true. I felt especially lucky to be at home for the New Year holiday.

Despite the pleasure of being home, there really was no forgetting the war. One day we had planned a picnic, but my wife was unable to go with us. She had to attend a meeting of neighborhood wives to discuss household brass and iron collections for the use of the military. The children and I had our picnic and a long walk in the pine-clad hills. On our return from the picnic I was vexed to find that my wife was not yet home. My daughter explained, "Do not be angry. Mother has to attend many long meetings these days. Remember, Daddy, this is wartime."

Later that same evening I had a Tokyo phone call from my old friend Commander Ko Nagasawa, who was working in the Personnel Bureau. He said, "This is an unofficial call, so don't get flustered. A group of our classmates are getting together tomorrow night for a *Bonenkai* (New Year's party). We have chosen Yokohama's Isogo-en as the meeting place. It is a good restaurant, just about halfway between Tokyo and Yokosuka. It is near your home so we are counting on your being there."

I arrived the next evening at the appointed hour of seven, to be greeted by Nagasawa and Commander Enpei Kanooka, who was naval liaison assistant to Premier General Hideki Tojo. I was surprised to see that Kanooka had been able to get this far away from his busy and important office, to attend an unofficial party. Seated next to him in our reserved room I said, "You must have had a hell of a time in your job recently with all the troubles we've been having down south."

"No, Hara, not at all," he replied glumly. "As a matter of fact, for the past five months General Tojo has asked me for no advice, no briefing, no business, nothing at all. The General seems to have no interest whatsoever in naval operations. My only duty in this time has been to attend nightly cocktail parties for VIPs. I don't like to drink, I'm bored to death, and the routine is killing me. With your capacity for alcohol, Hara, maybe you should replace me."

Ordinarily soft-spoken Kanooka had raised his voice quite noticeably during this harangue; and grim-faced Nagasawa, of the Personnel Bureau, had listened in silence. (A short time later Kanooka was ordered out of Tokyo to take command of cruiser *Nachi*. Nagasawa had evidently taken him seriously.)

Otherwise everything was quiet and sedate, unlike the riotous parties of our younger days. About 20 of us were gathered that evening, commanders and lieutenant commanders, and the talk was concerned almost entirely with the war. When asked to describe the situation in the Solomons, I was happy to oblige.

"I don't know how you who are stationed here view things from the homeland, but it is hell at the front. As professionals you all know better than to base your judgments on the official bravado announced by headquarters in Tokyo. We have had some tactical victories, but we are suffering a strategic defeat. Our destroyers and submarines in the Solomons are now being used as transports, and ineffective ones at that."

The entire party was listening as I described actions I had seen. There was interest in my candid account, but someone reminded us that this was a party and we should stop talking shop.

A few jokes and wisecracks were exchanged, and someone told about an affair with a geisha girl in Sasebo. But there was no real mood for merriment. We all knew our dismal prospects for the future.

I truly wanted to let them know what we had experienced in the south, what my own reactions were, and my opinions. I knew that a party was no proper place for such topics, and yet there was no other chance. And it was disappointing to see the world-weariness of my classmates.

There was much drinking but little sign of drunkenness when the party broke up at a fairly early hour. Farewells, outside in the cold starlit night, were spiritless mutterings, "See you again." This was said without conviction. Very few of that group survived the war.

Tojo might ignore his Naval liaison officer, but there was no ignoring the formal representations of the Naval high command. The ranking officers of the Army and Navy were huddling daily in secret strategy conferences at Tokyo. The last of a series of these conferences took place on December 31 in the Imperial Palace, attended by Emperor Hirohito. The conference decided unanimously for the withdrawal of troops from Guadalcanal.

The rest of the holiday with my family passed happily but too quickly and I returned to Kure on January 7. Three days later I got orders relieving me from command of *Amatsukaze* and assigning me to duty at the Yokosuka Naval Station. This was only a few miles from my home!

Within a week of my departure, I was again settled comfortably at home, and then I fell ill. The doctor said it was exhaustion resulting from extended rigorous duty at sea. I was confined to bed for two weeks.

Adding to my misery, further orders came on the 25th, naming me Commander of Destroyer Division 19 with instructions to take its four modern ships to sea two days later. I phoned Nagasawa to report my inability to accept the post. Understanding and comforting as only a good friend can be, he assured me that there would be other such posts available when I recovered.

My convalescence seemed terribly long. I had never felt fatigue in battle. At sea a few hours sleep would always refresh me. Now, suddenly, I was aware of how exhausting my sea duty had been, and realized why Admiral Nagumo had looked so worn in November when I saw him at Truk.

As my strength returned I took long walks. The hills and the beaches were beautiful. In the woods I gathered pine cones each day and carried them home for fuel. They burned well enough to be used for cooking, and that helped. But it was depressing to realize how scarce all basic commodities were.

By the end of February I was fully recovered and called Nagasawa to ask about my next assignment. His vague reply made me uneasy that the Navy had forgotten about me. I called daily, without an encouraging word until early March, when Nagasawa informed me that I was to command Destroyer Division 27.

"What?" I shrieked belligerently. "Why the 27th?"

"Just a minute, now, Hara. Calm down and listen for a minute. I know the 27th has a bad reputation, but this assignment is all the more a credit to you. The admirals feel that only a man of your ability and experience can whip this division into shape as a fighting unit."

My first reaction was the product of shock. I was not really upset. After all, when a man is assigned to command four ships for the first time, it is an honor no matter what kind of ships they may be. Then too, I had missed the earlier attractive assignment through default. I had nothing to complain about.

The 27th was composed of four old 1,700-ton destroyers whose best speed was 30 knots. Their crews, strictly second class, were the object of derision to men of other ships. It really was a greater challenge for me.

With this in mind I replied to Nagasawa, "Don't misunderstand me. I welcome the assignment and will do my utmost to make it the best outfit in the Second Fleet. I am happy to have this command. When and where do I report?"

"I'm glad to hear you talk like that, Hara. Three of your ships are at Truk. Flagship *Shigure* (Autumn Rain) is waiting for you at Sasebo. When can you leave?"

"As soon as transportation is available."

"Good. You'll have a reservation on tomorrow's express train leaving Tokyo Central Station at 1330."

I arrived in Sasebo on March 9 and went immediately to my flagship for a tour of inspection. My first look at the crew convinced me that I was in for a real job. I thought back to the tribulations of my experience in training the crew of *Amatsukaze* in time for the Midway operation, and realized that compared to my present crew those men had been crack experts from the outset. *Shigure*'s crew looked like an ill-disciplined bunch of landlubbers. But I looked on their clumsiness and ineptness with mixed feelings, confident that I could work them into competent fighting sailors. At least I was not discouraged, so my feeling was worlds apart from what it had been six months earlier in *Amatsukaze*.

As to my flagship, having served in much newer destroyers, I found *Shigure* quite decrepit. She was old, sadly in need of maintenance, and, worst of all, she could do no better than 33 knots. The newest destroyers could make at least 38 knots, and my old battle-tested *Amatsukaze*, now back in service, was capable of 34 knots. But I pushed aside these vagrant thoughts, and my hopes were high that *Shigure* might prove worthy in battle despite her apparent shortcomings on this first day of our acquaintance. But even with my high hopes, I never dreamed that her exploits would earn for her the nickname of "Indestructible," and fame as the most publicized destroyer of the Pacific War.

Escorting two transports, *Shigure* left Sasebo to join the other three ships of my command. We arrived at Truk after a quiet voyage. Entering the spacious atoll I had the feeling that nothing had changed in my absence. *Akashi*, the old repair ship, still moored where it had been four months earlier when *Amatsukaze* limped in from the Solomons, was busy as ever.

I was wrong, however, in thinking that nothing had changed. Truk was as before, but the war situation to the south had undergone drastic changes in the brief period of four months, as I shortly learned. I reported to Vice Admiral Nobutake Kondo in *Atago*, flagship of the Second Fleet, as soon as we had anchored.

Entering his cabin, I was shocked at the haggard appearance of this man who had always been noted in naval circles for his excellent grooming. His appearance shocked me as much as Admiral Nagumo's had five months earlier. He motioned me to a chair. His voice was hoarse and low and he spoke slowly as if with great effort. "Hara, you have all my sympathy in your new assignment. It is a tough one. I can only say, take care of yourself. Use every possible caution."

I had certainly not expected such a greeting from my commanding admiral. Kondo's statement was so startling that I was at a loss for a response.

He continued, almost painfully. "Although you are a division commander, we are so short of ships that three of yours are being used by other commanders. It may be months before you have your full division under your command."

He paused and mused briefly, while I sat in uncomfortable silence, then he continued, "Above all, Hara, do not be impatient. I intend to keep you here for at least three months so that you can get acquainted with and train your subordinates, and also familiarize yourself with the rapidly changing war situation."

Kondo was a remarkable man and he was wonderful to me. Thus it was with great reluctance that I had to criticize his combat ability earlier in this writing. On this particular day, however, I was dazed and stunned in leaving his cabin.

At his suggestion I studied his flagship records of the war during the past five months. The most outstanding occurrence was the withdrawal from Guadalcanal. At Kamakura, while recuperating from my illness, I had heard radio announcements of a spectacular and perfect victory. Imperial Headquarters, loath to use the word "withdrawal," had coined and applied to this operation the word "*tenshin*" (turned advance), without providing any details.

As a result of the Palace decision at the New Year's Eve meeting, Imperial Headquarters issued an order on January 4, 1943, for the withdrawal of all troops from Guadalcanal, to begin the later part of the month. Plans were worked out accordingly, and secretly, while making every attempt to convince the enemy that we were about to make an all-out, determined stand.

American intelligence, which had been so successful in detecting Japanese plans for the Midway battle, failed utterly to anticipate the withdrawal plans for Guadalcanal. It is still one of the miracles of the war to me that this should have remained such a successful secret. The marvel of this increases when one considers that the enemy enjoyed absolute supremacy of the air in the vicinity of Guadalcanal at this time.

Starting in mid-January, Japanese air activities in the area were sharply increased. On the 30th a task force of two carriers, two battleships, and more than a dozen other warships steamed out of Truk and headed for Guadalcanal in a decoy movement to attract the attention of the U.S. Navy. Meanwhile, during the evening of the 28th, 300 fresh troops were landed on Russell Island, just to the west of Guadalcanal.

Needless to say, the Guadalcanal garrison was heartened by news of the planned withdrawal. They fought with surprising determination and strengthened their dogged resistance against enemy reinforcements. Considering their deprivations and pitiful shortages they fought valiantly right up until the end.

On the nights of February 1, 4, and 7, a total of 22 destroyers ran in to the very shores of the island to effect the evacuation of 12,198 Army and 832 Navy men. The destroyer crews were appalled at the sight of these troops, most of whom were living skeletons. They had not eaten for days and were so weak and emaciated that they could not even express joy at their rescue.

The withdrawal was a phenomenal success in which Japan's only losses were destroyer *Makigumo* sunk and three others damaged. That marked the conclusion of a six-month operation which left 16,800 Japanese bodies strewn in the tropical jungle, and scores of warships sunk with their thousands of sailors around this bitterly contested island. The many pages of reports on the subject all boiled down to one fact: Japan had lost the Battle of Guadalcanal.

I turned next in my reading to operations in New Guinea and found them almost equally depressing. The Army had tried to march a division from Buna, on the east coast of Papua, across the Owen Stanley mountains to reach Port Moresby. Most of the troops perished in the mountains. While the Navy was having its troubles on and around Guadalcanal, the Army's expeditionary force was starving to death in Papua. Meanwhile the enemy was making steady advances in the Papuan jungles of New Guinea, reducing Gona on December 9, 1942, Buna on the 14th, and Madang and Wewak four days later.

More shocking to me than the amounts of these land losses, however, was the Battle of the Bismarck Sea. Japan's defeat there was almost unbelievable.

Japan's two main airfields in eastern New Guinea, at Lae and Salamaua, were turned over to the Army on November 15. The Army decided to reinforce these positions with a division of troops from Rabaul. These troops were loaded in eight transports which departed Rabaul on February 28, escorted by eight destroyers.

The force commander, Rear Admiral Masatomi Kimura, had counted on sufficient air cover for his ships, but in broad daylight on March 2, and again the next day, more than 100 enemy planes attacked the convoy unopposed, sinking all eight of the transports and four of the destroyers. The second day of the action there were 26 planes of the Imperial Navy flying high cover for the convoy, but they were unable to break up the attack by low-flying bombers. More than 3,500 soldiers perished in this operation.

Never was there such a debacle. It was the complete opposite of the successful withdrawal operation from Guadalcanal. Now I could understand why Admiral Kondo had been in such a funk when he greeted me in his cabin. I paced the small cabin trying to figure how such a thing had come to pass. Rear Admiral Kan Takama entered in search of a document and I asked if he could explain the terrible defeat of the Bismarck Sea.

He said, "I can't criticize without knowing all the facts, Hara, but after reading these official reports, I don't understand it. The operation was carried out with all due care and caution, but the air cover was completely inadequate. At Guadalcanal our planning was right, the withdrawal was carried out in full secrecy, and the enemy was outfoxed. It may be that this spectacular success caused the Army leaders to think that they could risk a precarious operation without full preparation and support. One thing is certain: the Army did not provide proper air cover for the Bismarck Sea convoy."

Admiral Takama left the cabin, droop shouldered, with his document, and I returned to reading the record of further shocking events. On March 5, destroyers *Mineguma* and *Murasame* were sunk in Kula Gulf before they had even fired a shot. The enemy success was the result of his radar-controlled gunfire.

I was totally depressed upon leaving flagship *Atago*, and ordered the launch to take me ashore. As I stepped on shore at Truk I realized how much things had changed. My shipboard impression of the atoll had been deceptive. Faces in the street bespoke the changes that had taken place in five months.

In the Officers' Club I was greeted by Captain Tomiji Koyanagi, Admiral Kurita's chief of staff, and we had a pleasant reunion. The disastrous Bismarck Sea battle being uppermost in my mind, I lost no time in asking for his views on it. "Admiral Kimura himself has told me of the new method used by the enemy bombers in attacking his convoy," Koyanagi said. "The big planes came skimming the waves, dropping their bombs to skip on the surface and hit into the side of the ships. Conventional evasive maneuvers proved utterly useless against these skip-bombing tactics. Kimura thought the enemy was using aerial torpedoes, and futilely maneuvered his ships accordingly. High-altitude bombing against ships at sea was ineffective, so the enemy developed this new tactic which foiled our every evasive effort. We now have the serious problem of how to oppose skip bombing. Have you any ideas?"

The day had been so full of shocking surprises for me that I was drained of ideas. I felt like a freshman on his first day in college, and returned to *Shigure* with a splitting headache. After arranging shore leave for the crew, I retired to my cabin and spent the next 24 hours in search of answers to the many new problems of the war. I finally gave up, realizing that these questions were lofty and esoteric compared to my own immediate problem of readying an untrained warship crew for battle. I had to begin with fundamentals. After the crew's day of rest ashore we started intensive training in the waters around Truk. I was grateful to Admiral Kondo as I found how shrewd his appraisal had been. It soon appeared that three months would be the very minimum needed for organizing this inept crew.

In my training plan, the first month was devoted to shipboard fundamentals and controlling my temper. If a drill fell short of my standard, I personally demonstrated and directed its rehearsal, dozens of times if necessary. I drummed it into the men that, in a life-and-death struggle, nothing short of perfection is adequate. At first they were bewildered by such high standards, but gradually they became willing and eager to carry out my orders. They were not as bad as I had originally feared. Yet, throughout all this training, I was haunted by the realities of the war situation as revealed in the combat records I had seen in cruiser *Atago*.

At the end of a month I began to feel that some problems were capable of solution. For one thing, a study of the past year's actions showed that many of them were patterned on the same formula. When a tactic succeeded it was likely to be used repeatedly and without change by the Imperial Navy, and this often proved disastrous.

Admiral Kurita's October incendiary bombardment of Guadalcanal from battleships *Kongo* and *Haruna* was a great success. One month later Admiral Abe, with battleships *Hiei* and *Kirishima*, was ordered to undertake the same kind of attack. Not only did the Imperial Navy fail to hit the island with a single shell, but a battleship was lost in the process.

The disaster of the Bismarck Sea in February cost Admiral Kimura 12 of his 16 ships in his unsuccessful attempt to bring reinforcements to Lae and Salamaua. He was merely trying to do what the Navy had done six months earlier, and successfully, when it reinforced Buna. But those six months had seen a build-up of enemy air strength in this area, and that had not been properly taken into consideration.

Admiral Tanaka carried out a series of brilliant transport operations to Guadalcanal in November and December 1942. When other destroyer groups, led by officers of lesser ability, tried the same kind of operation it frequently led to such debacles as the March 5 massacre in Kula Gulf.

Such inflexibility was stupid. It appeared that the Imperial Navy felt the enemy was gullible enough always to play our game. The situation reminded me of the passage from the memoirs of Musashi Miyamoto, the superb medieval swordsman.

> In fighting it is bad to repeat a formula, and to repeat it a third time is worse. When an effort fails it may be followed with a second attempt. If that fails, a drastically changed formula must be adopted. If this fails, one must resort to another completely different formula. When the opponent thinks high, hit low. When he thinks low, hit high. That is the secret of swordsmanship.

I was impressed with the applicability of this advice to our present situation, and determined to convey my ideas to Admiiral Isoroku Yamamoto. I could not simply walk into the office of the Commander in Chief of Combined Fleet and set forth these opinions to him directly, so, on April 24, 1943, I went to flagship *Musashi* to explain my views to his chief of staff, Vice Admiral Matome Ugaki.

At the ramp of the huge battleship there was only one warrant officer to meet me. This was extraordinary and not in keeping with Navy protocol for greeting a flotilla commander. My announced desire to see Admiral Ugaki was met with such a blank stare that the man seemed doltish. After a long pause he asked me to follow him and we began walking through the maze of passageways and ladders of the giant ship. No officers were in evidence along our route, and the men I saw looked bewildered and depressed.

When we reached the cabin marked "Commander in Chief" my guide opened the door and silently gestured for me to enter. The smell of burning incense wafted out from the softly lit cabin. The center of the chamber was filled with a large, draped table on which were aligned seven coffins. I turned questioningly to the warrant officer.

He lowered his head and answered quietly, "Last Sunday Admiral Yamamoto and his staff flew south from Rabaul in two bombers. As they neared Buin the bombers were ambushed and shot down by P-38s, apparently from Guadalcanal. These are the remains of our Commander in Chief and six of his staff officers. Admiral Ugaki and the others were critically injured."

It seemed beyond belief, and yet there was no doubting what I could see and what I had just heard. My eyes filled with bitter tears as I offered a prayer for the repose of the dead.

part four

AGAINST THE ODDS

1

My promotion to captain came on the first day of May, 1943. *Shigure*'s skipper, Lieutenant Commander Kimio Yamagami, gave a party in my honor. The officers crowded the gun room to congratulate me and toast me with *sake*. After a couple of drinks Yamagami said hesitatingly, "The crew has been working hard for the past 40 days without any real relaxation. I see that factory ship *Akashi* is showing a movie tonight. Do you think I might allow the men to go see it?"

It pained me to refuse this reasonable request, but I explained, "I know we are on a rough schedule, seven days a week, but it is necessary. Do not think me harsh, but we cannot afford to let up one bit at this critical time."

That silenced Yamagami, a very mild man, but Lieutenant Toshio Doi, the torpedo officer spoke up, "Captain Hara, forgive my bluntness, but I don't understand why the men can't have some respite. They'd be invigorated by a little recreation, and they certainly deserve it."

"Doi," I answered, "this may also seem blunt, but our crew has never been in battle, where the slightest mistake may mean death for ship and shipmates as well as oneself. They may curse me now and think me harsh for imposing this rigorous training. But I want you, their officers, to understand that I insist on this regimen because it is better for them to suffer here in training than to be killed by the enemy."

The brief, clumsy silence that followed was broken by Lieutenant Hiroshi Kayanuma, the chief engineer. "Gentlemen, I share Captain Hara's feelings. In recent months many of our destroyers have been sunk, and Captain Hara has seen it happen. We are lucky to have a division commander of his experience. Let us set a proper example, quit beefing, and take advantage of his skill and experience. Those of us who do not know enough to appreciate him now, will find out before long how grateful they should be to Captain Hara."

Yamagami proposed a final toast to me, in which all the officers joined. The party broke up and we all went to night combat stations. Walking back to the bridge I said to Yamagami, "I feel sorry for you, Skipper, having to put up with a sonofabitch like me who dictates so concerning your crew. Normally a division commander leaves the running of a ship to her captain. I cannot explain further why I am compelled to take charge in *Shigure*. But I do appreciate your co-operativeness, and hope that you will some day understand."

Yamagami nodded meekly. Had he been forceful or obdurate as *Shigure*'s skipper, he could have made my task most unpleasant. Fortunately for me he was most co-operative and obliging.

After six weeks of training, *Shigure* was assigned to guard duties at Truk. This involved escorting transport ships in and out of the harbor, and also being on the lookout for enemy submarines. These light duties did not interrupt my training program in any way.

Meanwhile, the over-all war situation was not improving for Japan. After withdrawing from Guadalcanal, Japanese forces fell back to dig in on other islands up the Solomons chain. But the enemy's offensive capability seemed to be growing far faster than Japan's defensive capability.

Admiral Mineichi Koga, who succeeded Admiral Yamamoto as Commander in Chief Combined Fleet, continued the tactics of his predecessor. Destroyers and light cruisers were committed piecemeal into battle. These "expendable" elements, working desperately day and night, scored occasional local victories, but failed to change the tide of the war.

With the retreat from Guadalcanal, Japan's most forward defense line in the Solomons lay in the New Georgia group. There were bases at Munda on the main island and at nearby Kolombangara, with a total of about 10,500 troops in the area. It was here that the U.S. Navy drove a wedge on June 30, 1943, with landings on the northern tip of Rendova Island, and at Vangunu Island.

These landings posed a threat to the Japanese bases, and Admiral Koga ordered maximum reinforcements for the garrison troops. Our destroyers were again called into action on "Tokyo Express" assignments for this ferry service. Carrying tremendous loads of men and supplies, these ships fought fierce battles against better equipped and numerically superior enemy forces on the 4th, 6th, 12th, and 19th of July. In spite of distinct disadvantages, these plucky little ships gave good accounts of themselves.

Particularly brilliant were the exploits of five destroyers in Kula Gulf on the night of July 12. Indeed, their success outshone the November battle off Guadalcanal in which I had taken part, and the famed Tanaka action of November 30 in the same vicinity.

In the Kula Gulf battle a Japanese force of light cruiser *Jintsu* and destroyers *Yukikaze*—my old teammate—*Hamakaze*, *Mikazuki*, *Ayanami*, and *Yugure* took on an Allied force consisting of two U.S. and one New Zealand cruisers, and ten destroyers. The engagement opened around midnight when *Jintsu* repeated battleship *Hiei*'s blunder of using searchlights and was promptly sunk by concentrated gunfire.

In the ensuing action cruiser *Leander* was knocked out by torpedoes. The Allies made the mistake of dividing into two groups. One of these, consisting of four destroyers, failed to engage any Japanese ships. The five Japanese destroyers, storming back and forth, completely outmaneuvered the other group, knocking out cruisers *St. Louis* and *Honolulu* and sinking destroyer *Gwinn*. In the confusion destroyers *Woodworth* and *Buchanan* collided, and the Japanese ships returned to base, damaged but triumphant. Yet the loss of that one cruiser was more costly to Japan than were the casualties *Yukikaze* and her colleagues inflicted on three cruisers and three destroyers of the Allies.

At Truk I heard of *Yukikaze*'s exploits with some envy. She had not had great achievement in battle when teamed with my *Amatsukaze* in late 1942, but she was the only ship to survive the Bismarck Sea battle without a scratch. With her Kula Gulf exploit she was becoming a ship of some note. I vowed to match her exploits with my *Shigure* when we were ordered to move to Rabaul on July 20.

I was glad to get the orders. So far I had been a division commander in name only, since all my ships but *Shigure* were assigned to other commands. Two of my destroyers, *Yugure* and *Ariake*, were at Rabaul. It was stimulating to think of having three of my ships together at one time. I knew that *Yugure*, having just come from earning glory with *Yukikaze* in the Kula Gulf battle would be a great asset to the division.

My feelings were shared by *Shigure*'s entire crew, and their morale soared when they heard of *Yugure*'s exploits. They were tired after almost four months of intensive training, but they rejoiced at the prospect of moving to the front and having the chance to engage in battle.

Shigure headed south at a steady 18 knots, loaded to capacity with plane parts badly needed at Rabaul. I thought of how the weeks of recent training had transformed *Shigure*'s sloppy, dispirited crew into a snappy, hard-working team. I had been very sparing with praise during their training, but they had done a good job. Still, experience had taught me that one real action teaches more than a thousand maneuvers. I would save my praise until they had withstood their baptism of fire, and hope that the acid test would not find them wanting. I was eager for battle. *Yukikaze* had been successful, and if she could succeed, we could.

The voyage to Rabaul was eventless and we arrived on July 23. I reported at once to the headquarters where a staff officer silently handed me a report. I scanned it hastily and was stunned. Destroyers *Yugure* and *Kiyonami* had been sunk south of Choiseul on the 20th. They were part of a transport mission to Kolombangara which had been thwarted a week earlier and were trying again. The entire crews had perished—228 in *Yugure* and 240 in *Kiyonami*. Thus the enemy had avenged their losses at Kula Gulf within a week.

As soon as *Shigure*'s cargo was unloaded I told the crew what had happened to the two destroyers. They listened in silence and, I gathered, began to feel that all their training had been worth the effort.

Destroyer Division 27 was still my command in name only. But *Ariake* returned on the 21st with two other destroyers from a successful supply mission to Kolombangara. This trio had chosen Vella Gulf as their approach route instead of Kula Gulf. A powerful enemy force of four cruisers and three destroyers were on the prowl in Kula Gulf, but they did not find out until too late that the Japanese destroyers had entered and departed on the other side of the island.

Rabaul—supply base for all Japanese forces in both the Solomon Islands and the New Guinea theaters—was a hectic place in the summer of 1943. Destroyer *Shigure* was allowed to rest—but check-ups, familiarization cruises, and the like, kept it from being a rest—for just six days when orders arrived to join with three ships of Destroyer Division 4 on a transport mission to

Kolombangara. We were to take the route through Vella Gulf that had been used so successfully by *Ariake* ten days earlier, because, headquarters said, "This route was safe enough."

I did not share this complacency, however, because of my observation that a repetition of the same operational formula usually ended disastrously. We should not expect that the enemy's cruisers and destroyers would again obligingly waste time and fuel in Kula Gulf. The tragedy of *Yugure* and *Kiyonami* should have been example enough that we could not count on the enemy for such stupidity.

On the 1st of August, we steamed out of Rabaul in a column led by *Amagiri*. As lead ship and scout for the force, she carried no cargo. The following three destroyers—*Hagikaze, Arashi, Shigure*—were loaded with a total of 900 troops and 120 tons of supplies. I was apprehensive on my first real sortie of the year.

In my absence from action, the seas of the Central Solomons had claimed many illustrious destroyers. *Kagero, Kuroshio,* and *Oyashio*—veterans of Tanaka's victorious battle off Savo Island—were sunk by mines and air attack on May 8, 1943. My Java Sea battle teammate, *Nagatsuki,* and *Niizuki* were lost in these waters in July. *Hatsuyuki,* hero of the October, 1942, Savo Island battle, was blasted into the ocean depths, near Bougainville on July 17.

I became lost in these contemplations on *Shigure*'s bridge, watching the darkening ocean, and wondered how many and which of the four ships on this sortie would survive. As night came I was relieved to see that it was pitch dark, and hoped that luck would be with us.

We entered Blackett Strait which threads between Kolombangara and three smaller islands to the southwest. Both sides of this hazardous, narrow waterway are lined for miles with dangerous reefs and shoals. Engines were stopped at the rendezvous point and our three loaded ships drifted in silence. Dozens of barges came swiftly out from shore to receive our cargo. Working very efficiently they cleared our ships of all troops and supplies within 20 minutes! It was a great relief to see *Hagikaze*'s hooded lamp signal, "Let's go home!"

Amagiri went ahead to lead the way while the other three of us warmed engines, and within five minutes we were headed back through the weird and treacherous waterway. I had alerted *Shigure*'s bridge and lookouts for any sign of danger. The enemy with his tight scout networks in this area must have detected our activities, and might spring out from any of the myriad shoals that lined the mazelike strait.

Ten minutes after getting under way from the rendezvous we were making 30 knots through the confined waters. This was a truly breakneck speed for such a dangerous waterway. In peacetime no ship would have ventured here at night in excess of 12 knots, even with all lights burning. We, of course, were running fully blacked out.

The night was sultry, but cold sweat stood out on every brow. We passed Arandel and Wana Wana, and caught up with *Amagiri* as we drew abeam of *Gizo*. We then drew into a tight column formation with only 500 meters between ships.

My eyes, well adjusted to the darkness, suddenly caught the movement of a small black object moving swiftly from the left toward *Amagiri* which was some 1,500 meters ahead of *Shigure*. I could not determine what the object was, but groaned, "Here it comes!" and braced for a fearsome explosion at any moment.

The black object melted into the darkness and was gone, with no explosion, no flash, no fire. It was mystifying. The suggestion of bustling activity on board *Amagiri* was borne out when her veiled lamp flashed a swift message:

"Enemy torpedo boats encountered! One rammed and sunk!"*

Hagikaze and *Arashi* machine guns suddenly barked and I saw them fire a torrent of bullets to starboard. Two violently burning torpedo boats came into view near the two destroyers. I gave the order for *Shigure's* guns to open fire, and the crews, who had been standing by with fingers on triggers, responded beautifully. The flaming craft disappeared into the black water as if they had never existed. [These two "burning torpedo boats must have been the two halves of *PT-109*"—R.P.]

Cheers of joy and laughter sounded and echoed in each of our destroyers as we continued running at top speed. I understood the elation at our good fortune, but could not join the merrymaking. My spine was still creeping at the thought of the close shave we had had, as I recalled the loss of *Terutsuki* in December, 1942, to motor torpedo boats. This new Japanese destroyer of 3,470 tons was sunk as the result of two hits by torpedoes delivered by a couple of 50-ton torpedo boats. The same fate could have just as well befallen us this night if the enemy had spotted us and reacted a few minutes earlier.

---

* This was *PT-109* (Lt. John F. Kennedy USNR) which was sliced in two by *Amagiri* in the early hours of August 2, 1943, and sank in position 08°03′S., 156°8′E. Two of thirteen crew members were lost, and the survivors were finally rescued on the 7th, thanks to the valiant efforts of her skipper, who later became President of the United States. For brief account see Appendix A.

Outside of Vella Gulf we slackened speed and returned uneventfully to Rabaul. Our crews were still exultant about the victory, but I was apprehensive and glum. Reason for the glumness appeared when I reported to headquarters and received an official report that awaited me.

Destroyers *Mikazuki* (Destroyer Division 30) and *Ariake* (Destroyer Division 27), while on a transport mission to Tuluvu, New Britain, grounded near Cape Gloucester on July 27 and were attacked next day by B-25s which demolished them completely. Only seven crewmen were killed.

I returned sadly to *Shigure*, once again commander of a one-ship division. How swift the tempo of attrition! Of the glorious quintet of July, only two ships remained a month later. How could both *Mikazuki* and *Ariake* have been so clumsy and inept as to run aground?

Depressed and dispirited, I downed several bottles of *sake* that night. Yamagami joined me in drowning sorrow for an hour or so and then retired. I stayed up and drank myself into a stupor.

Two days later, on the morning of August 4, Captain Kaju Sugiura, commander of Destroyer Division 4, invited Yamagami and me to his flagship to attend a conference. The day was sunny and we had a pleasant boat ride over to destroyer *Hagikaze*. The conference table and chairs set up on the foredeck were shaded by a small awning. We were the last to arrive and the skippers and execs of the other destroyers gave us a cordial greeting. Sugiura, several years my senior and a staff college graduate, opened the conference with a general greeting and then stated the business of the day.

"Gentlemen, I am very happy to report that our last transport mission to Kolombangara was a complete success, thanks to your splendid co-operation. Both the Navy and the Army high command are gratified and have asked me to extend their appreciation to you. They have also ordered that the mission be repeated the day after tomorrow. *Kawakaze* will replace *Amagiri* whose nose was bruised in ramming that torpedo boat. I invite discussion and will welcome your opinions and suggestions."

Looking around I saw that the skippers of Sugiura's destroyers were listening with impassive obedience. They would offer no dissenting voice to anything Sugiura said. Yamagami, of my *Shigure*, was squirming uneasily. Being the only other officer of captain rank in the conference, I spoke up:

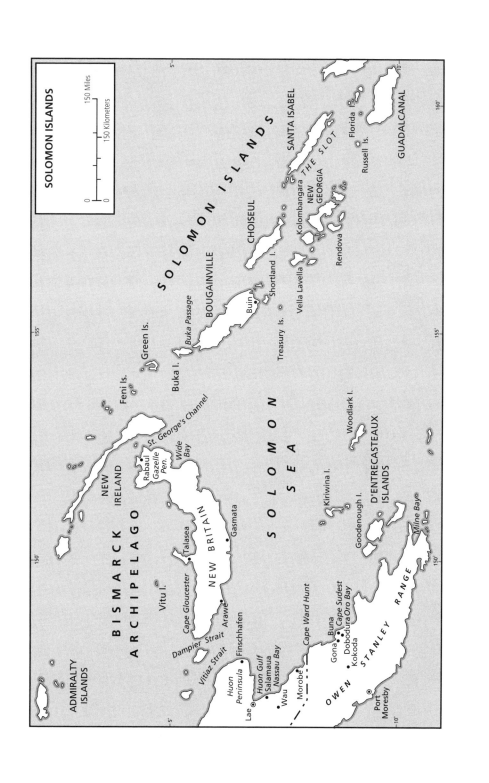

SOLOMON ISLANDS

150 Miles

150 Kilometers

ADMIRALTY ISLANDS

BISMARCK ARCHIPELAGO

NEW IRELAND

Feni Is.

Green Is.

Rabaul
Gazelle Pen.
St. George's Channel
Wide Bay

Buka Passage
Buka I.

BOUGAINVILLE

SOLOMON ISLANDS

Buin

Shortland I.

Treasury Is.

CHOISEUL

THE SLOT

SANTA ISABEL

Florida Is.

Russell Is.

GUADALCANAL

Kolombangara
Vella Lavella
NEW GEORGIA
Rendova

Talasea

Vitu I.

NEW BRITAIN

Gasmata

Cape Gloucester

Arawe

Dampier Strait

Vitiaz Strait

Finschhafen

Huon Peninsula

Lae
Huon Gulf
Salamaua
Nassau Bay
Wau
Morobe

Cape Ward Hunt

SOLOMON SEA

Woodlark I.

Kiriwina I.

Goodenough I.

D'ENTRECASTEAUX ISLANDS

Milne Bay

Buna
Gona
Cape Sudest
Dobodura
Oro Bay
Kokoda

OWEN STANLEY RANGE

Port Moresby

"Captain Sugiura, I understood you to say that we are to repeat the mission. Does that mean we are to conduct this operation in the same way as the last one?"

"Yes, Hara. We shall go through Vella Gulf and Blackett Strait again, and unload at the Kolombangara anchorage at 2330, exactly as we did last time."

"Begging your pardon, Sugiura, I do not think it wise to repeat the exact same formula again. This same procedure has already been used twice in Vella Gulf. Can't we vary the course somewhat this time? Blackett Strait by itself, with all those reefs and shoals, is unhealthy enough, without using the identical route for getting there again. How about feinting through Gizo Strait before sneaking into Blackett? Or how about just changing the timing by two hours either way?"

"Hara, I see your point but I already have my orders. To alter them in any detail such as you suggest would involve great changes for all parties concerned, especially in communications. And you know how poor the Army garrison's communication system is. If Blackett Strait is unhealthy for us, it is dangerous for the enemy too. Their torpedo boats can get lost in the maze of reefs before they spot us."

Sugiura's three skippers meekly nodded their agreement. It was plain that any counterproposals I might make would be opposed by everyone except Yamagami. I felt a bit dizzy. My ears heard the din of the words from Musashi Miyamoto's memoirs:

. . . it is bad to repeat a formula, and to repeat it a third time is worse. . . .
When the opponent thinks high, hit low. When he thinks low, hit high.

Sugiura was no stranger to me. We had been friends for many years. He was highly regarded by our superiors. There were already indications that he would reach flag rank. A man in such circumstances seldom argues when the high command gives orders. He broke the silence and continued in a conciliatory tone:

"If it is agreeable with you, Hara, I should like to have *Shigure* be scout ship for the force. That will free you from carrying burdensome cargo and give you a free hand. The former scout ship, *Amagiri*, has been replaced by *Kawakaze* and the crew lacks experience. With your experience and skill, you would do a perfect job of scouting for the force."

This was a clever move on Sugiura's part. It tended to place me, his only vocal opponent to following the operation orders, in the position of having to accept from him a favored position of responsibility in this operation. All eyes were on me, awaiting my response. Fortunately I was able to answer with complete truthfulness, "I appreciate your consideration, Sugiura, but cannot accept your proposal."

My listeners could not have been more surprised, and the skippers looked appalled at my having answered in this fashion. I continued, "*Shigure*, a sluggish and creaking hulk, is the oldest of our four. Its 42,000-horsepower engine needs overhaul so badly I doubt if she can make 30 knots. She is unfit for scout duty. I recommend that this duty be assigned to Commander Koshichi Sugioka in *Arashi*. His new ship, with its 52,000-horsepower engine, can easily make 35 knots."

Sugiura squirmed slightly as an awkward silence prevailed. He looked at Sugioka who averted his gaze and said nothing. Mild-tempered Sugiura finally broke the silence with a sigh of resignation.

"Very well, gentlemen," he said, "flagship *Hagikaze* will lead the column and serve as scout ship, but she will carry her share of troops and supplies. Following her will come *Arashi*, *Kawakaze*, and *Shigure* will bring up the rear, with 500 meters' distance between ships. This will give us a compact but maneuverable formation. Is that satisfactory, Hara?"

In view of his tolerance and patience with me, I had to agree with this arrangement. It was obviously futile to question the wisdom of the operation itself. The conference moved into a discussion of technical details.

The plan was to leave Rabaul early in the morning so as to arrive in the area covered by the enemy's Russells-based air patrols after nightfall. Sugiura assumed that these U.S. patrol planes covered a range of 300 miles.

His assumption was probably right as of a week earlier. But we had no right to assume that patrols might not now come from the more advanced base at Rendova, which had been in operation since early July. Also, our force could be spotted by enemy submarines, but this was not taken into consideration. The more I thought about these things the more upset and uneasy I became. Still too clear in my mind was the miserable fate of the two ships of my division which were lost while under another command.

The conference lasted about two hours. I remained silent and glum as we departed for *Shigure*. In the boat Yamagami said, "Captain, I was surprised at your courage in speaking up like that. But I'm afraid those Destroyer Division 4 officers took a dim view of your contentions."

"It was not a matter of courage so much as saying what I had to say. As to what they think of me, I do not care. But I do care for men's lives. This operation, at best, is unreasonable. Now I simply pray that luck will be with us."

I have always looked back on that conference with deep regret. I should not have yielded to the idiotic policy of the high command. Had my views prevailed, hundreds of lives might have been saved in a single operation and many times that number in ensuing months. Yet under the strict hierarchy of command prevailing in the Navy there was no way my objections could have any effect. I learned later that even my futile protest at the beginning of the conference aroused much criticism of me when word of it spread among the officers at Rabaul.

We sortied from Rabaul on August 6 at 0300 and headed southward in a calm sea. The cloudy sky offered intermittent rain squalls and brief glimpses of sunshine. We were passing Buka Island at 1430 when an enemy patrol plane was seen disappearing into the clouds. Our radiomen reported hearing an "Urgent" coded message, which must have been the plane's report of our approach. Clearly, our operation would not take the enemy by surprise.

I kept close watch of flagship *Hagikaze* to see how Captain Sugiura would react to this development. It grieved me to see our same speed of advance and course maintained, even after we had been sighted by the enemy. I gritted my teeth and followed along.

We entered Bougainville Strait at 1900 and, turning to a course of 140 degrees, boosted speed to 30 knots. Two hours and twenty minutes later we were directly northeast of Vella Lavella Island. *Shigure* was falling behind the formation as the 30-knot speed proved too much for her. The navigation officer, Lieutenant (j.g.) Yoshio Tsukihara, came to report to me.

"Sir, we are lagging 1,000 meters behind *Kawakaze*. Shall we use the overboost to gain back our lost 500 meters?"

"No," I roared, "this is good enough. To hell with the prescribed 500-meter distance. Don't overboost the engine!"

Kolombangara loomed to starboard, its towering volcanic peak overhung with ominous black clouds. To port I could see nothing but blackness, from which anything could emerge at any moment. It made my spine creep.

I shouted new orders. "Stand by for action! Aim all guns and torpedoes to port. Set gun range of 3,000 meters. Set torpedoes to run at two-meter depth, angle 20 degrees. Double all lookouts!"

For the next ten uneasy minutes I peered searchingly to port for some sign of activity or movement to betray the presence of the enemy. Visibility was no more than 2,000 meters in this direction. The growing tension was shattered by the voice tube from torpedo control where Lieutenant Doi asked if it was all right to return the tubes from portside to their original starboard position.

I shrieked an emphatic "No!" and followed with a more controlled explanation, "No, Doi, for heaven's sake, no! Starboard visibility is so good that we can see the reefs of Vella Lavella. To port we see no more than 2,000 meters, and we don't know where the enemy is. Stay trained to port and be ready for action at any moment."

This bit of instruction was hardly finished when lookout Yamashita called, "White waves! Black objects! . . . Several ships heading toward us!"

I called at once for full starboard helm, and ordered torpedoes launched at port-side targets. The white waves were plainly visible. I shuddered and glanced at the three leading destroyers. They were proceeding straight ahead, oblivious of the closing enemy ships. Damn! Damn! *Shigure* was now 1,500 meters behind *Kawakaze*. Forty-five seconds after the order was given, *Shigure* began swinging to starboard as her torpedoes leapt in rapid succession into the water. The time was 2145.

As the eighth torpedo was about to be released I caught sight of telltale white torpedo tracks fanning out in our direction, the nearest within 800 meters. I shouted again for hard starboard helm. In the same moment I saw a pillar of fire shoot up from amidship of *Arashi*, and two from *Kawakaze*. Lead ship *Hagikaze* was beyond and in line with these two victims so that I could not see her.

Looking again at the water, I held my breath. Three torpedoes were streaking toward *Shigure*'s bow, which was swinging rapidly to the right.

My knees almost gave in as I clutched the handrail. The first torpedo passed 20 meters ahead of the bow, the second was closer, and the third appeared certain to hit. It did not, however, or if it did it was just a glancing blow on the skin of the rapidly turning ship. I thought I felt a dull thud from aft but could not be sure. Looking around again I saw several torpedoes running 30 meters or more in front of the bow, as the ship was completing a full circle in its desperate evasive turn.

I called for a reverse turn. "Port helm, half!"

When a destroyer is running at 30 knots, it takes the better part of a minute for the helm to answer the wheel. I looked around anxiously. Fortunately there were no more torpedoes in sight, and I had a chance to look at my watch. It was 2147. Those two minutes just passed were the most breathtaking ones of my life.

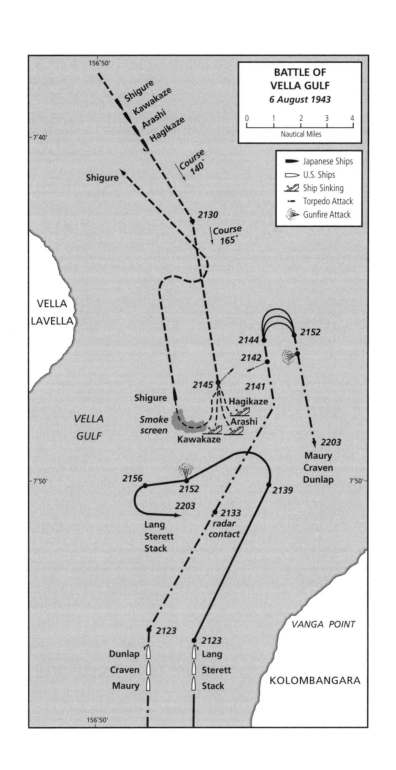

156°50'

Shigure
Kawakaze
Arashi
Hagikaze

−7°40'

Shigure

Course 140°

2130

Course 165°

**BATTLE OF
VELLA GULF**
6 August 1943

0   1   2   3   4
Nautical Miles

▬ Japanese Ships
▭ U.S. Ships
🚢 Ship Sinking
➤ Torpedo Attack
💥 Gunfire Attack

VELLA
LAVELLA

2144   2152

2142

VELLA
GULF

Shigure   2145   2141

Hagikaze

Smoke
screen   Arashi

Kawakaze

2203
Maury
Craven
Dunlap

2156   2139   7°50'−

−7°50'   2152
2203

Lang
Sterett
Stack   2133
radar
contact

VANGA POINT

2123
Dunlap
Craven
Maury   2123
Lang
Sterett
Stack

KOLOMBANGARA

156°50'

Lookout Yamashita announced gleefully that one of our torpedoes had scored a hit, raising a great explosion amid the enemy ships. This was a needed shot in the arm for the men and officers of *Shigure* who had been wondering when their own ship would be hit. Shouts of joy were short-lived when it appeared that no enemy ships had been hit.

It was later ascertained that the exploding torpedo observed by Yamashita had been triggered upon crossing the wake of one of the enemy destroyers. The Japanese oxygen-fueled torpedoes were so sensitive that they often exploded upon hitting a ship's wake. But no American ships were hit in the action. The enemy performed superbly that night, and did everything right.* I felt certain that some of my torpedoes were going to hit, but the enemy destroyers made a 90-degree turn to the east just in time to evade us.

I asked the radio room what had been heard from our other destroyers. The reply came back at once, "*Arashi* and *Kawakaze* sent brief messages saying they were hit by torpedoes. We have heard nothing from *Hagikaze*."

After ordering that efforts be continued to keep contact I ordered a smoke screen to mask our movements. Then I wondered what to do next. *Shigure* was heading northwest, away from the battle zone. I could not quit like this.

A quick review of the situation convinced me that the enemy had ambushed us brilliantly, and that *Shigure* was now at a distinct disadvantage. I recalled the night off Guadalcanal when my ship made a solo run against the enemy column and sank destroyer *Barton*. Now the tables were turned. The enemy was coming at me, and it was no solo run for them. Judging from the many torpedo tracks we could see, several ships must have fired in concert. The hits on *Arashi* and *Kawakaze* were phenomenal. Never before had I seen such marksmanship by the enemy. We had been taking altogether too casual a view of his torpedo technique.

The Americans took full advantage of the situation this night. I could not leave my friends in the lurch, and yet there was little I could do against an opposition greatly outnumbering us. With no message from *Hagikaze*, there was always the chance that she was still afloat. I ordered torpedoes prepared

---

* The U.S. naval force operating near Bougainville that night was Task Group 31.2 (Commander Frederick Moosbrugger), consisting of Destroyer Division 12—destroyers *Dunlap, Craven* and *Maury*—and Destroyer Division 15, comprised of destroyers *Lang, Sterett* and *Stack*.

and announced that we were going back to fight. It was 2151 as *Shigure* turned around.

A minute later tremendous fireworks filled the sky some three miles ahead. Torrents of flares and flaming projectiles shot up in every direction with blinding brightness. The enemy was bombarding our destroyers, which were soon in their death throes.

While *Shigure* made way toward this holocaust I asked for reports of radio contacts with our other ships and of our own readiness for battle. There was no answer to our call, and I learned that *Shigure*'s rudder was not functioning properly. The thought came back to me of the ominous thud I had heard earlier. It was not until *Shigure* went into drydock four months later that we found in the rudder a hole nearly two feet across. An American torpedo had passed right through it without exploding.

I was in agony on the bridge. Handicapped with a load of 250 troops and tons of deck cargo, how could this destroyer fight singlehanded against the odds of an apparently undamaged enemy force? At Guadalcanal I had made three mistakes and lost 43 men. How many mistakes would there be this time, and how many men would I lose?

Shigure was still approaching the scene of action when the gunfire ceased abruptly at 2210. The area was thrown into complete darkness and it seemed certain that our three companion ships were sunk. The triumphant enemy must be waiting in the darkness for just the right moment to jump *Shigure*. When a final check showed no response from our other ships, at 2215 I gave the order to withdraw. It was a hard decision but there was no alternative.

We informed Rabaul that we were ready to leave the area and requested instructions. Headquarters came back at once saying, "Return to base. Ask Kolombangara to rescue survivors."

Thus ended the Battle of Vella Gulf in a perfect American victory. Three Japanese destroyers were sunk. Of their 700 crewmen and 820 troops, only 310 survived. Among them was Captain Sugiura. He had drifted ashore some 30 hours after the sinkings and roamed the jungles for a week before being rescued by a search party.

It pained me to see Sugiura when he returned to Rabaul on August 20, emaciated and ashamed. Survivors recounted how they had seen the fatal torpedoes only within a few hundred meters of their ships. Two torpedo hits on *Hagikaze* had instantly silenced her radio. *Arashi* was hit by three torpedoes and *Kawakaze* by two. It was one of the most astounding torpedo successes in history.

An eighth enemy torpedo hit *Shigure*'s rudder. Had it not been a dud, *Shigure* would have shared the fate of the three destroyers of Destroyer Division 4. The American score for this action was very high by any standard, and it was shockingly so to Japanese experts who thought the enemy weak in torpedo effectiveness.

It was not until after the war that I read American versions of this battle and found how the victory had been won. Our destroyers had walked into a shrewdly laid trap which took full advantage of the cloaking Kolombangara mountains.

The enemy had learned of our approach early and kept track of our force throughout the day. Six American destroyers had left Tulagi at 0930, and they were well informed of our movements toward Vella Gulf. In the gulf these ships' radar picked us up at a range of almost 10 miles. Thereupon the enemy force split into two groups of three ships each. *Dunlap*, *Craven* and *Maury* were to make the first torpedo run, the others to follow as needed. The shooting of the first group was so good that the second group needed to join only in the finishing gunfire.

The victory would have been perfect if they had pursued *Shigure*. But our smoke screen must have been effective in making the enemy think we were done for.

The significance of the American victory was finally realized at Rabaul. Never again did headquarters try to reinforce Kolombangara through Vella Gulf.

2

Shigure returned late in the night of August 7 to Rabaul, where headquarters was in a turmoil. Our loss of Munda on the 4th, followed by the unprecedented defeat of our destroyers in Vella Gulf was a shock to everyone. Across the narrow Blackett Strait from Munda was the main Japanese bastion of the Solomons, Kolombangara. I could understand why the enemy destroyers opposing us at Vella fought with such authority.

I was greeted ruefully by the Eighth Fleet commander, Vice Admiral Tomoshige Samejima, but he said not a word of criticism of my actions. He was remorseful at having sent Destroyer Division 4 into a trap, on a foolish repeat mission.

On return to my ship I had the 250 Army troops and their supplies put ashore. Most of the soldiers were terribly sick after huddling more than 40 hours in the cramped, stinking spaces below deck. They shouted with joy as they staggered down the ramp to solid land. They realized what a narrow escape we had had, and bowed a grateful farewell to *Shigure* and her crew as they marched away. It made me feel that my decision had been the right one.

I gave my crew the next day off and let them go ashore, one third at a time. It was their first real rest, and a well-earned one. When I saw Petty Officer Yamashita, the lookout who had discovered the enemy, among the first group to go ashore I called him to my cabin. There I handed him my silver watch and said, "You did a great job. I want you to have this. It is not much. I bought it 20 years ago, at Wanamaker's Department Store in New York City."

"I cannot accept it, sir," Yamashita protested. "I must not take a thing of such special significance for you. I merely fulfilled my duty. If my act deserved a reward, it should come from headquarters."

"Take the watch and stop arguing with me, Yamashita. The high command will not give you anything. They have actually denied our claimed torpedo hit because your sighting was not witnessed."

"Oh, Captain Hara, that is wrong. I saw the torpedo hit just as I saw the approaching enemy. I have never lied in my life, and will fight anyone who calls me a liar."

"Come, now, Yamashita. You know how the service can be. Forget it. Go ashore and have a good time."

I put the watch in his pocket. He looked bewildered for a moment, smiled, saluted, and withdrew.

I sat down to the difficult job of writing a detailed action report of the Vella Gulf battle. I had to be honest and at the same time I wanted to defend my colleagues. Hours passed before the work was completed.

As I stepped out on deck to relax, the first shore party was returning. Yamashita stood out from the rest of the group because of his disheveled uniform, swollen face and blackened eye. When I called for an explanation he stammered, "It is nothing, sir. I just stumbled and fell."

"You said this morning that you do not lie. Don't try to fool me. Do you think I cannot tell when a man has been beaten up?"

"I am very sorry, sir. Forgive me for telling you the first lie of my life. I tangled with some bastards ashore, but they did not beat me up."

"Come to my cabin and explain what happened."

This usually cocky young man followed sheepishly to my cabin. There I demanded a full explanation.

"Well, sir, I had a few drinks and was having a good time. Maybe I got a little drunk. I showed off the watch you gave me. Then some son of a bitch said that *Shigure* had retreated in shame and was a disgrace to the Navy. Another joined in saying that Destroyer Division 27 was a bunch of bums. That did it. I lit into both of them and gave them what they deserved. The bastards!"

"Shame on you, Yamashita. Do you think *Shigure*'s action was wrong?"

"No, sir. I believe your judgment was absolutely right. That's why these bastards made me mad."

"You should have ignored them. We are here to fight the enemy, not our countrymen. Don't feel bad about it now. Blow your nose and go to sick bay for treatment. Next time you will know better."

The atmosphere in *Shigure* changed radically after Vella Gulf. The crew was transformed overnight into a proud, tightly woven team. No more beefing, no more sullen faces. This happy development made our whole ordeal of training and battle worth while. This team would have confidence in its next battle. And it was not long in coming.

The Americans continued their advance and carried out a new landing operation on August 15 at Biloa, near the southern end of Vella Lavella. This new beachhead and the one at Munda formed a pincer on our 12,000-man garrison at Kolombangara. The reaction of the Japanese high command was to throw in all available aircraft over Biloa and then land reinforcements at Horaniu, on Vella Lavella, to counterattack the new enemy beachhead.

On the morning of August 16, Yamagami and I attended a conference in destroyer *Sazanami*, presided over by the commander of Destroyer Squadron 3, Rear Admiral Matsuji Ijuin. It had already been announced that he would lead the Horaniu operation in person.

"When ordered to direct this operation," Ijuin said, "I urged the high command to discontinue the use of destroyers for transport purposes. Accordingly our destroyers will function purely as escorts. Escort squadrons of a year ago never had fewer than eight destroyers, but we must be content with four because of the high attrition rate of recent months. But I have hand-picked these four outstanding ships, and I know that their fighting strength will be as the strength of eight."

Ijuin then asked me to brief the conference on the Vella Gulf action, and he listened just as intently as the others. When I had finished he spoke again.

"I wholeheartedly endorse Hara's remarks and I commend to you his actions in that battle. Remember his cautiousness and flexibility. In the present operation our duty is to guard the convoy, not to seek duels. I disapprove of the dogged inflexibility which has proved such a detriment to our Navy."

This reference to the four ships as the best at Rabaul was no mere flattery. My *Shigure* was the only one which was not of the very latest type. *Hamakaze*, hero of the July 13 battle at Kula Gulf, was one of the rare Japanese warships to be equipped at this time with radar. She and sister-ship *Isokaze* formed Destroyer Division 17, commanded by Captain Toshio Miyazaki. These and Ijuin's own flagship, *Sazanami*, formed the escort for the operation. This little squadron could boast the rare line-up of a rear admiral and two captains. Furthermore, Ijuin, with his stress on flexibility, gave each of us captains a free hand in making preparations. And the freedom allowed to Ijuin by the high command showed how impressed they had been by the Vella Gulf debacle.

This four-ship squadron left Rabaul at 0300 on August 17, and sped southward to rendezvous with our convoy of 20 small landing barges. They set out from Buin, Bougainville, at 1027 the same day, carrying 400 reinforcements for Horaniu.

We were still within 100 miles of Rabaul when our radio intercepted a message from an airplane very near by. Since the enemy thus knew of our movements, it was essential that we learn what we could of his. Accordingly, Ijuin promptly radioed the Buin air station to double its scout plane missions.

The first message from any of our scout planes came at 1330, just as Bougainville appeared on the southwestern horizon. The sighting report said: "Three large enemy destroyers in Gizo Strait headed toward Biloa."

This information was received in our force with mixed feelings. I was relieved to know something about the enemy's movements. It was so much better than my last mission when we had to advance with no knowledge of the enemy deployment.

Our ships were bent on 28 knots toward Bougainville Strait. We had to rush lest the enemy maul the unescorted convoy which was advancing slowly along the Choiseul coast.

The sun set while we sped through Bougainville Strait. The night's full moon was obscured by heavy weather. Clouds hovered at 1,500 feet, and visibility was no more than three miles. These conditions favored the enemy with his vastly superior radar, and we knew it.

At 2100 Vella Lavella loomed dead ahead on the horizon. We were near-ing our goal and, very likely, a showdown with the three enemy destroy-ers. The tense silence of our march was suddenly broken by the booming voice of lookout Yamashita: "Enemy plane!" A sleek bomber swung overhead and disappeared into the low clouds. Just as suddenly, another plane, which appeared to be an Avenger bomber, edged out of the clouds to drop a white flare directly above *Shigure*.

Our destroyers broke column instantly and spread out, with all guns barking at the enemy plane. We zigzagged at 30 knots and laid smoke screens, each destroyer following prescribed procedure.

Another bomber came out of the clouds and dove toward *Sazanami*, almost scraping the flagship's masts as it flew over and released several bombs.

"Skip bombing!" I thought and clenched my fists in anxiety. It had been a constant nightmare for me in the five months since I had first heard of this new air attack method. My wrestling with the problem of how to evade such assaults had failed to produce any solution.

The bombs aimed at *Sazanami*, however, did not skip. They were dropped in a conventional dive bombing and they missed, raising several white col-umns of water around the flagship. *Sazanami*'s guns replied but failed to score on the daring attacker.

I relaxed with relief that our ships were undamaged and the plane gone. But there was now great likelihood that more would return. Far ahead we caught sight of the convoy we were to guard. It would be an hour before we could catch up. I tried to figure what we would do if the enemy came back with many planes, but such thoughts were broken by another shout from Yamashita. This time there were two enemy planes.

One twin-engined bomber dived on lead ship *Sazanami*, the other struck the opposite end of our column, at *Shigure*. All our guns greeted this auda-cious pilot who dove literally between our masts in laying his deadly eggs, before zooming up in a sharp climb. Some of our shells must have caught that bomber for, as it was about to disappear into the clouds, we saw the left wing spurting fire.

When the bombs missed *Shigure* I looked toward *Sazanami*. She was wreathed in a very thorough smoke screen. I knew she'd be safe from the attack of such mediocre bomber pilots as these. Before it was over, a total of eight bombers assailed us in this running battle which lasted almost until we reached the mouth of Vella Gulf. As the last of the planes departed, the ominous, black silhouette of Kolombangara towered over us from the east. Everything was again in pitch darkness. Were we walking into another enemy trap?

From the radio-room voice tube: "*Sazanami* orders 180-degree turn to the west, because of poor visibility on Kolombangara side."

I was happy to obey that order, and *Shigure* turned immediately. Our four destroyers rejoined and started a westward march. We had gone nearly 30 miles when *Sazanami* signaled: "Four enemy ships bearing 190 degrees, distant 15,000 meters."

Admiral Ijuin had kept us out of an enemy ambush.

Sazanami's stern signal light kept blinking: "Form combat column. Prepare for torpedo attack to port!"

Ijuin later told me how overjoyed he was to find that the enemy was pursuing us. "I was positive that the enemy, overconfident after his phenomenal August 6 victory, had decided to ignore the vulnerable unescorted convoy, and challenge us to a duel. I headed north to lure the enemy into battle at a safe distance from the convoy."

At 2232 our destroyers turned 45 degrees to a northwest heading, while every eye was glued to the movement of the enemy. The "combat column" order had shifted the positions of our ships so that radar-equipped *Hamakaze* was closest to the enemy and covering *Sazanami*, and my *Shigure* was another 1,000 meters northward.

The enemy's continued speeding to the northeast indicated that he was not yet aware of our irregular turn-around. The distance between our forces was shrinking steadily when, at 2240, a brilliant blue and white flare blossomed above the enemy column. That signal dropped by one of our scout planes meant: "Enemy ships are destroyers!"

The U.S. column started a rapid, sharp turn to the west. This was a shock to Ijuin who realized that the enemy was breaking off his chase of our destroyers. This meant that the enemy would charge against our unprotected barges.

Ijuin immediately ordered a 90-degree turn to the southwest for his destroyers, and called for a calculation of the enemy's speed. It appeared shortly that our destroyers could not possibly reach the enemy destroyers before they lit into our defenseless barges. Ijuin ordered: "Fire torpedoes on long-range setting!"

He estimated the distance between *Sazanami* and the enemy to be 8,000 meters. To me it appeared to be more than 10,000 meters. At such a range

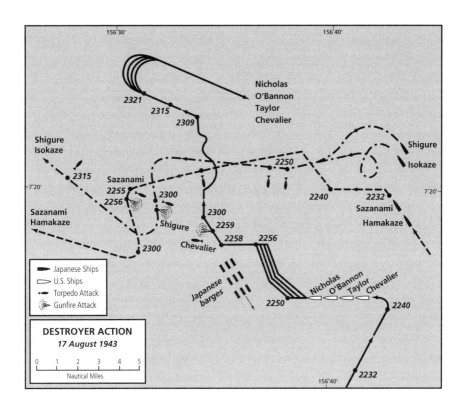

there was practically no chance of scoring hits. The American ships were on an almost parallel course and making better than 30 knots. Nevertheless, a catastrophe appeared imminent and Ijuin decided to release torpedoes. At 2252 they were launched and sped on their deadly way, two meters beneath the surface.

The 23 oxygen-driven torpedoes were about halfway to the targets when suddenly one of them leaped upward, breaking the surface of the water and raising white, billowing waves of fluorescent spray which stood out in the dark of night like a lighted signboard. The enemy column saw it too, and made a rapid right turn, followed by another right turn, and our torpedoes missed completely. Admiral Ijuin watched impassively through his binoculars and said, "What an evasion! But at least we distracted them from the convoy."

At 2255 *Sazanami* released her eight remaining torpedoes. The distance was still a difficult 7,000 meters, but the admiral did not care. The enemy reacted with another sharp turn to the right and again evaded all torpedoes.

"All guns," Ijuin roared, "open fire!" *Sazanami* and *Hamakaze* rushed precipitously toward the enemy with guns blazing. But, without searchlights, the guns were poorly aimed. Also, the distance was too great for the small 12.7-mm. guns of our destroyers.

Isokaze and *Shigure* raced forward but held fire, while the two opposing groups swiftly closed. It was 2059 when I gave my next battle order: "Ready four torpedoes portside!"

The next moment *Shigure* was straddled by enemy shells which fell 20 to 40 meters from the ship, kicking up pillars of water and spray. Another barrage, seconds later, bracketed our ship even more closely; and the third just barely missed us.

I craned my neck and strained my eyes for gun flashes which simply did not appear. I realized now that we were confronted with the enemy's new flashless powder we had all heard rumored about. That, combined with his radar-controlled guns, presented a formidable opposition. Forgetting my own plans for a torpedo attack, I ordered smoke and a zigzag course.

Shigure weaved back and forth through the thickening smoke screen at her full 30 knots. But no matter which way we turned shells kept falling around us every six or seven seconds with breath-taking, uncanny tempo. Tension rose as we realized that any moment might bring a direct hit.

My torpedo and gunnery officers were crying for permission to open fire, but I knew we must hold off until the most opportune moment. We held fire while the enemy shelling continued. The enemy ships were approaching on a bearing of 60 degrees. I wanted to launch torpedoes before opening gunfire because the guns would tend to spoil the accuracy of our torpedo launchings.

Enemy salvos were falling so close that they splashed water in my face. When the enemy range had closed to 5,000 meters I gave the word to launch and turn away. I watched the torpedoes speed on their way and, at the same time, waited for the feeling of *Shigure's* response to her helm which was slow in coming. A salvo of enemy shells hit farther away, and then another close by.

I called for gunfire and *Shigure's* hull quivered like a leaf with the first barrage. The din was deafening. While we continued to fire at the enemy and he at us, not a single shell hit our ship. As my ears adjusted to the roar and clatter of guns I became aware that the masthead lookout was shouting: "One torpedo hit the second enemy ship. Our guns are getting the range on the third."

I could see no vestige of this through the smoke of battle, but the news brought cheers from the crew on deck. The next piece of news, the most surprising of the day, was from *Hamakaze* whose radar had detected the

7

approach of a powerful enemy force. Captain Toshio Miyazaki suggested retirement to the northwest.

A message from Admiral Ijuin expressed his concurrence with Miyazaki's proposal. I immediately sent word of my complete agreement.

We turned northwest at 2300, followed by *Isokaze*. *Sazanami* and *Hamakaze*, moving together, also sped on a retirement course. Shells continued to fall about us for another ten minutes. None hit *Shigure*, but *Isokaze* was less fortunate. She desperately launched eight torpedoes at the pursuing enemy who swerved to the right, evaded them, and continued on. Near misses on *Isokaze* at 2312 injured some of her crewmen and set small fires. *Hamakaze* was also slightly damaged, but *Sazanami* and *Shigure* were unscathed. This was the second straight battle for *Shigure* in which she and her crew had not received a scratch.

Lieutenant Commander Toshio Niwa, who commanded the convoy, later told me that his barge crews and passengers enjoyed a grandstand view of the eight destroyers in their running battle. The men applauded and cheered when they saw hits made on the American ships.

The 20 barges, meanwhile, inched along the coast as the U.S. destroyers—*Nicholas*, *O'Bannon*, *Taylor*, *Chevalier*—were being lured seaward by our destroyers. The 400 troops had to spend the following daylight hours in the barges, nestled along the coast, but they were put ashore at Horaniu when night fell. The landing operation was an unquestioned success. By the same token, it must be concluded that Captain Thomas J. Ryan's destroyers failed and, in so doing, left some unexplained puzzles.

His ships paralleled our course until 2321 and then made two 90-degree right turns to head back toward the convoy. Some reports say he gave up the chase because his ships could make only 30 knots against the 35-knot speed of the Japanese destroyers. *Shigure*'s maximum speed was 30 knots. With her poor rudder response at the time, I know that she and *Isokaze* were running at no more than 28 knots. Furthermore, the course of his column and my pair of ships, as checked by action reports of both sides, do not support his claim of having chased us.

Captain Ryan's force did not even give determined chase to the barges of the convoy. It is said that his destroyers had spent all their ammunition, but they must still have had some machine-gun bullets left, and that was all that would have been needed against the unarmed barges. As it was, only two of the barges were sunk, and no lives were lost in them.

It may be that Ryan thought this was one of the familiar "Tokyo Express" runs in which the destroyers were serving as transports for the main portion of the landing troops. When we withdrew he may have retired satisfied that he had successfully foiled our landing operation.

During the battle, neither I nor any of my colleagues saw a single American torpedo. This puzzled us too, especially since this encounter came only ten days after an epochal U.S. torpedo victory in this same area. Ijuin said afterward, "I believe the enemy ships must have been cruisers, not destroyers, because they preferred to fight with guns at long range."

The claim by *Shigure*'s lookout that one of our torpedoes had hit the enemy was never verified. It may have been an illusion. More likely it was an explosion, induced by a destroyer's wake. The somewhat halfhearted enemy maneuvers after the reported hit led me to believe this latter possibility.* Ijuin, of noble birth and used to having his way, was in a buoyant mood. He would hear nothing of my doubts and skepticism. Accordingly, his report to Imperial Headquarters said: "The outstanding destroyer of this force is *Shigure* which sank an enemy cruiser by torpedo attack."

The most criticized part of the entire action was the Japanese break-off, which was sparked by *Hamakaze*'s radar-detection of a powerful enemy force in the vicinity. There is only one explanation for *Hamakaze*'s error in this regard. Japanese radar was so unreliable in those days, it must have mistaken our convoy of barges for a nonexistent enemy fleet.

Since the end of the war I have observed strong American criticism of Ijuin for his withdrawal, forsaking the barges he was supposed to protect. Strangely, however, there seem to have been no voices raised against the U.S. commander for his failure to follow through in this action.

It is my feeling that both commanders approached this action prejudiced and preoccupied. The August 7 debacle at Vella Gulf was obviously a strong influence on Ijuin. And Ryan had commanded one of the destroyer squadrons in the Kolombangara battle of July 12. In that battle, one of his ships had been sunk and three others turned in a poor performance as an outnumbered Japanese force inflicted heavy damage. Historians and critics too often overlook the state of mind of the commanders in judging a military or naval action.

---

* No Japanese torpedoes scored hits, though some were evaded only by skillful maneuvering.

3

Our four destroyers returned to Rabaul on August 18. *Shigure*'s proud and happy crew was given the next day off. In those days of high attrition it was a real wonder for a destroyer to go through two battles in a row without a scratch. On our previous return there had been raised eyebrows that *Shigure* should be the sole Japanese survivor. This time no one could even suggest a doubt about her valor.

Admiral Ijuin lunched with Captain Miyazaki and me at the officers' club. They praised *Shigure*'s performance until I was pleased to the point of embarrassment. Ijuin noted how greatly *Shigure* had changed under my command, and he concluded, "I regret, Hara, that as a division commander you have had but a single ship, and that one much older than your *Amatsukaze*. But be patient. You will soon have other ships to command."

Admiral Ijuin was a remarkably congenial and friendly person despite his noble rank of Baron. Born with a silver spoon in his mouth, he had achieved a Navy-wide reputation as an excellent navigator. It was gratifying to know that a man of his ability and rank was interested in one's welfare.

Rabaul was enjoying a comparative quiet spell from air raids so we left the club after lunch and went for a stroll. A balmy southeasterly breeze rustled the coconut trees. There was little fuss about formalities at this tropical base.

We wore plain shirts and shorts and ordinary straw hats. Accordingly, sailors passed us without saluting for a change, and it was fun to walk unnoticed.

Stores conducted business as usual and most of them were owned by Chinese. What a tenacious people! While Japan and the Allies were engaged in savage battle the calm Chinese of Rabaul seemed interested only in strengthening their control of the local economy.

Passing an alleyway we were attracted by a crowd gathered in an inner yard. The bystanders were watching the spirited dancing of some 40 native men. They wore nothing but feathers in their hair and colorful sarongs around their waists. The rest of their sepia bodies was covered with brightly-hued powders and paints. With only drum for accompaniment they danced so vigorously that they streamed with perspiration. From time to time native women threw bananas or other fruit to the dancers. This was devoured while the dance continued. Occasionally they gave out loud shrieks which sounded like the quacking of ducks. We did not learn the occasion for this dance but it was fascinating. For half an hour we watched as the young men kicked up their feet, waved arms, and jerked their heads from side to side. It was monotonous but strangely appealing.

Miyazaki said, "These people are content with their primitive way of life—bare subsistence food, crude dwellings, coarse garments—and they seek nothing more. By our standards they are lazy. But who is happier?"

Ijuin finally suggested a move, saying, "I enjoy this dancing, but would like to visit the hot spring baths we saw earlier. Will you join me?"

This proposal took Miyazaki and me by surprise. We had visited the hot spring and commented in passing with the admiral about what a good bath place it was. Now Miyazaki recovered voice before I did, and said, "Begging your pardon, sir, that spring is right out in the open. I have never seen an admiral bathing there."

"But you have bathed there, my dear Captain," Ijuin retorted, "and if you can enjoy the pleasures of the large outdoor bath, why should I have to be content with my narrow and uncomfortable shipboard bath?"

There was no arguing with an admiral, especially when his words were so full of pleasant logic. Taking advantage of the volcanic formation of New Britain the Navy had built open-air bath houses over the hot springs. Large metal drums in each enclosure served as tubs. Each bather filled his own with the clean, hot spring water. A rinsing wash, followed by a Japanese-style soaking in the tub, and the bather emerges lobster-red and refreshed.

It was the most popular place in Rabaul for ships' crews. Anyone with a shore pass could bathe free of charge, and, after days at sea with no bath, this was a welcome treat. But high-ranking officers had their own baths on board ship. Thus it was surprising for an admiral, let alone one who was also a baron, to visit these public baths.

When we started to fill our drums with the hot water, two young men leaped from their tubs, saluted, and took over our work. We had returned their salutes automatically but Ijuin quickly said, "Take it easy, lads, we can fill our own tubs. Stark naked there is no difference of rank."

But the young men would not listen. When the drums were filled they disappeared. Ijuin sighed, "We seem to have spoiled their pleasure. I should not have come."

The baths were wonderful. Before they were over, we had scrubbed each other's back, lined up in a row like three monkeys. It was most undignified for naval officers, but we did not care. In the course of this relaxation, Ijuin said, "Professor of Torpedoes Hara, I'd like to have your critique of my action in this last operation. *Sazanami*'s eight fish were wasted. How could we have done better?"

"Well, in the first place, I do not think they were really wasted. Our first spreads were detected when that one torpedo malfunctioned and broached. Had it not been for that, I believe we would have had some hits."

Ijuin conceded that, and further mused that the distance had been too great for even our long-range torpedoes. I continued, "That's right. With the phenomenal success of the enemy's radar, I fear that all of my formulas will need adjustment. When the enemy can fire at us with the advantage of radar-controlled range finders, it is virtually impossible for us to close him to within 3,000 yards."

"That is true," Ijuin said. "The enemy now has the upper hand, and it would be wiser for us not to try for a smashing victory every time. It does not pay to sink an enemy ship if it costs us too dearly in men and ships."

The Allied offensive was growing constantly stronger, gaining momentum, and becoming more and more difficult to oppose. On the very day of our return, while we were relaxing at Rabaul, Japanese troops started a withdrawal from Santa Isabel, a long, slender Solomons island due east of and parallel to the islands of Vella Lavella, Kolombangara, and New Georgia.

We had three days' rest at Rabaul before Miyazaki and I were ordered to take three destroyers and pick up as many troops as possible from Rekata on northeastern Santa Isabel. Of 3,400 troops at Rekata, some 600 had been removed by an earlier group of destroyers.

Once again *Shigure* was teamed with *Hamakaze*. Damaged *Isokaze* was replaced by *Minazuki* and the three ships sortied in the morning of August 22. We were loaded to capacity with food and supplies for those who could not be evacuated. Our three ships could each carry only 250 passengers.

Our mission was a tough one under any circumstances. The previous evacuation, carried off just four days earlier, made our task all the more difficult. The enemy was alerted. We had to be prepared for the worst.

The approach to Rekata was dangerous because of its countless unposted reefs and shoals. Our charts, copied from British ones made in 1939, carried this note: "These islands have been only partially surveyed and, the larger portion of them being quite unknown, great caution is necessary while navigating in this vicinity."

We were not 100 miles out of Rabaul when three enemy planes flew over at 20,000 feet. Our guns fired at them immediately, but could not reach that altitude. It was most distressing.

The enemy planes dropped no bombs but they harassed us almost as effectively by circling overhead, out of reach, in taunting fashion. After about ten minutes six Zero fighters from Buka appeared on the scene. They climbed frantically to attack the bombers and made a number of firing passes. But the enemy planes, which appeared to be B-24s, kept on going, completely unperturbed. Our gunners rotated their guns skyward, ready to shoot if the enemy planes came within reach.

But they went away after mocking our ships and planes for an exasperating 20 minutes. Our own planes continued southward with us until nightfall, when they returned to base. Uneasy hours followed then, as we had to maintain our own alert. Fortunately, no more enemy planes came. We advanced slowly along the Bougainville coast, fully realizing the risk we ran in these dangerous waters.

We were stealthily nearing the jutting rocks and shoals around Choiseul when an urgent radio message came from Rekata. None of us who heard it will ever forget that message: "Four enemy cruisers and several destroyers sighted near the mouth of Rekata Harbor."

I groaned. Our heavy-laden ships, hampered by the dangerous reefs, had been making only ten knots. In our close approach to Rekata we were supposed to slow to six knots. That would set us up like big clay pigeons for the shells and torpedoes of the enemy.

While we struggled over the various possibilities, *Hamakaze*'s veiled signal lamp blinked a message: "Put about at once and head out to sea at 24 knots, until we learn the movements of the enemy."

Our consequent turn away from the coast to head toward the north made us a clear target for the radar of the enemy. We had not been on our new course more than ten minutes when a radio intercept indicated that an enemy scout plane had spotted and reported our change of course. What could we do against such an opponent?

A study of the chart showed the enemy to be just 30 miles distant. Should we hug the island coast to confuse his radar? Make a run for it? Attack? By attacking we could surely knock out an enemy ship or two, but there was no chance of defeating all the enemy ships. The blue signal lamp in *Hamakaze*'s stern began to blink.

"Rabaul orders immediate return to base without engaging. Return to Rabaul at 30 knots."

I breathed a deep sigh of relief and looked at my watch. It was almost midnight as we headed toward Rabaul, where we arrived in the afternoon of August 23.

We barely had time to recover lost sleep when two days later we left again for Rekata. This time we got a break with murky weather which kept us from being spotted by the enemy. There was intermittent rain during our southward run and visibility was down to a few hundred meters by nightfall.

Weather conditions were the same when we arrived at Santa Isabel. We now wished, since there was no sign of enemy warships, that the weather would clear. We slowed to six knots and threaded the reefs of Rekata Harbor at this snail's pace, pausing every hundred meters to check on our situation. This was as enervating as enemy action. We groped thus for almost two hours, until a dim light appeared. It was a garrison soldier, marking the harbor mouth. Our three ships had successfully negotiated the treacherous shoals, and we were relieved to ease into the narrow port.

By 0100 of August 25 we had started to unload cargo. Several hundred troops waited on the blacked-out pier for their time to embark. The silence of the night was suddenly and violently shattered by two bomber planes, which roared in at masthead height and zoomed away into the low-hanging clouds. In the same instant their bombs began to detonate, raising huge pillars of water all around.

A quick survey showed no damage, but the poorly aimed bombs did serve to speed up the unloading process. As the decks were cleared of cargo the waiting troops flew up the ramps. The ships were soon jammed with eager passengers and we were on our way again. It was still pitch dark but now we could navigate the reefs without pausing. As soon as we sighted the signal light at the mouth of the harbor we gained speed. By 0230 we were up to 30 knots, certain the enemy planes would soon be after us again, and in greater numbers. We wanted to be as far away as possible by daybreak.

Dawn came within an hour of our reaching the open sea. We were then running along the coast of Choiseul. Another hour passed and we reached Bougainville Strait, and so did the enemy planes!

Luckily we spotted their approach and were able to put up a smoke screen as we scattered. *Hamakaze* and *Minazuki* revved up to their maximum of 35 knots. *Shigure* panted along at her best speed of 30. There were at least a dozen enemy planes and they seemed to be everywhere. They swooped and banked all around us. Our guns roared skyward ceaselessly, but made no effective hits. We zigzagged and weaved at top speed as the bombs came curving down, but *Shigure* was exasperatingly sluggish in responding to the helm.

An intense five minutes passed and the planes were gone. Fortunately for *Shigure* the bombardiers did not have her number. The various ship sections reported no damage or casualties. No bombs had even come close.

As we were clearing our own smoke screen the two other destroyers showed up some 3,000 meters ahead. When all smoke had cleared I saw that *Hamakaze* was in trouble. There was fire in her forecastle and she was limping at greatly reduced speed. *Minazuki* appeared to be intact and was standing by.

Shigure closed quickly while *Hamakaze* sent us a flag signal: "One direct hit on forecastle, 36 casualties. Speed restricted to 20 knots. Am considering heading for Shortland. Miyazaki."

Our nearest base was at Shortland, not more than 30 miles away. But I knew it was not safe for warships because no air cover was available. Accordingly, my signalman waved a message: "Captain Hara strongly objects to your plan. Shortland base no longer safe. Let us return to Rabaul at 20 knots. If trouble develops, *Shigure* is prepared to tow you. Please reply."

Miyazaki promptly approved my suggestion. *Hamakaze*'s fire was put out and we continued northward together. The rest of the voyage was agonizingly slow, but luckily no more planes came to attack, and we made it to Rabaul.

Waterfront hands gaped to see *Shigure* heading the column composed of *Hamakaze* and *Minazuki*. If any of these three should have been a victim, it was rickety old *Shigure* and not a new, fast ship like *Hamakaze*. Every man in *Shigure* was happy and proud. We had not forgotten the jibes and jokes aimed at her in the past.

I felt sorry for Miyazaki when we met the next day at headquarters. After an excellent career and brilliant performances as a destroyer man, he had been directly in line for promotion to flag rank while still in his forties. Now, as hapless commander of a destroyer division whose every ship (*Yukikaze*, *Isokaze*, *Hamakaze*) was under repair from battle damage, his chances of making admiral seemed much more remote. This day he was sullen and shamefaced.

Ijuin greeted him by holding out a piece of paper and saying, "Don't scowl, Miyazaki. Read this and cheer up."

His hands trembled as he read the paper and passed it to me with a wan smile. It was a radio message from Shortland saying that the base was being ruthlessly pounded by a heavy air attack. Miyazaki shook my hand and said, "Hara, you saved me and *Hamakaze* with her crew and hundreds of passengers. Had I gone to Shortland we would have been blasted to bits by now."

Four days later Admiral Ijuin summoned me and *Shigure*'s skipper to his office. Our squadron commander appeared moody and spoke somewhat hesitatingly. "*Shigure* is to make a solo transport run to Tuluvu. I hate to give you this assignment, but I have been ordered to take all our other destroyers with me to evacuate Rekata. *Shigure* has been chosen for the lone mission because we know that you are on board, Hara, and we believe that if any man can make this run with a single ship, you can. It is a difficult assignment, and I promise that at least one more destroyer will be added to your division when you return from this mission."

"I am flattered, Admiral Ijuin, to be given this assignment. It is a matter of great honor for Yamagami and me to take *Shigure* on this lone sortie."

Ijuin's face brightened with relief. In sudden good humor he spoke again. "Hara, you have worked wonders with *Shigure*. She has earned a nickname in the fleet as 'The Indestructible Destroyer.' I am proud to have her in this command, and I hope we can sortie together the next time."

At Tuluvu, on the northern tip of New Britain's Cape Gloucester, Japan maintained a small air base. Although the enemy now held air superiority in this vicinity, Tuluvu was important as an advance lookout post for Rabaul. There was no overland route between Rabaul and Tuluvu, so all supplies had to be brought in by ship. Food and ammunition had been in short supply at this little base for some time, but its repeated requests for supplies had gone unanswered because of the pressure of the Solomons operations. Now Tuluvu could no longer be ignored if Japan wanted to keep it.

The name had an ominous sound for me. Tuluvu sits at the western mouth of the Bismarck Sea where, in early March, the enemy had introduced skip-bombing to sink four of eight destroyers and eight out of eight transports, from our sixteen-ship convoy. It was off Tuluvu that *Ariake* of my own division sank on July 28, along with *Mikazuki*. The two destroyers had run aground on a reef while dodging enemy bombs.

Tuluvu was fully within range of daily Allied air patrols. Any Japanese ship venturing in those waters could expect enemy bombers to provide an "all-out welcome," including their phenomenal skip-bombing. Try as I had for a defensive solution against this form of attack, here we were, almost certain to face it, and I still had no idea of how skip-bombing could be thwarted.

Bismarck Sea survivors had reported how ineffective conventional evasive tactics had proven to be. Perhaps if the target ship turned directly toward the attacker, the plane's timing would be thrown off. But there was no way to find out except by the test of battle. And that involved the lives of my ship and its crew of more than 200 men.

Shigure left Rabaul at noon, September 1, on her sortie for Tuluvu. At 18 knots we moved along New Britain's northern coast, as treacherous as any in the Solomons. Here also were many uncharted rocks and shoals.

Night came as we approached Cape Hollmann, at the northern tip of Willaumez Peninsula, roughly midway between Rabaul and Tuluvu. *Shigure* was entering the danger zone. The radio room announced that an enemy plane was transmitting from nearby. This news came a little earlier than anticipated. I ordered the lookouts to watch for enemy planes, despite the heavy clouds and darkness.

An hour later the radioman called out, "An enemy plane is sending again. Directly overhead. We cannot decipher the message, but it seems to refer to our position, direction, and speed."

The weather and visibility worsened as we continued westward. It was becoming sultry. Sweat stood in beads on my face. Minutes passed and the radio room called, "An enemy plane is again reading our course."

Tension and silence mounted on the bridge. I took out a handkerchief and wiped my face. Never had the atmosphere been so tense. Lieutenant Tsukihara, the navigation officer, observed approaching rain, and he was right. It came, cutting visibility to a few meters. It was 2000 hours. We dropped speed and turned southwest for an approach to the craggy coast.

The radio room reported that no enemy planes were audible. "Good," said Tsukihara. "This glorious weather has discouraged the enemy."

The tension on the bridge was easing. Officers and men chattered in whispers. They yawned and stretched when 20 minutes had passed with no enemy communications detected in the vicinity.

Arms froze in the air and jaws fell agape, however, at the sudden high-pitched, jarring sound of dive-bombing planes. We all crouched and ducked. With a spine-shivering roar, a plane whizzed directly over the bridge. There was a monstrous, deafening detonation followed by several explosions. Another plane thundered by the mast.

I staggered to my feet. Where were the enemy planes? I saw Yamagami grope for and press the warning button, and klaxons whined their belated warning of an air attack throughout the ship. *Shigure* was swinging sharply to port when a water pillar rose within her turning circle, not more than 10 meters from the ship. It cascaded smack onto the forecastle. The bridge was inundated.

Shaking off the water I shouted, "Hard right rudder! Immediate overboost! Flank speed!"

Tsukihara looked at me incredulously and said, "Flank speed with immediate overboost?"

"Immediately!" I roared.

Pale and trembling, Tsukihara pushed the engine-room communicator lever full to the bottom, and closed his eyes. At the same time Yamagami called into the engine-room voice tube for an immediate overboost, and mumbled, "Oh God!"

Their reactions were perfectly natural. I had never before given such an order. Most naval officers go through their careers without ever giving such an order. Under normal conditions, it requires half an hour to go from a cruising speed of 12 knots to a maximum speed of 30. Under combat conditions this kind of speed increase should take fifteen minutes. My "immediate" order ignored all normal procedures, and ran the risk of breaking turbines and engines of our venerable *Shigure*. This caused a flurry below decks that is hard to imagine. The greatest anxiety of the engine-room gang was that this sudden call for power might shatter the fins of the turbine as the engine valves were opened. All hands performed their emergency duties, as ordered, in full expectation that this would happen.

Everyone on the bridge awaited the momentary appearance of more enemy planes. Yamagami, who was looking toward the stern, suddenly shouted and pointed toward the stack which was belching long steady streams of flame. The excess fuel poured on was being burned in the funnel, whence the flames ominously illuminated the entire after part of the ship.

Bombers could never miss such a target. Anxious minutes passed. They seemed like hours, and then the radio-room voice pipe boomed: "Enemy plane, in plain language, reports direct hits amidship on a destroyer, setting it afire and leaving it sinking."

Unable to believe my ears, I asked for a slow repeat of this message. Yamagami and Tsukihara shouted with joy when they heard the amazing report.

Another voice broke through the hilarity as the engine room asked if the emergency overboost was to continue. I was delighted to reply that it was no longer needed, and that we could slow to 12 knots again. The flames from the stack subsided quickly, and we continued in the safety of darkness.

No more planes came after us. The enemy had written off *Shigure*. The rest of our voyage was easy and pleasant, after our hair-raising experience. We landed supplies at Tuluvu and left amid joyful cheers from the garrison.

Again we returned undamaged to Rabaul. There I met Ijuin next day. He had got back safely and successfully from his Rekata operation. When I told of our experience he laughed until he almost choked, and said, "I guess we can now call you the Miracle Captain, Hara. No one but you could have thought of such an unconventional and successful tactic on the spur of the moment."

I was pleased at his considerateness, and said, "War does seem to involve many illusions. Luck had a large part in this one. I doubt that the same ruse will work again."

4

As soon as Admiral Ijuin read my report of the Tuluvu mission he ordered a complete check and inspection of my ship. As a navigation expert he was concerned about the effects on *Shigure* of the "instant" overboost she had experienced.

After a test run and rigid check the maintenance engineers submitted a report which fully justified Ijuin's apprehensions. The destroyer was declared unfit for combat. The report noted that an overhaul was long past due, the engine was on the point of breaking down, the ship did not respond properly to helm and rudder, the hull was heavily encrusted with barnacles, and all precision machinery was badly in need of repair and adjustment. The report concluded: "It is recommended that all possible repairs be made at Rabaul so that *Shigure* may proceed to Sasebo for complete overhaul at earliest opportunity."

When a copy of the report reached *Shigure*, it was circulated through the ship. Reactions of the crew were varied but basically the same. Not a man wanted to go home. After repeated battles without loss of a life, morale in this ship was at the peak, and the men roared in anger at the report. They booed, cursed, shook their fists, and howled threats at the "fathead mechanics." Admiral Ijuin, of course, approved the engineers' recommendations.

When the repairmen came on board the crew's attitude quickly changed. They became all sweetness and light, offering to co-operate with the workmen in every way. Lieutenant Hiroshi Kayanuma, *Shigure*'s chief engineer, was particularly effective. A foot-long beard gave him the fierce appearance of a cave man, but he was shrewd and intelligent, in addition to being one of the ship's heaviest drinkers. Kayanuma befriended the repair foremen, bought them drinks each day, tried to cajole them into making a new recommendation for *Shigure*. "Rabaul is short of warships," he pleaded.

"Even this rickety old tub is in better shape than ones which have received direct hits. We want to fight. Give us an early chance to sink enemy ships!"

Such was the general attitude of my crew. How they had changed in the last six months! I was now proud of them, knowing that they could succeed in any battle with their fine spirit.

The repair job took much longer than anticipated. There were additional defects which needed the repair crew's attention.

During our first week of enforced idleness I fell sick. Throughout the active month of August we never had more than a brief rest between strenuous battles which entailed long, nerve-wracking hours and many sleepless nights. In such rest periods as we had, I took to drinking heavily before retiring. By the end of August I was consuming almost a gallon of *sake* to get to sleep. After a week of idleness and drinking I had fears of becoming an alcoholic, and tried to cut down. I developed a terrible case of nerves, not serious enough to confine me to bed but enough to make me moody and irascible.

I brooded about the war situation. Why did not Japanese statesmen negotiate for peace before it was too late? I could not sleep well. When I did sleep it was only to have bad dreams and awaken in a cold sweat.

Looking back on this period, I am grateful for Ijuin's awareness of my need for rest. I was still strong, in my early forties, and yet command of a ship in wartime was a grueling task. I can only imagine how much more difficult it must have been for higher ranking officers. Historians, often critical of commanding officers, are apt to overlook the strains and heavy responsibilities of a battle command.

My brief rest was a lifesaver. Those two weeks of recuperation saved me from having a nervous breakdown. By the time our repair job was finished in mid-September, I was fully back in form, physically and mentally.

Meanwhile the war situation for Japan had deteriorated. Lines of communication were being cut and outpost garrisons were being strangled. Accordingly, the high command decided on another withdrawal operation. The Kolombangara area was to be evacuated.

I returned to action just in time for the Buka transport operation. This Solomon island is the closest of that group to Rabaul. Ijuin had decided that this easy operation would provide a good warm-up for me. The Kolombangara pull-out began September 21. On that date the Japanese contingents were withdrawn from Arundel and Gizo, which flank Kolombangara on the south and southwest. On the 27th, the Buka operation completed, I joined in the evacuation of the 10,000-man garrison from Kolombangara itself. This job was successfully completed in early October with a loss of only 66 men.

Vella Lavella was next on the program. From there, as from the other evacuation points, the troops were pulled back to assemble at Bougainville. Ijuin was ordered to direct the evacuation of some 600 troops from Horaniu, Vella Lavella.

For this withdrawal operation Ijuin mapped out an elaborate plan calling for three support groups of nine destroyers. Compared with the total of only 25 destroyers used in evacuating 10,000 troops from Kolombangara, this was an extraordinarily strong force. Ijuin explained that though the Kolombangara operations had met with surprisingly little opposition, the enemy was now aware of our strategy, and we had to be ready for much stronger opposition.

The ludicrous character of this particular operation is highlighted by the fact that the 600 troops on Horaniu were to be transported to Buin in southern Bougainville, a distance of no more than 50 miles. Furthermore, and ironically, 400 of these soldiers comprised the group whose landing on Horaniu had been supported by Ijuin just a month and a half earlier.

The resultant destroyer battle of October 6–7 was one of the most confused encounters of the Pacific War. From the very beginning, the fight was conducted by men consistently obsessed with illusions and miscalculations, but some points are certain. The Americans had a correct appraisal of Japanese strength at Horaniu, and they were aware that an effort to withdraw these few isolated troops was imminent. The enemy also knew that a year of attrition warfare had seriously depleted Japanese surface strength. But the American high command did not dream that the Japanese Navy would throw nine destroyers, four sub-chasers, and twenty barges into such a small operation.

Admiral Ijuin had been through many naval actions in recent months. He was a tired man. While I was able to recover from my weariness, he had no chance to rest from the mental and physical strain of protracted battle. This was an important factor in the ensuing engagement.

Admiral Ijuin's evacuation force for Vella Lavella, which departed Rabaul in the early morning of October 6, was organized as follows:

SUPPORT GROUPS, Rear Admiral Ijuin
1. DD *Akigumo, Isakaze, Kazegumo, Yugumo*
2. DD *Shigure, Samidare* (Cdr. Hara)
Destroyer Transport Group, Captain Kunizo Kanaoka
    DD *Fumizuki, Matsukaze, Yunagi*
Sub-chaser Transport Group, Captain Shigoroku Nakayama
    4 Sub-chasers and about 20 barges

Ijuin led the force in destroyer *Akigumo*, followed by experienced Captain Miyazaki in his *Isokaze* and the rest. Had Ijuin sailed in *Isokaze* he could have relied on Miyazaki to assist in making important battle decisions. In *Akigumo*, with her less experienced captain and officers, Ijuin was forced to make all decisions for himself.

Contrary to the opinions of some Americans concerning this action, Ijuin was ready and willing to fight. The very number of ships he brought attests to that. Being a navigation expert he was inclined toward elaborate maneuvers, and the memory of having successfully outmaneuvered the enemy in the same area seven weeks earlier could not but influence him further. Tired as he was, new concepts could not be expected.

The four ships of his first group were capable of making 35 knots. Accordingly, in our conference on tactics, Ijuin had told us that he would maneuver to lure the enemy into position where my two destroyers could make a disconcerting thrust so that the third group of destroyers could reach the transport convoy without opposition. Our nine destroyers were thus deployed in separate groups to confuse the enemy as to our actual strength. The Americans did underestimate our total fighting strength, but they did not fight according to Ijuin's script.

The day was cloudy with intermittent rain. We found comfort in the squalls which provided a measure of concealment. We were skirting the eastern coast of Bougainville at noon when our radios picked up an enciphered enemy message. It came from either a patrol plane or from some clandestine lookout planted in the Bougainville jungle. We had no way of knowing if the spotter was reporting all or just some of our ships, then spread over many miles in their three separate groups; but it was disconcerting to know that our presence had been detected so early.

On receipt of this message, distance between our ships was increased from 500 to 1000 meters in preparation for an air assault. Several planes did approach from the direction of Choiseul about 1500, just as we encountered heavy rain squalls. The storms provided welcome protective darkness for half an hour or so, in which time the planes gave up the chase. When we emerged into clear weather they were nowhere to be seen.

At sunset I received a message from Ijuin saying that his group was rushing ahead toward Vella Lavella, and directing the rest of us to "slow to nine knots and stand by east of Shortland to meet the barges" which were expected to come out soon. Ijuin thereupon sped down Bougainville Strait with his four ships at 26 knots. Darkness added considerably to the hazard of these waters but his ships made it without incident. It was a fine demonstration of his talent as a navigator.

My two ships moved slowly through the strait and met the transport convoy east of Shortland on schedule. We then proceeded southeast at a leisurely nine knots.

Ijuin had arrived almost at Horaniu when he spotted "four" destroyers through the darkness. A sudden rain squall cloaked everything from sight, this time favoring the enemy, who had not yet sighted Ijuin. Groping in the utter darkness, and preoccupied with dire thoughts about the enemy's radar-controlled guns, Ijuin hesitated. At that moment he was handed a message from the radio room:

"A scout plane from Rabaul has spotted four enemy cruisers and three destroyers cruising westward north of Vella Lavella."

Ijuin nodded gravely and quietly gave the order for his group to be ready to reverse course. This completely erroneous sighting report thus caused most of the ensuing Japanese blunders. How it came to be credited and disseminated has never been determined. It is my assumption that the scout pilot was sadly lacking in experience. He probably saw the group of three American destroyers intermittently through the clouds. Seeing them in various positions and on various courses he could easily have mistaken the one group for two or three different ones, and he so reported. It was a grave error indeed.

Had this first sighting report been accurate, the entire picture of the battle would have been different. A cruiser packs ten times the firepower of a destroyer, and Ijuin must have been thinking of this and recalling how accurate radar-controlled guns can be. Ijuin knew that in rain and darkness, without effective radar, his warships would be no match for so powerful an enemy force. He could thus come to only one decision.

When the fateful message came to *Shigure*, I was surprised at the early appearance of the enemy but had no reason to doubt the accuracy of the sighting report. I could fairly visualize Ijuin's chagrin at thus having his schedule disturbed. His dilemma was a harsh one. Should he follow the logical choice of canceling the entire show, or should he try to continue as planned? His force was disproportionately strong for the minor evacuation effort on which he was embarked. Cancellation would mean a terrible loss of face. Also, there was no reason to think that postponement of the evacuation attempt would result in meeting a lesser enemy force the next time.

While Ijuin wavered, debating the various possibilities, his group of ships continued southward at 26 knots. And while he wavered, Captain Walker, leading a column of three destroyers in flagship *Selfridge*, spotted what he determined to be an enemy transport convoy at 2131 (local time). While Walker ordered his own ships to race toward the "convoy" at 33 knots, he called in another group of three U.S. destroyers which were then off the northern coast of New Georgia, some 20 miles west of his position.

Visibility this night was variable and changing. Clear air brought objects into view from a range of up to 15,000 meters. But frequent mists and vapors reduced local visibility to practically zero. Thus it was that Captain Walker had sighted Japanese ships from afar, while Ijuin was still unaware of these American destroyers.

Walker's ships were closing rapidly on the Japanese destroyers when Ijuin issued his next order, which was for my two destroyers to join him "as quickly as possible." I received this message at 2010, and hastened to comply by ordering our full speed of 30 knots.

Ijuin was then still ignorant of the enemy's location and movements. This rapidly closing threat was hidden from him by the hazy night air. But, trying to facilitate the joinder of my ships, Ijuin turned his group westward at 2029. Six minutes later I radioed an appeal: "Cannot find you because of poor visibility. Request that *Yugumo* hoist a blue stern light." At this time, 2035, Ijuin put his ships into a sharp left turn as *Yugumo* hoisted the requested identification lamp.

Ijuin's column took two more left turns in rapid succession, the last at 2038, when I caught sight of the blue signal light. One minute later Ijuin finally sighted the enemy column approaching from the east. The four fast

Japanese destroyers picked up to 35 knots and sped southward. The night's misty vapors hindered visibility as Ijuin squinted and glowered at the enemy column which he still believed to consist of four cruisers and three destroyers. Through the haze he estimated the range of the wraithlike enemy ships to be 10,000 meters, and he decided to repeat his tactics of August 17.

He planned, accordingly, to head west southwest at high speed for a torpedo-firing run. But, as is so often true at sea, these targets appeared to be closer than in fact they were, and Ijuin misjudged the distance.

He dashed briefly to the south southwest, on course 235 degrees, altered at 2040 to south by west. A message from the commander of the four sub-chasers reported that the convoy was headed directly for Horaniu, from which he was then about 20 miles to the southwest. This news pleased Ijuin for it meant that the convoy would pass safely to the rear of the enemy formation.

At 2045 Admiral Ijuin discovered his miscalculation. The enemy column appeared to have maintained its course, but it was still farther away than it should have been. He quickly altered course to SSE and then, seeking to correct the error and carry out a torpedo attack plan, at 2048 he ordered a simultaneous right turn of 45 degrees for all ships.

Here Ijuin made another mistake. A simultaneous turn is an extremely difficult maneuver. It requires precision timing and is even more difficult of execution by destroyers speeding in tight column formation. In order to execute this movement it is absolutely essential that the flagship be fully aware of the exact situation and attitude of every ship in the column. As a result, all flagship communication lines were tied up in talking with each of the other three ships, and contact was lost with *Shigure* and *Samidare* of the second group.

After his miscalculation of the enemy distance, followed by the error of ordering the simultaneous turn, Ijuin called his ships into a column formation heading momentarily southward. Surveying this situation, he paled upon realizing that his ships were now a perfect target for the enemy force. He remembered the swift deft right turn made by the four American destroyers in his August 17 encounter. Such a move at this time would permit a devastating blow at Ijuin's column followed by a northward dash to wipe out the Japanese transport convoy. Impelled by this dread possibility, exhausted, battle weary, and without opportunity to seek or hear advice from his most experienced subordinates, Admiral Ijuin next made the greatest of his blunders. He ordered his ships into another simultaneous turn, this time to the

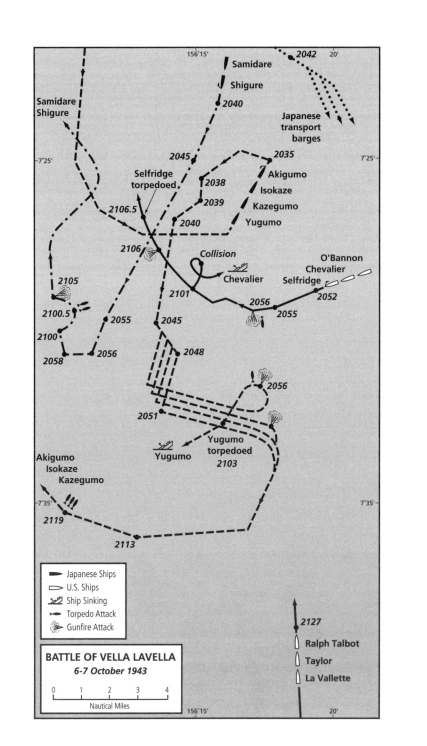

156°15'   20'

2042

Samidare

Shigure

2040

Japanese
transport
barges

Samidare
Shigure

7°25'

2045

2035

7°25'

Selfridge
torpedoed

2038

Akigumo

Isokaze

2039

Kazegumo

2106.5

2040

Yugumo

2106

Collision

O'Bannon
Chevalier
Selfridge

Chevalier

2101

2056

2055

2052

2105

2055

2100.5

2055

2045

2100

2056

2048

2058

2056

2051

Yugumo
torpedoed
2103

Yugumo

Akigumo
Isokaze
Kazegumo

7°35'

7°35'

2119

2113

Japanese Ships

U.S. Ships

Ship Sinking

Torpedo Attack

Gunfire Attack

2127

BATTLE OF VELLA LAVELLA
6-7 October 1943

Ralph Talbot

Taylor

0   1   2   3   4

Nautical Miles

La Vallette

156°15'   20'

left. This put his ships in staggered line abreast, heading east by south, and setting them up as a perfect target for the enemy.

Ijuin has never offered any reason, excuse, or alibi for this action other than to acknowledge his mistake. It is my belief that he made this move to lure the enemy southward and thus insure that the Japanese convoy remain free from attack.

At 2056 Ijuin's ships took a simultaneous right turn to the south which put them again into column formation, sterns to broadside of the enemy ships, with *Yugumo*, at the end of the column, only 3,000 meters distant from the enemy's radar-controlled guns.

At this same time the enemy ships opened gunfire and launched torpedoes. Destroyer *Yugumo*, hit by five shells at the very outset, whipped desperately out of column to the left, fired a barrage from her guns, and released eight torpedoes. *Kazegumo*, next forward, joined in the barrage but could not loose torpedoes for fear of hitting her damaged colleague. *Isokaze* and *Akigumo* could not even fire their guns.

Yugumo, quickly blasted by many shells, lost all rudder control and drifted off to the southwest. At 2103 she was hit full in the starboard side by at least one American torpedo. *Yugumo* exploded almost immediately, staggered drunkenly for several minutes, and sank. Not one of the crew of 241 appeared to have survived. Ijuin's three remaining ships fled the immediate vicinity in chaotic disorder. It took ten minutes for them to regroup, after which they pursued an orderly westward movement.

The three American destroyers, which had thus far maneuvered brilliantly, now appeared to fall victim to their own confidence. It was 2056 when they swung to the right after opening fire and releasing torpedoes at *Yugumo*. Had they continued on course they would very likely have survived. But after running for about a minute and a half, they discovered the other two Japanese destroyers—*Samidare* and my own *Shigure*—some 13,000 meters dead ahead. They swiftly turned to a reciprocal course, paralleling these new targets, in preparation for attack. This, of itself, was a correct maneuver, but it did not take into consideration the very real danger of torpedoes from dying *Yugumo*. In the excitement of their good fortune, the three American ships swung right and started to level their superior guns at the two new victims, ignoring the possibility of the approaching oxygen-driven torpedoes which they could not see.

One of *Yugumo*'s torpedoes struck *Chevalier* and detonated in her powder magazine at 2101. The American destroyer blew up two minutes before

Yugumo's own fatal explosion. Some American reports insist that *Chevalier* was preparing to machine-gun some torpedo boats at the time she was torpedoed. This unreasonable assertion must be put to rest as the product of sheer illusion or as a fiction made up for wartime home consumption. Not a single Japanese torpedo boat was operating in the area at that time.

At 2105, the very moment *Yugumo* sank into the depths, the American force suffered its second disaster when destroyer *O'Bannon* bashed smack amidship into the starboard side of dying *Chevalier*. The excuse that *O'Bannon* collided with exploding *Chevalier* because of a signal lamp failure, does not make sense to me. It is much more reasonable that the pall of smoke between the two ships, and the sudden sharp turn of *Chevalier* when hit by the torpedo, made the collision unavoidable.

Selfridge, the third American destroyer, and the only one still undamaged, proceeded on course toward *Shigure* and *Samidare* with guns blazing ineffectively. This gunfire, which she opened at 2104, had continued only two and a half minutes when her bows were rent by a torpedo. This was one of sixteen long-range torpedoes launched several minutes earlier by *Shigure* and *Samidare*.

Having covered the essentials of this action as they occurred to Ijuin's four ships up to this point, let us consider them from my viewpoint as I stood on the bridge of *Shigure*. At 2038, three minutes after asking that a signal lamp be hoisted in *Yugumo*, I sighted a dim blue lamp at some 15,000 meters and ordered full speed ahead.

Suddenly a black object appeared to port, like a small island. But there were no islands in that location. As I wondered what it could be, lookout Yamashita shouted, "Unidentified objects, 50 degrees to port. They appear to be cruisers or destroyers, apparently hostile, approaching!"

I took a look through the huge 20-centimeter binoculars. There they were. I could not count the ships because their column formation was heading almost directly at us. A flash from *Samidare* at 2040 showed that she too had made the sighting, "Enemy ships bearing 115 degrees relative."

The enemy was closing rapidly. I peered through the binoculars and considered what to do. The range was now 13,000 meters. I decided that a long-range torpedo attack was our best bet. Our heading was SSW; while that of the enemy, now 11,000 meters to the east and still closing, was SW. We were within ten degrees of being on parallel courses. This left me with a very poor launching angle, so I ordered a gradual turn slightly to the left, to improve our position for firing torpedoes.

By 2055 the range was down to 10,000 meters and we were within reach of the enemy's radar-controlled guns. I could no longer see *Yugumo*'s blue signal lamp. As the vital distance shrank to 9,000 meters it became clear that the enemy was trying to drive a wedge between Ijuin's four ships and my two. I ordered an immediate hard right rudder at 2056, and *Samidare* followed suit. My decision was made with the idea of avoiding danger from enemy guns and further improving my own torpedo-firing position.

As *Shigure* and *Samidare* went into their sharp right turn we did not observe the exchange of torpedoes between *Yugumo* and the enemy. The visibility was too bad at the moment for us to observe any of this engagement.

I felt that my own two ships were being pressed hard. How could we best oppose the "powerful" enemy force, still believed to consist of four cruisers and three destroyers? If the enemy took the initiative he could wallop us. How could we seize the initiative? In the excitement I had the feeling of not being able to breathe deeply enough, and suddenly realized that I was panting.

Seeing the enemy column take a right turn, I ordered another hard right at 2058. We were 8,500 meters from our intended targets. The idea of running parallel and ahead of the enemy column was one of the formulas worked out in my torpedo manual. My running ahead discouraged the enemy from attacking with torpedoes, and permitted me to choose my own time and angle for launching at him.

My order, "Prepare guns and torpedoes for fight to starboard!" was sent to *Samidare* by signal lamp and radio. At the same time the enemy was bringing his portside to bear on us so that he could make full use of his guns. Realizing this I ordered another hard right at 2059, to close the enemy as rapidly as possible and thus throw off his aim and timing. I was infuriated when *Samidare*'s skipper stupidly asked by radio if we were going to fight on this new course. With all the restraint I could muster I thundered, "Tell him we will turn left again before opening on the enemy!"

We ran some 500 meters in closing on the American force before I ordered a left turn and release of torpedoes. It was 30 seconds after 2100. The enemy was 50 degrees to starboard, an ideal torpedo angle, and distance 7,500 meters. Sixteen fish shooshed into the water from my two ships, and torpedomen immediately began to reload the tubes.

No sooner were the torpedoes on their way when water pillars rose on both sides of my ships. The first enemy salvo had straddled us. The enemy's aim—undoubtedly radar-controlled—was spectacular, but neither of my ships was hit. The straddling shots continued while my torpedomen fumbled and struggled to refill the tubes. I waited for them to complete this work until time began to run out and, abandoning the second torpedo attack, finally gave the order for guns to open fire.

Shigure jerked throughout her length with the sudden deafening roar of her 12.7-cm. (5-inch) guns, and the violent muzzle blasts were dazzling and blinding to eyes that had become accustomed to the dark of an ocean night. Billows of smoke served momentarily to cut off all visibility from the bridge. The first sound to emerge from the din and obscurity was the voice of lookout Yamashita, who shouted that our torpedoes had hit home.

As my eyes adjusted to the scene I could make out an explosion in the lead ship of the enemy column, but nothing else. The two other ships which had been in line only a few minutes before were nowhere to be seen. A check of the lookouts confirmed that only one enemy ship was visible. This led us to the belief that all three of the enemy ships had fallen sudden victim to our torpedoes. And that was the opinion rendered by our cohort *Samidare*. We simply could not imagine that *Chevalier* and *O'Bannon* were stranded 6,000 yards astern of their lead ship. General poor visibility, worsened by gunfire and smoke I was responsible for the illusion and the mistake.

Still with faith in the reported cruisers, I wondered where they could be. I ordered all guns rotated to starboard and peered vainly through binoculars for a glimpse of these nonexistent ships. Through the haze and darkness I finally caught sight of tiny specks and, influenced by my preconception, decided that these must be the cruisers. They appeared so small that I concluded they were fleeing. The specks were actually the two enemy destroyers: crippled *O'Bannon* and sinking *Chevalier*.

In an attempt to check the results of our torpedo attack I turned my ships to the right. Visibility was worsening and we could see nothing. After searching fruitlessly for about ten minutes I ordered a 90-degree turn to port and headed home.

The erroneous report given by the scout plane of enemy cruisers and destroyers continued to plague Ijuin's ships. They ran in wild disorder for several minutes after the loss of *Yugumo*, until 2113 when lookouts observed the erratic movements of *Chevalier* and *O'Bannon*. Still bewildered and disturbed by the sudden loss of *Yugumo*, the three Japanese destroyers saw these as the four enemy cruisers and judged they were approaching for a showdown.

At 2119 the three ships released 24 torpedoes against mirages which yielded no scores. Wishful crewmen observed through the misty night the fires raging in *Selfridge* and *Chevalier*, and reported that their torpedoes had sunk "two cruisers or large destroyers." Another complete illusion.

With this supposed success, Ijuin turned his ships northward for the return to base. Meanwhile the Japanese transport convoy had reached Hora-niu without interference. Within two hours the entire garrison of 589 troops had been evacuated, without the loss of a single life.

A second group of American destroyers—*Ralph Talbot*, *Taylor*, and *La Vallette*—speeding from New Georgia waters, arrived on the scene of combat just after the last Japanese warship had cleared for home. They sighted no enemy, but *La Vallette* delivered the *coup de grâce* to *Chevalier* with a well-placed torpedo, The three fresh destroyers rescued survivors and then some-how nursed crippled *Selfridge* and *O'Bannon* back to their Tulagi base.

Thus the battle ended with United States losses of one destroyer sunk and two severely damaged, as against Japan's loss of one destroyer sunk. American loss of life was slight compared to Japanese deaths in the sink-ing of *Yugumo*. But, unknown to us at the time, about one third of *Yugumo*'s crew was rescued by American destroyers. Most important of all, however, was that despite his many blunders, Ijuin's escort mission worked out pretty much as planned. And so it was his victory.

It is my opinion that the Americans could have won this battle decisively if Walker's three destroyers had turned south instead of north. He would have had a field day chasing the three terrorized Japanese destroyers. Such a chase would not have permitted the use of American torpedoes, but the radar-controlled guns could have worked havoc on Ijuin's fleeing destroyers. But this is only conjecture, and naval battles are always filled with blunders, illusions, and surprises.

On returning to Rabaul, I found Ijuin shaken and ashamed. He was not openly rebuked, but the high command showed its appraisal of the action by presenting a ceremonial sword to me and daggers to Lieutenant Commander Kinuo Yamagami of *Shigure* and Yoshiro Sugihara of *Samidare*. No rewards or citations were given to anyone in Ijuin's group for the action, Japan's first naval victory in the theater in almost three months.

5

The naval victory of October 6 was celebrated the next day with a sword presentation ceremony and dinner. The party was held at the swank officers' club, with practically all of the top officers on Rabaul in attendance. These included Vice Admirals Jinichi Kusaka, Commander Southeast Area Fleet and 11th Air Fleet; and Tomoshige Samejima, 8th Fleet Commander.

Great quantities of *sake* were served, and the party got really gay when several hostesses joined. These were the usual geisha girls assigned by the Navy Ministry to the major forward bases as morale boosters.

Although the party was in my honor, I was still under a strain and was not enjoying it as much as the others. I just wanted to get drunk and kept drinking *sake* at a great rate.

Kusaka made a speech praising *Shigure*, saying, "The life expectancy of Rabaul-based destroyers has averaged something under two months. Yet one old ship has now fought steadily for almost three months without a scratch or the loss of a single member of her crew. Let's drink a toast to Captain Hara, Commander Yamagami, and all the men of the great *Shigure!*"

It dawned on me then why my mood was so dark. The party really ought to have been for my fine crew of 240 men instead of all the top brass. While I brooded about this the party became quite boisterous, and then one of the staff officers spoke up: "Admiral Kusaka, I have long desired, but never dared, to ask certain questions. May I ask them now?"

The room fell silent at this effrontery, but Admiral Kusaka nodded, and the young man continued: "You have just noted the brief life expectancy of a destroyer. Must we put up with such a situation? Why do all our big ships just sit at Truk? Are we going to celebrate next October 26 as the anniversary of the last battle in history in which our carriers took part? During the past year our destroyers have not only been conducting their unglamorous transport missions, but they have also been bearing the full brunt of all actions in these waters. Forgive my rudeness. This is no criticism of you, but we all know that your 11th Air Fleet has been shore-based since the start of the war. In this critical theater, why do destroyers have to shoulder the entire burden without the support of our carriers, battleships and cruisers?"

This rambling series of questions was far more than had been expected, but it expressed the feelings of most in the crowded room. There was awe-stricken silence as the full impertinence of the drunken officer struck his more inhibited colleagues. Kusaka was glumly silent. Admiral Samejima broke the mounting tenseness. "I understand that Commander in Chief Koga is preparing for a decisive naval action in which all our big ships will be deployed."

The young officer shouted uncontrollably: "When? When are these ships going to do something? They have been out of action for a full year, and that year has been like a century for our destroyers. In this time the enemy has caught up and surpassed us!"

A fellow officer tried to quiet his friend, suggesting that it was late and time to go home, But the drunken harangue continued: "And what is Imperial Headquarters doing in Tokyo? Announcements blare every day that we are bleeding the enemy white in the Solomons. It is we who are being bled white, not the enemy."

Two friends carried and dragged him from the room while he burst into tears and sobbed, "*Yugumo* is sunk. Poor *Yugumo* is sunk with so many of my friends."

The episode had a strange effect on me. I too was drunk, but managed to stagger to my feet clutching the long ceremonial sword which Admiral Samejima had just presented to me. I walked over to him and said, "I wish to return this sword, Admiral, because I do not deserve it. Even if I did deserve it, what use is a sword on board ship?"

While everyone gasped in astonishment at my outburst, Captain Miyazaki recovered quickly from his shock and came to my side, saying, "You are tired, Hara. Let us go home and get some rest."

I waved him aside with, "No, thank you, Miyazaki," and continued, "I want to exchange this sword for *sake* for my wonderful crew. They are the ones who should be rewarded. Not me. Admiral Samejima, buy drinks for my men."

With this Admiral Ijuin, my own commanding officer, came to my side and tried to cajole me. "All right, Hara. I'll buy drinks for your men, but now we are all tired and it is time to turn in."

I awakened next morning with a terrible hangover. Commander Yamagami woefully recounted how the other officer and I had made spectacles of ourselves, and how Ijuin and Miyazaki had dragged me bellowing from the party. Such behavior by ranking officers was unheard of in the Imperial Navy, and dire misgivings added to my discomfort from overindulgence.

Curiously, I was never rebuked for my misconduct. I later learned that when news of my performance spread to the enlisted men it boosted my popularity with them. The fact that nothing happened to me would seem to indicate that my superior officers shared the general dissatisfaction with the high command.

Naval Headquarters in Tokyo had ordered our withdrawal to Bougainville as the final defensive line. This did not encourage optimism in the combat area. Bougainville is almost three times the size of Guadalcanal. Its long coast line, largely unexplored, offered many potential landing spots for the enemy. The occasional discovery of American ration boxes scattered in the jungle made it clear that enemy operatives on the island were selecting the best invasion sites.

Combined Fleet Headquarters at Truk did nothing to add to our peace of mind. Our new top commanders were no better than their predecessors. Admiral Mineichi Koga, who had succeeded to over-all command upon Yamamoto's death in April 1943, had done practically nothing. No great victories had been achieved by Vice Admiral Jisaburo Ozawa since he had replaced Nagumo as carrier force commander in November 1942. And Vice Admiral Nobutake Kondo, ailing and weary of his Second Fleet command, had just been relieved by Vice Admiral Takeo Kurita in August 1943.

These three new commanders worked diligently and hard, but they could not work miracles. The basic defect was in Tokyo where Imperial Naval Headquarters was still run by Admiral Osami Nagano.

Half a year had passed since the death of Yamamoto, and yet his policies were still being followed. In the Java Sea battle of February 1942, I had learned that combat teaches more lessons than a thousand exercises. Unfortunately, the commanding admirals did not share this view. They kept Japan's main naval strength at Rabaul or, still worse, in homeland waters "to conserve the ships and train the men." The result was that both ships and men proved unfit when they were finally forced into action.

The aggressive enemy took no pause. We had scarcely returned from our "triumph" at Vella Gulf when we were made acutely aware of how critical the situation really was. On October 12, a record raid of 349 land-based planes swarmed over Rabaul. The high-altitude bombing was not very accurate, however, and only one transport was sunk.*

So huge a raid on a main Japanese base was very impressive, and it shocked Truk headquarters. But Admiral Koga still wavered. If the enemy could fly so many land-based planes against Rabaul, the Solomons was not a favorable stage for a fleet engagement.

Another large-scale air assault was made on October 18 against Rabaul and Buin, the main air base on Bougainville. Koga at last ordered two heavy

---

* Hara means one Navy transport, 5,879-ton *Keisho Maru*; but also sunk by this raid were Army transports *Tsukinada Maru* (526 tons), *Kamoi Maru* (548 tons), *Fuku Maru* (132 tons), and Navy patrol boat *Mishima Muru*. Three destroyers, three submarines, an oiler, and a survey ship all received minor damage.

cruisers and a squadron of destroyers to go from Truk to Rabaul. This followed the familiar Yamamoto pattern of piecemeal reinforcement. It was a move which Koga would have cause to regret.

Air assaults in strength were resumed five days later and continued daily until Buin lay in ruins. Meanwhile the surface units arrived at Rabaul on October 21. Among the newcomer destroyers was *Shiratsuyu*, which had been on detached duty, and now rejoined my command. I was elated finally to be in charge of three ships, six months after my appointment as a division commander. In those days very few Japanese destroyer divisions actually had as many as three ships.

Shiratsuyu, 1,980 tons, was a sister ship of *Shigure* and *Samidare*. Although built in 1933, she had the appearance of being brand new. She had been badly damaged by enemy bombs near Buna, New Guinea, in November, 1942, and had to be practically rebuilt at Kure.

In spite of my elation, I was apprehensive about this ship. She was manned almost completely by inexperienced sailors and I doubted that *Shiratsuyu* would prove much of an asset to my division.

On October 23 I took my three ships on a transport mission to Iboki, about 50 miles east of Cape Gloucester. The first of a series of daily air raids hit Rabaul and Buin that day, but enemy planes still gave my ships a warm reception during the dark of morning. My destroyers scattered to run independently, and the planes gave up the chase at daybreak. My ships reassembled in good order, and I was relieved to find all three intact. *Shiratsuyu* showed more promise than I had anticipated.

Six days later I took *Shigure* and *Shiratsuyu* on a transport assignment to Garove Island, north of Willaumez Peninsula. A few enemy planes made passes at us but no heavy action was involved. Nevertheless, *Shiratsuyu* performed so well that I decided she was an asset to the division. How wrong I was!

Meanwhile, on October 27, the enemy made another landing, this time on Mono Island, a small base 20 miles south of Bougainville. The following day enemy paratroops fell upon Choiseul,* and Admiral Koga realized that the time had come for a showdown, whether he liked it or not. Imperial Headquarters demanded that he hold Bougainville until October 30, at all cost.

---

* These were paratroopers from the 2nd Paratroop Battalion, First Marine Amphibious Corps—but they came in by boat.

Koga immediately ordered Ozawa's three carriers, with their 173 planes, to Rabaul. At the same time he ordered Rabaul to mount a full-scale counteroffensive around Bougainville.

But the American timetable was not waiting for Koga. Carriers *Zuikaku*, *Shokaku*, and *Zuiho* were still far north of Rabaul when powerful enemy forces invaded Cape Torokina, on the western coast of central Bougainville. The invasion, which commenced at 0700 on the first day of November, was practically unopposed. Admiral Kusaka rushed all the planes of his 11th Air Fleet to Torokina, but these 104 fighters and 16 bombers were unable to stem the enemy tide which flooded onto the island. Ozawa's three carriers, concerned primarily with their own safety, launched their 173 planes while still 200 miles north of Rabaul.

Admiral Koga, at Truk, wanted to avoid the mistakes of 15 months earlier, when the enemy had landed at Guadalcanal. On that occasion Admiral Mikawa led his seven ships to a phenomenal victory, but he failed to sink any of the enemy's transports. Accordingly the decision was now made to throw all available ships at Torokina, and follow up with a convoy of troop-laden transports for a counterlanding.

Koga appointed Rear Admiral Sentaro Omori to command the operation. Omori, newly arrived at Rabaul, had been in the homeland or at Truk for many months with his two 12,374-ton cruisers, *Myoko* and *Haguro*. Yet in this operation Omori was expected to outdo Mikawa's Guadalcanal feat. That is, he was to wipe out enemy transports in addition to sinking warships.

Omori's two heavy cruisers were supported by two screening units. The left flank, consisting of Ijuin's light cruiser *Sendai* (5,595 tons) and my three destroyers, was the only combat-seasoned element of the formation. The right flank screen under Rear Admiral Hiroshi Matsubara in light cruiser *Agano* (7,170 tons) included destroyers *Naganami*, *Hatsukaze*, and *Wakatsuki*. None of these ships had ever operated together before, and Matsubara was inexperienced in night battle.

In a short briefing conference held in flagship *Myoko*'s gun room, Admiral Omori said. "We have never teamed together before, and this can be a serious detriment in battle. But Admiral Mikawa managed without a previously trained team, and so can we. I have firm trust and faith in the skill of each of you commanding officers and in the ability of your men. I believe we shall win."

As the meeting broke up, Ijuin tapped my shoulder. "Hara," he said, "this will be a tough one. I shall be relying on you."

I laughed. "Let's be prepared for a swim and take along plenty of shark repellent." But I saw at once that Ijuin was in no mood for a joke.

He mumbled glumly, "I do not like cruiser *Sendai*. She is now nine years old, and so sluggish."

I know what he meant. He had not used this cruiser in many months, although she was flagship of his Destroyer Squadron 3. He preferred to sail in destroyers.

Ijuin added, "But then *Sendai* is younger than your *Shigure*. I am uneasy about this operation, and hope that the ships from Truk will do a fine job. Their crews, though inexperienced, are young and fresh. They are not as tired as we are."

We walked in silence to the ramp where Ijuin offered his hand and said, "Brooding will do us no good, Hara. We must fight and fight desperately. Japan will topple if Bougainville falls."

Returning to *Shigure*, I could not keep from brooding. I did not understand how Omori could have been selected to lead such an important operation as this one. Until recently, he had been instructing in tactics at the Torpedo School and had never been in a major naval action.

Our ten warships steamed out of Rabaul at 1520 on November 1. Immediately clear of the harbor we went into regular cruising formation with Ijuin's *Sendai*, followed by my destroyers—*Shigure, Samidare, Shiratsuyu*—in a tight single column to the left and slightly ahead of *Myoko* and *Haguro*. On the right flank of these heavy cruisers was Admiral Matsubara's light cruiser *Agano*, followed in column by destroyers *Naganami, Hatsukaze,* and *Wakatsuki*. The convoy of five troop-filled transports and their five destroyer escorts followed at a distance of several miles.

The day was cool but drizzly and murky, and visibility was limited. Beneath a mild southeasterly breeze the sea was calm. Our force had no more than cleared St. George Channel when our radios began picking up nearby enemy transmissions. We could see nothing, but it was evident that radar-equipped scout planes had spotted us from above the clouds.*

At 1945 one of the SB-24s broke through the clouds to make several bombing runs on Sendai, but it scored no hits. By this time our own scout

---

* These were two radar snoopers (SB-24) of COMAIRSOLS' 5th Bombardment Group, which kept Admirals Halsey and Merrill well informed of the movement of these Japanese ships toward Empress Augusta Bay. The SB-24s located and first reported these ships about 15 miles east of Cape St. George.

planes were reporting on the enemy situation to the south: "Three battle-ships, many cruisers and destroyers at Empress Augusta Bay near Torokina." This was much greater strength than we had anticipated. The enemy seemed to be ready and waiting for us.

Omori consulted with Rabaul headquarters, where at 2130 Admiral Kusaka ordered the transports to turn back. He concluded that a counter-landing in the face of such a strong enemy deployment was impossible. But he told Omori to go ahead with his force and sink enemy ships.

The ten ships in their three columns continued through the steady driz-zle, which limited visibility to 5,000 meters. I was in the column nearest to Bougainville, but could discern nothing along that black coastline. I thought of how closely this resembled the situation at Vella Gulf on August 6, and how disastrously that had turned out. Our speed of advance continued at 18 knots, while I brooded about our blind left side. Enemy ships, with their all-seeing radar, could use the darkness as a perfect cloak and attack us at will.

At 2324 another SB-24 swooped out of the darkness to drop bombs at *Haguro*, but again no hits. The enemy was keeping close track of where we were and where we were going. When this attack ended, *Haguro* catapulted a scout plane which reported 14 minutes later: "One cruiser and three destroy-ers spotted 50 miles, 330 degrees from Cape Mutupina."

The indicated position was only 20 miles south of our formation. Omori ordered the plane to search for other enemy ships and put his formation into a simultaneous turn-about to mark time while awaiting a further report on enemy ships. The ten ships, maintaining their tight formation, turned 180 degrees, steamed about 10,000 meters and turned again to resume their southward course. This maneuver worked well in throwing the enemy off his timing in 1942, when he had to rely on sighting reports. But the maneu-ver was ineffective in 1943 against an enemy continuously and accurately informed by radar.

During the turn-around we eagerly awaited further reports from our scout planes, but none came. We had not the slightest idea that Admiral Merrill's force of four cruisers and eight destroyers, fully informed of our approach, was rushing northward at that very moment to oppose us.

At 25 minutes past midnight, as we were resuming course after the sec-ond turn-around, I saw a dim red flare in the sky ahead. The bearing of this light, 70 degrees to port, jibed with the position of the enemy force reported by the *Haguro* plane. The flare was so dim that I estimated the distance to be about 20,000 meters. It disappeared after two or three seconds. I continued to look for it during precious minutes in which other factors were ignored. This was my mistake.

Had I looked nearer at hand at this time I would have seen our own formation in disorder and dangerously jammed together, as a result of the complex turns we had just completed. *Samidare* was out of column to starboard and our other three ships had closed to within 300 meters distance instead of the prescribed 500 meters.

I decided that the flare had been dropped by one of our scout planes to mark the enemy's position. I dictated an urgent message to all ships, "Enemy sighted 70 degrees to port!" and ordered it prepared for immediate transmission upon my next instruction.

Not a soul in our force even dreamed that the main enemy force was approaching from the south and was at that moment directly ahead of our position. When my lookout called out, "Four ships, 70 degrees to port!" I told the radiomen to send my prearranged message. It was then 0045 hours of November 2.

It was my judgment that the four ships had continued straight ahead from the position indicated by the first dim flare. Actually, four of the eight American destroyers had swerved from their south-to-north movement, while I was peering toward the dim flare. They reappeared to us only after completing their turn to launch torpedoes.

My lookout reported, "The enemy force has split into two groups. One going away, the other paralleling our course. They are destroyers! Distant 7,000 meters!" I shuddered at the realization that they must already have released torpedoes. The initiative was in the hands of the enemy.

In that instant I yelled two orders: "Launch torpedoes! Hard right rudder!"

There was prompt response and *Shigure* started a right turn as her eight torpedoes plopped into the water at two-second intervals. I watched more calmly then, satisfied that we would be able to evade any torpedoes the four enemy destroyers might have fired before they split up. Turning from watching our own torpedoes for a moment, I was petrified to see *Sendai* heading straight for my ship. Simultaneously with *Shigure*, the cruiser had also turned right, but in an exceptionally fast and violent manner. I paled to see how close she was. This huge cruiser, nearly three times the size of *Shigure*, was coming head-on for our portside.

"Full starboard helm!" I screamed. "Full speed!"

Icy sweat coursed down my back at the swift approach of *Sendai*'s hulk. I held my breath: like a drowning man as I watched the approach of her towering bows and felt the snakelike pace of *Shigure*'s evasive effort. I braced for the impact of collision as *Shigure*'s frail stern passed within ten feet of the speeding cruiser.

With the danger passed I turned anxious eyes toward *Samidare* and froze again in anxiety. This following cruiser, turning sharply right to avoid *Sendai*'s crazy rush, sideswiped *Shiratsuyu*, last in line. Her portside hull and deck crumpled under the impact of *Samidare*'s hull, and in that instant all of her guns and torpedo tubes were smashed beyond use.

Newcomer *Shiratsuyu* had proved she was no asset to my division. But most shocking to me at that moment was *Sendai*'s sudden turn without notice to our following ships. Aghast at the unexpected response of his ship, Ijuin ordered the helm reversed, and I watched *Sendai* swing back to the left immediately after she had so narrowly missed hitting *Shigure*.

One moment I sighed with relief, and in the next instant caught my breath as I saw a flight of falling shells, one of which hit full amidship into *Sendai*. The cruiser, in its erratic movements, had walked into the very first salvo from the American cruisers! I had never seen such spectacular accuracy—a first salvo hit!

Second and third salvos also struck the fated cruiser with fantastic precision, and she flamed like a giant torch. Her vitals smashed, the ship staggered and slowed, but managed still to clear eight of her torpedoes in the general direction of the bombarding ships.

The huge flames from *Sendai*, 500 meters distant, blinded me from seeing the source of the enemy shells. But *Samidare*, 500 meters farther away, was able to judge the position of the enemy ships. Her seasoned skipper, Lieutenant Commander Yoshiro Sugihara, released a brace of eight torpedoes at 0052.

The four unseen American cruisers were then 15,000 meters away. They made an all-ships-right maneuver at 0051 and successfully evaded the 16 long-range torpedoes. Destroyer *Foote*, however, the last ship of the second American destroyer column, turned erratically into the course of a torpedo at 0108. She was put out of action but did not sink.

I was suddenly overjoyed when, at 0052, a lookout announced that *Shigure*'s torpedoes had accounted for two enemy destroyers. Actually the separation of the enemy's four-destroyer group was a maneuver unknown in the

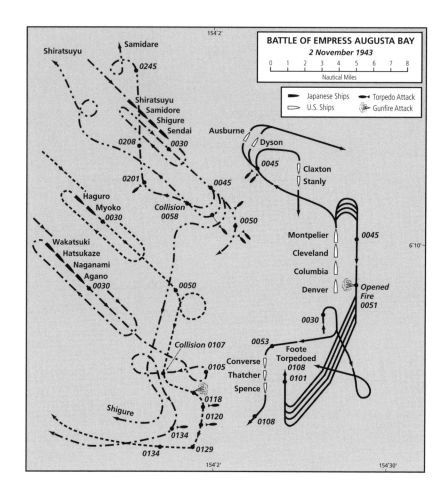

Imperial Navy. We thought two of them were closing in a hyperbola to parallel our own course, and so wrote them off when they failed to appear in the position we had anticipated. Instead they were all running in the same direction, away from our course. This novel American tactic created an illusion that was deceptively effective.

The jubilation raised in my destroyers was thus entirely unwarranted. Meanwhile chaos and consternation reigned in the two other Japanese columns.

Admiral Omori could see no enemy ships at the time of my 0045 sighting report. Five minutes later he saw *Sendai* erupt in flames. She was supposed to be at least 1,000 meters ahead and on course parallel to his *Myoko*. Instead he found her burning on his port beam.

Omori knew then he had been taken by surprise. His reaction—influenced by the "conservation" idea so prevalent in command circles—was to adjust his formation to its original deployment, and he ordered a turnabout.

This action has been widely criticized, but Omori has never seen fit to discuss it. The turn-about might have worked if all ships had responded properly. But two of the columns were manned by officers inexperienced in night action, and the result was chaos. Admiral Matsubara's third column made a further blunder.

Although he lacked battle experience, Matsubara was known for his dogged aggressiveness. On hearing my sighting report he put his column into a full-speed dash to engage the enemy. He continued thus for ten minutes without result. When he finally saw the turn made by heavy cruisers *Myoko* and *Haguro*, he put his own ships into the awkward movement, committing the most serious error of the night.

When cruiser *Agano* and her three following destroyers had headed north after completing their turn, Matsubara did not notice that his column was crossing the course of Omori's *Myoko* and *Haguro* at a right angle. The result was that 12,374-ton *Myoko*, crossing in front of *Hatsukaze*, third ship of the Matsubara column, brushed the tender nose of that 2,500-ton destroyer. The two following ships, *Haguro* and *Wakatsuki*, barely avoided making it a quadruple collision.

Panic-stricken, Matsubara again circled to get back to his crippled destroyer. A quick survey was enough to convince him that nothing could be done for her in the height of battle, and he turned again to withdraw on a course parallel to that of the two heavy cruisers.

At 0115 American shells straddled *Myoko* and *Haguro*, and the cruisers opened fire blindly with their big guns, in the general direction of the enemy. In the next few minutes they also released a total of 24 torpedoes which were entirely wasted.

Enemy radar had wrested from the Japanese Navy its former supremacy in night action.

While Omori and Matsubara were experiencing these travails I was suffering agonies of my own. We were standing by burning *Sendai* which had stopped dead. The enemy bombardment continued to batter the crippled ship so incessantly that *Shigure* could not close for rescue operations. I watched glumly as *Samidare* and *Shiratsuyu* received Omori's approval to withdraw. The American destroyers had done a very effective job, even though their ten torpedoes had missed. Three Japanese warships had been put out of action at one stroke.

My bridge lookout noted a distress call from Sendai's stern lamp which blinked: "*Shigure*, approach me . . . *Shigure*, approach me . . . *Shigure*, approach me. . . ."

My ship was still 500 meters on *Sendai*'s starboard beam. No enemy shells had reached us, though they continued to cascade onto the stricken cruiser. My best friend, Ijuin, was pleading for help, and yet *Shigure* would not have a chance in approaching that inferno. I stood frozen on the bridge. Still vivid in my mind was the year-old memory of losing 43 *Amatsukaze* men when we drew concentrated fire from cruiser *Helena* as a result of my error. I had pledged to the spirit of those men not to repeat such a mistake.

Shigure's skipper yelled impatiently, "Let's go, Captain Hara. Let's approach *Sendai*. The Squadron Commander has given us an order."

Commander Yamagami's imploring tone and words had an effect on me contrary to what he had expected. Casting indecision aside, I replied, "No, Yamagami, I have decided not to. If we go to *Sendai*'s aid we too will be pinned down by enemy gunfire. We might take off a few crewmen, but all of us would perish."

"But we have orders!" Yamagami shouted heatedly. "Orders? You are right!" I thundered. "And let's get on with them. Our primary orders are to strike at the enemy. In battle rescue is always secondary. Let's go!"

"But our friends are asking for help," pleaded Yamagami. "They are dying before our eyes."

This angered me and I roared, "Shut up! This is no place for sentiment or debate. This is my responsibility. Don't interfere with authority!"

Yamagami was stunned into silence, and I gave ship orders, "Port helm! Full speed ahead! We attack!"

Shigure's engine roared up to her maximum speed of 30 knots. It was my thought to join with any other ships still capable of fighting and strike back at the enemy. But neither Omori nor Matsubara had notified me of their movements and I was unable to find them. When no friendly forces appeared I spent ten minutes in frantic search of targets. I then tried to find targets by following gunfire traces, but this did not work. *Shigure* advanced on a southerly course until 0134 when we got Omori's withdrawal order and returned to Rabaul.

Omori decided to break off because he believed we were fighting a two-column force consisting of seven cruisers and nine destroyers, and that they were heading south on a course parallel to his own. This misjudgment stemmed from early reports of the enemy formation, and the erroneous report by the spotter plane.

The two Japanese heavy cruisers fought a mirage which existed only in the minds of their commanders. The four American cruisers had turned from their southerly course at 0101 and headed north. This resulted in the illusion that Omori had sunk one cruiser "instantaneously" and damaged two others. So Omori did not realize that his ships had been groping about like blind men, simply wasting ammunition and fuel.

My heart was heavy as *Shigure* followed sluggishly after the five fast ships. Looking in the direction where we had last seen *Sendai*, I felt miserable. Thinking of the sideswiping which had put *Samidare* and *Shiratsuyu* out of action, I realized that some of the enemy ships must have gone in hot pursuit of those cripples, and could only hope for the best. In the silence of *Shigure*'s bridge, the men about me shared my lugubrious thoughts.

On our way north I thought of Admiral Koki Abe's distressing return from Guadalcanal. The tactics employed by Abe on that occasion had been sharply criticized ever since. And here, more than a year later, Omori had repeated the same errors. Both admirals had adopted and clung to a complex formation, failing to shift to a combat deployment when engaging the enemy. In Abe's case we were fortunate that the enemy had outblundered us, but against Omori the Americans no longer blundered.

When I had brought *Amatsukaze* back it was with 43 of my crew dead, and the ship severely damaged. Now *Shigure* was intact and had suffered no casualties. It was some slight solace to think that I at least had not repeated my mistakes. This reminded me that *Samidare*, too, had survived the Abe sortie of a year ago, and I cheered up at the thought that this combat-seasoned destroyer would pull through this time as well.

About *Shiratsuyu*, on the other hand, my thoughts were considerably gloomier. Had she not sideswiped *Samidare* I felt sure that my three ships could have confused the enemy, just as I had done at Guadalcanal in the Abe sortie. The four destroyers which had just stormed us were not as skillful as the ones I had opposed at Vella Gulf on August 6, 1943. Here, despite the enemy's absolute advantage, all their torpedoes missed, and by so big a margin that none of us even saw them pass.

From the vantage point of hindsight I know that in this battle the advantage lay with the American force. There was not the slightest chance for a Japan victory. But I know, too, that we could have done better than we did.

Ijuin was responsible for the debacle that befell his column. He was a tired, weary, and exhausted man. And, with the loss of cruiser *Yugumo* a month earlier, he had lost confidence in his own ability. An aristocrat often breaks down quickly in the face of adversity.

Still greater responsibility rests with Admiral Omori. His turnabout in the face of the enemy served to tie Ijuin's hands, severely limiting his possible courses of action.

On the other side of the picture, the Americans do not seem to have fought very brilliantly in this battle. They could have sunk many more Japanese ships, if they had not been satisfied with just finishing off the two cripples. I do not understand why their spectacular bombardment of *Sendai* was not repeated against the other Japanese ships which lay in such confusion.

These are thoughts that have occurred to me in the years since this battle. As *Shigure* returned to Rabaul that day I had more immediate concerns. The engines were acting up, probably as a result of her having run at full speed for almost an hour during the battle. The Rabaul mechanics were apparently quite right when they had recommended her complete overhaul in the homeland. The high-speed run had been too much for her and we now had to reduce speed to 18 knots.

Somehow, this did not disturb me. Perhaps my anger at the outcome of the action made me hope that some enemy ships would catch up with us, so that *Shigure* could engage them and show the kind of stuff we were made of. Nevertheless, I radioed our situation to Admiral Omori, adding a request that he arrange for the rescue of *Sendai*'s survivors.

Omori replied promptly: "We are slowing to 12 knots so that you may catch up. I have already asked Rabaul for a submarine to pick up crews of *Sendai* and *Hatsukaze*."

At his reply I grinned for the first time in many hours. It was so typical of his conscientiousness.

Shigure joined *Myoko*, her engines functioning well at the reduced speed, and we reached Rabaul at 2000 on November 2. I was relieved to find that my two other destroyers had made it to Simpson Harbor. All things considered, *Shiratsuyu* was in fair shape, but *Samidare* was badly beaten up.

As soon as *Samidare* sighted *Shigure* she signaled a report of her actions. Starting at 0154 she had engaged enemy destroyers in a running battle which lasted for an hour. Five men were killed and five injured by two direct hits which also knocked out her steering control. She made it back to Rabaul by hand steering. Her skipper concluded, "We returned gunfire and launched six torpedoes at the enemy, and believe we inflicted as much damage as we received."

Shiratsuyu expressed regret for the sideswiping and delighted us all in *Shigure* with a closing remark: "Our withdrawal was easy. Enemy gunfire simply failed to catch up with us!"

A message from *Myoko* brought mixed relief and sorrow: "Submarine *I-104* reports the rescue of Admiral Ijuin and 37 others from *Sendai*, but none from *Hatsukaze*."

Early next morning *Shigure*'s skipper suggested that we visit *Myoko* to deliver a full report to Admiral Omori. I said, "We can do that later, Yamagami. It would not be wise to leave our ship right now. Rabaul is no longer a safe place. The enemy will probably send a heavy air attack today and we must be ready for them. Prepare *Shigure* for an all-out aerial attack."

American planes had struck Rabaul four times in the past week. When November 3 broke clear I had a strong hunch that they would return this day. With this in mind, I also instructed *Samidare* and *Shiratsuyu* to prepare as best they could.

All my crews worked feverishly, and it was well they did. The enemy came, and in strength, approaching from the north at a height of no more than 50 meters over the water. Previous attacks on Rabaul had all been made from high altitude, but the tactics were changed this day. The ensuing battle was the most spectacular action of my life.

Shigure was the first ship to get under way, closely followed by *Samidare* and *Shiratsuyu*. All guns were pointed skyward when the first wave of planes came in, and the gun crews worked like fury. They fired everything without pause, seeming to vent the general anger pent up after our unhappy return from Empress Augusta Bay. A total of 80 B-25 bombers and 80 P-38 fighters hit Rabaul that day, and most of them skimmed past the masts of my destroyers. Three little ships speeding out of the harbor must have been something that the American pilots and bombardiers had failed to reckon with.

The American bombardiers were not ready or perhaps disdained to use their bombs on our small ships. Few bombs were directed at our ships, *Shiratsuyu* being the only one damaged, and then but slightly by a near miss. On the other hand, our guns were telling. The enemy formations were shredded as they passed us.

Considering the size of his effort, the enemy achieved very poor results with that raid. It netted 18 Japanese planes destroyed, and only two small merchant ships and one subchaser sunk. For these minor spoils the Americans paid with eight B-25s and nine P-38s definitely shot down, and many more planes which limped back to base with wings and fuselage so badly riddled that they crashed on landing.

Gunfire from surface ships is usually of little effect against fast airplanes. But it was different that day. The enemy planes practically flew right into our gunfire. I saw at least five planes knocked down by *Shigure*.*

When my destroyers returned to Rabaul shortly after noon every man of the crews was justifiably proud and jubilant. The depressed mood of the morning was completely gone. Officers and men alike were able to joke and laugh again. In the late afternoon I went on board flagship *Myoko*, feeling a little easier about the unpleasant duty of reporting on the Empress Augusta Bay battle.

Admiral Omori greeted me warmly as usual. After listening to the details of my report on the activities of the Ijuin group, he spoke reassuringly: "I think you did the right thing. You were correct in moving away from *Sendai* while she was under concentrated attack. On another score, I wish to thank you for the radio message of 0045, reporting your discovery of the enemy ships. No one else had then seen the ships. Without your sighting report our whole group would have had a much worse time of it."

When I asked permission to leave and turned toward the door, Admiral Omori called me back. He pulled out his wallet and emptied it on the desk. "Here's 30 yen ($15)," he grinned. "It isn't much, but take it along as my token toward buying drinks for your men."

I must have looked startled at this, for he laughed. Then we shook hands and laughed together. The episode of my returning the sword and request-ing money for drinks in its place must have reached his ears, though it had occurred before he ever came to Rabaul.

The battle of Empress Augusta Bay ended in a very one-sided victory for the United States. Destroyer *Foote*, which took a *Samidare* torpedo, was badly

---

* Captain Hara is quite right about the effectiveness of his destroyers' AA fire this day. It is noted in the official history of the Army Air Force as follows:

> . . . Two destroyers off the mouth of the Warangoi River, directly in the path of the approaching planes, caused some confusion as their fire, together with that of intercepting fighters, forced the B-25s to break formation and attack in two-plane or individual bombing and strafing runs.

The Army Air Forces in World War II, The Pacific—Guadalcanal to Saipan, Vol. IV, 326.

damaged but managed to get home. In this important action the Americans lost fewer than 40 men killed and injured.

Japan lost light cruiser *Sendai* and 335 men of her crew, and destroyer *Hatsukaze* with her entire crew of 240. Direct hits on heavy cruisers *Myoko* and *Haguro*, and destroyer *Samidare*, did some damage to these ships but resulted in total casualties of only six men killed and seven injured.

Omori was shortly relieved of his command and returned to the Torpedo School as its Superintendent. Matsubara was also relieved of his post and assigned to shore duty.

Submarine *I-104* arrived in Rabaul on November 3 with *Sendai* survivors, and I was on hand to greet them. Admiral Ijuin was a pitiful sight as he staggered onto the pier. I approached him with apologies for my failure to come to his aid.

He responded with great feeling, "Don't say that, Hara. I am ashamed of my behavior. Never mention an apology for that again. I was a coward. You did the right thing. I must have been out of my mind."

Soon afterward Ijuin was returned to Tokyo. After a few months of rest he came back to the South Pacific and fought valiantly. On May 24, 1944, he was killed while escorting a convoy when his flagship, frigate *Iki*, was torpedoed and sunk by United States submarine *Raton*.

6

If the fighting ability of Rear Admiral Matsuji Ijuin was open to any doubt, his prediction that Japan would topple after the loss of Bougainville proved to be spectacularly accurate.

Rabaul weathered the November 2 air attack with little loss, but suffered a disaster three days latter. Americans think of the Pearl Harbor attack as a catastrophe, but the November 5 air attack on Rabaul was far worse. A fleet of cruisers, zealously conserved for more than a year, was put out of action in a single day.

How could such a thing happen? The Rabaul debacle of November 5 was an immediate outgrowth of the nightmarish battle of Empress Augusta Bay. Battle lessons that should have been learned were ignored. Errors were repeated, until they became fatal.

Japan should have realized the inadequacy of its reconnaissance efforts. Not only were too few planes allocated for search purposes, but pilot proficiency fell as the more skilled flyers were lost in combat. The high command must have been aware of this, but the situation was not corrected.

If our battle reports of the Empress Augusta Bay action tended to deceive the high command, we were not entirely to blame. Other factors added to the deception.

Submarine *I-104*, in accounting for its rescue of the *Sendai* survivors, stated: "We saw many enemy seaplanes and surface ships busily engaged in rescue operations, indicating that a number of enemy ships were sunk in the battle."

Our delayed transport convey left Rabaul November 2, escorted by only four destroyers, and succeeded in landing 930 troops at Torokina. The convoy commander reported happily, "We met no surface opposition. The enemy fleet was obviously mending the wounds it had received from the Omori force."

The fact is, however, that the Americans had chosen to trap the Army troops after they had landed, and did so quite effectively. But that was an Army problem, and the Japanese Navy could not be bothered with it.

The illusory scores claimed by the Omori force were thus substantiated. Accordingly, when Omori returned to Tokyo after the operation he suffered no disgrace. Instead, he was promoted to Vice Admiral and reassigned to the Torpedo School as its superintendent.

Admiral Koga, Commander in Chief of the Combined Fleet, accepted Omori's report at face value. He felt that patient waiting had paid off and that his chance had come for a showdown with the enemy in the Solomons. It was on this basis that on November 3 he ordered seven cruisers south from Truk. Neither Koga nor any of his staff had been in combat recently with the increasingly powerful enemy. Consequently, complacence reigned.

Admiral Kusaka at Rabaul was disturbed when he heard of the plan to send the cruisers, and he tried to discourage the idea. But he could not explain his skepticism of Omori's claims or his general uneasiness in terms convincing and meaningful to Koga. And so the cruiser fleet came south—under constant surveillance by American scout planes.

Vice Admiral Takeo Kurita, who had replaced Kondo as Second Fleet commander, shared Koga's complacence. He had heard much about the recent intense bombings of Rabaul which failed to score a single direct hit on a warship. It was more than a year since Kurita had been in battle. The Japanese fighters he remembered were those of 1942, when Japan still boasted clear superiority over America in plane performance and pilot skill. His confidence of those days persisted, but now it was without foundation.

Kurita's force arrived at Rabaul's Simpson Bay early in the morning of November 5. I gaped as flagship *Atago* nonchalantly dropped anchor in the narrow harbor, now jammed with seven cruisers and some 40 auxiliary ships. These new arrivals made me apprehensive and uneasy.

At 0700 that same morning a patrol plane reported an enemy force of five heavy cruisers, seven destroyers, and two transports in position 150 miles distant, bearing 140 degrees from Cape St. George. Rabaul headquarters concluded that these ships presaged a landing attempt. Reactions were casual since staff officers had become accustomed to enemy landing operations in recent months. No one at Rabaul dreamed that the two "transports" were aircraft carriers *Saratoga* and *Princeton*.

Japanese flyers had not seen American carriers for many months. Even the crack pilots of the Coral Sea battle in May, 1942 had trouble recognizing American carriers. But no one at Rabaul remembered that. Kusaka ordered other scout planes to scramble and shadow the American movements. They scrambled but they could not locate the task force in time to do any good.

Air raid alarms in Rabaul were not sounded until 0900. My *Shigure*, already standing by, was under way rapidly and weaved out of the harbor amid many ships still at anchor. The big cruisers were still weighing anchor when the carrier planes stormed the base at 0915. Some 50 Japanese ships were sitting ducks to the 23 Avenger torpedo planes, 22 Dauntless bombers, and 42 Hellcat fighters. Some 70 Zero fighters were airborne but they could not stop the torrential rain of American bombs.

While steaming out, *Shigure* opened up with all guns at the swift targets. I saw two planes knocked down by our ship's fire and crewmen claimed hitting two others. The day's catastrophe might have been prevented if the whole fleet had moved out as *Shigure* had done. But no other ships got out that day. My own *Samidare* and *Shiratsuyu* were not at Rabaul, having left the previous day for overhaul by repair ship *Akashi* at Truk.

We returned to harbor around 1000 and I was stunned at what had happened in less than an hour. I recalled grimly the debacle of January 1942, when American planes had damaged cruiser *Myoko* at Malalag Bay. And here we were, almost two years later, pulling the same blunder. What a disgrace!

Flagship *Atago* was burning, and her sisters *Maya* and *Takao* were damaged. These three heavy cruisers, each packing the firepower of a squadron of destroyers, were disabled in one raid, after having been conserved for a full year without ever engaging the enemy on the high seas. Also damaged were heavy cruisers *Mogami* and *Chikuma*, and light cruisers *Agano* and *Noshiro*, as well as destroyers *Fujinami* and *Amagiri*. I rubbed my eyes and wondered if this could be real.

It was all too real. At Rabaul headquarters the ordinarily mild Kusaka was furious. He bellowed imprecations at everyone.

Meanwhile, Rabaul airfields buzzed like a stirred-up hornets' nest. Every possible plane was airborne in pursuit of the attackers. About 100 Japanese fighters and bombers finally succeeded in locating the enemy task force, distant some 235 miles on a bearing of 145 degrees from Rabaul. They reported "sinking one large carrier, two cruisers, and one destroyer, in addition to damaging one medium carrier."

This claim proved to be totally exaggerated. When a man is tottering, it is impossible to remain cool and objective. Objective double-checking of war claims is possible only when one is winning. So these illusions went into the official record unchecked, as had so many before them. Admiral Kusaka, who survived the war, explained: "I was skeptical of these claims, as of Japanese claims generally at this time, knowing full well the marked drop in the skill of our pilots during the past year. But to question the claims, or request verifications, would simply have frustrated the men, who were doing the best they could."

The next day, November 6, cruisers *Atago*, *Takao*, and *Mogami* limped out of Rabaul for Truk, escorted by uninjured *Suzuya*, and *Chikuma* which had suffered only superficial damage. It was sickening to watch the departure of these five cruisers, when one considered that their sortie probably was the most fruitless of the entire war. Only three days earlier I had been distressed at the departure of two crippled cruisers and my two destroyers.

One heavy cruiser, *Maya*, remained in the harbor. Her vitals were destroyed. Light cruiser *Agano*, nearby, was barely afloat. The futility of our losses and the stupidity of our high command struck me forcibly, and I cursed aloud while wondering what Japan could do.

At noon that day I was summoned to headquarters where Admiral Samejima greeted me glumly and said, "I want you to take *Shigure* and *Yubari*, which is the only operable cruiser we have, on a mission tonight. The situation is bad. We may be forced to give up Bougainville, but we must hang on to the nearby base of Buka. It has been decided to reinforce the defenses at Buka."

The decision did not surprise me. I saluted and turned to go, but Same-jima called me back. "I must also tell you, Hara, that this will be your last assignment in my command. I hate the idea of having you go, especially at this time, but *Shigure* is badly in need of dry-dock repairs, and you are enti-tled to a rest."

Buka is closest to Rabaul of all the Solomon Islands. *Shigure* and *Yubari* crept to its coast that night and landed 700 troops of the 17th Army Division, and 25 tons of supplies.

Throughout this brief operation tension ran high in both ships. There was no opposition to our landings, but we returned exhausted to Rabaul the next day. I reported to headquarters and said good-bye to Admiral Samejima.

"Our assignment turned out to be very easy. But," I cautioned, "the next one like it will not be easy. Repeated tactics always seem to backfire."

Samejima nodded and said, "I appreciate your warning and will pass it on to other ships making the same mission. I am really going to miss you, Hara. We have lost so many experienced officers and men. I certainly want you to come back."

In conclusion he asked me to alter my schedule to allow for "a slight detour." The detour involved a stop at Kavieng, New Ireland, with two trans-ports *Shigure* was to escort to Truk. He explained unhappily that Rabaul, after the November debacle, was so short of ships that even poor *Shigure* had to be pressed into service on her way home for overhaul. The mission appeared much easier than any I had had in recent months, and I accepted it cheerfully.

Shigure left Rabaul at 0530 on November 7 with transports *Ontakesan Maru* and *Tokyo Maru*. As day dawned I gazed at the towering volcanoes behind the port. Rabaul was a drab and dreary place. But having been based there since July, I had developed a deep feeling for the place without real-izing it. There was nothing attractive about Rabaul, but, when we sortied, we always hoped desperately to return. Now we were leaving for home and would probably never see Rabaul again.

In three brief months we had lost island after island in the Solomons group, until only Buka remained in Japanese hands. Buka might fall any day and then Rabaul would fall too. We did not talk of this possibility but every-one was aware of it.

I thought of many friends who had perished in the savage battles in this area, and also of the many others who were staying behind, and tears came to my eyes. Looking around I saw that my feelings were shared by others in *Shigure*. Men on deck waved frantically at the few standing watch in ships we passed on our way out. From somewhere came the lilting tune, "Saraba Rabauru-yo, mata kuru made wa . . . " (Farewell, Rabaul, see you soon again . . .). This sad song had become a hit all over the Pacific in a very short time, though no one knew just where it had started.

We reached the open sea quickly. The day was bright and sunny, the water calm. Everything was as pleasant as a holiday cruise. Enjoying the fresh breeze on the bridge, my thoughts turned to my many missions and sorties while based at Rabaul. My arrival at Truk on March 21 and that day's revealing talk with Admiral Kondo had made me realize some of the many difficult problems which faced us. Two of the biggest problems were the enemy's radar-controlled gunfire, and skip-bombing.

It was with satisfaction at having whipped the first problem that I considered my encounters with radar-controlled gunfire from enemy ships, and how *Shigure* was the only ship to come through this trying period without the loss of a single man. The other problem—how to deal with skip-bombing—I had not solved. Many times *Shigure* had encountered enemy planes, but they had never tried to skip-bomb her. I wondered what could be done against such an attack.

At sunset we were still navigating along the southwestern coast of New Ireland. It takes many hours to cover 250 miles when the pace is set by transports, whose cruising speed is 12 knots. The weather was fair and clear, and the sky twinkled with myriad stars as we entered Ysabel Strait. The three ships were just turning east for Kavieng when the radio room reported undecipherable messages being sent from nearby, indicating that enemy planes were operating in our vicinity. The holiday cruise was over! I remembered how I had once foxed an attacking enemy bomber by an instant overboost from 12 to 28 knots. Such a ruse would not work with *Shigure*'s tired engines. Moreover, *Shigure* had been alone on that mission, now there were the transports to protect.

I increased speed to 18 knots and ordered a smoke screen for our two charges, while every lookout scanned the skies. The transports ran desperately eastward at their top speed of 16 knots. I ordered a further build-up of speed as *Shigure* ran erratically in and out among the slow ships, billowing out rolling clouds of smoke.

A lookout suddenly announced two planes, 50 degrees to starboard, and I saw them. Definitely bombers. Making directly for *Shigure*. I was thinking of my next move, grateful that the attackers were not striking at the transports. Then the planes had a sudden change of heart. They swung parallel to *Shigure* on a reciprocal course and disappeared far astern. As I wondered what they were up to, the lookout called, "Planes returning on port quarter!"

They were approaching steadily, and flying low! I tensed at the realization that they were going to skip-bomb *Shigure*! At last I was faced with the unsolved problem. In that same instant a solution flashed to my mind, and I yelled at the top of my voice: "All guns prepare for antiaircraft fire 150 degrees to port!"

Turning then to Lieutenant Tsukihara, the navigation officer, I said, "No zigzagging. We will follow a straight course!"

Shocked at my order, Tsukihara stammered, "What, what, Captain, aren't we even going to try to evade?"

"I'll explain later, do as I say!" *Shigure* had built up speed to nearly 30 knots while the bombers were choosing their approach angle. All guns followed as the black monsters swooped in on us. They were only a few hundred feet away and I could hear their engines as I gave the order to fire. Guns and machine guns responded instantly, and amid their deafening reports I heard Tsukihara scream, "Do we still go straight?"

In that tense kill-or-be-killed moment there was no explaining the reflex formula that had suddenly occurred to me. I simply shrieked, "Go straight!"

Now, years after that memorable encounter, it is simple to explain. Enemy planes were known to approach close in, to minimum range, before making their drop in skip-bombing. The apparent and logical evasive effort for a ship is to zigzag as violently as possible. But a zigzag movement slows a ship, and bombardiers figure on this slow-down in planning their bomb run. I was thinking, too, of *Shigure*'s very slow response to helm and rudder. By eliminating the zigzag we would not only speed up the ship, but also throw off the bombers' calculations. Another advantage to following a straight course is that the ship's guns can fire more accurately, as zigzagging disturbs their aim.

With shrieking, spine-quivering sounds the bombers flew past our masts from port to starboard and two bombs fell. They skipped all right, but over the ship, missing their target by seven or eight meters, as *Shigure* roared along at full speed. The bombs exploded, shooting up two high columns of water as the planes banked and pulled away to the south. The gunners halted their barrage but stood by to resume fire as necessary.

An uneasy five minutes passed in which there was no sign of the planes. Then word came from the radio room: "Enemy pilots are transmitting in plain language."

Ensign Hiroshi Chosa, our English expert, jumped to his feet, saying, "OK boys, I'm coming to hear what they have to say." And he darted from the bridge.

A minute or two later Chosa announced through the voice pipe, "One enemy plane reporting its controls are damaged, is giving its position in code. Another plane says its left wing is damaged and it is going to ditch."

The bridge roared its jubilance. Tsukihara, who had been so greatly concerned, was literally leaping with joy.

Chosa continued, "The enemy base replies that a flying boat is rushing to the rescue. The locations, unfortunately, are given in unreadable ciphers. Wait . . . The planes say, 'Thank you,' and they are now ditching!"

I sighed with relief. I had not expected my new formula to work with such telling effect. *Shigure* slowed down and rejoined the transports. We resumed our "holiday cruise" toward Kavieng, unloaded our consignments there, and departed for Truk early in the morning of November 8.

The holiday mood was again broken with the announcement at 1000 that *Shigure*'s sonar gear was out. Our technicians worked all day but could not revive the sensitive, long-overworked system. With no sonar it was most uncomfortable to recall that enemy submarines were known to be lurking in this vicinity. How could our "deaf" destroyer hope to protect the slow transports during a three-day voyage? The submarines would certainly be out to avenge the bombers we had knocked down.

I ordered an emergency setup with all depth-charge men standing by. The two transports were told to spread out with a distance of 1,500 meters between them. *Shigure* took position to starboard. The "holiday" cruise had turned into a raw-nerve run.

Nothing happened during the rest of the day or night. The following day, a Tuesday, was also quiet. My crewmen were dead tired after their long watch, but if we could go one more day without incident we would reach Truk safely.

All Wednesday morning I carried out intense antisubmarine exercises. The weather was cloudy and the sea was getting choppy. At 1130 I ordered a recess from the exercises.

Just as the men spread out on deck to relax, I saw the telltale wake of a torpedo crossing in front of *Shigure* from starboard to port. Instead of reacting promptly, I stood for several seconds watching the track of the torpedo as it headed for *Tokyo Maru*, then some 700 meters ahead and on the port bow of *Shigure*. The torpedo caught *Tokyo Maru* smack amidship. The shock of the explosion was felt in *Shigure*, and it brought me to my sensess. I called for fighting speed (24 knots), ordered depth-chargers to stand by, and sent *Shigure* racing down the track of the torpedo wake, toward its source. We launched six charges but no results were observed.

The submarine had gotten away. Not surprising, I thought, with a skipper clever enough to score with just one torpedo. I stood stunned and angry on the bridge. My sluggish reaction had let the submarine escape.

Shigure kept circling the transports, but the sub did not come back for a finishing attack. There was no fire in *Tokyo Maru* but her engine room was, filling with water through the, gaping hole in her side. She was still able to stay afloat but had no power. Accordingly, *Ontakesan Maru* took her in tow and we headed again toward Truk at seven knots.

While our little convoy sailed on, *Tokyo Maru*'s list increased steadily. After eight hours it was clear that she was sinking, and her skipper ordered "Abandon Ship." *Shigure* closed to receive her 70 men and officers just before the 6,486-ton transport slid beneath the waves.

This was a sad occasion for me. It was the first time I had ever lost a transport under my escort. Had the attack come a few hours later the freighter could have reached Truk, even in her damaged condition. But then, had he enemy sub used a few more torpedoes, *Tokyo Maru* would have sunk instantly. I took further solace in knowing that there were no casualties, in her torpedoing or sinking, and her cargo had already been safely delivered to Kavieng.

Shigure's score for this mission was two enemy bombers knocked down, in exchange for one transport sunk; no casualties on either side. In monetary value it may be figured that this was about even, but a big freighter meant much more to Japan in those days than the shooting down of two enemy bombers.

I was provoked with the attacking submarine for many days, whenever I thought about it. But now that years have passed I would like to salute that submarine and her skipper for the skill of the approach, torpedo firing, and evasion in the attack on *Tokyo Maru*. I do not know if more than one torpedo was fired, but that was all I saw. The sub did a very good job.* On that day, however, I could not look on the event with such detachment.

Shigure and *Ontakesan Maru* reached Truk around noon of November 11. I visited cruiser *Atago*, the Second Fleet flagship, a couple of hours later to make my uncomfortable report to Vice Admiral Takeo Kurita. I also wanted to see his chief of staff, Rear Admiral Tomiji Koyanagi. I still remembered vividly our conversation of eight months earlier, in March, at this same base, and the many problems he had posed at that time. I now had answers to some of those problems.

Atago had been damaged in the November 5 raid on Rabaul, and was being repaired by factory ship *Akashi*. Everything on board was in a turmoil. Staff officers were running around and would not even listen to my report. Kurita, they said, was "tied up," and Koyanagi was with him. I finally got a word with Koyanagi by hailing him as he was going into the head. We shook hands and he smiled, saying, "I'm glad to see you again, Hara."

I quickly recounted my experience with the two bombers off Kavieng and my regrettable loss of *Tokyo Maru*. Koyanagi waved his hand and said, "That's all right, perfectly all right. You did a wonderful job. No one else could have done better. I am glad you had no casualties."

I then went into detail about my technique for fighting against the enemy's range-finding radar, and my formula against aerial skip-bombing. But Koyanagi did not seem to be listening. In fact, he looked stunned, or completely lost in his own thoughts. Wondering what the matter was, I paused. He suddenly realized that he had been turning a deaf ear to me.

"Oh, I beg your pardon," he stammered. "My apologies . . . well, Hara, let me explain my rudeness. The enemy struck Rabaul again, this very morning, and mauled it badly. That's why we've all been tied up, and . . . well . . . indeed, upset."

A total of 128 planes from three American carriers—*Essex, Bunker Hill, Independence*—had swarmed over Rabaul starting at 0830. Kusaka had learned of their approach in time to send out 68 Zero fighters which met the attackers over Cape St. George, but the enemy planes got through to Rabaul and sank destroyer *Suzunami*. Destroyer *Naganami* was heavily damaged, and cruiser *Agano* was hit by a torpedo. More than 100 Japanese planes pursued the

---

* It was USS *Scamp* (Lt. Cdr. Walter G. Ebert) and she fired seven torpedoes, claiming one hit and the sinking of a 7,000-ton freighter. Now retired, R. Adm. Ebert lives in Muncie, Indiana.

task force. They claimed damaging two carriers and one cruiser—purely illusory—and 41 Japanese planes were lost.

"Excuse me, Hara, I must get back to the strategy conference. Oh, say, Admiral Kurita wants you to escort cruisers *Myoko* and *Haguro* when they leave tomorrow morning for Sasebo. Good luck. See you again." And with these words, Koyanagi literally ran away.

I stood there for a while, my ears ringing. *Suzunami* sunk at Rabaul! What a shame! And it was astounding to learn that one of the most famous destroyers in the Navy was badly damaged. *Naganami* had been Tanaka's flagship when he led the eight ships of his Squadron to victory at Tassafaronga in November, 1942. Only a week had passed since I had watched the many cruisers clumsily absorbing enemy bombs and torpedoes in clogged Simpson Harbor. They were large ships and simply could not maneuver in that crowded area. But how could swift destroyers be so inept as to fall victim to air attack!

With weary heart I returned to *Shigure* and gave orders to prepare for a hasty departure. At 0800 on November 12 we steamed out of Truk in escort of the two heavy cruisers. Our departure coincided with Admiral Koga's decision to withdraw the remainder of the Japanese fighters and bombers from Rabaul, where they had arrived only two weeks before from the three carriers. Koga had abandoned the idea of a showdown with the U.S. Navy in the Solomons. He evidently realized that his "conservation" tactics had failed.

At Truk, the *Akashi* technicians worked on *Shigure*'s sonar equipment without success. Their verdict was that the instruments would have to be replaced in Japan. But this did not disturb me since all gear on the two cruisers was in good order and *Shigure* could keep pace with their cruising speed of 18 knots. I felt easier than on my last mission because cruisers, unlike transports, pack their own wallop.

The five-day voyage was quiet. We dropped anchor at Sasebo on November 17, 1943. This was much more pleasant than my return to Kure in December 1942 with the cenotaphs of my 43 dead crewmen. In eight months of duty at Truk and Rabaul *Shigure* had not lost a single member of her crew. My men shouted and jumped with joy on entering our home port. During savage actions in the Solomons we had often despaired of seeing it again.

After two days of red tape and rigmarole, *Shigure* entered dry dock. As water was pumped from the dock and the destroyer's bottom became visible, every onlooker gaped in astonishment. In the center of the rudder was a hole at least two feet in diameter. Engineers closely examined the hole with its overgrowth of barnacles and shells and proclaimed that it must have been caused by a torpedo at least three months ago.

"Oh, yes," I recalled, "it must be from the Vella Gulf battle of August 6–7. That was the only time that torpedoes came near us."

"But," said one of the engineers, "how could you have navigated the ship since then in this condition?"

"The rudder has been sluggish in recent months," I replied. "But we've been on dozens of missions since then and pulled through, as you can see."

News photographers and reporters swarmed into the shipyard next morning and almost mobbed me. They interviewed *Shigure* crewmen and took pages of notes on our activities for hometown newspapers.

Shigure's glory, as the most famous destroyer in the Imperial Navy, dated from that time. Local papers splashed the *Shigure* Saga over a full page. It embarrassed me to read some of the exaggerated accounts, and I tossed them off as mere morale boosters. I soon learned, however, what the story meant to the people of this port city.

That evening there was a homecoming party for *Shigure*'s crew at the Mankiro restaurant. A popular place with the Navy crowd, it was run by an old woman whom we all knew as Oseki-san. This celebrated character was very outspoken. She treated every guest like a child, calling even admirals by their given names. This seeming rudeness was not offensive because she had a kind heart.

On entering the restaurant I expected her to shout my name and clap me vigorously on the shoulder as she had always done when I returned after a long absence. Thus I was flabbergasted to be greeted by Oseki-san, in her finest garb, kneeling and bowing to me. She spoke in a tone I had never heard before:

"Captain Tameichi Hara, welcome home. It is a great honor for this humble place to have been chosen for the homecoming party of the great crew under your honorable command. Please accept my humble appreciation."

"What's the matter with you, Oseki-san? You look strange. Don't you feel good? Are you mocking me?"

"I am serious, sir. We are so proud of you. You are famous. I never imagined what a great officer you are. I am ashamed for having been impolite to you in the past."

"What are you talking about, Oseki-san? I am the same Tameichi, the perennial drunkard, who often failed to settle accounts with you. I'll bet I still owe you some money."

"Oh, Tameichi-san, now you are mocking me. Any outstanding bills for you or your men are now written off. I proclaim a moratorium on *Shigure*. And tonight your party is on the house."

I laughed and said, "Now I know there is something wrong with you."

"You still do not understand. I know of the many destroyers that have been lost in battle. But your *Shigure* has survived its ordeals without losing a single one of our boys in all of its dazzling exploits. In catering to the Navy for 50 years, I have not accommodated so great an officer as you since the days of Admiral Heihachiro Togo when he triumphed at Tsushima Strait in 1905."

"I see now, Oseki-san, that you have been reading the newspapers. Do not believe half of what you read. If *Shigure* pulled through her missions it is because her officers and men worked hard and were lucky. Or perhaps because you prayed hard for our return so that you could collect our outstanding accounts."

With this we both laughed, but she emphatically repeated that this party would not cost *Shigure*'s men a penny. As she ushered me into the banquet hall she whispered, "Every geisha in Sasebo volunteered to entertain at this party—without fee! They say they would not serve those characters of *Myoko* and *Haguro* for any price."

Needless to say, that night's party was a most successful and happy one.

The following day I arranged for all *Shigure* crewmen to have ten days of home leave on a rotation basis. It was a great joy to see the first contingent of about 80 men leave Sasebo the following morning.

But my happy days were numbered. On November 25 a staff officer at the Naval Station showed me the latest action reports. There was a depressing account of one of the most disgraceful destroyer defeats in the history of Japan's Navy. I read it over and over again.

Five destroyers led by Captain Kiyoto Kagawa had left Rabaul on the 24th at 1530 on a second transport mission to Buka. (The first had been carried out by cruiser *Yubari* and my destroyer *Shigure*. We had met no enemy opposition.) Kagawa, who was not a specialist and had no night battle experience, seems nevertheless to have made a correct appraisal of the danger. He divided his five ships into two groups: his own *Onami* and *Makinami* as the scout-fighting ships and the three others as purely transport vessels.

No opposition was encountered on the way in and the three transport destroyers—*Amagiri, Yugiri, Uzuki*—landed their 920 troops and 35 tons of supplies on Buka Island shortly before midnight, without incident. These three destroyers took on board some 700 sick and ailing troops for return to Rabaul.

Kagawa, with *Onami* and *Makinami*, some eight miles ahead of the three transport destroyers, was taken by surprise with a torpedo attack from five destroyers under Captain Arleigh A. Burke. *Onami* sank before she could even return fire, and *Makinami* broke in two, under enemy shellfire and sank shortly afterward.

The Americans then observed and pursued the other three. *Yugiri*, at the tail of the column, turned to engage the pursuers but came under deadly U.S. destroyer gunfire which sank her. *Amagiri* and *Uzuki* managed to escape.

The results of this action were especially saddening for me because *Onami*'s skipper was my old friend, Commander Kiyoshi Kikkawa, who, along with Kagawa, went down with his ship. He was neither stupid nor timid. His performance as skipper of destroyer *Yudachi* off Guadalcanal had won him a deservedly high reputation. But even a man of his prowess and bravery was helpless before an enemy whose technical superiority provided accurate vision and aim in the dark of night.

What would be the enemy's capability compared with my own when I returned to battle? The thought disturbed me greatly. I went back to the dockyard and pleaded for *Shigure*'s swift repair. The repair chiefs replied that they would do all they could but, at best, it would be a month before my ship was fit for combat.

On November 26 I was pleasantly surprised by a phone call from Vice Admiral Chuichi Nagumo, who invited me to dinner. I was delighted to accept.

As Commander in Chief First Air Fleet, Nagumo had commanded the Pearl Harbor Striking Force and subsequent carrier operations through the battle of Midway until July 1942, when he took command of the Third Fleet. In November 1942, he was appointed Commander in Chief Sasebo Naval District, and in June 1943, he was moved to the Kure Naval District. Now I had just learned of his reassignment as Commander in Chief First Fleet (a homeland training organization), and was as flattered by his invitation as I was eager to learn his views and plans.

His health was restored. He looked much better than the sorry man I had last seen at Truk a year earlier. But his conversation lacked spirit. In fact, all through our long dinner he urged me to speak of my experiences. He listened intently, complimented my work, and finally said, "But the heyday of our destroyers ended with the battle of Cape St. George. Things might have been different there and after if we could have had a dozen destroyer skippers of your caliber."

I did not know it at the time but, despite his return to health, this wrinkled old officer was forlorn. In times since I have realized that he must have then foreseen his own destruction and that of the Imperial Japanese Navy as well.

That was the last time I saw him. In March 1944, he was transferred to Saipan as Commander in Chief Central Pacific Area and 14th Air Fleet, and there he fought until his death the following July.

On the next day, I joined the second group of 80 officers and men from *Shigure* in taking a 10-day home leave. And such a home leave "never was before." By ones, twos, threes, and fours, my men and officers came morning, afternoon, and evening, always with large bottles of *sake*, to do me honor in my home. Some rode several hours by train to reach Kamakura in order to make the gesture. Accordingly, I sat and drank with them, day and night.

They always apologized to my wife for intruding and begged forgiveness for their seeming rudeness. But, they explained, "We have gone through the bloodiest of battles and emerged unscathed. It was miraculous, and possible only because of your husband. He is the greatest officer in the Imperial Navy. We gladly give up part of our time with our families to honor our esteemed Captain in his home. Do not be harsh with us."

They did all kinds of work around the house, running errands, and playing with the children. For me the steady bout of drinking made it the wettest few days of my life. It is a wonder I did not drown in *sake*. Secretly, my wife, and especially my two daughters, pronounced it a terrible home leave, but they put up with it. My son loved the robust guests.

On December 6 I returned to Sasebo accompanied by a record-breaking hangover which took a week to wear off. *Shigure*'s overhaul and repair were completed on the 20th. Our two-day shakedown cruise proved her fit for combat and I reported to the high command that she was ready to return to the South Pacific. I was ordered to stand by.

After sweating it out for three days, in which every minute dragged like a week, I was summoned to Sasebo Naval Headquarters. The deputy commandant personally delivered orders which assigned me as an instructor to the Torpedo School!

I was infuriated, and let it be known. "Shore duty for me? What's going on? Admiral Samejima himself told me that he needed me and was awaiting my return. I want to get back—I insist on it!"

"All right, Hara, now calm down. Before you lose your temper there is something else you should know. Your assignment to the school as an instructor is no reflection on your service record, as is sometimes the case. This matter is still highly classified, but I can say that you will be in charge of a new school for training torpedo-boat men. Headquarters has decided that only you can fulfill a vital Navy need by training men to be torpedo experts. Don't scowl. You will be shouldering one of the most important tasks in the Navy."

I did realize what the rear admiral was driving at, and was in agreement with the need for trained torpedo-boat men. This need was one that the Navy had been slow in accepting.

"Hara," he continued, "you once revolutionized the torpedo doctrine of the Imperial Navy. You are now expected to revolutionize a phase of surface doctrine and tactics. You know better than anyone else that destroyers have had their day. You were chosen for this highly classified assignment upon very strong recommendations from Admiral Ijuin in Tokyo, Admiral Nagamo of the First Fleet, and Admiral Omori of the Torpedo School. Congratulations. Let me wish you every success."

On returning to *Shigure* I called the crew to assemble at the forecastle and spoke to them: "Shipmates. I have been relieved as Commander Destroyer Squadron 27 and must leave immediately for Yokosuka and my new assignment. The past ten months, in which we have lived and fought together, has been the happiest and most satisfying time of my career. I have been proud of you, and can now say that I have never commanded such a fine crew. Keep up your spirit and your skill and I know you will continue to win with your new commander. Good luck. I shall miss all of you, but will always be wishing you well. Good-bye."

I walked around to shake hands with everyone. Some mumbled farewells, some were silent, but very few cheeks or eyes were dry. Several men dashed off after shaking hands, to relieve comrades who were standing watch. The duty men thus came in for their turn.

I had my bags packed in half an hour and went over *Shigure*'s side for the last time. I stood up in the boat for a farewell look as we pulled away from my proud ship. The scene was one I had never heard of in the cold, harsh-disciplined Imperial Navy. The crew lined the railings and clung to every vantage point of the superstructure and riggings, waving and shouting their farewell. I started to wave but my heart was so full I had to sit down and weep.

part five

THE LAST SORTIE

1

I reported to the Yokosuka Naval Station personnel office on December 27, 1943, and was brusquely told that my formal appointment was not yet ready and that I should come back after the New Year holidays. The only semblance of work in progress was people clearing off desks, apparently in preparation for their holiday. How could they be so concerned with holidays at this critical period of the war?

"You just go on home and take it easy," the officer continued in a cajoling voice. "It's wonderful that you can be home on New Year's Day, isn't it? I guess it's a gesture on the part of the high command in recognition of your exploits."

To me this attitude was shocking and disgusting. I glared my displeasure and almost roared in anger to remind these people of our serious setbacks in the Solomons. Instead I turned and strode from the room.

The Naval Torpedo School was located at Oppama, just north of Yokosuka. There I stormed into the commandant's office and unleashed my pent-up anger to Vice Admiral Sentaro Omori. He was embarrassed, but after listening patiently to my outburst he said, "I know what you mean, Hara, but these people at home can never know the vital urgency of war as do we who have been in battle. You must learn, as I have, that we cannot change the world, but must be patient and do what we can when we can."

I returned to Kamakura, just 20 minutes by train from Oppama, with a bad taste in my mouth. I looked at the streets for the first time in many months and was shocked. Kamakura, one of the beauty spots of Japan, was a ghost town. No bombs had fallen, but the stores were empty. People on the streets appeared depressed and hungry. Our enormous shipping losses in the Solomons were beginning to tell in the homeland, dependent as it was on imports.

My anger abated then, giving way to depression, and I arrived home with mixed feelings. When my wife and children rushed out to greet me joyously, I shook off all unpleasant thoughts, thankful for the chance to be home.

On January 10, 1944, the same date Admiral Koga decided to move his Combined Fleet Headquarters from Truk to Palau, I formally became senior instructor of the Naval Torpedo School.

It is strange that Japan had not used torpedo boats earlier in the war. In its preoccupation with big ships, the Navy high command had not developed torpedo boats and their tactics. Japanese naval officers were appalled at the brisk activity of American torpedo boats in the Solomons, and at the rapid attrition of Japanese destroyers. To this situation the natural reaction was to build torpedo boats and train crews for them, but Japan's decision was too late.

Such miscalculations on the part of the Japanese Navy were by no means restricted to torpedo boats. The problems of aviator training and radar development were also neglected too long. By late 1943 Japanese electronic factories were working day and night to build radar sets; but by then too many Japanese warships had been sunk in the Solomons.

In prewar days Japan trained very few flyers out of thousands of applicants. The Navy did not change this policy until late in 1943, when most of its crack pilots, who should have been teaching, had already been killed in action. When the Navy belatedly started to train aviators on a mass-production basis, it discovered that the aircraft factories were unable to keep pace with the demand for planes.

All 100 of my students at the Torpedo School were college and university graduates who had originally volunteered for flight training and duty. After three months of preliminary air training, these men were all switched to surface assignments, and thus to my torpedo-boat class, simply because of lagging airplane production.

My students were all in their early twenties. They were serious and enthusiastic but, being reservists, complete amateurs, and totally unlike the Academy men to whom I had taught my destroyer-torpedo formula in this same school some years before. I quickly discovered a great need for patience.

In teaching professionals I was very stern and never hesitated to criticize ineptness. The professionals all had years of training and experience and thus expected strict discipline. But my present group of reservists were like caricatures of students. I found it of no use to scold no matter how clumsy and stupid they were. How could such amateurs be made into efficient torpedo-boat men in the prescribed three months of training? Many times I thought of resigning, out of sheer desperation.

Our equipment was deplorable. We had only ten small, dilapidated torpedo boats, barely capable of making 18 knots. Almost every day I prodded Admiral Omori for better ones, but they were slow in arriving. Because of the Navy's tardy interest in torpedo boats, the arsenals were slow in producing the small but powerful engine they required.

The first new boat arrived at the school in February and I was totally disgusted with its performance. After a test run of the 20-ton craft I returned it to the pier and ranted, "This is no torpedo boat. It is nothing but a barge. This scow would be of no value in a real fight."

Omori and my instructors were glumly silent. The designer, visibly pale, stepped forward and explained apologetically that this boat was equipped with an old airplane engine. "We simply cannot produce the new engine needed for this type of boat. There are too many bottlenecks, including a critical shortage of materials."

Too angry and discouraged to speak, I stalked away. The next few "torpedo boats" to be delivered were no better. Insofar as I know, only 200 or so boats, ranging from 15 to 30 tons, were produced under the emergency wartime program beginning in 1943. All were equipped with old aircraft engines, and none could make better than 25 knots. Their V-shaped hulls of steel or wood were 45 to 55 feet overall. Manned by a crew of seven, these boats were armed with two small torpedoes and one 13-mm. machine gun. But none ever came up to the standards I would have desired. It was painful to consider that the nation which could produce the world's greatest battleships was unable under pressure to produce a single satisfactory torpedo boat.

The training program for my first class of 100 students was extended for a few weeks and they were graduated at the end of April 1944. My remarks to them on that occasion made Admiral Omori and my teaching colleagues quite unhappy: "Your boats are, unfortunately, inferior to any fighting craft of the enemy. As I have tried to drum into you every day, you will have to rely on stealth. You will not be able to outfight the enemy. You will have to take advantage of every use of camouflage or ruse to be successful. Otherwise you will be nothing but practice targets for the enemy guns."

Teaching was a wearying job. The classroom windows overlooked the calm port of Yokosuka and the view made me long for life at sea. Hard and harsh as destroyer life had been in the Solomons, I looked back on it as a time of happiness, with its thrills and exultations all of which were completely lacking in the school.

News from the war front was frequently long delayed and usually incomplete, but I went to Yokosuka headquarters for occasional information about my former ships.

Amatsukaze served as escort to transports plying between the homeland and the Southwest Pacific without incident during 1943. But shortly after the start of my school I was shocked by news that she had been torpedoed 250 miles north of Spratly Island in January, 1944, and that 80 members of her crew had been killed.* Although badly damaged the destroyer was able to reach Saigon. Emergency repairs there enabled her to be moved to Singapore for further work which was not completed until March, 1945, when she was again seaworthy.

Shigure was also used on escort duty after leaving Sasebo with her new squadron commander on board. I was saddened to learn that she was hit February 17, 1944, by an aerial bomb which did only minor damage to the ship but killed 21 of her crew. The most shocking part of this news was that she had been hit at Truk, which I knew as a calm haven, immune from air attack. There must have been a shocking laxity at Truk if *Shigure*, which had survived so many attacks in the Solomons and at Rabaul, could fall victim to air attack there.

Further horrifying news followed shortly. On March 30, an American task force under Admiral Raymond A. Spruance struck the Caroline Islands, shredding the defenses at Palau. Admiral Koga took off that evening from

---

* This attack was by USS *Redfin* (Cdr. Robert D. King) on her first war patrol. Four torpedoes were fired and King claimed four hits and a sinking.

Babelthuap, to transfer his Fleet Headquarters to Davao in the Philippines, and was never heard from again.*

Meanwhile I was ordered to Kawatana, near Sasebo, immediately after graduation of my first class. My assignment was to set up a new torpedo boat school there, because Oppama could not accommodate the increasing number of students assigned. I was probably chosen for the transfer because of my continual griping about conditions and equipment at Oppama, which tended to spread discontent.

Whatever the reason, I welcomed the change. I was tired of griping, and the prospect of being commandant of an independent school was pleasant.

Kawatana is a small fishing village on the shore of Omura Bay. The Navy had maintained a small torpedo testing range there for many years, but it had not been used recently. I arrived on May 3, to find the most decrepit barracks of my experience. I was met by a dozen maintenance men who must have wondered what made me chuckle as I inspected the ruins which were to serve as billet and school for the "revolutionizing" of the Navy's surface tactics. It struck me as being very funny.

A petty officer in charge of the maintenance crew told me that Admiral Koga had been given up as lost and that Admiral Soemu Toyoda had been named his successor as Commander in Chief Combined Fleet. This surprised me even more than my school's miserable facilities, but I could see nothing funny in it. I felt strongly that Admiral Toyoda was not the man for this job. He had been commandant of the Yokosuka Naval Station when I left Oppama. Prior to that he was a member of the Supreme War Council, and still earlier, at the start of the war, commandant of the Kure Naval District. He had never seen action in this war. Just as Koga had been plucked from quiet China waters to succeed Yamamoto, his successor was also a man without battle experience. Why at this time did the high command pick as Commander in Chief a man totally unknown to most of the sailors at the fighting front? I wondered often about this while organizing my new school.

---

* They flew in two flying boats which met storms over the Philippines. The second plane, carrying V. Adm. Shigeru Fukudome, skirted the typhoon, which apparently accounted for Koga's plane, and made a forced landing near Cebu Island. Koga's death was not publicly announced until May 5, when Admiral Soemu Toyoda was announced as his successor. V. Adm. Shiro Takasu, Southwest Area Fleet commander, had interim command of the Combined Fleet.

A week later 200 students arrived for torpedo-boat training. Like my class at Oppama, they had all been transferred from aviation schools. With six assistants, three of them picked from the Oppama graduating class, I resumed the frustrating profession of a teacher.

My premonition about Toyoda soon proved sadly true. He was not the man for the job. On June 19–20, Vice Admiral Jisaburo Ozawa's carrier task force suffered a disastrous defeat at the hands of the Americans in the so-called Marianas Turkey Shoot. Ozawa tried to engage the enemy by making use of his longer-range Japanese combat planes. But Admirals Toyoda, Ozawa, and Kurita, who mapped out the strategy of this operation, did not reckon sufficiently with the effectiveness of enemy radar and the enemy's increased pilot skill and plane capability; nor with the correlative decrease in the skill of Japanese pilots. The result was that Ozawa lost three carriers and 500 planes, and the Navy lost its last real task force. Four months later Ozawa took three empty carriers on a "decoy mission" to the Philippines, and lost them all without achieving anything.

Almost every day brought shocking news, and all too often it touched me closely. A radio newscast in the evening of July 10 reported that Saipan had fallen to the enemy the previous day, and that Vice Admiral Chuichi Nagumo had died there.* I was standing in my room, stunned at this news, when a wire message from Yokosuka was delivered. It was a directive for me to "train students henceforth for the main purpose of fighting the enemy on the coasts of Japan."

My reaction to this order was something I will never understand, but it affected me most strangely. My hands trembled and my face turned scarlet in anger. I tore the message into bits, threw it into the wastebasket, and sat down at my desk to write a petition to Emperor Hirohito. It was a preposterous thing to do, but I simply could not control myself.

I wrote that Japan had already lost the war, and I appealed to the Emperor to see the situation realistically. I pointed out that the ranking positions in the Army and Navy were held by superannuated officers unfamiliar with modern warfare, and that continual bickering between the Army and Navy leaders blocked efficiency of operation both in the military and in industry, as exemplified by our lagging production in planes and torpedo boats. I urged the Emperor to consider a termination of the war and, as a first step, to dismiss all incompetent admirals and generals.

---

* Nagumo took his own life on July 6 with a pistol shot.

I had become a hotheaded revolutionary. Perhaps it was the long-continued frustrations of my teaching job which caused me to suddenly write this petition. My act was not only insubordination but treason as well, according to Naval Regulations, and I could be court-martialed for it. But I did not think of such a possibility. I forgot everything except that the nation was tottering to a catastrophic fall.

When my petition was completed I boarded the first train for Tokyo. On the 12th of July, I stomped into the Navy Ministry where the first person I saw was Rear Admiral Prince Takamatsu, the second brother of Emperor Hirohito. I dashed up to him.

"Prince Takamatsu, may I have a man-to-man talk with you?"

The Prince looked at me and probably thought me a little daft, but he nodded and I followed him to his office. There I offered the petition, requesting that he present it to the Emperor.

"May I read it before doing so?" he asked.

"Certainly, Your Highness."

He slowly unfolded the paper and manned its contents. His brow wrinkled and he appeared disturbed by what he read. He looked at me again, probably wondering just how insane I really was, and put the petition in his pocket.

"All right, Hara," he said as he stood up, "take good care of yourself."

I never found out what Prince Takamatsu did with my petition, but he must have been discreet about mentioning it in Navy circles. Had word of my writing ever reached the Navy Minister or the high command I would have been dealt with in summary fashion.

Immediately after delivering the petition to the Prince I took the next train back to Kawatana, to await the Emperor's reaction. When nothing happened I came to my senses gradually and realized how outrageous my action had been. Neither the Emperor nor any other member of the royal family could take action on my petition. He was, after all, a constitutional monarch, and under the constitution could not initiate any action. This rule was broken a little, more than a year later, however, when he personally decided in favor of the surrender of Japan.

With grim resignation I attended the graduation of my 200 students at the end of July. On August 1, the barracks were jammed to overflowing by 400 new students, like the others, transferred from aviation schools. When I saw them, some without blankets, sleeping on the floor, packed like canned sardines, I decided to quit my griping and be a devoted teacher. These youngsters were serious-minded patriots and they deserved my best efforts regardless of their professional limitations.

The training period for these 400 students was drawing to a close when action erupted in the Philippines. American landings at Leyte on October 20 led to a series of naval engagements which decimated what remained of the Imperial Navy. On the 27th an unprecedented communiqué announced the formation of the Kamikaze Corps, a volunteer suicide aerial attack unit.

This stunning news horrified the Kawatana school. It was also a blow to me since I had always preached that men's lives should be spared. Since I drilled into my students the idea of attack and return, these new tactics were to me inhuman and intolerable. My ideas of revolt subsided, however, when I read the detailed reports of how the pilots had actually volunteered for these sure-hit but sure-death attacks. In the solitude of my room I wept aloud.

My 400 students were graduated at the end of October in a ceremony which greeted the arrival of another 400 new students. In the same week our school had an unexpected visitor in the person of my old friend from Rabaul, Captain Toshio Miyazaki. This former commander of Destroyer Division 17 was now senior instructor in the Torpedo School at Oppama.

Announcing his arrival in person, Miyazaki confided that he had come by special train, carrying a surprise cargo, and he asked me to accompany him to see it. In the railroad yard he led me to a freight car guarded by an armed detail which had accompanied it from Yokosuka. The cargo was transferred to the old torpedoing range, where it was opened to reveal three small torpedo boats and a dozen sets of lightweight diving gear.

The boats, made of plywood and powered by an automobile engine, looked like ordinary motorboats. Their novelty lay in their "warhead" bows filled with high explosives. When Miyazaki whispered, "This craft is a surface kamikaze," I could only groan in anguish.

To break the awkward silence, I asked about the diving gear. "That," explained my friend, "is for frogmen who will walk the bottom of the sea with their own supply of oxygen, carrying a compact explosive charge to be attached to the screw or rudder of an enemy ship."

He walked silently back to my quarters where Miyazaki went into more detail. The tiny one- or two-man torpedo boats and the frogman ideas had been approved by the high command about the time I was sent to Kawatana. The suicide tactics were the subject of long and heated debate until the initiation of the kamikaze units in the Philippines, and then there was a sudden decision in favor of their adoption.

"Knowing you as he does," Miyazaki continued, "Admiral Omori detailed me especially to come here and present this explanation. Knowing you as I do, I realize how awkward this mission is. I will listen to anything you wish to say, but I must advise you again that this tactical formula has already been adopted."

I considered his remark and thoughtfully replied, "I know how you feel, Miyazaki, and am in no mood to argue with you. But you know as well as I do that the hurriedly trained graduates of this school will be little more than cannon fodder when they go into action in these slow barges called torpedo boats. I have known all along that they have little chance of survival. Yet, even against their overwhelming odds, that is different from asking boys to commit suicide. How can we ask them to kill themselves?"

Miyazaki was solemn. "Hara, during the past 50 hours on my sleepless ride here from Yokosuka in those freight cars, I have been thinking long and hard about this. The only thing for us to do is to honestly explain the harsh realities of the situation. I plan to tell your students how the men in my destroyer division were killed, despite their skill and long years of experience. Now we are dying in the Philippines. All servicemen must face death. I hear that the kamikaze pilots volunteered unanimously for their unconventional sorties after hearing how 500 comrades with hundreds of hours of flying experience were killed like flies in the Marianas. These are rationalizations, to be sure, and I know what your feelings are. It is because of your acknowledged genius in bringing men back alive, even from the savage Solomons battles, that Omori sent me to you on this unenviable mission. And it is because I know and understand you that I was willing to come."

Miyazaki, usually a swashbuckling, devil-may-care sort looked beaten and miserable. I thought over the many things that occurred to me and finally said:

"I thank you, Miyazaki, for your trouble in coming here. I know that neither the circumstances nor the conditions were pleasant for you, and I appreciate your kindness. In thinking of the things you have just said, I recall my combat-seasoned destroyer *Samidare*. I have just learned that despite all her great exploits, she was torpedoed and sunk near Palau with the loss of half her crew. A destroyer bagged by a submarine! That's a cat eaten by a mouse! What irony!

"*Shiratsuyu* fared even worse. This ship of gallant early actions turned sour after sideswiping *Samidare* at Empress Augusta Bay. I hear that she collided with a tanker off Mindanso last June and sank with a lost of 224 men.

"My old flagship *Shigure*, the 'miracle destroyer,' barely survived the Leyte Gulf battles, as the sole survivor of the Nishimura Force. But I have the firm feeling that her time will come soon. That fine ship, with all my old shipmates. . . . What a war this is!"

With that Miyazaki and I had nothing more to say to each other. We shook hands and parted for the night. Next morning I summoned a full assembly of the school. Miyazaki spoke first to explain the new weapons and their use. The atmosphere in the dilapidated barracks hall was tense, and the audience sat incredulously silent.

When Miyazaki finished I trudged to the podium and said: "I have no orders for you. You came here to prepare yourselves for conventional torpedo boats. You have just learned of two other weapons that have been authorized for study in this school. Starting tomorrow either of the three courses of study will be open to you. You have a free choice of which class you wish to attend, according to your own aptitude and inclination. I want your choice to be made without compulsion or influence from anyone, according to the dictates of your own conscience. This is my ruling. I will be in my office this afternoon and evening, as long as is necessary. Each of you will report to me personally on your choice. There will be no questions asked or explanations required as to why you make the choice you do. That is all."

One by one, the 400 students came to my office. The last one did not leave until 0400 the next morning. When they had all reported, I called Miyazaki and we sorted out the papers containing each name with the student's course preference. Our tabulation showed that 200 had chosen the conventional torpedo boat course, 150 elected for duty in the suicide boats, and the other 50 as frogmen.

Miyazaki, exhausted after long sleepless hours, heaved a deep sigh. So did I.

The suicide boats were given the poetic name *Shinyo*, which means literally "Ocean Shaker."* The frogmen were called *Fukuryu*, which has the literal meaning of "Crawling Dragon."

Considering their aggressive purpose, the "Ocean Shakers" were not an effective craft. Shortly after the three boats arrived at Kawatana I asked the

---

* About 6,000 of these small motorboats were built by dozens of manufacturers. The craft varied in length from 16 to 18 feet, and in weight from 1.35 to 2.15 tons. Most of them were powered by a single automobile engine and could make up to 26 knots; others having two engines could do 28 knots. A few were made of steel, but most were wooden, and fragile to a degree that belied their imposing name.

nearby Naval Air Station at Omura to send a fighter plane over for a practice encounter. An instructor manned the boat into open water but he jumped overboard when the plane swooped low directly over the craft. On the next pass the fighter sprayed machine-gun bullets into the flimsy shell, smashing it to bits.

The "crawling dragon" equipment was even more useless. The 50 men, all expert swimmers, had trouble with it throughout the course. Even the tanked oxygen supplied to the school was no good. Several student divers fell sick from it on the very first day.

What could these crude efforts do against a powerful enemy supplied with the finest of modern scientific equipment? Bitter pessimism shriveled my heart. Each day of the school was more depressing for me, and I took to drinking heavily again.

About 100 graduates of the conventional torpedo-boat school were sent to the Philippines and Okinawa—many to die without any significant achievements. All of the other graduates were held in preparation for opposing the anticipated invasion of the homeland. It has been some consolation to know that most of my fine students were not sacrificed in suicide missions.

On December 20, 1944, Miyazaki relieved me as commandant of the depressing school at Kawatana, and my new orders were for sea duty as commanding officer of light cruiser *Yahagi*. That was my happiest day of a very unhappy year.

2

It was a joyous commanding officer who climbed the ramp of light cruiser *Yahagi* at Sasebo on December 22, 1944. I was back where I belonged, with a chance to fight again, freed of the frustrations at Kawatana. My appointment to this command was a great honor.

The ship's senior officers turned out to welcome me. Commander Shinichi Uchino, the executive officer, announced excitedly, "*Yahagi*'s crew is overjoyed at having you as our new skipper. The youngest recruits are already speaking proudly of our 'Miracle Captain.'"

I expressed pleasure at my good fortune in being given command of *Yahagi,* and said, "Never having commanded such a big ship, I will have plenty to learn from each of you."

My remarks were received appreciatively and everyone appeared elated with my arrival. If it was a morale booster for the ship, it was needed.

Just returned from the disastrous Leyte Gulf battle, *Yahagi* had been flagship of a support group in Vice Admiral Takeo Kurita's Second Fleet. Details of that battle were still unknown, even to the Japanese who had taken part in it. But many knew that the Japanese Navy had taken a beating and that the United States was winning back the Philippine Islands.

When Admiral Kurita made his celebrated retirement on October 25 after inflicting heavy damage on an escort carrier force—though he failed to disrupt the landing operations at Leyte Gulf—*Yahagi* and three accompanying destroyers were still some ten miles away. From that extreme distance *Yahagi* and her companions released torpedoes, all of them wasted. The sluggish performance of these ships was a disappointment to all who were aware of it.

Rear Admiral Susumu Kimura, commander of Destroyer Squadron 10, which included *Yahagi* and six destroyers, was relieved of his post after the battle. He was an expert navigator but not a fighter.

Kimura's disinclination to battle had been clearly illustrated as early as November, 1942, when his light cruiser *Nagara* failed to engage the enemy off Guadalcanal. Yet almost every other Japanese warship in this action fought at point-blank range. To use him thereafter in such an important battle as Leyte illustrates again, but does not explain, the mysterious mental processes of the Japanese high command.

An even more serious blunder was the retaining of Admirals Kurita and Ozawa in command positions. Both of them survived the war and they are still alive. I do not like to criticize men of their integrity, but the retention of these two tired and aged admirals on active duty was a great factor in the disastrous defeat at Leyte.

Kurita has told me, "I made that blunder (of retiring) out of sheer physical exhaustion."

On the subject of Leyte, Ozawa has admitted to me, "I am ashamed to have survived the battle."

This greatest of all naval actions in history has been the subject of extensive writing. I disagree with many of the opinions expressed, but I agree wholeheartedly with C. Vann Woodward when he concludes in his *The Battle for Leyte Gulf*: "What was needed on the flag bridge of *Yamato* on the morning of the 25th was not a Hamlet but a Hotspur—a Japanese Halsey instead of a Kurita."

Kurita had shown frightful ineptness when he took his Second Fleet to Rabaul in November 1943, only to be shot up. But he, like Ozawa, was retained. As a consequence, the two of them were in command of the Japanese forces which took such a trouncing in the Marianas battle of June 19, 1944. They were still retained after that debacle, for reasons I have never understood. Both men were tired from the beginning. Sending them to Leyte was bound to be disastrous, especially since neither of their fleets was provided with effective air cover.

The greater responsibility, however, rests on Admiral Soemu Toyoda, Commander in Chief Combined Fleet. Arriving in Japan on October 18 from Formosa, he directed the battle first from Yokosuka and then moved 30 miles inland to Hiyoshi to carry on his duties. Thus this unrealistic operation was planned and directed on land, by an admiral who had never taken part in a naval action.

The causes of Japan's defeat in the battle of Leyte Gulf are numerous, but high on the list must be mentioned her deficiencies in airplanes, radar, and communications. The dying Japanese fleets fought well, considering that in addition to being without aerial defense or striking power, they were practically blind and deaf.

Japan's war was lost with the fall of Saipan. Thereafter, her many battleships and heavy cruisers, long conserved, were merely thrown into the slaughter at Leyte.

Kurita was replaced as commander of the Second Fleet by Vice Admiral Seiiehi Ito, on the day I joined *Yahagi*. Like so many other high-level decisions of the time, this one too astounded me. Ito had been on the Naval General Staff since the start of the Pacific war. He had had no sea duty whatsoever, let alone any combat experience, during the war.

The Personnel Section of Naval Headquarters seemed to be unreasonable in most of the assignments of those days. Kurita, with all the blunders of his career, was made commandant of the Naval Academy on his return from Leyte. Ozawa was promoted to become Commander in Chief Combined Fleet in May 1945. It is remarkable that most of the commanding officers who survived the Leyte battles were promoted.

Meanwhile, Second Fleet remnants limped home by twos and threes. In mid-January *Yahagi* joined *Yamato* and five destroyers at Hashirajima anchorage near Hiroshima. Remembering the sight of hundreds of warships filling this wide harbor just four years earlier, I was saddened to view these few leftovers that now comprised the scaled-down Second Fleet—a fleet that hardly deserved the name.

While we drilled I kept an eye out for either of my old ships, which might arrive to join us. *Shigure* had been a part of Nishimura's force when he led his two battleships, a cruiser, and four destroyers in a mysterious, unco-ordinated approach to Leyte Gulf on October 25, 1944. Every ship of this force except *Shigure* was sunk. By surviving, she became the target of harsh criticism and evil rumor which I could not believe. I wanted to talk with her crew and learn the truth. Instead of the long-awaited reunion, however, word came that *Shigure* had been torpedoed and sunk by an enemy subma-rine north of Singapore on January 24.* What a shame that such a fine ship should fall victim to a submarine. This word was followed shortly by news that *Amatsukaze* was staying in China waters, and so would not be able to join the Second Fleet.

But not all news was bad. New weapons and equipment for *Yahagi* arrived almost daily. There were proximity fuses, homing torpedoes, and, most important of all, efficient radar sets. Gun crews began to learn how to use radar-controlled gunfire. Many of these devices were still in the experi-mental stage, but their appearance was a sign that Japanese technology was moving forward. Too late to catch up with the enemy, to be sure, but it was a tremendous morale booster in those days of adversity.

All training, however, was limited to the narrow Inland Sea. I asked why we did not go to the open sea to engage in some high-speed combat exercises, and was told that our limited fuel supplies would not permit it. I knew that fuel supplies were low, but was staggered to know that there was not even enough for essential basic training.

After heavy preliminary bombardment, the Americans began the inva-sion of Iwo Jima on February 19, 1945. Not a single Japanese warship was sent to oppose this enemy landing, only 700 miles from the homeland.

Meanwhile the bombing of Japanese cities by B-29 Super-forts from Mar-ianas bases continued with increasing intensity. The high command returned to its old formula of conservation—this time of fighter planes. They were put under camouflage or hauled away into revetments safe from air attack, leav-ing the enemy unopposed in his bombing of the homeland.

---

* *Shigure* was sunk by submarine *Blackfin* (Crd. W. L. Kitch) in position 06°00′N., 103°48′E.

In Imperial Headquarters hot debate raged for many days on what should be done with the remnants of the Combined Fleet. Admiral Ito reported on March 1 that training exercises were completed and his force of one battleship, one cruiser, and ten destroyers was ready for action. But the high command was still undecided whether to use the impoverished Second Fleet for present attack or save it for homeland defense against invasion.

While angry arguments continued in Tokyo headquarters, the Second Fleet entered Kure harbor and took on its meager allotment of fuel. The Navy argued for conservation of its dwindling strength. The Army pointed to Leyte Gulf as showing the folly of conserving ships until they merely fell prey to enemy air attack. On March 19, the Army argument finally prevailed, for on that day an American task force closed the home shores and hurled hundreds of planes in an attack on shipping, at Kure and Kobe. No ships were sunk in these assaults, but seventeen warships were injured including slight damage to six carriers and three battleships, among them *Isa* and *Hyuga*, which survived the action at Leyte Gulf only to be hit while docked at Kure.

The Army generals nodded derisively at these losses which were increased when the carrier plane attacks continued on the 20th. The 5th Naval Air Fleet, newly organized in February 1945, fought back with hundreds of kamikaze planes. Its commanding officer, Vice Admiral Matome Ugaki—who had been Yamamoto's chief of staff—issued a report saying, "Our special attack planes accounted for seven enemy carriers, two battleships, and one cruiser either sunk or badly damaged." This exaggerated report helped restore the Navy's falling stock in Tokyo headquarters, but it backfired. Top strategists naively believed the report and placidly concluded that after such a setback the enemy task force would have to retire to Ulithi for repairs before it could strike again.

Three days later, on March 23, hundreds of American carrier planes began making daily strikes all over Okinawa. This assault was followed directly with bombardment of the island by American warships. Japanese staff officers were stunned, but took no action. Instead they predicted wishfully that landing operations would not be carried out until much later. But the American task forces were not just visiting in Okinawan waters. They had come to stay.

Imperial Headquarters finally ordered all-out aerial opposition on March 26. The American hordes walked ashore on April 1, practically unopposed. Lieutenant General Mitsuru Ushijima, commanding the defending 32nd

Army, had wisely learned that defense in depth was more effective than trying to annihilate the enemy at the water's edge. The Navy cried, "Why doesn't the Army put up a fight?" To which the Army retorted, "Why don't Navy ships sink the enemy task force?"

This kind of haggling achieved nothing, but Admiral Toyoda, who had endured Army nagging for five months, finally gave in on April 5 and decided to use the Second Fleet, four full days after the enemy invasion had begun.

That day is notable for two other events of consequence to Japan: Prime Minister (General) Kuniaki Koiso resigned and was replaced by retired Admiral Kantaro Suzuki; and the Soviet Union notified Japan that it would not extend their nonaggression pact.

I knew nothing then of these behind-the-scene moves. On that hazy morning the Second Fleet was moored near Tokuyama in the Inland Sea. From light cruiser *Yahagi*'s bridge I was looking idly around at giant battleship *Yamato* and our eight destroyers (two had been docked at Kure because of engine trouble) that swung at anchor. They were organized as follows:

SECOND FLEET

Vice Admiral Seiichi Ito*
Battleship *Yamato*,* Rear Admiral Kosaku Ariga*
Destroyer Squadron 2, Rear Admiral Keizo Komura in *Yahagi*
Destroyer Division 17, Captain Kiichi Shintani*
    Isokaze,* Commander Saneo Maeda
    Hamakaze,* Commander Isami Mukoi
    Yukikaze, Commander Masamichi Terauchi
Destroyer Division 21, Captain Hisao Kotaki*
    Asashimo,* Commander Yoshiro Sugihara
    Kasumi,* Commander Hiroo Yamana
    Hatsushimo, Commander Masazo Sato
Destroyer Division 41, Captain Masayoshi Yoshida
    Fuyutsuki, Commander Hidechika Sakuma
    Suzutsuki, Commander Shigetaka Amano

Japan's great Second Fleet of the early part of the war was now reduced to these few ships. My musings on past glories and present weakness were interrupted by the approach of a seaplane from the southeast.

---

* Sunk or killed in the ensuing action.

It came in swiftly for a smooth landing and taxied to the side of *Yamato*. I watched several figures scramble up the accommodation ladder of the huge battleship. Even as I wondered who they were, *Yamato's* signal flags announced, "Operation *Ten-go* now in force!"

Almost immediately there was bustling activity in every warship, for the *Ten-go* operation meant that the Navy would make an all-out effort at Okinawa. Rear Admiral Keizo Komura, who had replaced Kimura in flagship *Yahagi* and had been sharing the bridge with me, was summoned to *Yamato*. He hurried into a waiting motorboat and was on his way. It was evident that the seaplane had brought high-ranking passengers with important information.

I kept an anxious eye on the battleship and, after two hours with no sign, was getting impatient. At 1130 *Yamato* signaled, "From Admiral Komura to all division commanders and ship captains. Meet Komura on board *Yahagi* for a noon conference."

Komura returned to *Yahagi* promptly, visibly excited but volunteering nothing to me. In answer to my question about the excitement he snapped, "Never mind, Hara, not now. Wait until they all arrive."

This startled me because he was an easygoing man who seldom showed his feelings. I left him alone and watched the eight boats from the destroyers as they approached *Yahagi*.

The conference started promptly at noon, with Komura addressing the group: "Gentlemen, you have all seen the signal that Operation *Ten-go* is now in force. Vice Admiral Ryunosuke Kusaka, the Combined Fleet chief of staff, has just come from Kanoya to confer with the flag-rank officers of our fleet."

His audience of four captains and eight commanders were deadly silent. After a short pause Komura continued.

"The operation formula proposed by Kusaka is an extraordinary one. The high command wants the Second Fleet to sortie for Okinawa, without air cover, with fuel enough for only a one-way trip. In short, the high command wants us to engage in a kamikaze mission.

"No, this is not even a kamikaze mission, for that implies the chance of chalking up a worthy target. I told Kusaka that our little fleet has no chance against the might of the enemy forces, and that such an operation would be a genuine suicide sortie. Aruga and Morishita agreed with me. Admiral Ito said nothing, so I do not know his opinion of the proposal.

"As you all know, I was chief of staff to Ozawa when he went on the decoy mission to the Philippines and lost four carriers. I have had to do with the killing of enough of our own men. I am not concerned with my death, but I do shrink from the wanton throwing of my own men into a suicidal sortie. Accordingly, I asked Ito and Kusaka for a recess in order to get your opinions."

With these words Komura clamped his jaw tightly and closed tear-filled eyes. There was a strained silence which I was about to break when Captain Eiichi Shintani, who a year before had relieved my friend Miyazaki as Commander of Destroyer Division 17, spoke up: "Has Kusaka come to cram these orders down our throats?"

Komura answered, "No one can tell another to kill himself. Kusaka has not mentioned orders. If he has them, he is not saying so. At this point we can only present to him our ideas and opinions."

Shintani blushed a deep scarlet, took a deep breath and declared, "I sortied with Kurita for Leyte the day after the Americans landed. It looks like the high command is pursuing that fatal formula again if they want us to thrust at the enemy's consolidated beachhead at Okinawa. The Kurita effort was more valid, however, because he at least had Ozawa as a decoy. Without a decoy we have no chance. Ours would be a ridiculous operation. If we try such a thing we will all perish, and then who will defend the homeland? I am opposed to it."

"I agree with Shintani," said Captain Hisao Kodaki, Commander of Destroyer Division 21. "The high command has been blundering now for many months. Why must we, who have been through many battles, blindly follow a bunch of inept, inexperienced leaders? Why are we not called upon for a proposal based on our practical experience?"

There were instant sounds of approval from the skippers under Shintani and Kodaki. This was rapidly becoming the liveliest naval conference of my experience. But Komura sat perfectly silent and motionless, his eyes still closed.

I felt impelled to say, "The realistic thing for us to do is to attack the enemy's overextended lines of supply. I would like permission to go on a lone-wolf mission. *Yahagi* now has radar and sonar equipment and I think she could go out alone and account for at least half a dozen enemy ships before they could get us. That strikes me as a worthwhile mission. The proposed fleet mission to Okinawa would, in my estimation, be just like throwing an egg at a rock."

Captain Masayoshi Yoshida of Destroyer Division 41 spoke up next. "Hara has expressed my opinion exactly. My destroyers *Fuyutsuki* and *Suzutsuki* are the very latest in anti-aircraft ships. These destroyers were built with blood, tears, and taxes of our impoverished nation, and have yet to be given a worthy assignment. I am positive that they could serve best on an independent mission such as Hara has described."

Commander Yoshiro Sugihara, skipper of *Samidare* when she sank in August, and now commanding *Asashimo*, vehemently seconded Yoshida's remarks. "I am living on velvet," he said, "and am prepared to die at any moment, but not meaninglessly as this action requires. My *Asashimo* is 2,520 tons of fighting warship. I would like a full chance to make her an asset to the nation."

The conference was interrupted when orderlies brought lunch, but the food was tasteless. During the meal the destroyer skippers voiced their opinions in the general vein of what had already been said. At 1300 Komura went back to *Yamato*. The rest of us waited grimly in *Yahagi* until he finally returned at 1600.

His face was haggard when he entered the salon slowly and said in a tired, croaking voice, "I have accepted the orders, which went into effect at 1530."

He seemed relieved to have gotten this off his chest. Then, looking around the room at each of us in turn, he gave a detailed account of the fateful meeting:

"I spent a full hour in conveying your opinions and my concurrence in them. Kusaka and the others listened to me intently. When I finished, Kusaka explained that this sortie was a decoy mission. He emphasized that it was not his plan, but that it had been worked out during his visit at Kanoya. While enemy carriers are occupied in opposing our fleet, Kanoya, as the southernmost airfield on Kyushu, will fling hundreds of kamikaze planes at Okinawa. Kusaka assured me that this decoy sortie will not end in vain as did my last one.

"Then he turned to Morishita and explained that the high command, and especially the Army members, had been dismayed by *Yamato*'s breakoff at Leyte. Kusaka said that he felt it was not Morishita's fault, for he had worked a wonder in dodging all torpedoes, while *Musashi* fell victim to them. Yet he said that Tokyo was displeased that *Yamato* had returned without firing her 18.1-inch guns at the enemy. Morishita took these remarks very hard.

"Kusaka said to Aruga that the whole nation would hate the Navy if the war should end with *Yamato* still intact. Through no fault of Aruga's, *Yamato* had been out of action for three years prior to Leyte, and was being spoken of as 'a floating hotel for idle, inept admirals.'

"Ito broke his long silence at this point and said, 'I think we are being given an appropriate chance to die. A samurai lives so that he is always prepared to die.' That ended all argument. When Morishita and then Aruga finally gave in, I did too."

Komura bent his head low at these last words, as if apologizing. We sat in stunned silence. As the hour-like moments passed I decided to face the reality of this most unreal situation.

"We appreciate your stand on our behalf, Admiral Komura," I said. "But orders are orders. We must now make the best of the situation."

Admiral Komura looked at me gratefully and said, "Thank you, Hara."

The three division commanders—Kodaki, Shintani, Yoshida—accepted the orders, subject to the approval of their skippers. The eight commanders chorused their unanimous acceptance.

This abrupt change of heart may be hard for Westerners to understand. Kusaka had made a painstaking effort to persuade the admirals to consider his officers' point of view. Because these were unprecedented orders, they could be carried out only if they were acceptable. But beyond this, we all knew that orders in the Imperial Navy were absolute.

Kusaka told me after the war that this was the hardest ordeal of his life. He explained further, "Ito was prepared for certain death when he took command of the shrunken Second Fleet. Having been a deputy chief of staff for so long, he evidently felt acute responsibility for our continuous defeats. Few people retained common sense in those days. A kamikaze spirit permeated the entire Navy."

Upon acceptance of the orders, all ranking officers attended a formal briefing in *Yamato*. It concluded with remarks by Admiral Ito who said, "In view of the extraordinary nature of this mission commanding officers will remove from their ships all cadets, the sick . . . and . . . er . . . any others who are considered unfit. This is a matter for your discretion."

Returning to *Yahagi* I called an emergency meeting of all officers and noncoms at the forecastle. I explained the orders to them, carefully studying the face of each man. The air was tense but, to my surprise and relief, no one appeared upset.

In conclusion I said, "These are extraordinary orders. But let me make this clear. If any of you believe you can be of better service by skipping this sortie you are to leave the ship along with the cadets, the sick, and others considered unfit for the mission. I request any such of you to call at my cabin immediately after this conference."

Mine was a broad interpretation of Admiral Ito's instructions, but I felt sure it was what he had intended. In my cabin I gazed forlornly at the picture of my family, and considered that most of *Yahagi's* men were family men, wondering how many would come to raise conscientious objections. The idea of herding 1,000 men to certain death did not appeal to me. I was ready for the knock at my door, but was surprised when my executive officer, Commander Uchino, entered.

"Captain, there are 22 cadets and 15 men who are sick."

"Is that all, Uchino? Are there none of the crew who wish to leave?"

"No, sir. Every man is eager to comply with the orders." I went out on deck where the 37 men were waiting, and said to them, "You are ordered to leave this ship now. I know that you will all be given a better chance later to fight for the cause of our country."

As I turned away a young man leaped from the ranks and cried, "Please allow me to stay, sir. I am not of much use, but will do any job if you let me stay."

Another lad wept, "Why must we be put off just because we are fresh from the Academy? We can surely clean latrines."

I groaned silently as the others fidgeted to burst out with further appeals. To ward this off, I cleared my throat and declared, "You joined this ship only two days ago. You have not even completed your introductory tour. As skippers of the future your lives must not be wasted. My orders are to put you ashore."

With that I turned and walked away to survey the bustling activity in *Yahagi*. Everyone was busy checking weapons and instruments. Almost 100 men were sharpening bayonets to be used after we went aground at Okinawa.

The 72,400-ton battleship *Yamato* came close to shore to pick up pipes from the Tokayama fuel depot, and the tanks of this huge oil center were soon drained.

While three barges alongside *Yahagi* were supplying fresh water, I asked Uchino about the state of our general provisions.

He replied, "We were full-loaded at Kure, and have on board at least 20 days of supplies for our 1,000 crewmen."

"In view of homeland shortages, why don't we put ashore all but five days' of our provisions? There is no need of taking along so much extra food on our one-way mission."

"I agree," said Uchino. "Let's ask the barges to relieve us of all extras."

The commander of the barges was bewildered by our request that he accept the bulk of our cargo. In fact, he objected, saying he had no authority to take our extra stores. Uchino and I could not explain our reasons, so we wheedled and cajoled until he agreed. When the surplus provisions had been removed, we pulled alongside *Yamato* for our last fueling. That done, *Yahagi* drew away to anchor, and the eight destroyer skippers and three division commanders were invited on board for a farewell party.

Admiral Komura, genial host on this occasion, no longer scowling and haggard, offered great quantities of *sake*. He poured each glass and the party turned into a curious drinking bout, with everyone striving for merriment and gaiety. Old, tired wisecracks were laughed at uproariously. Some officers sang or did tricks or sleight of hand, and each was greeted with cheers and applause. Meanwhile the *sake* supply dwindled, yet no one got drunk. The alcohol had no effect. There was boasting of romantic prowess and successes. But despite all efforts, there was no spontaneity in the laughter, and the gathering broke up a couple of hours before midnight, leaving 30 large, empty *sake* bottles. Yet every man walked straight and sober to the ramp and into waiting boats to return to his ship.

When the guests had gone, Commander Uchino invited Admiral Komura and me to join a party in the wardroom. There some 20 of *Yahagi's* senior officers were gathered. We exchanged drinks and toasts with them, and absorbed more pints of *sake*. We sang Navy songs and laughed with these officers, who were less subdued than the older skippers.

Uchino joined Komura and me to go to the gun room next, where the junior officers were having their final party. We had a drink and joined in a song or two. By 2330 all celebrating in *Yahagi* was ended and the celebrants had retired.

When Komura, Uchino, and I were finally alone I knew they shared my concern at how *Yahagi* would respond to the ordeal ahead. The officers all seemed composed enough, but what about the men? We decided to visit their quarters. Lights were out in the cramped, narrow spaces, filled with hundreds of occupied hammocks. There was no sound but the regular drone of snoring as the men slept peacefully.

We tiptoed back to the upper deck and Uchino said, "They are all right. They sleep like children with full trust and confidence in you. They know that you will take care of them no matter how hazardous our mission."

I was overwhelmed and tremendously happy. The vast quantities of alcohol began to work and I felt dizzy, I staggered, and was suddenly drunk. Tears streamed down my cheeks as I clung to a post and shouted, "Nippon Banzai! *Yahagi* Banzai! Nippon Banzai! *Yahagi* Banzai! Nippon Banzai! . . . "

And that was the last I remember of that unforgettable night. Uchino helped me to my cabin where I collapsed on the bed.

The next day was Friday, the sixth of April, and I awakened at 0600. The weather was glorious when I stepped out on deck and breathed deeply. I shook my head vigorously and was surprised to find no trace of a hangover.

A soft breeze whipped up small waves on the calm Inland Sea. A few thousand meters away, radiant cherry blossoms dotted the shore and distant mountains sparkled under the cobalt sky. This beautiful homeland is worthy of our sacrifices!

All ships were abuzz with activity. *Yahagi* was still occupied with the off-loading of nonessential supplies. Small barges and lighters were coming and going all around.

Uchino approached and greeted me, "Good morning, Captain."

"Good morning, Uchino, beautiful day, isn't it?"

"A bit too beautiful, sir. A B-29 flew over at 0100, and there were two others at 0400. The enemy is keeping close watch on our movements."

I nodded silently. This was what I had expected. After standing at the railing for a few minutes looking at the homeland, I dashed to my cabin. There was no time to waste. This was going to be a busy day.

Following the daily shipboard routine, we had morning exercises before breakfast, and then the crew lined up on deck to salute the Rising Sun flag as it was hoisted at the bows of our ship.

I returned to my cabin after the ceremony to catch up on accumulated paper work. There were messages to be read and scores of papers requiring my signature. At 1000 hours an orderly came to my quarters to say, "Captain Hara, the last courier boat leaves for Tokuyama in 15 minutes. Do you have anything to send?"

"Nothing, son, nothing at all." Alone again, I realized that there should be a farewell letter to my family. There was so much yet little to say, and time was fleeting. In a hasty note, which my wife has to this day, I wrote:

The Combined Fleet has shrunk unbelievably in the past two years. I am about to sortie as skipper of the only cruiser in this fleet—8,500-ton

Yahagi. With my good friend Rear Admiral Keizo Komura on board, we are going on a surface special attack mission. It is a great responsibility as well as a great honor to be skipper of a ship in this sortie to Okinawa. Know that I am happy and proud of this opportunity. Be proud of me.

Farewell.

I sealed the letter and ran with it to the ramp just before the boat pulled away. Returning to the cabin, I was no longer worried or upset. The sortie no longer occurred to me as a one-way mission. Determined now to fight to the last, I felt we could do it. I looked at the eight destroyers lying nearby and thought of past days and what these ships had been through.

Yukikaze (Snow Wind) had survived many hard battles. She had vied with my *Shigure* for indestructibility. I recalled the song that had been so popular at Truk and Rabaul:

Sasebo's *Shigure* and Kure's *Yukikaze*,
Immortal and indestructible destroyers!
You fulfill the miracle dream of sailors,
Two ships which always return from battle.

That song had been a great morale booster for my men. Now *Shigure* was gone, but *Yukikaze* would surely continue the miracle.

I looked at *Suzutsuki* (Cool Moon), 3,470 tons, and thought of her amazing record. Completed in late 1942, she had been hit by two torpedoes from a submarine on January 16, 1944, near Shikoku, off Bungo Channel.* Her bow and stem were shot off but the "Cool Moon" refused to sink and somehow made it back to Kure. Nine months later this same ship was hit by a submarine torpedo off Toizaki, again near Shikoku, and its bow was blown off, but again she made it to Kure and was repaired. "A thing repeated will occur a third time," I thought, and chuckled, little knowing how true this would be in the case of *Suzutsuki.*

Hibiki should have been in this force, but she had hit a floating mine early in the morning of April 5, and limped back to Kure. I felt a particular attachment to this little 1,980-ton destroyer and regretted her absence. When the mine-hitting incident was reported, it angered all of us. What a shame that a Japanese destroyer should be damaged by a mine in the Inland Sea.

---

* By submarine *Sturgeon* (Lt. Cdr. C. L. Murphy, Jr.).

But B-29s had dropped many mines there and in the Sea of Japan. Even home waters were no longer safe. Perhaps this fact had influenced the decision to throw our few remaining ships at Okinawa.

Looking at *Hatsushimo* I had no suspicion that she would survive this "one-way" sortie. But she did, only to hit a mine in the Japan Sea on July 30 and become the 129th and last Japanese destroyer sunk in World War II.

At 1600 the signal was given to weigh anchor and the ten ships of the Second Fleet commenced their "special attack" sortie. *Yahagi* moved out first, followed by the three "Wind" destroyers—*Isokaze, Hamakaze, Yukikaze*—and *Yamato* sandwiched between the two "Moons"—*Fuyutsuki, Suzutsuki*—with *Asashimo, Kasumi* and *Hatsushimo* in column astern.

As we advanced at a slow 12 knots, to avoid the hazard of mines, I surveyed our puny column of ships and realized this would be the last sortie of the Imperial Navy. It made me proud to be in the lead ship.

Two hours later we entered Bungo Strait, between Kyushu and Shikoku. Barely discernible to port was the long cape which formed the westernmost stretch of Shikoku. I bade a silent farewell to this island of my birth.

Past the narrow strait, the mine hazard was behind us, and we increased speed. But new hazards soon appeared. Two B-29s, flying high out of gun range, dropped several bombs at our formation. They scored no hits, but their challenge was a grave presentiment of what lay ahead. It made me uneasy to consider that, of our ten ships, only *Yamato* and two destroyers had antiaircraft radar. The sets in *Yahagi* were useful only against surface targets.

But there was no time now for such concerns. In each ship the crews were called to the forecastle. On *Yahagi's* spacious deck her 1,000 men collected while I briefed them on our mission and read a special message from Admiral Soemu Toyoda:

The Imperial Navy is mounting a general offensive against the enemy at Okinawa by mustering in concert with the Army all of Japan's air, sea, and ground strength to render this operation a turning point of the war.

Every unit and every man is expected to put up an inspiring fight and annihilate the enemy, thereby assuming the continuance of our Eternal Empire. The fate of our nation rests on this operation.

There was no sound but the murmur of engines, the slap of water, and the flutter and snap of the Rising Sun flag at our bows. I continued:

"You have just heard the message from our Commander in Chief. I wish to add a few words about our special attack mission.

"As you know, hundreds of our comrades have flown bomb-laden planes on one-way missions against the enemy. Thousands more of these flyers are standing by at every airfield. Hundreds of our comrades are ready in submarines to man one-way torpedoes. Thousands of others will drive explosive torpedo boats or crawl the bottom of the sea to fasten explosive charges against enemy ships.

"Our job in this mission is part of the same pattern. Our mission appears suicidal and it is. But I wish to emphasize that suicide is not the objective. The objective is victory.

"You are not sheep whipped to a sacrificial altar. We are lions released in the arena, to devour the enemy gladiators. You are not to be slain merely as sacrifices for the nation.

"Do not hesitate to come back alive. We must force our way against any enemy effort to intercept our mission. But you must not give up your lives cheaply. Once this ship is crippled or sunk, do not hesitate to save yourselves for the next fight. There will be other battles. You are not to commit suicide. You are to beat the enemy!"

A pale spring moon shone between the clouds, lending an appearance of statues to my motionless, silent audience. The almost visible tension mounted until it was, broken by an officer in the front row who said, "Captain Hara, may I ask a question?"

I nodded assent to Lieutenant Kenji Hatta, who continued. "During my four years at the Academy we were taught to live and die with our ship, which suggests that we should not abandon our ship under any circumstance. May I ask for clarification of your remarks which seem confusing in this regard?"

It was clear that Hatta's confusion was shared by many of his shipmates, so I replied, "That is a very good question. I will try to answer it. If our ship is stricken you are to abandon her immediately, without any qualms. This may seem contrary to what you have been taught in the past, but I will explain.

"We have reached a point of great adversity in this war. The material strength of the enemy is tremendous. But more crucial is our lack of skilled personnel, because of our many losses in battle. It takes five years to train an officer, so they cannot be replaced quickly. This ship may sink but there will be many more. Many fine Japanese sailors have died because they were too willing to give up their lives. If we are to win this war we must be tenacious.

"In feudal times, lives were wasted cheaply, but we are in the 20th century. The code of *Bushido* (the way of the samurai) says that a warrior lives in such a way that he is always prepared to die. Nothing has been so abused and misinterpreted as this adage. It does not mean that a warrior must commit suicide for some slight reason. It means that we live so that we shall have no regrets when we must die. Death may come to a man at any moment, no matter how he lives. We must not forfeit our lives meaninglessly.

"*Bushido* does call for atonement by suicide in case of gross negligence, and we can commit suicide at any time. But we are going on this mission not to commit suicide but to win, and turn the tide of war. We are to win this war and not think of dying. Does that answer your question, Hatta?"

"Yes, sir, it does," he shouted. "And I share your views entirely. Thank you very much." And he saluted.

I shouted, "Let us all do our best and turn the tide of war."

This curious briefing was broken up by the tumultuous shouting of the entire crew as they joined me in three cheers for the Emperor and *Yahagi*.

On our way, a final assault exercise was conducted. *Yamato* was the hypothetical enemy and each of her escorts made a "firing" run against her. We simulated the runs we would make against enemy targets next day. It was my first chance to run *Yahagi* at her maximum speed of 35 knots, but the time allowed us was short and we had to resume column formation for our southward passage.

Our radios soon picked up nearby transmissions from an enemy submarine. *Yamato* ordered a column-right turn to close Kyushu for the protection of its eastern coast. Moonset left the ocean in pitch darkness, as the weather turned bad. Lookouts strained their eyes but could see nothing. Everyone was tense, but there was no submarine attack.

Unknown to me, my old destroyer *Amatsukaze* was that day blasted into the East China Sea by American bombers, as if in prelude to the greater catastrophe that was about to befall the fleet of which I was a part. But even had I known of *Amatsukaze*'s misfortune, the news would have had no portent for me. As I had told my crew, my thoughts were all on the success of our operation. There was no room for defeat.

3

Our fleet advanced in column formation, zigzagging at 10 knots, and skirted the southeastern coast of Kyushu. At 0700 on the morning of April 7, we turned again to 210 degrees as if heading for Sasebo at the northwestern end of Kyushu. While making this feint, the ten ships shifted slowly into a ring formation around *Yamato*, on a 2,000-meter radius.

Yahagi took position directly ahead of *Yamato*. Counting clockwise, the eight destroyers formed the rest of the circle as follows: *Asashimo* at $7\frac{1}{2}$ minutes, *Kasumi* at 15, *Fuyutsuki* 21, *Hatsushima* 27, *Yukikaze* 33, *Suzutsuki* 39, *Hamakaze* 45, and *Isokaze* $52\frac{1}{2}$.

As soon as the ring was formed the ships boosted speed to 24 knots and resumed their zigzag advance. The first zig of 45 degrees to the right placed *Asashimo* in lead position. The ensuing zag of 90 degrees brought *Isokaze* to the front. This formation movement requires the utmost in precision maneuvering. It provides good protection against attack by submarines, limited as they are in mobility for attack. But the zigzag ring formation is relatively ineffective against attack by swift planes which can rapidly shift to any attack angle.

The ring formation and zigzag pattern for the Special Attack Force had been decided upon at Ito's conference, as soon as the orders had been accepted. It would soon prove to be a poor decision.

The beautiful weather of our departure day changed completely over night. It was unseasonably cool. Leaden clouds covered the sky and hung low on the sea. Not a beam of sunshine pierced the thick cloud layers. Rain could come at any moment. It was a dismal day.

The coast of Kyushu disappeared quickly when we turned southward into the East China Sea. An uneasy feeling came over me, for the first time since our departure, when I considered that this was the worst possible weather for a surface sortie. Daylight visibility of only 20,000 meters offered a distinct advantage to the enemy with his excellent radar. A blinding rainstorm would work to our advantage, but I knew that we could not expect it in this latitude. I wondered why we could not have chosen more advantageous weather for our desperate mission.

Lookouts posted on *Yahagi*'s decks gleefully announced the appearance of 20 Zero fighters from the north. They flew low past us and circled to come over again, darting in and out of the low cloud banks. Uchino asked if they had come to fly cover for our force.

"No, Uchino, they are not for us," Komura replied calmly. "We will have no air cover. They are on a routine training flight. Kusaka probably told these young pilots to fly over and bid us farewell."

Glum silence prevailed on the bridge until *Yamato* signaled that she was catapulting one of her two remaining planes to go to nearby Ibusuki air base, and ordered *Yahagi* to send off one of hers. *Yamato* normally carried seven planes, but five had been off-loaded at Kure. The sixth was being released now, as well as one from *Yahagi* because Admiral Ito did not want them to be wasted on our sure-death sortie.

One of *Yahagi*'s pilots reported to me just before taking off. He stood at stiff attention and said, "Under orders I am now going to Ibusuki. But there I shall join a kamikaze mission and be seeing you soon again."

When his plane was catapulted he circled three times over our ship and then headed back toward Kyushu. Men on deck waved him a last farewell.

The next message from *Yamato* was that her last plane and the last one from *Yahagi* should now be launched to return to Kyushu. But this order was rescinded shortly when two unidentified planes were sighted to the north. Our ship-based scout planes would have no chance against enemy fighters.

Uchino grumbled, "Why didn't those Zero fighters hang around to fight enemy planes?"

Komura answered him calmly, "Take it easy, Uchino, hold your temper. You know those youngsters wouldn't have a chance against the seasoned enemy pilots."

The clouds lowered, the weather grew worse, and at 0800 it started to drizzle. Our ring formation of ten ships advanced steadily toward their doom, observed constantly by enemy scout planes. At the same time Japanese planes calmly winged their way on a training mission. I had seen many kinds of operations, but never one like this. It was weird.

At 0900 destroyer *Asashimo*, right of *Yahagi*, slowed down. Through binoculars I could almost make out the face of my old friend Sugihara on her bridge, where there was a flurry of excitement. Her signal flags announced engine trouble. Greatly disturbed to see her fall behind, leaving a breach in the ring formation, I sent a message requesting further information.

Asashimo replied, "Rushing repairs. Hope to rejoin soon." But she fell farther behind, and by 1000 hours was completely out of sight. Komura ordered *Kasumi* to move up into the vacancy and the next four destroyers shifted their positions accordingly. This adjustment was no mean feat while the formation continued its zigzag course.

It had meant a lot to me to know that my old friend Sugihara was supporting my right flank. It was dismaying to realize that this place was now occupied by the second smallest ship of our force.

Our radios presently began to pick up enemy messages again, this time transmitted from aircraft near at hand. It was clear that our feint course had served no purpose. The enemy was aware of our force.

A pleasanter matter was the appearance of three 2,000-ton freighters to port. They presented a cheery aspect as they saluted us. Someone remarked that he didn't realize we still had transports of this size.

At 1130 a seaplane was detected 20,000 meters to the east. It approached to within a safe distance and circled leisurely about our formation, giving detailed reports of our movements. What a pity we did not have fighters available to shoot down this threat to our safety. While we watched wistfully this plane cruised beyond the range of our anti-aircraft guns. The radio suddenly boomed: "Amami Oshima lookout station reports 250 enemy planes heading northward."

"Here they come!" said Komura with a wry smile.

Amami Oshima is an island midway between Kyushu and Okinawa. Without even looking at a chart, every bridge officer knew that these enemy planes would be overhead within an hour.

Yamato ordered distance between ships increased to 5,000 meters; a standard procedure against air attack. Yahagi and the seven destroyers poured on fuel, and gun crews readied their weapons.

Yahagi's six big 150-mm. guns, four 80-mm. antiaircraft guns, and 40 machine guns pointed rapidly skyward. Ammunition supplies at hand, the gunners stood alert at their positions. When noon came and there was no sign of an attack, orderlies brought lunch to the combat posts. Everyone ate hurriedly, washing down the food with steaming green tea. I watched the efficient preparations with great satisfaction. My uneasiness vanished and I knew that Yahagi would give a good account of herself.

At 1220 Yamato signaled her radar findings: "Large group of planes distant 30,000 meters, bearing 35 degrees to port. All ships, full speed ahead! Prepare for antiaircraft action!"

The orders were hardly necessary. All ships were making nearly 30 knots. With Komura and other officers I climbed to Yahagi's antiaircraft command post behind the bridge. Yamato raised huge bow waves as she pushed through the water at her maximum speed. The 72,000-ton battleship presented a striking inspiration to every man in the force.

Navy men had an almost religious faith in Yamato. This feeling was heightened when she returned intact from the Leyte battle, even though sister ship Musashi was sunk there. Rear Admiral Nobuei Morishita was on board as Ito's

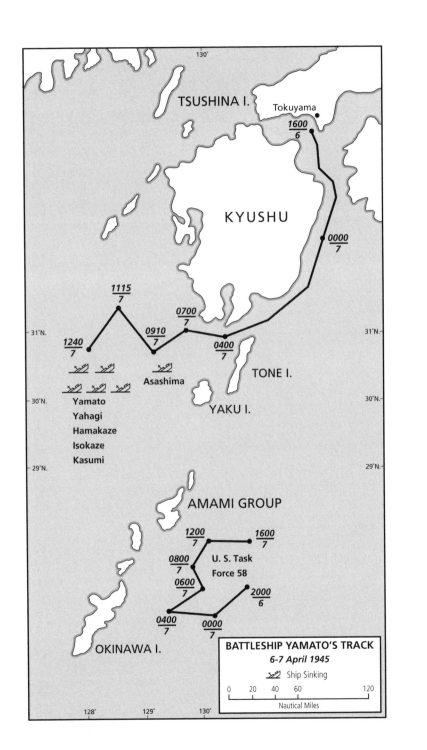

TSUSHINA I.

Tokuyama

$\dfrac{1600}{6}$

KYUSHU

$\dfrac{0000}{7}$

$\dfrac{1115}{7}$

$\dfrac{0700}{7}$

31°N.

$\dfrac{1240}{7}$

$\dfrac{0910}{7}$

$\dfrac{0400}{7}$

31°N.

Asashima

TONE I.

30°N.

YAKU I.

30°N.

Yamato
Yahagi
Hamakaze
Isokaze
Kasumi

29°N.

29°N.

AMAMI GROUP

$\dfrac{1200}{7}$

$\dfrac{1600}{7}$

$\dfrac{0800}{7}$

U. S. Task
Force 58

$\dfrac{0600}{7}$

$\dfrac{2000}{6}$

$\dfrac{0400}{7}$

$\dfrac{0000}{7}$

OKINAWA I.

BATTLESHIP YAMATO'S TRACK
6-7 April 1945

Ship Sinking

0   20   40   60   120

Nautical Miles

128°   129°   130°

chief of staff. He had been in command of *Yamato* at Leyte and, I thought, would surely bring her good luck again. Who could imagine that this greatest battleship ever built would be sunk within two hours?

Even from the command post we still could not see any planes approaching. The cloud cover had descended to 1,500 meters and a sudden rain squall blurred out everything around us. The situation couldn't have been worse; and now the planes must be overhead, above the clouds. Though *Yahagi* had practiced firing control with her new radar, it worked only against surface targets. Her sets were useless against planes. I realized woefully that our manually operated guns would not even have time to aim, once enemy planes popped out of the low clouds.

A lookout shouted, "Two planes on part bow!"

I looked up to see not two, but twenty, forty, and more planes spilling out of the thick clouds. It was 1232 when I ordered, "Open fire!"*

I had expected the planes to swoop down at us immediately. Instead they began circling clockwise, just below the clouds. Then I saw that one of the three groups was circling counterclockwise. This strange activity was completely baffling. Gun crews fumbled trying to set ranges, and then they seemed too bewildered to fire.

The confident enemy was methodically sizing up his victims. While they circled, the flight commanders must have been assigning planes to specific targets.

There was brief sporadic fire from a few of our ships when all the planes first came into view and started their merry-go-round. *Yamato*'s nine 18.1-inch guns roared off a few rounds of Type-3 shells which scattered in the sky, but even these fell miserably short of the intended goals. Suddenly the planes whirled and came thundering down toward their selected targets. Many ships' guns were still swinging into position.

The first planes to pick on *Yahagi* were four Avenger (TBM) bombers. Our cruiser rattled and roared, firing with all guns, but with little aim, as the bombs came curving down toward our portside. I called for hard right rudder and *Yahagi* responded beautifully. The bombs, dropped from about 500 meters, raised water pillars all about, but none hit.

The next group, Hellcat (F6F) fighters, dove defiantly lower. I could see the face of one pilot who jerked his stubby plane upward scarcely ten meters in front of me. The deadly whine and thud of machine-gun bullets beat like

---

* All U.S. planes in this day's action were from the carriers of Task Force 58.

hail through the length of the ship, but none hit my men. The gun crews stuck to their posts and fired steadily, but they also failed to score.

I looked hastily about to see all ships dashing at full speed, kicking up white waves and shooting with everything they had. In the water I caught sight of the weird crossing of foamy lines which spelled aerial torpedoes.

"Right rudder! Full speed!" I shouted as another dozen planes came at us. Black bombs sent white spray towering a hundred meters into the air. Fighters came careering down, fanning us with bullets and prop wash as they pulled out at masthead level. *Yahagi*'s guns returned a curtain of steel. Still neither side scored.

A lookout shrieked, "More bombers coming!"

"Hard right rudder!" I thundered, and the 8,500-ton ship jerked and wheeled in response, staggering a moment in her violent turn. Our guns missed again, but so did the enemy planes.

Yahagi's fourth group of attackers was coming in when the radio room reported that *Asashimo* was under attack. No time to think of that lone crippled ship as I streamed out orders to keep us from being hit. We wove through that rain of bombs and bullets, again without getting hurt. But what about *Asashimo*? With her engine trouble, *Sugihara* would have little chance to oppose an attack. It was fantastic that the enemy could be striking our main force so heavily and still have planes free to spring on a straggler more than twenty miles away.

Yamato was plowing ahead at full speed. Destroyers were corkscrewing violently here and there, appearing and vanishing in tremendous waves punctuated by mushrooming bursts from bomb hits, misses, and near misses. The spectacle was at once thrilling and terrifying.

More planes swinging low over *Yahagi* brought me sharply to action as near misses jolted the ship, but we were still uninjured. It gave me a feeling of relief to realize that our sharp twists and turns were effective in dodging the enemy's attack. If that was an unguarded moment it was my undoing.

A scream from portside, "Torpedoes!"

I shouted helm orders, looked down, and in the same moment let out a gasp. Three torpedo wakes were streaking toward us from only a few hundred yards away. The launching Avengers whizzed past the deck, zoomed and thundered triumphantly away. This time I did not follow the planes, but looked steadily at the eerie lines of approaching foam. *Yahagi* again staggered for a moment in the midst of her violent turn, then shuddered as a torpedo caught her portside, amidship just below the waterline.

It is hard for me to believe to this day the occurrence of the next event. *Yahagi* stumbled crazily for a few minutes and then shuddered to an abrupt and horrifying halt! It was inconceivable that a speeding warship of her size could be brought so suddenly dead in the water by just one torpedo. My stupefaction was increased if possible when I looked unbelievingly at my watch to find that it was 1246 hours. We had been fighting for only twelve minutes.

I grabbed the engine-room voice tube and called for a damage report. No response. I tried the phone with the same result. Then came the realization that the torpedo had hit the engine room, and I groaned. But the enemy allowed no time for lament. Another six planes swooped down to release bombs. I saw one hit and explode on the forecastle, felling at least a dozen men and blowing six bodies into the air. A detonation astern rocked *Yahagi* and caused a violent tremor throughout her length.

Biting my lip in agony, I saw again the sinking *Tokyo Maru*, victim of a single torpedo hit in the engine room. In the same instant I thought of Britain's mighty *Repulse* and *Prince of Wales* sunk by a force far smaller than the one that now confronted us. Suddenly my bolstered confidence was shattered.

An orderly came panting to the command post and reported, "The torpedo exploded in the center of the engine room, killing everyone there. The compartments are flooding."

"What about the watertight bulkheads?"

"The damage control crews are working, sir."

The ship was listing noticeably to starboard. I heard Komura say, "*Hamakaze*'s done for." Looking to port where Komura was staring I caught sight of the ship's red-painted belly as it sank beneath the waves.

A new attack came before our wounded had even received first aid. Uchino ran down the ladder shouting orders to the gun crews. That was the last I ever saw of my worthy exec. All operable guns opened fire and, for the first time in this action, I saw *Yahagi* strike back effectively as two planes were knocked down.

The ship itself, dead in the water, absorbed many bullets and bombs as group after group of enemy planes came driving in. A dozen to starboard winged low directly into the gunfire barrage. The enemy pilots certainly had guts.

The stalled cruiser rocked violently again with a tremendous explosion in the stern. I looked back and saw three mangled bodies hurled 60 feet in the air. And another torpedo exploded in the starboard bow.

Yahagi quivered and rocked as though made of paper. Clinging to the rail of the trembling command post, I saw that the torpedo hit had blasted a huge hole in the bow and the ship's list was increasing. Still another group of fighters and bombers came to concentrate on that shattered bow. The deafening drum of machine-gun bullets was climaxed by a direct bomb hit on No. 1 turret which wiped out its entire crew and smashed men on the forecastle. Strangely, no one on the bridge or in the command post was hit. But rivets popped as steel plates worked loose and the bridge shook so violently that it might collapse at any moment.

The structure of No. 1 turret was still intact, but the force of the 250-pound bomb explosion had cracked the thick steel of the surrounding deck. Yellow, acrid smoke drifted slowly up through the cleavages. Amid all that devastation I was surprised to hear the voice of the gunnery officer, Lieutenant Hatta, shouting from his post to open the water cocks in No. 1 magazine. For a wonder the valves still worked and the inrushing water quenched the fires in that magazine as Hatta had figured. With fires out, the yellow smoke stopped. Had that magazine exploded, the ship would have sunk quickly with no chance of survivors. But, of course, the flooding magazine accelerated the listing of the ship.

Still the planes kept attacking, and the next group hit with more bombs than I was able to count. When the explosions ended I shuddered to find that several gun posts and crews had vanished. How long can one endure the horror of his men being torn to shreds? And still there were no hits on the main bridge and command post.

I was jolted back to my duties when the torpedo room voice tube squawked my name. It was Lieutenant Commander Takeshi Kameyama requesting permission to empty the torpedo tubes. He said, "If they are set off it will blast everything."

"Okay, dump the fish!" I shouted. Almost at once sixteen powerful homing torpedoes slithered unarmed into the water. I thought wistfully of what damage might have been done to enemy ships by these deadly weapons we now had to waste. It was another last-minute reminder of our doom.

Kameyama acted not a moment too soon. The last torpedo was barely in the water when bombs blasted the tubes and rooted out *Yahagi*'s stern mast. Looking aft from the command post, still miraculously intact, I saw that the catapult was a shambles. The ruins of twisted iron looked like melting candy bars. The lone airplane, untouched just a minute ago, was a mass of cinders.

A few guns barked as their burned and blood-soaked crews still manned their posts.

Avengers came in skimming over the waves and dropped torpedoes. Three, four, I could not tell how many found their target. Our dying ship quaked with the detonations. The explosions finally stopped but the list continued as waves washed blood pools from the deck and dismembered bodies fell rolling into the sea.

And now the second wave of some hundred planes had done their work and gone. I looked around. All gun posts lay in ruins. My proud cruiser was but a mass of junk, barely afloat. Strangely, I thought, there are no fires. Through this weird sight my dazed brain raced back to see cruiser *San Francisco,* the phantom-like ship my *Amatsukaze* almost crashed into that pitch-dark night off Santa Cruz. Now *Yahagi,* too, was a phantom ship. Nothing stirred on her main deck. Many of her crew had perished.

On the bridge not a man had even been injured. "Hara," said Admiral Komura, "I guess we better get out of here. It looks like now or never. The 250 planes reported by Amami Oshima seem to have done their job."

There was nothing for me to say. I bowed and mumbled, "I'm very sorry, Admiral."

"Let us shift my flag to one of the destroyers, and force through to our goal at Okinawa. What do you think?"

What could I say? I was limp with the burden of responsibility at having lost my ship and crew.

"Look, Hara, *Isokaze* is still operating!"

It was astonishing to find her to port in her original position of the ring formation, about 3,000 yards away. She appeared in good shape and was coming in our direction. It was one of the few heartening moments of the action.

"All right, Admiral, let's abandon ship. Signalmen, raise *Isokaze,* urgent!"

At my command the powerful signal light began blinking, and a signalman also went to work with a pair of hand flags. Word went through *Yahagi* to prepare to abandon ship, and survivors were made ready for evacuation. *Isokaze* responded to our signal and kicked up high waves as she raced to the shattered hulk of our cruiser *Yahagi.* The destroyer slowed down 1,000 meters away for a cautious approach, and drew slowly closer. I ordered "Abandon Ship."

"Enemy planes!" a lookout cried, and one minute later the third wave of fighters and bombers was overhead. *Isokaze* had approached to within about

200 yards. Scores of planes broke off from attacking *Yamato* to head for the hapless, slow-moving destroyer. Her engines roared into full power as she frantically took evasive measures. But the planes were everywhere, spewing their torrents of bullets and bombs. Explosion followed explosion until *Isokaze* disappeared in a billow of black smoke.

Yahagi had doomed her own destroyer. It was what had almost happened to my *Shigure* when *Sendai* was under murderous attack at Empress Augusta Bay, but I had refused to take *Shigure* into that slaughter. Now I hoped that *Isokaze* would ignore my request and escape. When it appeared that the destroyer was done for, the planes came to work over what was left of *Yahagi*. Our floating junk pile was raked and combed by machine-gun bullets. *Yahagi* twisted, rivets popped, plates buckled, and I clung to the bridge rail in desperation.

As *Yahagi*'s convulsions subsided I raised my head and was surprised to see *Isokaze* emerge from the dissipating wall of smoke and water which had surrounded her. Injured, but still alive, she was speeding frantically away. Again scores of planes swooped over *Isokaze* which was again lost in a cloud of smoke.

After swinging past *Isokaze* each plane felt obliged to pay its aggressive respects to our sinking ship. We could do nothing but hang on. The missiles of the enemy were no more frightening than the trembling of our ship in its final throes.

Lieutenant (j.g.) Yukio Matsuda, a navigation officer, had rounded up a dozen wounded men and was trying to get them into a lifeboat. This activity drew the attention of three more fighters who concentrated their fire, smashing the boat to bits and dropping the unlucky thirteen dead in pools of their own blood.

Elsewhere men were jumping from the ship into the water. The enemy allowed no time for breath. A fourth wave of about 100 planes arrived to pound and batter everything that still moved. Komura, a few other officers, and I remained unscathed in the command post which still stood miraculously intact on the crumbling debris of what had been light cruiser *Yahagi*.

Looking out to sea I knew that *Isokaze* was in trouble. Her speed had fallen off and, though not on fire, she staggered like a drunk. *Suzutsuki*, farther off, was afire and pouring out billows of thick, black smoke. *Kasumi* limped helplessly out of control, her flags signaling, "Rudder trouble."

Yamato still appeared to be in good shape. At a distance of three miles I had no way of knowing that this pride of the Navy was as badly off as *Yahagi*.

Destroyers *Yukikaze* and *Fuyutsuki* flitted nimbly about in a valiant effort to protect the huge ship.

The fifth wave, of more than one hundred planes, showed no mercy to *Yahagi* in her final agonies. Bullets hissed and whined all about me. Not caring now, completely dazed, I gritted my teeth and mumbled, "All right, you Yankee devils, finish us off!"

The whine of a bullet and a sudden sting made me think I was done for. But in knocking me down it roused me from a daze. I examined and dismissed as neglible a wound on my left arm, and then noticed that waves were lapping the deck of the command post where Admiral Komura and I now stood alone.

"Well, Hara, shall we go?" he asked calmly.

"Let's go."

While we were removing our shoes, I noted the time—1406. Planes roared overhead. Waves were up to our knees when we jumped into the water. I swam only a few meters when some gigantic invisible force dragged me under. I resisted and struggled, but the sucking whirlpool of a sinking ship is irresistible. I gave up and passed out, accepting death.

My next awareness was of being released from a viselike hold. I was kicking and writhing. Around me was complete darkness, but it was thinning. Fuzzily I admired a mass of bluish beads as they drifted up in front of my face. These were bubbles of air from my clothing and my lungs. Pain of suffocation forced me to swallow a huge gulp of sea water, and then my head broke the surface. I breathed deeply again and again in a great void in which there was no sound, no light, no feeling, no anything. Dazed, not knowing what I was doing, I managed to stay afloat.

Gradually, my eyes began to focus, and I was aware of daylight. A buzzing sound turned into voices and, looking around, I saw heads floating on the water. They were all black. In my stupor I felt it must be a Negro bathing beach where I was enjoying a pleasant swim. My brain revived, but slowly.

I was still dazed. The fatigue and tension of two hours of battle, followed by tremendous shock and collapse, were too much. Then I heard someone shout, "Hara! are you all right? Hara! Do you hear me?"

I peered in the direction of the voice, saw a black-faced man shouting at me, and recognized Admiral Komura. His wind- and sun-tanned face was so dark that he was recognizable at a distance of 30 feet, even though heavily covered with black oil.

"I'm all right, Komura," I answered. "How about you?"

"Yes, I'm quite all righ!"

So the "Negroes" around me were my own men. I patted my face and found my palm covered with heavy oil. The surface of the water was covered with this oil from *Yahagi*. To my surprise there were many men clinging to bits and pieces of wood. I thought that the crew had all perished.

As my vision returned, I caught a glimpse of *Yamato*, still big and impressive even at a distance of six miles. Rolling waves occasionally hid her but, when a crest raised me high, I could see scores of planes swarming about her like gnats.

While I floated, wondering what would happen, a log drifted by within my grasp. I clutched at it, grabbed and clung to it tenaciously. With my security thus improved I considered what my next move should be.

"Hey you, move over, make room for me," shouted someone behind me. A young man was trying to reach the log. I moved slowly to one end to permit him a hand hold. He caught the log and looked at me gratefully.

"Who are you? What's your name?" he asked as soon as he caught his breath.

"My name is Hara. I'm from *Yahagi*."

My new neighbor gasped and was suddenly speechless. He stared at me for some moments as though in a trance. "I'm very sorry, sir," he mumbled. "Forgive my rudeness. I am Second Class Seaman Daiwa . . . I'd better find another log, Captain Hara. This one isn't big enough to support both of us."

He looked around uneasily and I said, "Don't be foolish, son. Hang on tight. We can manage. Are you hurt?"

"No, sir, not at all. My friend Asamo and I decided to die quickly when *Yahagi* was doomed. We went to No. 3 magazine and mounted the shells, waiting to be blown to bits. But Petty Officer Yamada came and ordered us up on deck. He said, 'This is my place." He was so furious that we raced up the ladder. I stumbled once and sprained my ankle, but that is nothing. I wonder what happened to Hanada and my buddy Asamo."

"Don't worry, Daiwa. Now think only of survival. You will get out of this if you don't give up."

We looked around and saw *Yamato*, still moving. What a beautiful sight. Suddenly smoke belched from her waterline. We both groaned as white smoke billowed out until it covered the great battleship, giving her the appearance of a snow-capped Mount Fuji. Next came black smoke mingled with the white, forming into a huge cloud which climbed to 2,000 meters. As it drifted away we looked to the surface of the sea again and there was nothing. *Yamato* had vanished. Tremendous detonations at 1423 of that seventh day of April signaled the end of this "unsinkable" symbol of the Imperial Navy.

I felt a sudden chill and realized for the first time that it was raining. As I thought of *Yamato* my tears mingled with the rain and the water of the sea.

After the war, my friend Rear Admiral Nobuei Morishita, one of *Yamato*'s 269 survivors, told me the details of her last minutes.

The fast direct hit on *Yamato* was by bombs at 1240, and the first torpedo struck the ship to port ten minutes later. In all, eight more torpedoes hit on the port side and two hit to starboard.

Captain Jiro Nomura, *Yamato*'s exec, determined at 1405 that the ship's trim could not be restored. Thereupon Vice Admiral Ito, who had been on the bridge throughout the battle, canceled the operation and ordered "Abandon ship."

Destroyer *Fuyutsuki* was called in to assist the evacuation, but it was impossible to approach the rapidly sinking behemoth. Commander Hide-chika Sakuma, skipper of *Fuyutsuki*, kept clear because he figured that his small ship would be dragged down as the big one sank.

Ito shook hands with the officers on the bridge and then withdrew to his cabin to die with the ship. *Yamato*'s skipper, Rear Admiral Kosaku Aruga, tied himself to the bridge binnacle to ensure going down with *Yamato*.

Morishita had to argue violently with the other officers who wanted to share the fate of Ito, Aruga, and *Yamato,* but he convinced them and they all left the bridge together. The ship's port list was increasing rapidly when the last torpedo hit at 1417. Three minutes later the list had reached 20 degrees, inducing explosions which sent the ship into a precipitous plunge. These same explosions saved Morishita and others, throwing them clear of the ship.

Clinging to the log, I was lost in gloomy thoughts for several minutes after *Yamato*'s sinking. I grieved at the loss of my cruiser and I grieved dou-bly at loss of the world's greatest battleship. Looking about, I could see no sign of Komura, and young Daiwa was no longer clinging to the other end of the log. There was no one in sight. I seemed to be riding a current which had carried me away from the others. Was I to die like this, alone? Then I heard voices singing, not too far away.

I thought of our survival instruction that men adrift in the ocean should stay quiet to conserve physical strength, and not exhaust themselves with singing and shouting. Since these men were singing they had probably decided that there was no chance of rescue and they might just as well give their spirits whatever lift might be derived from song. The sound grew stronger as more voices joined. I heard it distinctly and recognized the Song of the Warrior, familiar to Japanese fighting men for hundreds of years:

> If I go to sea,
>   I shall return a corpse awash;
> If duty calls me to the mountain,
>   A verdant sward will be my pall;
> Thus for the sake of the Emperor
> I shall not die peacefully at home.

As the song was repeated, I found myself joining in. From time to time there were hoarse shouts of "*Tenno heika, Banzai!*"—Long live the Emperor—which suggested that the exhausted or seriously wounded singers were dropping out of the chorus to their death. I closed my eyes and the song grew faint in my ears.

I knew that I was going to die. The distant melody, wavering like a lullaby, brought back my childhood and my mother's songs, my grandfather, school days, the Academy, our world cruise, shopping in a New York department store, young officer days, my affair with the geisha girl. This kaleidoscope changed into a vivid picture of my mother, overlapped by one of my wife, and then my last formal officer portrait, which was replaced by the faces of my children.

I came out of this weird reverie with tears streaming down my cheeks. Thinking of my last home leave, just four months ago, and the children and my wife, I realized that they would face many hardships after my death. I cried aloud for their forgiveness and hoped they would try to understand. It was selfish of me to have married Chizu, taking her away from the comfortable life she had known. Now I was leaving her widowed, with three children. Forgive me, Chizu.

The singing had stopped. The water and the air seemed colder. I shuddered, chilled to the bone. My hands were going numb, and I was having trouble keeping my grip. Something drifted by and I picked it up. Nothing but a piece of black paper. I started to throw it away but instead shoved it in my raincoat pocket. Them I felt something else and pulled it out. It was a four-foot piece of rope. I had no idea of how it got there, but this rope changed my entire outlook.

I tied myself so that, even if I passed out, the log would still keep me afloat. And there was always the chance that my body would wash ashore on the coast of Japan.

Planes were overhead again, probably the last attack wave, but in my increasing torpor they were a matter of indifference, until several fighters began to spray the sea with machine-gun bullets. They concentrated on the large group of survivors, still separated from me, but some bullets came my way too. None hit me, but the whine and swish of bullets awakened me to anger against the pilots. Hating them, I found unrealized strength which let me duck and twist around, and my numbness soon vanished.

No more fighters came but, to my astonishment, a Martin (PBM) flying boat swooped low and landed on the water about 300 meters away. I ducked again, but the Martin paid no attention to me. It taxied slowly to a patch of water dyed brilliantly green, picked up an American pilot who had been drifting in a life raft and took off again.* I watched that operation with feelings of envy.

The feelings of another *Yahagi* survivor, Ensign Shigeo Yamada, who was also close to the rescue, were quite different. He was born in Hawaii and, being proficient in English, served as a communication officer. He later told me: "I was afraid of being taken prisoner, because of my background, and hastily tore all insignia of rank from my uniform and threw them away. But the flying boat and her crew did not come near me."

Yamada survived the war and in 1958 was working in the Japan Air Lines offices in Chicago, Illinois—a prospect not readily envisaged that April day of 1945.

The area was all quiet again. I felt easy for the first time, and began to reflect coolly on the day's actions. My anti-aircraft maneuvering had been clumsy. In a destroyer I would have pulled through, without any doubt. So my true caliber was that of a destroyer skipper—nothing more.

But that was wrong. I blundered in forgetting the solution used successfully off Kavieng when *Shigure* had bagged the two bombers. *Yahagi* was much faster and more agile than *Shigure*. Why had I kept the cruiser in the outmoded zigzag pattern which let the torpedo catch us?

---

* Avenger pilot Lt. (j.g.) W. E. Delaney USNR from CFL *Belleau Wood* was thus rescued by a PBM piloted by Lt. James R. Young USNR.

Yes, I had blundered, but I was rusty after a year ashore. If only the high command had kept me at sea instead of diverting me to that useless and ineffective shore assignment.

All our practice and training—with homing torpedoes, proximity fuses, and radar-controlled gunfire—had been of no use in this day's action against hundreds of planes. Everything we did seemed to be wrong. This very operation itself, without aerial protection of any kind for the ships, was a grotesque mistake.

I had no idea of how many hours had passed since *Yahagi*'s sinking. It was dark and the wind was rising. I shuddered with cold and began to get drowsy. I fought against sleep, knowing that with sleep would come an end to my cares. But, after all, a samurai lives so that he is always prepared to die. I could wait quietly for death, without regret or remorse.

Around me I saw nothing but rising waves, and heard nothing but the sound of the water slapping against my log. I closed my eyes and slept, with my head resting against the wood. I dreamed of days gone by. I was crossing from Shikoku to Honshu for the first time, to apply for the Academy entrance exams. The engine of the ferry boat had a distinctive sound and I could hear it clearly again. It did not seem like a dream.

I opened my eyes and the sound continued. I saw a destroyer a mile away and thought it must still be fighting off the persistent planes. My head sank down again on the log, but the engine noise kept me from dozing. It sounded too close to be the destroyer. I looked up and saw a motorboat This small craft, the kind normally carried by a destroyer, was not more than 200 meters away, and readily visible between wave crests. I wondered what it was doing here.

The boat disappeared. I craned my neck for another sight of it. After some minutes it emerged again, this time only 50 meters away. The boat was circling, looking for survivors. Suddenly I was terrified. I wanted desperately to live and was afraid they might miss me. I yelled at the top of my lungs, but the boat completed its circle without noticing me.

In desperation I untied myself from the log and thrashed the water with my arms and legs. That did it. They noticed the splashing and turned in my direction. It seemed an eternity before they reached me. I was too weak even to grab the side of the boat, but four strong hands quickly hauled me in.

It was curious, but as soon as my feet were in the dry boat my exhaustion vanished. I stammered gratitude to my rescuers and was surprised to see that there were no other survivors in the boat. The crew chief explained that they had already brought many survivors to the destroyer and this was their last trip.

They searched for another 15 minutes without further success, and headed back to destroyer *Hatsushimo*. My surge of energy gave out when I tried to climb the ladder. My feet simply would not move. Two husky sailors boosted me to the destroyer deck.

Hatsushimo's skipper, Commander Masazo Sako, greeted me, "Welcome home, Captain Hara. We had almost despaired of finding you. Admiral Komura is resting in my cabin."

I mumbled my thanks to Sako, and was grateful that darkness hid my face, which must have reflected how badly I felt. Sako took me to the sick bay where my water- and oil-soaked clothes were removed. Skilled corpsmen gave me first aid and a massage, which did much to restore me. I thanked them and asked for a glass of *sake*.

The doctor laughed and said, "Yes, Captain Hara. Ordinarily I might object, but I am sure that *sake* is just what you need."

The drink revived me quickly, and they next gave me a steaming bowl of soup. While I drank, the medical officer briefed me on events as seen from his ship.

"I'm afraid that *Hatsushimo* did not contribute much to this mission. The attackers passed us by to strike at *Yamato*. As a result we did not suffer a direct hit of any kind. Two of our sailors were slightly injured, but not a man on board was killed. *Hatsushimo* is probably the only undamaged ship of our force. That's why we stayed here looking for survivors. *Fuyutsuki*, *Suzutsuki*, and *Yukikaze*—all damaged—left for Sasebo two hours ago. *Fuyutsuki* is not in bad shape; she was hit by two rockets, neither of which exploded, but a dozen of her men were killed by machine-gun bullets. *Yukikaze* is not badly damaged but she lost three men killed by strafing. *Suzutsuki* was hit by a bomb which knocked off her bows and she had to return stern first to Sasebo.

"*Isokaze* was not so lucky. She suffered no direct hits, but near misses holed her, flooding the engine room and killing 100 of her crew. When there was no hope for her, she was dispatched by *Yukikaze* who took survivors.

"*Kasumi* was badly disabled and had 17 killed. Her survivors were removed by *Fuyutsuki* who then gave her the *coup de grâce*."

I thanked him for the information, and had nothing else to ask except, "Did you rescue a sailor named Daiwa?"

The medic checked a list and replied, "Yes, Sir. His name is here. In fact, he has been asking about you ever since he was picked up two hours ago." He called an orderly. "Tell Daiwa that Captain Hara is safe."

Destroyer *Hatsushimo*, loaded with hundreds of *Yamato* and *Yahagi* survivors, returned to Sasebo at noon on the 8th of April. An orderly knocked at the captain's cabin as soon as we had anchored, and delivered a message to Admiral Komura. He read it, grimaced and handed it to me. It was a citation for the Second Fleet from Commander in Chief Combined Fleet, commending our force for "its gallant self-sacrifice which enabled the Special Attack planes to achieve a great war result."

What was this great war result? The air attack effort that day consisted of 114 planes. The 60 fighters, 40 bombers, and 14 kamikazes succeeded only in damaging carrier *Hancock*, battleship *Maryland*, and destroyer *Bennett*, at a cost of nearly 100 planes.

The Second Fleet had sortied with one battleship, one light cruiser and eight destroyers. It was attacked over a period of two hours by a total of 386 carrier-based planes. Ten of these planes and twelve American lives were lost to antiaircraft fire from our ships. Of the Second Fleet only three destroyers survived. Japanese lives lost in the action came to 2,498 in *Yamato*, 446 in *Yahagi*, and 721 in the destroyers.

These simple but astounding statistics tell the story of who won and who lost the last aerial-surface engagement of the war. The powerful navy which had launched the Pacific war forty months before with the attack on Pearl Harbor had at last been struck down. On April 7, 1945, with the sinking of battleship *Yamato*, the Imperial Japanese Navy died.

Appendix A

SINKING OF PT-109 AND RESCUE OF SURVIVORS*

In anticipation of a Japanese supply effort to Vila on the southwest corner of Kolombangara Island, fourteen boats of MTB Flotilla One were on patrol in Blackett Strait on Sunday night, August 1, 1943. They had departed from their Rendova base at 1830 and arrived at stations two hours later. *PT-109* (Lieutenant (jg) Jack Kennedy, USNR) was patrolling Blackett Strait about 0230 at idling using only one of her three engines, when a dark shape loomed up on her starboard bow at a distance of no more than 300 yards. At first this shape was taken for another PT boat, but it was soon identified as a *Hibiki*-type destroyer of the *Fubuki* class, and bearing down on *PT-109* at high speed.

The torpedo boat started a starboard turn preparatory to firing torpedoes, but had swung through no more than 30 degrees when the destroyer struck forward of the forward starboard torpedo tube and sheared off the starboard side of the boat aft, including the starboard engine. Scarcely ten seconds elapsed between time of sighting and the crash. The destroyer neither slowed nor fired as she split the PT.

A surface gasoline fire ignited immediately about 20 yards from the remains of the boat which were still afloat. Lieutenant Kennedy ordered Abandon Ship as it appeared that the fire was approaching. When this danger

---

* Derived from Intelligence Officers' Memo to ComMTB Flot One of 22 August 1943, by Lieutenants (jg) Byron R. ("Whizzer") White and J. C. McClure, both USNR, on the basis of interrogations of the survivors. Made available to this work by the Office of Naval History, Department of the Navy.

passed they crawled back on board except for three men 100 yards to the southwest, two to the northeast, and two who did not respond to shouts and proved to be missing.

Kennedy swam toward the group of Harris, McMahon, and Starkey; while Ensigns Leonard J. Thom and George H. R. Ross struck out for Zinser and Johnson. McMahon was helpless because of serious burns and Kennedy had to tow him back to the boat, which took an hour because a strong current impeded their progress. Kennedy then returned for the other two men. He traded his life belt for Harris' useless waterlogged life jacket and together they towed injured Starkey back to the PT.

Meanwhile, Thom and Ross had reached Zinser and Johnson, who were both helpless because of gasoline fumes, and towed them. Both men regained consciousness by the time they got to the boat.

Within three hours after the crash all survivors who could be located were on board *PT-109*. Marney and Kirksey were never seen after the crash. During the three hours it took to gather survivors nothing was seen or heard to indicate other ships in the area. No Very pistols were fired for fear of giving away their position to the enemy.

All classified gear and publications on board were sunk in the deep waters of Vella Gulf. When daylight of August 2 arrived the eleven survivors were still on board. It was estimated that the boat then lay about four miles north and slightly east of Gizo Anchorage, and about three miles from the reef along the northeast side of Gizo Island.

Despite the fact that all water-tight doors were dogged down at the time of the crash, *PT-109* was slowly taking on water. It was obvious that the boat would sink on the 2nd, so it was decided to abandon it in time to reach one of the tiny islands east of Gizo before dark. A small island 4 miles southeast of Gizo was chosen rather than a closer one which it was feared might be occupied by Japanese.

At 1400 hours Lieutenant Kennedy took the badly burned McMahon in tow and set out for land, intending to lead the way and scout the island in advance of the others. Ensigns Ross and Thom followed with the other men. Johnson and Mauer, who could not swim, were tied to a float rigged from a 2″ x 8″ which was part of the 37-mm gun mount. Harris and McGuire were fair swimmers, but Zinser, Starkey, and Albert were not so good. The strong swimmers pushed or towed the float to which the non-swimmers were tied.

The men had shed most of their clothes; Ensign Thom was the only one who still wore shoes. By way of arms the group had six 45s (two of which were lost before their rescue), one 38, one large knife, one light knive, and a pocket knife. They had one flashlight, but the first aid kit was lost in the collision. All of the group, with the exception of McMahon, who suffered greatly from burns, were in fairly good condition, although weak and tired from their swim ashore.

That evening Lieutenant Kennedy decided to swim into Ferguson Passage in an attempt to intercept PT boats proceeding to their patrol areas. He left about 1830, swam to a small island 1/2 mile to the southeast, proceeded along a reef which stretched out into Ferguson Passage, arriving there about 2000. He saw no PTs, but did observe aircraft flares which indicated that the boats were operating that night in Gizo instead of Blackett Strait and being harassed as usual by enemy float planes. Kennedy began his return over the same route but was caught in a current which swept him in a two-mile circle into Blackett Strait and back to the middle of Ferguson Passage, where he had to start his homeward trip all over again. He stopped on the small island just southeast of "home" where he slept until dawn before covering the last mile to join the rest of his group. On his return to the group he was completely exhausted, slightly feverish, and slept most of the day.

Nothing was seen on August 2 or 3 that gave any hope of rescue. On the night of the 3rd Ensign Ross swam into Ferguson Passage in another attempt to intercept PT patrols from Rendova, without success.

The total diet of the group, on what they called Bird Island (because of its abundance of droppings from the feathered creatures), consisted of coconuts, as long as they lasted. When the supply ran low, and in order to get closer to Ferguson Passage, the group left Bird Island at noon of August 4; and, using the same arrangements as before, headed for an islet west of Cross Island. Kennedy, with McMahon in tow, arrived first. The rest of the group again experienced difficulty with a strong easterly current, but finally made the eastern tip of the island.

Their new abode was slightly larger, offered brush for concealment and a few coconuts, and had no Japanese tenants. The night of August 4 was wet and cold, and no one ventured into Ferguson Passage. The next morning Kennedy and Ross swam to Cross Island in search of some help for the party. Before they left, a New Zealand P-40 was seen making a strafing run on that island, indicating the possible presence of the enemy. But so acute was their food shortage that the two men set out, swam the channel, and arrived on the island about 1530. They sneaked through the brush to the east side of the island and surveyed the beach. They spied a small rectangular box with Japanese writing on the side, and furtively pulled it into the bush. It contained several dozen bags of candy and crackers. A little farther up the beach they found a one-man canoe and a barrel of water alongside a native lean-to. At the same time they sighted two natives in a canoe, who, despite all efforts by Kennedy and Ross to attract their attention, paddled swiftly off to the northwest. Nevertheless, having obtained a canoe, food and water, Kennedy and Ross considered their visit a success.

That night Kennedy took the canoe to venture again into Ferguson Passage. When no PTs had appeared by 2100 he returned "home" by way of Cross Island where he picked up the food but left Ross who had decided to swim back the following morning. When Kennedy returned about 2330 he found that the two natives he had sighted near Cross Island had circled around and landed on his "home" island. Ensign Thom finally convinced them that he and his colleagues were Americans, and they then landed and performed every possible service for the survivors.

The natives were sent with messages to friendly Coastwatchers, informing that the crew of *PT-109* was on Cross Island. After the natives left, Ross and Kennedy remained on the island until evening when they set out in the two-man canoe to again try their luck at intercepting PTs in Ferguson Passage. They paddled far, saw nothing, and were caught in a sudden rainsquall which capsized the canoe. Swimming to land was difficult and treacherous. The sea swept them against the reef on the south side of Cross Island, and Ross received numerous cuts and bruises, but both managed to make land where they stayed the rest of the night.

On Saturday, August 7, eight natives arrived bringing a message from a coastwatcher instructing the senior officer to go with the natives to Wana Wana. Kennedy and Ross had the natives paddle them to the island where the rest of the survivors were, and all were made as comfortable as possible.

That afternoon Kennedy, hidden under ferns in the native boat, was taken to the coastwatcher, arriving about 1600. There it was arranged that PT boats would rendezvous with him in Ferguson Passage that evening at 2230. Accordingly he was taken to the rendezvous point, finally made contact with the PTs at 2315, and directed the boats to the rest of the survivors. Their rescue was effected without mishap and they returned to the base at Rendova at 0530 on August 8, seven days after the ramming of *PT-109* in Blackett Strait.

Appendix B

NOMENCLATURE
OF JAPANESE WARSHIPS*

The system of nomenclature recently in use (with occasional exceptions) is thus:

Battleships: Named after ancient provinces and mountains.

Aircraft Carriers: Named after mountains, dragons, and birds.

Heavy Cruisers: Named after mountains.

Light Cruisers: Named after rivers.

Destroyers (First Class): Meteorological names in poetic style.

Destroyers (Second Class): Named after trees, flowers, and fruits.

Torpedo Boats: Named after birds.

Minelayers: Named after islands, straits, channels and (formerly) birds.

Color of Ships: Dark gray usually.

---

*From *Jane's Fighting Ships* (1941), p. 280.

Appendix C

Japanese Vessels Sunk in World War II*

Sinking Agent	Naval		Merchant		Total	
	Number	*Tonnage*	*Number*	*Tonnage*	*Number*	*Tonnage*
U.S.	611	1,822,210	2,117	7,913,858	2,728	9,736,068
Allies	45	69,636	73	211,664	118	281,300
U.S. & Allies	10	14,864	12	57,923	22	72,787
Marine casualty	13	50,338	97	268,948	110	319,286
Japanese mines			21	67,197	21	67,197
Unknown	7	8,598	26	98,519	33	107,117
TOTAL	686	1,965,646	2,346	8,618,109	3,032	10,583,755

*From Joint Army-Navy Assessment Committee, *Japanese Naval and Merchant Shipping Losses During World War II*. U.S. Govt. Printing Office, Washington, D.C.

Major Warship Losses

	On Hand Dec. 1941		Commissioned Dec. '41–Aug. '45		Lost Dec. '41–Aug. '45		On Hand Aug. 1945	
	U. S.	*Japan*	*U. S.*	*Japan*	*U. S.*	*Japan*	*U. S.*	*Japan*
Battleships	17	10	8	2	2	11	23	1
Carriers*	7	10	26	15	5	25	28	4
Cruisers†	37	38	46	5	10	39	73	4
Destroyers	173	111	261	52	54	135	380	28
Submarines	112	64	172	97	50	131	234	30
TOTAL	346	233	513	171	121	341	738	67

*Including CVs, CVL, and CVE.
†Including light and heavy cruisers.

Merchant Shipping Losses*
Ships of 500 tons and over

	Number of Ships	Tonnage
U. S.	98	519,772
Japan	2,346	8,618,109

*Including losses in Pacific and Indian Oceans.

U. S.-Japan Statistics of World War II
Personnel in Armed Services

	U. S.*		Japan	
	Dec. 1941	*July 1945*	*Dec. 1941*	*July 1945*
Army	1,332,000	5,924,000	2,100,000	5,710,000
Air Force	354,000	2,262,000	(included in Army and Navy)	
Navy	380,000	3,410,000	291,359	1,663,223
Marines	75,000	477,000	(included in Navy)	
Coast Guard	28,000	171,000	(included in Army and Navy)	
TOTAL	2,169,000	12,244,000	2,391,359	7,373,223

*In all theaters.

Casualties

	U. S.*			Japan		
	Killed	*Wounded*	*Total*	*Killed*	*Wounded*	*Total*
Army						
(incl. AAF)	41,686	109,425	151,111	1,289,605	53,028	1,342,633
Navy						
(incl. C.Gd.)	31,485	31,701	63,186	298,209	7,844	306,053
Marines	19,733	67,207	86,940			
TOTAL	92,904	208,333	301,237	1,587,814	60,872	1,648,686

*Pacific and Asiatic Theaters only.

Aircraft

	On Hand	Wartime Losses	On Hand
	Dec. 1941	*(Combat and Operational)*	*July 1945*
United States			
Army	12,300	13,055	66,000
Navy	5,300	8,500	41,000
TOTAL	17,600	21,555	207,000
Japanese			
Army	4,826	15,935	8,920
Navy	2,120	27,190	7,307
TOTAL	6,946	43,125	16,227

INDEX

FRED SAITO was born in 1917 and has lived most of his life in Tokyo. Though his family, like Captain Hara's, were members of the Japanese samurai, Saito turned to a career in journalism and broadcasting. From 1948 to 1960 he was with the Tokyo office of the Associated Press. He is the author of many magazine articles published in Japan and co-author (with Saburo Sakai and Martin Caidin) of *Samurai!*, the personal story of Japan's greatest living fighter pilot (Ballantine Books). At present, he is on the staff of the Japan Broadcasting Company. In translating and expanding *Japanese Destroyer Captain*, Mr. Saito spent more than 800 hours interviewing Captain Hara so that the book would be a full and accurate account of the many battles that Captain Hara mounted from the Japanese side.

ROGER PINEAU is a commander in the United States Naval Reserve. After service in World War II, he was a member of the U.S. Strategic Bombing Survey in Japan and later assisted Adm. Samuel Eliot Morison in preparing of the authoritative *History of United States Naval Operations in World War II*. His knowledge of the Japanese and their language, together with his own naval background and experience, makes him particularly well qualified as co-author of this book. In addition to checking the accuracy of Japanese battle accounts, he has added footnotes giving, where possible, the names of U.S. ships and commanders engaged by Captain Hara's forces in the Pacific. A frequent contributor to the U.S. Naval Institute *Proceedings*, Mr. Pineau is co-author of *The Divine Wind* and *Midway*, both written in collaboration with Japanese authors.

The **Naval Institute Press** is the book-publishing arm of the U.S. Naval Institute, a private, nonprofit, membership society for sea service professionals and others who share an interest in naval and maritime affairs. Established in 1873 at the U.S. Naval Academy in Annapolis, Maryland, where its offices remain today, the Naval Institute has members worldwide.

Members of the Naval Institute support the education programs of the society and receive the influential monthly magazine *Proceedings* or the colorful bimonthly magazine *Naval History* and discounts on fine nautical prints and on ship and aircraft photos. They also have access to the transcripts of the Institute's Oral History Program and get discounted admission to any of the Institute-sponsored seminars offered around the country.

The Naval Institute's book-publishing program, begun in 1898 with basic guides to naval practices, has broadened its scope to include books of more general interest. Now the Naval Institute Press publishes about seventy titles each year, ranging from how-to books on boating and navigation to battle histories, biographies, ship and aircraft guides, and novels. Institute members receive significant discounts on the more than eight hundred Press books in print.

Full-time students are eligible for special half-price membership rates. Life memberships are also available.

For a free catalog describing Naval Institute Press books currently available, and for further information about joining the U.S. Naval Institute, please write to:

Member Services
U.S. NAVAL INSTITUTE
291 Wood Road
Annapolis, MD 21402-5034
Telephone: (800) 233-8764
Fax: (410) 571-1703
Web address: www.usni.org